The
HOW•TO•DO•IT
Manual for Small Libraries

Edited by Bill Katz

The
HOW·
TO·
DO·IT
MANUAL
for small libraries

Edited by Bill Katz

Neal-Schuman Publishers, Inc.
New York   London

Published by Neal-Schuman Publishers, Inc.
23 Leonard Street
New York, NY 10013

Library of Congress Cataloging-in-Publication Data

The How-to-do-it manual for small libraries.

Includes bibliographies and index.
1. Small libraries—Administration—Handbooks, manuals, etc. I. Katz, William A., 1924 – .
Z678.H73   1987   025.1   87-12390
ISBN 1-55570-016-0

Contents

iii

Preface

Bill Katz

The How-to-Do-It Manual for Small Libraries is written by and for people working in small rural or urban libraries who must deal with everything from limited staffs and budgets to automation and demand for bestsellers. All 35 chapters are original to this book, the framework for which is based on the areas of interest and value indicated by librarians working in small libraries who responded to a questionnaire and informal poll. Although many of the authors are currently working in small public libraries, most of the material is applicable—and important—equally to the person employed in the small special, school, or academic library.

The *Manual* is organized into five parts so that the reader moves from the general to the specific, from umbrella type reports to individual concerns. Part one presents the outlook from the field, with five reports on what it's like to manage a small public library, school library, four-year college library, two-year college library, and a special library.

What it takes to administer a small library is discussed in part two, covering, for instance, staff and personnel issues, budget preparation, the physical plant, and creating and working with a library board of trustees. Also considered here are library cooperation, the importance of planning, writing and designing a procedure manual, using national standards, and evaluating library services.

Collection development and technical services are dealt with next. In addition to a thorough account of coping with questions of censorship and access, a variety of print and nonprint materials are examined, and cataloging, weeding, and circulation procedures are outlined. A concise description of bibliographic utilities is also presented.

The variety of library services that can be captured under the rubric public services are described in part four: reader services, service to adults, service to children and young adults, reference services, and library instruction. Also included in this section are chapters on conducting community/user studies, the importance of library promotion, and working with Friends of the library groups.

Questions of automation and the use of electronic databases and other new technology are addressed in part five. Specifically, the importance of microcomputers and the new laser technology are discussed, always with the small library's limits on staff size and budget in mind.

These major sections are followed by a bibliographic essay on the literature on small libraries over the past ten years, a general bibliography that is keyed to the major sections of *The How-to-Do-It Manual,* and a subject index.

DEFINING A SMALL LIBRARY

There are almost as many definitions of small as there are of libraries, but consider the term in relation to budget. There are some 9,500 to 10,000 public libraries in the United States, but less than 1,000 have book funds over $50,000, and the majority must get along with $1,000 to $5,000 a year for purchasing materials. Of the 2,600 college and university libraries, less than one-half can boast materials budgets of over $25,000. One suspects these figures and ratios hold true, too, for special and school libraries.

Herbert Goldhor, Director of the University of Illinois Library Research Center, approaches the descriptor from the point of view of those served. A rural public library is defined "as a library which serves fewer than 10,000 people and is located in a county which either has fewer than 150 persons per square mile or has over 80 percent of its land in farms."[1]

In an urban center the familiar breaking point for population served is under 100,000, but that figure is much too high. Most experienced librarians would agree with Diane Kadanoff that "those libraries serving populations of less than 25,000 are what truly qualify as small public libraries."[2] In a general way, of the close to 10,000 public libraries, more than one-half (5,495) serve populations under 10,000, while another 1,454 serve populations from 10,000 to 25,000. At the other extreme, only 140 of the 10,000 are in areas with populations over 250,000. These figures do not include branches, which are slightly over 6,000 and bring the total number of public libraries to 15,000.[3]

In the number of books available, figures vary widely and are not entirely reliable because of such well-known variables as the age of the books, the amount of circulation, and whether or not the library has ready access to larger stocks of books via interlibrary loan, larger systems, etc. Still, in one study of 101 Washington, D.C., public branch libraries, it was found that "almost half had 50,000 volumes or less."[4] An unscientific study of the *American Library Directory* reveals that holdings of from 15,000 to 35,000 are typical of small libraries.

Small budgets, a limited number of people served, and less-than-impressive-sized materials collections all add up to the typical small public, special, school, or academic library. To this one should add an equally small staff of no more than one to two professionals and several full- or part-time aids.

Unfortunately, this often tends to be equated with something less than desirable. It's probably not more than the American notion that the bigger it is, the better it is, and "small" in describing a library is not considered by many as a descriptor of praise. However, this is changing, and "small is beautiful" is not just an idle phrase anymore.

WORKING IN A SMALL LIBRARY

Why do professionals work in small libraries? Reality indicates there may not always be an initial choice. There is a shortage of well-paid positions in major libraries. Beginners are likely to find more employment opportunities in the small library. Still, given the chance to move on, thousands choose to spend their lives in small libraries. Many do it out of an old-fashioned notion of service and reward— service to the community and personal reward. Judy Smith of the South Mississippi Regional Library explains the joys of independence: "We have a freedom in small libraries that may be lacking in larger ones. I can be any type of person on any given day, which makes for an interesting work life. . . . Nothing is the same every day. I don't feel cheated not being the supervisor of dozens. . . . I enjoy this. What else is there?"[5]

Thomas Aud, the director of the Tennessee Jackson/Madison County Library, adds that the decision to work in a small library is based on more than financial rewards. "It is the commitment to serve in a community one enjoys. . . ."[6] Aud notes, too, that it helps to be "adept at minor repairs, plumbing, and electrical systems." William Muller of the Welch, West Virginia, McDowell Public Library, confirms that "small library work, like fishing, is dirty work, but somebody has to do it. And, like fishing, you have to love it to do it."[7]

If working in a small library has numerous benefits, what about the drawbacks of limited staff and budget? This need not be, for as Diane Kadanoff puts it, "small may imply limitations imposed on the library itself, (but) it does not necessarily mean limitations on the skills, talents, and creativity of the professional staff."[8]

In fact, the constraints of size often work for the benefit of the library and its users. Materials must be selected with particular care and the result often is a connoisseur's collection rather than a grab bag. The staff working closely with the collection and patrons can be more human, more personal, and finally more helpful.

The enthusiasm for the small library is reflected in all of this book's chapters. While no one is satisfied with sometimes overwhelming odds, all express understandable pride in overcoming those difficulties. The result is twofold—the librarian is happy and the patrons served are even more pleased. *The How-to-Do-It Manual for Small Libraries* is not only a testimony to excellent service, it is a guide to help you, the reader, find some of the joy and delight in working in the small library.

A word of thanks to all of the contributors who so generously agreed to share their experiences with the reader. We are all richer for it. My particular gratitude to Pat Schuman and Andrea Pedolsky who encouraged the concept of the book and helped to insure its success.

References

1. "What is a rural public library?", *Library Journal* (July 1986): 11.
2. Diane Kadanoff, "Small libraries—No Small Job," *Library Journal* (March1, 1986): 72.
3. *The Bowker Annual, 1985* (New York: R.R. Bowker, 1985), pp. 415, 434.
4. Mary Jo Detweiler, "The Best Size Public Library," *Library Journal* (May 15, 1986): 34.
5. Judy Smith, "Freedom in Small Libraries," *Library Journal* (June 1, 1986): 12.
6. Thomas Aud, "Larger not better," *Library Journal* (June 1, 1986): 18.
7. Ibid.
8. Op. Cit., Kadanoff, p. 73.

1
Managing the Small Library

The Public Library

Kathleen Stipek

A year or so into my first professional job as director of a small public library, I brooded on the wrong my library school had done me. What was it? I had been sent out into the cold, cruel world with a head stuffed with management techniques, information theory, and laws of library science. I was the cutting edge of information services. By George, I was going to show this town what real library service was! And then I walked in the front door.

The small are different. A good three-quarters of what is taught in library school either doesn't work or doesn't *quite* work in a small library. That is not to say, as I often did that first year, that my professors swindled me. They didn't. They were teaching for the medium-to-large library, which is where most MLS's go and where most library professors come from. They didn't tell me either because they didn't know or because they knew that I wouldn't believe them. After all, who would believe that one might need to know how to quell a riot over bunny cut-outs in story time or how to get a snake off the front sidewalk? (A bunny riot is quelled by making the worst offenders give up their bunnies and then threatening everyone else's. The snake responded well to a blast of cold water from the garden hose.)

The first thing to remember in running a small public library is that there aren't enough people for a hierarchy or a neatly-defined chain of command. There may be a general or habitual division of labor, but if something needs doing, you do it or it might not get done. You are the Departments of Administration, Reference, Reader's Advisory, Book Selection, and Public Relations—with a smattering of Bibliographic Instruction. You are also relief charge clerk, carder, shelver, and shelf-reader; back-up bookkeeper and interlibrary loan clerk; emergency plumber, furniture mover, and mechanic; and your own typist. That's not the whole list, but you get the idea.

The administrator of a small library does not have the luxury of looking like a textbook administrator, either. We all have our sincere, successful suits, but not for daily use. Suits are for meetings, important visitors, and those occasions which won't run up the dry-cleaning bill.

Kathleen Stipek is Head of Adult Services at Central Florida Regional Library, Ocala, Florida.

When, in the course of a day, you shelve books, set up a room for a program, plunge out a toilet, and unload boxes of donations, you want something comfortable and easily washed. Good-looking clothes along those lines are practical investments, as are sensible shoes. I know those are the shoes of the cliché librarian beloved of cartoonists, but they are essential. You will be amazed and horrified to find out how much time you spend on your feet. You, and your feet, will need all the support you can give them.

You also can't just take your MLS and retire in splendid isolation to The Office to plot grand strategy. There is always something that needs doing out front or someone who needs attention. That something or someone is more important than almost anything you could be doing in the office. Save your journals and catalogs for the slow days. That is when you catch up on your back reading.

Reading journals, reviews, and catalogs is important. The administrator of a small public library, who may well be the only MLS on the staff, is isolated professionally, and reading helps. Meeting with local professional groups is important, too. They may seem to be more social than professional, but a few hours' contact with colleagues is useful, even if it's only to swap war stories. There is nothing wrong with picking colleagues' brains for solutions to your problems. Just remember to give credit when you are retailing your triumphs.

INTIMACY AND COMMITMENT

While "Reader's Advisory" may no longer be done in a large library, it is in a small one. It's unavoidable. When somebody asks you what's a good book, it helps to have a fast answer. Many patrons assume that you have read every book in the place, and nothing you say will change their minds. In time, as you learn your collection, you will learn the popular authors and their read-alikes. You will learn about your patrons as well, especially the regulars, better than most large-library directors can.

This intimacy is hard on you in many ways. Some of your most memorable patrons are the difficult, the demanding, and the strange. You will know them all too well. Worse, people you know will ask your help in finding information on very intimate matters. I have heard about ailments of parts of the human body that I didn't even know existed, and about things that people do to each other that would shock a soap opera writer. It is hard enough to retain your detachment in such matters in the Reference Room, but when you meet the same people in the grocery or the post office, the front is almost impossible to hold up.

The intimacy can also be the source of your highest professional satisfaction. When kids come in after you've helped them on reports to show you their "A's," you glow for a week. When a child drags a parent up to you in the supermarket to introduce him or her to the "library lady," you grin the rest of the day. Seeing in people's faces that you have helped them justifies your existence and choice of profession.

Intimacy also leads to over-commitment, both at the library and in the community. There is always a need in small towns for people to serve on committees and take an active part in groups, and you may want to do it all. Face facts—you can't. Find one or two things you enjoy doing and do those. If they have nothing to do with the library, good. Not having someone to talk shop with also has its points.

At the library, there is a temptation to put in long days and take work home. Resist it. Work has a tendency to fill up your available life, which makes the job less satisfying and you less competent. I have found, though, that catalogs from exotic or offbeat publishing houses make great bathtub reading.

When it comes to relations with your local government, a certain realism is also appropriate. Most governments do not know what librarians and libraries do. Consequently, if you want to do anything, you have to explain it very carefully. If administrators and politicians have any notion of a library at all, it is a vague one of a marble-columned Carnegie, run by a severe librarian whose purpose is to check out books. If the former librarian got along without a VCR, computer, or decent budget—why can't you? The reply that while your predecessors over the years may have gotten along on scraps, scrounging, and the occasional windfall, they didn't like it, will be dismissed. They never complained; you'll wish they had. People do not understand that books in a library work differently from books in the home. It is nearly impossible to explain that books for the library are like the sports equipment for the recreation center that wears out, gets stolen, or gets damaged. They don't understand that books go out of date, especially reference books.

Stoicism is fine in the movies, but in real life, you have to put up a struggle. It won't always get you what you need. But in time, you will come to regard a budget that isn't increased, but hasn't been cut either, as a victory.

BOARDS—GOOD AND BAD

Boards, whether governing or advisory, are a fact of life. You can't have your board abolished, so you must work with it. If properly handled, it can be helpful. Members can lobby the government that pays your bills, they can talk up the library in their social and business circles, they can convey public sentiment to you, and they can support you in bad times, like fiscal crises and censorship incidents. At least they will listen sympathetically to your triumphs and tragedies. These good people do their job without pay in the hope of doing their civic duty by an institution they prize.

And then there are Those Other Boards. One hears about them from colleagues. They, too, are trying to do their duty as they see it, but they combine bossiness, ignorance, and caprice in equal parts. They take every opportunity to make life hard for the librarian. They seek to run the library themselves using you as a glorified clerk. Just remember: nobody's term on a board is forever.

PROBLEMS AND POLICIES

Staff problems also are aggravated by intimacy. People working at close quarters are bound to get on each other's nerves from time to time. Disciplinary problems may be complicated by social and political history that goes far back in time. It is a minefield which could easily blow you out of your job. Provided that the work gets done and the patrons are helped, there is a lot that you are wise not to see. On the other hand, with a small staff you get a degree of involvement that you can't get from a larger, more compartmented one. You also get information undistorted by layers of administration. Not only can an idea for a new procedure be presented to you directly, you can test it and implement or discard it without significant cost or effort, which is always a consideration when you have very little money and few people-hours to spend.

The watchword on developing policies and procedures is "simplicity." Those things that you have to do by your government's rules, you do that way. In-house, keep it simple. It saves time and effort. Rules are a necessary evil because you do need some control over what goes on in the library. Simple rules are easiest to enforce because they are easy to remember. All rules should flow from the "three don'ts": Don't tear up the books, don't tear up the furniture, don't tear up each other.

Quiet, the religion of the cliché library, is essential in certain places, in even the smallest library. Mark those places clearly and enforce quiet, by expulsion if you have to. Provide an alternative area where some noise is permissible: the children's room, the lobby, the front yard. The same rules that apply to children must apply to adults.

Just because you are in a small library doesn't mean you won't attract some strange characters. There are several varieties, similar to those encountered in large libraries. They are entitled to courtesy and assistance. Of course, if they smell awful enough or act strangely enough to cause comment or seem to be turning dangerous, you may have to ask them to leave. A show of courteous firmness is often enough. At times, though, you will be dealing with someone whose behavior seems ready to shift from eccentricity to violence. Clear the area and call the police; this is no time for heroics. You are not equipped to deal with violent people—the police are. Be prepared to sign a complaint and to testify in court, if it comes to that. If the officers settle the problem without an arrest, thank them and send a letter to the department.

More difficult to handle are the "ordinary" problem patrons. They come in several varieties, each enough to make you crazy. A sampler: The Last-Minute Researchers come in a half-hour before closing time with a research problem that would tax the resources of the Library of Congress. Tell them politely but firmly when closing is, and turn out the lights on them, if you have to. The Monomaniacs don't understand why you don't devote the collection to their particular cause. Don't argue with them—they'll just start yelling. The Bestseller Readers are the plague of your Monday mornings with clippings from the Sunday book section firmly in hand. Put them on the waiting lists for the bestsellers, and don't suggest that they read anything else. If Stephen, Danielle, and Louis didn't write it, they don't want to read it, nor do they want last year's model, either. In a tourist area, you will get the summer or winter crowd who regale you with stories about how great the library "back home" is. Listen—you will make homesick people very happy.

REALISTIC SELECTION

When you select for a small library, there are always more books to get than money to get them with. You must make choices. Even some best-selling authors will not go over in your library. Other books, ones that would gather dust in the library down the road, will move like mad, as will certain subjects. This is where being the relief charge clerk and carder comes in handy, especially since you can't afford surveys. You will see what is in demand, what people are asking about. Your financial restrictions will limit your risk-taking, but reserve a little money for it. I've discovered that there is a demand for anything on the Vietnam war and that we need more books on Alzheimer's disease. You listen, you learn, and you buy.

Salespeople don't make your job any easier. Each one has that one book that will make your library perfect, but you have to buy it right now. It usually won't, and you can't afford it anyway. There may be a small public library that could use a Code of Hammurabi with facing pages in Babylonian and English, but it's not mine. That sales call will be wasted, and so will your time. Salespeople will eat up your time if you let them, especially those who drop in and expect you to go through several hundred remainders. They get angry if you don't buy, even if you were frank about your financial limitations. They get even angrier if you won't consent to pay for this year's purchases with next year's anticipated funds. I know that salespeople must have their employer's interests at heart, but I must keep my library's budget firmly in mind. If I can get the same book at a better price somewhere else, that's where I go. My favorite salesperson who represented a business service we subscribed to called twice a year, checked on my satisfaction with his service, mentioned any new products he had, never used my given name, and took perhaps ten minutes of my time all year.

There are some dishonest publishers out there, you'll see their names in journals and newsletters from time to time. Everybody gets stung, and if you can hold the sting to under $100, you're lucky. I have heard of worse. Once in a while, you get your money back. With the help of colleagues and the writing of a few threatening letters, I did. Most people aren't that lucky. Like overdue books, some things cannot be recovered without more expense than the original loss.

Before the sale comes the selection, which brings up the question of what is suitable for your library. The conservatism imposed by your financial limits will solve some of the problems for you. You won't buy an author nobody reads, a subject nobody asks about, or specialized technical works. Nor will you buy many $100 books, except reference books, and those only in alternate years. That still does not address the problem of "questioned" books. What about those?

It is probably not true that every human being has a perfect mate, but I think it is true that every book has an enemy. You cannot select books to placate the enemies of books. If you do that and also yank from the shelves all the things that someone thinks should be yanked, you will be left with a couple of atlases and the phone book. You cannot do this and keep your doors open very long. You need a selection policy, and a policy and procedure on questioned books. Your board should be on record as approving both. Then let the procedure take its course. If the book is defeated and must be withdrawn, you have a difficult choice to make: resign on principle or stick it out and try to win the next one.

I once heard it said that any use of interlibrary loan was an admission of failure on the part of the book selector. This is nonsense because it assumes that a mere mortal librarian is both rich and omniscient. If you begin to get a lot of ILL requests on a particular subject, you will have to examine your buying plans, but it doesn't mean that you have failed. It means that the patrons have taken up something new. Learn from it. In Florida we can borrow large-print books on ILL, and they have proved to be quite popular. I am now buying more large-print books, and the result is gratifying.

ALL'S FAIR IN REFERENCE

Reference in a small public library is easy, but not as easy as it looks. Most questions are simple and easily answered; an encyclopedia, an almanac, a dictionary, Bartlett, and Stevenson will handle them. The local telephone book will handle most local questions. The whole collection works immediately as a reference collection because it doesn't matter where you find a fact as long as it's the one the patron needs. All's fair in love, war, and reference.

One thing they told me in reference class was true: People frequently do not know what they want to know, and if they do, they can't put it into words. Persistent but tactful questioning will almost always get you a question you can answer. It's no different from a large library reference process, including remembering that you have no right to express an opinion of the question or the questioner. It may be dumb to you, but it isn't to the patron who wouldn't ask if there wasn't the need to have an answer.

Sometimes you don't have the answer or a source. It happens, especially in a small library. Don't hesitate to say so. People are amazed and delighted by honesty, and if you combine this with an offer to seek the answer outside your library, you will make a friend.

Reference work includes helping children who are doing their homework. It is legitimate for students to get help in using the library's resources. It is your business, not theirs, to know the collection. You must not turn them off by saying "Look it up" and wave at the card catalog. The student may never have been taught how to use one. This is where you come in. Showing a child, or any patron, how to use the library's resources is not intellectual dishonesty. It is bibliographic instruction.

THE CHILD PATRON BECOMES THE ADULT PATRON

Children's work is important. The child patron grows up to be the adult patron. If children are happy and comfortable in a library, they'll be back when they grow up. A public institution like a library should be as interested in developing repeat customers as any commercial concern.

A separate room is helpful since children's voices don't have reliable volume controls. The room should be cheerful and contain toys and games for the children who do not or cannot read. Bookshelves must be accessible to small persons, just as the furniture must be their size. This is their room, and they must be made welcome in all things. Besides the usual signs on restroom doors, one library also displays posters of Kermit the Frog and Miss Piggy. Preschoolers don't know "Men" and "Women" yet, but they know those two.

If you don't do programs for anyone else, do them for children. Story times and summer programs give you a way to separate the library from automatic association with school. Many programs can be put on for little or no money if you exploit local resources. There are treasures in every community that only need a little prospecting. This allows you to budget for those programs for which you must pay full fare. Your state library agency may also coordinate programs and provide free or low-cost materials.

GOOD FRIENDS AND GOOD INTENTIONS

Your state library agency can be a good friend. In Florida, the agency provides ILL, film loans, reference help, and consultations—among other things. It is worth your while to find out what your state library can do for you and then take advantage of those services. They are yours for the asking.

No library should be without its friends, organized or not. They can supplement your budget and complement your efforts. Friends care about the library. They want it to succeed. Their energy and good will are invaluable to you.

Other people with good intentions will donate books or magazines or try to. Since you have limited space, you have to decide what to take and what to reject. Whatever you do will make somebody angry. Taking everything will eat up your time in getting things sorted and stored. Much is not usable anyway—outdated books, marked-up textbooks, books you already have, old books of no antiquarian interest. Your Friends group can sell some. You may find a book you can use or a magazine to complete a run, but not often.

Sometimes what people say they want to donate is really what they want to unload. I once rejected an entire pick-up truck full of paperbacks that I was assured were "just a little damp." They were crawling with mildew, but the prospective donor couldn't understand that I didn't dare accept them because mildew is as deadly to books as smallpox is to people, and as contagious. The "donor" went away mad. So do the people who want to donate several years of the *National Geographic*. Since they don't sell well locally, and we have our own subscription, I generally suggest giving them to a nursing home or a school or throwing them away. The latter shocks people. Would-be donors sneak them into the library or the bookdrop anyway, in parcels neatly tied up with string. This makes them easier to take out to the dumpster.

It's hard to make people understand that they aren't doing you a favor by donating long runs of the *Geographic* or a 1962 encyclopedia. They mean well, and you don't want to hurt their feelings. All you can do is wait until they have left the building before you put the donations in the dumpster. Some donors, of course, are looking for appraisals for tax donations. Unless you are a professional appraiser on the side, don't do it. Life is tough enough without adding the IRS to your problems.

Paperbacks are another problem. Sometimes the only way you can get a book is as a trade or mass-market paperback, or that's the only format you can afford. If so, that's what you buy, but what do you do with the donations of formula fiction and assorted other stuff? Once you've culled what you can use and the obviously crumbling, you can sell the leftovers or have a paperback exchange. The latter involves very little work and space. All you need do is shelve the books on old drugstore paperback racks. It can be a straight one-for-one honor exchange, and only what goes out for circulation need be counted. Some people never use any other part of the library. Some exchange people eventually get library cards. Patrons with cards often take the exchanges on vacation because they're cheaper to replace than regular books if they lose them at the beach.

LOSSES AND THEFTS

People lose books. They damage them. They keep them out too long. Short of sending an enforcer out to bring the books back, there isn't much you can do. Sending overdue notices and freezing borrowers' cards will get some books back. You can call the offending patrons, but this will also get you a lot of abuse. The only cure is to remain calm and quote the price of the replacement books. This should bring in some strays: A $2 fine is preferable to a $19.95 replacement charge.

Of course, an extreme recourse is to place the matter in the hands of the police or your government's attorney. But this can only be done if your city or county is willing and able to prosecute. If not, all you can do is refuse to loan the patron any more books and swallow your loss.

Theft is all too common in all libraries. Anatomy books, PDR (the *Physician's Desk Reference*), the *Merck Manual,* and test preparation books are popular targets. The only solution, unless you have an unlimited budget, is to keep them behind the front desk and make patrons sign for them. Sometimes you wonder if it might not be a good idea to have an enforcer in your budget after all.

BUDGETARY TRUTHS

Small library budgets are not devised in response to carefully delineated objectives as part of an ongoing program of fiscal control. Large systems may have something like that with a certain impersonality governing the budget process; if your budget gets cut, the odds are that everybody took a cut. In a small system, that's not how it works. Department heads may work out budgets carefully, but what gets funded will reflect the opinions of one or two people who have influence rather than the real needs of your department. Sometimes your board can lobby the right people or the appropriating body, but success is not guaranteed. Libraries are placed not only behind police, fire, and water and sewer, but also behind recreation and landscaping. All too often, you have to settle for last year's budget and no inflation increase. You can supplement your budget with gifts and donations, but an appeal requires front money you may not have. If you do manage to raise money on your own, you may find that your budget has been reduced by just that amount. If you don't have an account tied to your department, your hard-raised money may be absorbed in general revenue or made over to some other department, and you never see a dime of it.

PROFESSIONAL PREPARATION

How do you prepare to be the administrator of a small public library? To coin a cliché, you don't have to be crazy, but it helps. It also helps to be a jack of all trades, or at least willing to learn. Whatever miscellaneous needs to be done will suddenly become your problem, even if it doesn't seem quite consonant with your librarianly dignity.

Get the MLS. More and more it is the minimum professional qualification. There are still some places that cannot or will not pay for an MLS, so there is and will be a place for the non-MLS librarian for some time. If there is a choice between no MLS and no service, there really is no choice.

A good liberal education is an asset. You will be the town's paid intellectual, and it helps to be able to act like one. Read omnivorously— magazines, newspapers, and books, besides professional reading. Often, the only clue you have to solving a reference problem will be a vague memory of something you read somewhere. Don't neglect that professional reading, though. There is always something you can use, if only the freebies that most journals list.

FRUSTRATIONS AND COMPENSATIONS

It can all be very frustrating. You always have more projects to do than hours to do them in. You always run out of money before you run out of needs. Parents treat you as a cheap babysitting service. Salespeople are after your money. Patrons drive you nuts. Book publishers produce ever more fragile books at ever higher prices. Periodicals change name, format, and state of being at the drop of a hat. Your feet hurt even in sensible shoes. Feminists demean your choice of profession if you're a woman. Men think you're a sissy if you're a man. Your professional schools and associations are overwhelmingly on the side of bigness. The technological revolution is too expensive for you to join. Big names in the business cheerily predict the demise of the public library, starting with the small ones. You have to make speeches. Some days all you want to do is run away and become a beach bum. But you don't. Why?

There are many reasons. There are the mechanics who scrub their hands almost raw before they come in to use the Chilton's manuals. There are the people who thank you for finding special books for them on ILL. There is the gentleman who brings roses for no reason and the lady who brings candy every Christmas. There are the people (the majority) who bring books back on time. There are the slow learners who have developed decided opinions about the books they are beginning to enjoy reading. There are the people who thank you for suggesting a book or who bring in friends to get library cards. There is the father who brought his four sons and signed them all up, and himself as well. There is the little boy who came to the summer program and then acted as a guide for a little friend's mother when she needed to find the library. There is the little girl who took a shy boy in hand and acted as his social sponsor at his first story time. The job has its compensations.

The most truthful book I have ever read about being a small-town librarian is *Diary of a Village Library* by Caroline Lord (Somersworth: New Hampshire Pub. Co., 1971, o.p.). You may not have to stoke a furnace or sweep down the building as she did, but her experiences are common to all small-town libraries. I think that if Ms. Lord had been asked, at the end of her nearly 20 years at the Francestown Public Library in New Hampshire, "Was it worth it?" she would have replied, "Yes, it was." It still is.

The School Library

Robert Skapura

A school library must be viewed as an extension of the classroom, and managing the library has only one purpose: to make education in that school more effective. The library then is both a place of learning and a place that houses the tools of learning; put simply, the school librarian helps teachers teach and students learn.

The resources of the library must be organized, but the role of the school librarian goes beyond organizational skills. In most states, the librarian must also have a teaching credential since the librarian is expected to participate both directly and indirectly in the learning activities that take place in that school. One of those activities is to teach students to find information and materials by themselves.

Probably the common thread that runs through managing small libraries of all types is that the managing librarian must wear many hats. In a large public or university library, tasks fall to various individuals or departments: young adult, periodicals, reference, technical services. The lone librarian managing a small library does all of these things, and part of the organizational skill lies in making sure that each task is done within the constraints of limited staff and budget.

The heart of any school is the curriculum; it must also become the touchstone for library policy and procedures. The collection must reflect the curriculum and satisfy the assignments teachers make or else the students go away frustrated.

Probably the most promising innovation introduced into school library management in the 1980s is the use of microcomputers. It's a rare school that does not now have micros for student use (usually Apple computers); even where there are only a few, they very often end up in the library. The microcomputers that are used by students during the day can be put to library tasks before and after school. There are a large number of computer programs designed specifically for libraries, easy to use by either the librarian, student aides, or parent volunteers. Microcomputer programs can generate overdues, print bibliographies, keep track of inventory, and produce flyers and lists of all kinds. A school librarian with no computer background can find ready help in getting started from both students and other faculty members. *Booklist, School*

Robert Skapura is Librarian at Clayton Valley High School, Concord, California.

Library Journal, Book Report, and *School Library Media Quarterly* regularly carry reviews of software for library applications. The Apple Computer Company publishes a free newsletter (*The Apple Library Users Group*) with articles and advice from librarians who use microcomputers for management tasks.

Few things are as important in managing a library as organizing it; this includes the physical plant, the procedures, and the people working there. If the library materials are well organized, everyone (not just the librarian) can easily locate things. If library procedures are well organized, tasks are done efficiently. If people (paid staff, student aides, and volunteers) are organized, they have a clear idea of what to do.

ORGANIZING THE PHYSICAL PLANT

From kindergarten through twelfth grade, there is a subtle shift in emphasis in terms of the role that the library and the librarian play in the school. In the early grades, the teaching of reading is probably the most important activity in the classroom. Encouraging reading and promoting activities that produce a positive attitude toward books must, therefore, be high on an elementary librarian's agenda. This frequently involves displays, story reading, contests, and games. Elementary students in the early grades come to the library as a class, usually the same time each week, to return books checked out the previous week and to check out new ones.

In late elementary through high school, the shift is away from reading as an activity separate from a particular subject, and the library is looked upon as a place to do what can loosely be called research. Students are sent to the library on assignment to gather information and to prepare for papers or presentations. Even selecting a fiction book is often an assignment and must satisfy a certain criterion, e.g., historical fiction, only American authors, more than 250 pages. This shift has implications in the ways in which an elementary and high school library are organized; not that the differences are drastic, just a matter of emphasis. The elementary library should be attractive and engaging, a place that invites youngsters to come in and promises delight. The high school library should be organized so that information is easy to find and the logical order is obvious.

Signs and Divisions

Most students are not regular library users. There might be months (or years) between visits. This makes it all the more important that the books and materials be clearly marked and organized logically. Two ways of doing this are through the use of signs and the grouping of materials in logical ways. The grouping must come first, and the signs designate the groupings. Other organizations that deal with large numbers of people trying to find things understand this, e.g., supermarkets, subways, and amusement parks.

First the *kinds* of books should be grouped, as much as possible by themselves: Fiction, Nonfiction, Biography, and Reference are the most common. Library collections grow organically over many years. Fiction sections have been known to outgrow their original wall shelving and snake across rooms to free-standing shelves far away; reference sections that begin in the middle of free-standing bookcases, continue to wall shelving, and then jump across a doorway to end up behind the charge desk. The librarian who has worked in the same library for over 20 years moves smoothly from one section to another; the student is simply confused. When divisions have outgrown their original place, the library has to be reorganized so that students coming through the entrance to the library have an immediate sense of order and quickly perceive the arrangement. Large bright signs should mark the sections. In addition to the four traditional divisions, a special place is frequently set aside for encyclopedias and the *Readers' Guide* volumes with tables or study carrels. Additional signs should designate the card catalog and the check-out desk.

The Classification System

Although most school libraries use the Dewey Decimal System with Sear's subject headings, there can still be wide variation in the call numbers that confuses students. Since there are a half dozen acceptable ways to designate (with call numbers) fiction books, biographies, and easy books, some agreement is necessary. Consistency should be the rule, first within the school system itself and then within the community. A student should not find one system in the elementary school, a second in the high school, and still a third in the local public library. Since most librarians inherit a system that has been established for years, the real decision is whether to continue it or change it. But if the system is different from the community library or other schools, the decision must be faced.

The Card Catalog

A case can be made for either a combined or divided card catalog. The combined card catalog contains author, title, and subject cards alphabetized by top line. The divided one separates the cards into two sections, author and title cards in one section, and subject cards in the other. Neither system is clearly superior.

AV Materials

Even after the media explosion of the 1970s, it is still true that most students gravitate toward printed sources when seeking information. Most frequently AV materials are used by teachers as part of a class presentation. Because of this, most school librarians place the AV materials (filmstrips, kits, prints, tapes, records, etc.) in a separate section of the library. It is extremely important, however, that these materials be cataloged and that subject cards are placed in the card catalog, so that students and teachers can find these resources when doing research. Librarians seem split on a circulation policy for AV materials. Some let students take items home; others let them check them out only to their classrooms or for use in the library.

Paperbacks

Students, especially teenagers, seem to prefer paperbacks to hardcover books when given a choice. It could be the size of paperbacks or the fact that they're less intimidating, but the fact is that students gravitate around the paperback spinner racks. School librarians seem to have varying policies on how to treat paperbacks, in cataloging, shelving, and circulating them. Frequently paperbacks are put on the spinner rack without being cataloged at all or only very briefly. A title card and perhaps an author card are put into the card catalog, but since a call number is not put on the spine of the paperback, the catalog card only serves the purpose of telling the student that the library has the book and that it is somewhere on the spinner racks. Sometimes a book catalog, in both author and title order, is printed, something a microcomputer does very easily. Since most paperbacks are selected for pleasure reading, the philosophy seems to be that paperback racks encourage browsing, and a more casual attitude is in keeping with that intention. In some school libraries, paperbacks are seen as almost disposable items, with checkouts and returns on the honor system.

Periodicals

In elementary grades, periodicals are generally few and selected to encourage reading. In most high school libraries, the periodical budget is a substantial portion of the total with titles a combination of pleasure reading and those needed for research. Many high school librarians selectively back up their hard copy titles with microforms (either microfiche or film), but when given a choice, most students prefer the hard copy to the microform. Magazine request forms should be printed up and kept near the *Readers' Guide* volumes. They should contain at least the following information: student's name, and magazine title and date. If students also copy down the pages of the magazine in which the article appears, this will save them time later. The forms are then presented at the desk. Most librarians box the periodicals in Princeton files, labeling them chronologically, and house them in an area accessible only to the library staff.

Allowing students to check out periodicals from the library is a policy decision that must be made by the librarian. Once an old magazine is lost or damaged, the fine paid by the student cannot actually replace the issue. Many librarians do not allow magazines to be removed from the library, but if there is a duplicating machine for student use at a reasonable price, this policy does not place a hardship on students.

ORGANIZING PROCEDURES

Checking Books Out and In

On a daily basis few tasks are as important as checking books out and back in again. The whole purpose of a library is to put resources into the hands of those who need them. It's important to have a simple, straightforward method for checking materials out because this task is frequently shared by student aides, volunteers, clerks, and the librarian.

Items are usually checked out for anywhere from one to three weeks, the length of time to be decided by the librarian. There may be fewer overdues in the three-week check-out period. Most school librarians place a charge card in the pocket of the book. The top of the card contains the author, title, and call number of the book, the copy number, and perhaps an accession number; this information is repeated on the pocket of the book. The card has room for the due date, and the student's name and location—a homeroom or teacher's name, the place to which the overdue can be sent. The location usually has to be squeezed in somewhere on the line; there never seems to be enough room.

Getting a clear signature on the charge card is always a problem and deciphering a name is a real challenge when doing overdues. Some school librarians employ a charging machine that uses a library card to imprint the student's name on the charge card. It solves the handwriting problem, but it's difficult to get students to carry their library cards. The due date must be stamped in two places: once on the charge card and once on a due date slip that is in the book.

At the end of each day, the charge cards from the day's checkouts are arranged in some order, usually kept separate by due date in an upright file. Within the due date, arranging the cards alphabetically by author is most common, but it can be done by call number or accession number order. In elementary grades, they are even sometimes arranged under the teacher's name. Each arrangement has its advantages.

Some librarians change the due date every day; others change it once a week which seems to work better. Once a week means that there are only four or five divisions in the file at the circulation desk, while daily due dates mean that there will be 25 to 30 small divisions. When looking for snags or mix-ups, four or five divisions make it easier. If the due date is changed only once a week, books checked out on any day during the week are all due on the same day.

Most libraries have items that are checked out for only one day, e.g., encyclopedias, reference books, vertical file pamphlets. An additional due date stamp should be handy so that the regular one will not have to be continually changed. This makes for fewer mistakes. There is usually a third category of checkouts for the faculty. Generally, courtesy is extended to faculty members, allowing them to sign the charge cards with no due date stamped on it, only the checkout date. Three divisions then are made in the file at the circulation desk: regular checkouts, overnights, and faculty.

When books are returned, the charge cards must be retrieved from the circulation file and replaced in the books. The due date slip is checked and the card should be located in that date division in the file at the circulation desk. This is a task that students or volunteers can do. In some libraries, the carded books are not immediately shelved; first the books are checked by either a library aide or the librarian before they are put on the cart for shelving. Student aides are not always observant of copy numbers or even different titles by the same author. A card mix-up at this point can cause serious problems later on.

Generating Overdues

There are almost as many ways of doing overdues as there are librarians. The principle, however, is the same everywhere: students who do not return books on time must somehow be notified. Very few librarians send overdues the very first day a book is overdue; most wait a few days. If individual slips are used, the charge cards can be taken out of the circulation file and the pertinent information copied onto the notices. Three-part commercial notices are available so that if a second or third notice is necessary, the information is already there. The individual notices are then grouped by room or teacher and distributed throughout the school.

Some librarians simply issue lists, either by room or one long master list. This works better in the elementary grades where students have the same teacher all day long. On the high school level, such lists raise an ethical issue. A list of overdues would invariably contain the title of the book checked out; if it doesn't contain the title, the student has to come to the library to see what he or she owes. Titles of books on sensitive subjects (venereal disease, teen pregnancy, drug abuse, homosexuality, etc.) which appear on a list opposite a student's name might cause embarrassment and raises the issue of a patron's right to privacy.

Microcomputers are a great help in doing overdues. There are a large number of commercial programs that generate overdues. Student aides or volunteers can type in the information, and the printer tirelessly generates individual notices (first, second, third bills) and prints lists sorted in a variety of useful ways. In one school of over 2,200 students, overdues are entered, printed, sorted, and distributed in less than two periods a week, which could not be done without a microcomputer.

Policies vary, but some librarians send only one overdue notice. The second notice is a bill, a copy of which is sent to the school treasurer. If the student returns the book, the treasurer is notified to clear the bill. The treasurer informs the librarian if the book has been paid for. A computer-generated master list of all students who owe overdues or bills can be kept at the desk. Most schools require students who are transferring to check out with the library before leaving the school; a master list is invaluable at such times. Without a computer, that kind of list would be very time-consuming to maintain.

Passes or No Passes

School libraries operate successfully at both ends of a pass policy. Some require all students who enter to present a pass at the desk. This seems more prevalent in the upper grades. Others require only good behavior while in the library. The library is an attractive refuge for students who, for whatever reason, are not in class. Only the librarian at a particular site can determine which policy best serves the goals of the school.

Lunches, Breaks, Before and After School

As a rule, the library should be open during at least part of the student lunch period and for some time before and after school. For many students, this is their only opportunity to use the library. Policies vary widely on this point. In my school, the library is open 20 minutes before and 45 minutes after school hours. The library is closed the first 15 minutes of the lunch period, a practice that has virtually eliminated the problem of students eating lunch in the library. It gives me a chance to spend 15 minutes in the faculty lunch room, a convenient time for the faculty to touch base with me and make requests for materials. The library aide takes her lunch after the students; I take mine before.

ORGANIZING THE STAFF

The range in staffing patterns among school libraries is very great. Some librarians have no paid clerical staff at all or only a day or two a week. A librarian may run more than one school. In some communities, it is very difficult to find outside volunteers or even reliable student aides. And then there are school libraries that have more than one full-time librarian, paid assistants, student aides, and many volunteers. Nevertheless, the goal in directing clerical help (whether paid or volunteer) is to free librarians to do the professional tasks for which they were trained. If there are no aides at all, books must still be checked out, overdues sent, and books reshelved. If there is no one else, the librarian must do these things taking time from activities that more directly contribute to education in that school.

Paid Assistants

The most successful school libraries always include an excellent library assistant who efficiently manages the clerical aspects of running the library, freeing the librarian to work directly with staff and students. Responsibilities must be matched with talent, but generally maintaining the files at the circulation desk, typing orders and correspondence, processing books, and overseeing the shelving of books and magazines are typical tasks for assistants. The microcomputer can help automate some of those tasks, although it takes a willingness on the part of the assistant to make that succeed.

The library assistant usually keeps an eye on supplies, ordering whatever is necessary from a local district warehouse or from a library supply catalog. In many school districts, a formal job description lists responsibilities and gives examples of how to complete forms, make out purchase orders, and submit reports. More important than any formal job requirements is the *relationship* between the library assistant and the librarian. The assistant should be made to feel part of a team with a common goal. The librarian should not hesitate to help out on occasion with clerical tasks when things get behind. The assistant should share in the library's success in the classroom or with student assignments, and be asked for suggestions when appropriate. For many librarians, no single factor is more important to a library running well than a good library assistant. It is the librarian, however, who is responsible for discipline in the library, not the library assistant. If students become angry or abusive, they should immediately be handed over to the librarian.

Student Aides

Upper elementary, junior and senior high school students are certainly capable of helping in the library. Typical tasks include checking books out, carding returns, pulling magazines that students request, shelving returned books, and generating and distributing overdues. Straightening the library at the end of the day and a little modest cleaning is also common. Students should only be given one task at a time to learn; after a few days, a new one can be added. The accuracy of most tasks can be easily measured, e.g., reading the shelves, verifying that the proper card is replaced in returned books.

In upper grades, student aides receive the same status as a classroom aide. A grade is given and attendance is kept, encouraging the students to do a good job. Student aides should have a clear understanding, at the outset, of what their grades will be based on to avoid an argument or a misunderstanding later. In some schools, students work every period; in others, only two or three periods a day.

Volunteers

It is not impossible but very difficult to run an entire library program based on volunteer help. Volunteers are there out of good will, and obligation and necessity sometimes override good intentions. Library aides are paid; student aides receive a grade. Both these things help regular attendance. Volunteers don't have such "easy" incentives.

The most successful volunteer programs involve specific projects with no immediate deadline. If the volunteer does not show up, the job can wait until later or next week. Such projects include targeting books for a detection system, labeling magazine boxes, making new signs for the library, reshelving magazines, helping with overdues, and the like. With a specific project in mind, a request to the parents club or a similar organization for volunteers usually produces results.

PROFESSIONAL ACTIVITIES

Managing the library is the first of the professional activities that a librarian is hired to do, but in a school library, this responsibility is not an end in itself. In a sense, managing tasks are secondary; teaching is primary.

In the context of the library, teaching usually takes one of three forms: 1) teaching a formal class on library skills or preparing a group to do an assignment in the library; 2) teaching indirectly by working with teachers on a specific topic, pulling pertinent resources, or selecting specific materials for an exercise; or 3) one-on-one teaching that continually takes place when working with an individual student.

Most school librarians develop a number of teaching units for the school year. Typically this involves using the card catalog, the *Readers' Guide,* specific reference books, or books on a particular topic. Many librarians have worked out library skills exercises that are taught to all the students at a particular grade level. Because there is no common call number notation in the United States and no group of books guaranteed to be in every library, commercial materials are usually vague, dull, and ineffective. Despite the difficulties, most school librarians have created a number of presentations that are polished and professional and very helpful in getting students off on the right foot.

In addition to the content being taught during such lessons, there is another effect that is beneficial to the librarian. Students and staff will perceive the librarian as a "teacher." Teachers respect few things as much as they do another teacher who's doing a good job.

Teaching classes is rarely done every day, but working with students is continual. When working with a single student who has made a request, there is always the temptation to go directly to the materials, retrieve them, and simply hand them to the student. In some situations, this is appropriate. But many times it's also an opportunity for instruction. No matter how many times the same explanation is repeated by the librarian, it may very well be the first time a particular student has heard it. The hardest part is to remain fresh and enthusiastic during such explanations, a problem teachers have in every subject area. This "teaching" aspect more than anything else marks the difference between a school librarian and a public librarian.

Teaching indirectly takes place when the librarian works with teachers developing a lesson or an assignment that involves the resources of the library. This requires two things from the librarian: rapport with the teachers and thorough knowledge of the collection. Both of these are acquired only after a length of time.

Few things are as important to a successful library program as the relationship between the librarian and the staff. Teachers must view the librarian not as a cataloger, an archivist, or a policeperson, but rather as *another educator.* The librarian's subject area is the resources in the library and how to find things quickly and efficiently. The librarian should willingly take on typical staff duties, for instance, sitting on committees, attending school activities, and helping out at functions outside the library. All of these activities reinforce the perception of the librarian as a staff member.

This relationship between the teachers and the librarian is important because much depends on good will. Something as simple as distributing overdues cannot be done without the cooperation of the staff. Working with a class in preparation for an assignment requires an invitation from the teacher, and teachers will not seek out the librarian unless they both respect the librarian's knowledge and feel comfortable working together. There's no magic formula, but clearly never leaving the library, never having coffee or lunch in the faculty lounge, and excluding oneself from outside school activities does not help build that rapport.

Promoting the Resources

It is not enough to wait for students and staff to come to the library. A school librarian should promote the resources in as many ways as possible. This includes publishing subject bibliographies, displays, announcements of new materials, reading contests, and participating on committees that develop curriculum or distribute funds. This is another area where a microcomputer can be a great aid. Special computer programs can be used to create flyers and posters, and both a word processing program and a database manager make publishing lists and announcements easy to do and professional in appearance.

Selecting and Ordering Materials

Few things have a longer lasting effect on the library than collection development. The librarian must be familiar with the school curriculum and have a knowledge of what materials are available for purchase. Working with the collection over the years provides the first; professional journals provide the latter. *Booklist, School Library Journal,* and *Book Report* are frequent sources for reviews of books K-12.

Some school districts allow the librarian to order books directly from a jobber such as Baker & Taylor or Demco, but most require that purchase orders be placed through a central purchasing office. This insures that the librarian does not exceed the allotted budget. If the titles selected are from a current periodical, it can be assumed that the item is in print. If the title being ordered is more than a year or two old, it's always a good idea to check *Books in Print* to verify availability.

Processing Materials

Most book and media jobbers offer processing as a service to librarians. For an additional charge they will provide a book jacket, book pocket, spine labels, and catalog cards with every book. There are other companies that specialize in selling catalog card sets by themselves. The quality of the cataloging varies, but if the school district does not process the books for the school libraries, this service should be seriously considered. Cataloging and processing new books is a time-consuming task and one that cuts into other activities of the librarian. There are also a number of microcomputer programs that generate all the catalog cards after only the information for the main entry card is entered. These programs usually print spine and pocket labels also.

Funding

Most schools receive their funds from a number of sources—local, state, and federal. There are no common funding sources that would hold true in school libraries everywhere. Some districts have a written policy requiring that a certain amount per student be budgeted for library materials. In other schools, the library depends solely upon the generosity of the parents' club. In some schools, there is truth to the joking reference to bake sales and book fairs. In most schools, though, the principal usually has a fair amount of latitude in spending funds. The principal also knows the various sources for money and which ones the library would qualify for: special state programs, federal funds, instructional budget, and organizations that contribute to the school. To win the support of the principal almost always assures adequate funding. Principals have an amazing ability to find money for projects they want to promote. To win that support, it is necessary that the principal be kept abreast of what takes place in the library and its most pressing needs.

Inventory and Weeding

Most school librarians find it almost impossible to take a complete inventory each year. Many divide the collection into three or four divisions, doing only one section a year. This is also the perfect time to weed the collection. In addition to the general criteria used for weeding collections in other types of libraries, the school librarian must consider the school curriculum and whether the item is regularly used in teachers' assignments. Only a librarian familiar with the collection and knowledgeable about school assignments can properly weed the books. When a book is removed from the collection, it should be remembered that all cards in the catalog must also be removed. Final exam week or the end of the term is the usual time for inventory.

It is not an accident that so many school librarians have themselves been classroom teachers. The characteristics that are admired in a good teacher are the same ones found in an excellent school librarian.

The Four-Year College Library

Terrence Mech

Library directors at smaller four-year colleges have a difficult task. Their libraries are staffed with three or fewer librarians, a few support staff, and a number of student assistants. Colleges that support these libraries are almost exclusively private or church related. Student enrollments are generally under one thousand, 500 being the norm. These colleges, frequently rural and isolated, have never really seen good times. Most have been struggling since they were founded; some have recently fallen on hard times and are shadows of their former selves. Deferred maintenance is a way of life for most.

Successful directors of smaller college libraries must be generalists and able "to do everything and do all at the same time."[1] A recent advertisement for a library director at a small college library indicated that the "Primary responsibilities include, in addition to usual administrative tasks, all technical services, staff training and development, and serials. Share public service responsibilities with other staff, including some nights and weekends."[2]

Small college library directors soon learn that there is more to do than any one person can do well, much less be equally successful in all areas of responsibility.[3] The key to success is realizing that one cannot do it all. Concentrate on what must be done and do it well; eliminate tasks that are not necessary and compensate for weaknesses.

Within academic librarianship, there is a definite pecking order among institutions by pedigree and size. At the top are large research libraries and Ivy League schools. Lower down are the bucolic, very selective, small regional colleges. At the bottom are the smallest of the small college libraries. Like anything else different or unique, smaller college libraries are frequently misunderstood by those who have infrequent contact with them.

Being small in American academia frequently means doing without and living with a sense of being in the academic minor leagues. In academia, bigger is supposedly better; however, Schumacher makes the point that small is beautiful.[4] Liberal arts colleges are resilient human organizations. Generally small and specialized (a characteristic which

Terrence Mech is Director of the D. Leonard Corgan Library, King's College, Wilkes-Barre, Pennsylvania.

makes them more vulnerable than diversified universities), they are easier to manage. They command a high degree of loyalty and commitment from their faculty and staff, who are generally willing to make personal sacrifices on behalf of the college. This intangible feature is a great asset.[5]

Because of the "bigger is better" bias, librarians and administrators at smaller colleges frequently fail to recognize the uniqueness of their missions and situations. They are not working in miniature universities, yet they exhibit a strong tendency to think and manage their college libraries as if they were university libraries. The "University-library Syndrome" is identified as "a pattern of attitudes which cause college faculty, administrators, and librarians to think of their libraries in terms of university libraries—and thus to imitate their practices, attitudes, and objectives."[6]

College libraries exist to do more than support the college's curriculum. They exist *primarily* for the students, and they are in a position to teach undergraduates independent research and intelligent library use. Because of their size and mission, colleges and their libraries can offer an undergraduate some totally unique educational experiences. Unfortunately, much of this potential is lost because librarians, college administrators, and faculty are often afflicted with University-library Syndrome. "College libraries are quite different from university libraries, not only in quantitative terms but in their educational roles. They have their own goals and purposes and unique opportunities to achieve them. Only if the differences are kept in mind can college librarians begin to work successfully toward these goals."[7]

AMBIGUOUS MANAGERIAL ROLE

Management is a difficult enough task. Much of the trouble academic library managers suffer from may be related to their weak grasp of what they are or should be.[8] Confusion about the managerial role is not unique to librarians. Misunderstanding about what a manager is and does is unfortunately quite widespread.

The library director's job is ambiguous with many conflicting aspects to it. Directors must identify with the faculty, yet manage one of the largest budgets and most complex operations on campus. Varied and unpredictable demands come from forces both inside and outside the library. The college administration wants a proficient manager; the faculty wants a scholar librarian; and the staff wants a supervisor. These conflicting expectations shape the director's job[9,10] and frequently place library directors in the middle between internal and external groups. The feeling of being "in the middle" seems to increase with the amount of time library directors spend with constituencies outside the library.[11]

Library directors at small colleges tend to concentrate their energy on internal library matters.[12] But while internal matters are immediate and not amenable to delegation because there frequently *is* no one else, relations with groups outside the library are important and cannot be neglected. As libraries grow, library directors find themselves forced to spend more time on external concerns.

Faculty, students, staff, administration, and library staff all have their ideas about what a library is and how it ought to be run. Library directors have their idea, too. Differences among these expectations frequently produce stress. Library directors need self-confidence, self-motivation, and a strong occupational self-identity to cope with this stress. "Librarians with strong professional identities, independent of their particular position, seem much less vulnerable to stress, much less prone to withdrawal and associated feelings of futility. They generally are satisfied with their performance, do not look to others to know what is expected of them."[13]

Because of the numerous inherent frustrations, limited resources, the size and diversity of their task, library managers occasionally retreat into the security of day-to-day operations. It is easier to simply survive one day at a time. It is exactly because things are less than euphoric at smaller college libraries that directors must not neglect leadership and management duties such as planning.

THE PLANNING IMPERATIVE

Making things happen, rather than watching them happen, is much more fun: Management on the offensive is more satisfying than management on the defensive. In theory, it is as simple as knowing where you are, where you want to go, and then deciding what you need to do and how you are going to do it. Without a course of action, a library will drift endlessly, using limited resources and going nowhere fast. Setting a plan to paper crystalizes thinking and allows one to clearly identify alternatives, resources, and the necessary steps. If a plan is not written down and tested in open debate, it is meaningless.

When resources are limited, it is imperative to plan and focus their use. If the library must suddenly reduce its budget in mid-year by 25 percent, it helps to have priorities already identified. When cuts have to be made, they should be made by the library director rather than the dean.

There is widespread agreement on the purpose and importance of planning, but there is no universal planning process. McClure[14] provides a good overview of various planning processes and their basic components. Planning gives the organization direction and serves as the basis for all other management functions.

Before planning, you must know the environment in which the college and library operate. Knowing the faculty is vital. How do they teach? What do they really want from the library? Forget what they say, what do their actions tell you? What do they demand from students? What do students tell you? Where do they come from? How prepared for college are they? What do they really want from college and what are they capable of doing? Similar questions are appropriate for administration. Find out who really calls the shots on campus. Get a feel for the institution and what goes on before starting to make changes. Frequently, new directors coming from larger institutions or fresh from graduate school barge right in because they supposedly see "so clearly what must be done." As a result, they miscalculate the problems, personalities, and resources and get needlessly mired in politics and land mines. Find out what your predecessor was really up to before launching anything. One of the first things a new director should do is find a number of reliable but politically neutral sources who can reveal "who's who" and "what's what" on campus.

Before the library can progress, it must be evaluated. How well is the library doing? What resources does it have available? Evaluation is still a subjective operation. Although "Standards for College Libraries, 1986"[15] exists, they are considered to be ideals rather than possibles by many college administrators. With that caveat in mind, standards can be used as a framework to provide an overview of the library and its operation. "An Evaluative Checklist for Reviewing a College Library Program"[16] provides an extensive framework for evaluation based on the "Standards for College Libraries."[17]

Another good source of evaluative information is comparative data. Rather than comparing your library against an abstract standard, compare it with other libraries of similar size and type. Basic data can be gathered from directories; more extensive data can be collected by questionnaire. It is important first to identify schools that your college administration considers its peers, or schools it wishes to emulate, and then what information you need—budget, staffing, space, circulation, collection, etc. Once you have identified the information, ask the other libraries for it. Resist the temptation to ask for too much. Chances are they will share their information willingly, in exchange for a copy of the results.

Is the library doing things that need not be done? Smaller college libraries do not need to duplicate the operations of larger libraries. Because your time and personnel resources are limited, do not waste them on unnecessary processes. Throw out the accession book. Just because others have always done it that way is not a good reason for continuing to do it. Keep operations lean and efficient.

Having assessed the college and the library, decide on the type of library service the college needs and can support, and what services the library can realistically offer. The library's mission statement is a concept of itself and its purpose and should conform with the college's mission statement. College libraries are not independent, self-sufficient entities. They exist to support the colleges' teaching/learning process.

Having determined what the library's role will be on campus, establish goals and objectives. Goals are general statements of the direction in which the library will move; they are not time-bound or measurable, e.g., our goal is to increase use of the library. Objectives are more specific statements of what the library will try to achieve within a certain time, usually a year. Objectives should be clear, measurable and have a deadline, e.g., our objective is to increase circulation by ten percent by the end of the fiscal year. Priorities are needed to assure that the most important objectives receive emphasis and resources.[18] Once you have determined what it is you need, develop your strategies. How are you going to increase circulation by ten percent?

Planning, with its goals, objectives, priorities, and strategies, is easier said than done. Lee[19] demonstrates that a plan does not have to be long and detailed to be effective. The purpose of planning is to move the library towards something better or at least prevent it from slipping. Even if your goal is to keep the doors open and get the newspapers out, you know what to concentrate on. You are not going to worry about *AACR2*.

Smaller college libraries can be very busy places, particularly when you have to do it all. When you have not seen the top of your desk for a week, the photocopier is down, your student aides did not show up, and the dean wants to talk to you about the noise in the library, you may lose sight of what libraries are supposed to be. Like the adage says, "When you are up to your butt in alligators, it is difficult to remember your objective was to drain the swamp." Planning allows you to focus your energies and resources.

Build success into your planning; it is good for morale. Keep your goals and objectives manageable, yet far enough out there so you must stretch a little. In preparing the budget, review the library's progress so that you can target your limited monetary resources and have a clear idea of what you want to accomplish. You are much more likely to receive administrative support if the administration sees or hears of tangible improvements.

MANAGING THE ADMINISTRATION

Library directors learn fast that there is very little real power attached to the position, particularly in a small library. The authority of the office is not the same as the power to make things happen. Most of the power that you develop in the position is only what individuals will give you based on your reputation and performance.

Library directors must spend considerable time dealing with individuals outside the library, especially their college administration, and their success or failure depends heavily on this relationship.[20] Much of the library directors' work depends on the cooperation of individuals over whom they have little or no control, such as deans, presidents, business managers, financial aid directors, maintenance supervisors, and faculty members. The ability to influence and manage relationships and get cooperation is important. Without the assistance and cooperation of others, there is very little that directors can accomplish.

Libraries by their nature have no inherent power because there are few real gut or pocketbook issues to galvanize a faculty or administration into action. Library directors have to earn their influence and cooperation by developing a solid reputation for doing a good job, presenting a balanced view, and delivering what was promised.

Effectively dealing with individuals outside of your span of control requires being willing and able to gain cooperation without formal authority. Working effectively with administrators means actually managing them. It is impossible to get things done without their support, which does not happen automatically unless you take responsibility for making it happen.[21]

Determine what you want from your administration and faculty. What most "librarians expect of their teaching and administrative colleagues (and do not invariably find) is a genuine understanding of the library's mission in higher education, a clearer recognition of the professional librarian's craft and an acceptance of the librarian as a peer in the educational enterprise, and a reliable flow of communication and consultation."[22]

Faculty attitudes towards the library are influenced by local conditions, particularly the attitudes of key college administrators towards the library.[23] Most college faculty have good feelings toward the library, but do not see the library as the heart of the college, nor do they view librarians as equal partners in the education process. Faculty are more likely to see librarians as something necessary, much like dorm directors, counselors, or athletic coaches.

Working relationships with key administrators are so important that they cannot be left to chance. No one says you have to like them, but you must be able to work with each other. To get the support, information, and resources you need to perform your job effectively, it is essential to develop and maintain good working relationships. Learn about the goals, pressures, strengths, weaknesses, problems, blind spots, and working styles of key administrators. Assess your own strengths, weaknesses, pressures, needs, objectives, working style, and dependence on—and predisposition toward—authority.

It may help to take one of several management style inventories, such as the *Managerial Grid* or the *Myers-Briggs Type Indicator*. The *Managerial Grid*[24] basically assesses a manager's concerns for production and people. Depending on their view, managers adopt a particular management style reflecting their degree of concern for people and production. Too much concern for one or the other can cause real problems.

The *Myers-Briggs Type Indicator* identifies 16 distinct personality styles, according to one's preference for thinking or feeling, and the use of intuition. Knowing your own preference and that of other people can help you understand where your strengths are, and how individuals with different preferences can relate to each other.[25] Use this information to create relationships that fit your needs and those of administrators you must work with. Develop relationships characterized by mutual expectations. Maintaining relationships demands that you keep individuals informed. Be dependable, honest, and use their time and resources selectively.[26]

Support from key administrators does not just happen. You have to make it happen. Find out what others expect from you. Keep them informed of what is happening in the library. Administrators on small college campuses hear enough bad news; try to provide them with something positive. It makes educating them about libraries all that much easier. College administrators generally hold quaint, narrow views of libraries and librarians based upon their limited exposure and experience. The feeling is frequently, "Well we have to have a library; let's hope it is not going to cost too much." Your good performance may not speak for itself; occasionally it must be discreetly publicized. Library directors, particularly on small college campuses, must maintain visibility, and must not confine themselves to the library.

To lead your staff and gain the support and cooperation of the faculty and administration, develop as much credibility as possible. Systematically use your performance, interpersonal and intellectual skills, and other personal assets and abilities, to establish a good reputation and earn their respect.[27] When new to a position, there is a "honeymoon" period when individuals will give you the benefit of the doubt. Use this time to establish good relationships with administrators, staff, and faculty. Anyone new to a position is subtly observed and tested. It is important to give a good performance during the "honeymoon" period because first impressions last a long time. On smaller college campuses, your reputation precedes you. People often know of you before they have met you.

During this period, identify relevant formal and informal relationships. Assess who may give you trouble, why, under what conditions. Wherever possible develop good relationships with individuals to facilitate communication, education or negotiation. Negotiation or bargaining is a powerful tool in which all aspects of the situation are under scrutiny and evaluation. In many cases, the ability and willingness to negotiate allow library directors to beat or make the best of a bad situation.[28] When things are difficult, that is not the time to get to know your adversary. However, there will be times when cooperation will not be forthcoming and it may be necessary to be forceful.[29] Be especially careful with faculty. Though observing the proprieties, their thin-skinned egos bruise easily. In the long term, you may lose more than you gain. Never really push an issue unless you are guaranteed a positive outcome or you have nothing to lose; victory is frequently just cutting your losses. Don't take confrontation personally, yet always proceed as though others do.

SUPERVISION

A library's staff is one of its major resources, but personnel issues are a director's greatest source of aggravation. Library staff are highly visible and frequent sources of contact for library users. To small college library users, the staff *is* the library.

The likelihood that directors will be able to motivate their staff with money is not great, because directors generally do not control salaries. What they do control is how much influence the staff has over their own work situation. Staff development is a fundamental management responsibility. Develop your staff so that they can effectively contribute to the library's problem solving ability. A director's job is to bring out the best in each staff member so that they do not really need a director. Work and talk directly with your staff, ask them where the problems are, and what their solutions are. Listen carefully to their responses; their insights will often go a long way towards solving problems.

Smaller college libraries need "working" directors, not bureaucratic dandies. A director's job is to make the staff's job easier. Eliminate unnecessary work. Do not waste their time and effort. Stay out of their way. Be a facilitator. Provide them with the resources to do their jobs. Encourage them to develop an easier way of doing things and let them do it. If you try to assume rigid control of staff instead of giving them freedom and authority to control their own work, a lot of time and energy will be wasted in trying to put down revolution. Remember that a good staff can cover for a bad director, easier than a good director can cover for a bad staff.

Concentrate on the staff's work, not their personalities. Learn to live with their idiosyncrasies. Most individuals are not difficult to get along with, but there are some who will create problems. There are ways of handling difficult individuals and a very helpful source of ideas is *Coping with Difficult People*.[30] Most people have a natural tendency to want to be accepted or loved. You must remember that you are not in your job to be loved.

Employees like to be told in advance of changes that will affect them. A good supervisor involves all the individuals affected in the planning and preparation for change. Employees feel that supervisors contribute to employee job satisfaction when they: provide freedom to work without interference and let them make independent decisions; listen to staff and are accessible, fair, consistent, honest, optimistic, friendly, and personable; respect employee opinions, give recognition for work well done, and teach and help employees.[31]

One task that library supervisors frequently do, but really dread, is training the new employee or student assistant. It is important that employees know and understand what their job is and how it fits into the total library operation. Staff manuals that are short, clear, and direct can help in the training, but most manuals are not kept current and as a result are worthless. With good manuals, no employee is indispensable because of their knowledge of operations.

Employee training should be carefully planned and guided by six basic principles: teach simple tasks first; break tasks down into basic components; teach only correct procedures; reinforce short teaching cycles with practice; develop skills through repetition; motivate trainees.[32]

On-the-job training—consisting of showing, telling, doing and checking—is a tried and true method of training employees. It works because it is common sense. In the box on page 36 is an outline based on the widely used on-the-job training system known as Job Instruction Training (JIT).[33] This system was developed during World War II as an efficient method to quickly train replacements for drafted workers and maintain production in critical war efforts. The system is still a simple yet effective way to achieve efficient, productive results.

FINANCES

Small college libraries are frequently considered by many administrators as an expense that must be controlled, but they also want to see

JOB INSTRUCTION TRAINING

Getting Ready to Instruct
1. Decide what the employee must be taught to do the job.
2. Prepare a training schedule which determines what skills you expect the employee to have by what date.
3. Make a written breakdown of the job listing key steps or areas.
4. Have the right equipment, supplies, and materials ready.
5. Have the work area properly arranged, just as the employee will be expected to keep it.

Prepare the Employee
1. Put the employee at ease.
2. Find out what the employee already knows about the job.
3. Get the employee interested in learning the job.

Present the Operation or Position
1. Tell, show, and illustrate one important step at a time.
2. Stress each key point.
3. Instruct clearly, completely, and patiently, one step at a time.
4. Check, question, and repeat.

5. Make sure the employee really knows.

Performance Try-out
1. Have the employee do the job.
2. Have employees explain each key point to you as they do the job.
3. Make sure employee understands. Ask questions beginning with why, how, when, or where.
4. Observe performance, correct errors, and repeat instructions if necessary.
5. Continue until you know the employee understands.

Follow-Up/Review
1. Put employees on their own.
2. Designate who they are to go to for help.
3. Check frequently to be sure they follow instructions.
4. Encourage questions.
5. Taper off extra supervision and close follow-up until employee is qualified to work with normal supervision.

their library perform because it is a visible indication of a college's health. A library's condition and levels of use tell a lot about the college and its student body. High levels of library use indicate some teaching and learning are going on and that the library has the appropriate materials in sufficient quantity to support that activity. A good library and high levels of library use are dependent on the library's collection, staff, and physical facilities,[34] which require a financial commitment from the institution. Money alone will not produce a quality library with the ability to meet its goals and objectives, but you certainly cannot do without it.

"There are no absolutes in measuring the adequacy of a library's financial support, because the amount of money needed depends upon the goals of the particular college and the extent and quality of service needed to support those goals."[35] No two colleges nor libraries are alike, but comparative library data from carefully selected peer colleges and libraries will give an indication of how similar colleges support their libraries. Institutional support for libraries is commonly expressed as a percent of the college's educational and general expenditure (E & G), excluding capital outlay, expenses, and auxiliary enterprises. This is a valid measure only if overall institutional support is adequate.

In the 1960s, it was felt that a small college should allocate between four and six percent of its total education and general (E & G) expenditures to the library;[36] in the 1970s the minimum acceptable figure was five percent;[37] and in the 1980s, six percent.[38] In reality, a number of smaller college libraries are quite happy to get three percent of their colleges' E & G.

Libraries are expensive to operate and require attention to financial detail in order to get the most per dollar spent. No matter how small, the budget is a means to achieve the library's goals. Rather than saying the library's budget ought to be five percent of the college's E & G expenditures, the administration should be told that the budget will enable the library to accomplish certain specific objectives. The budget should be used to move towards goals, no matter how modest, rather than doing all things poorly.

Rarely is a budget adequate to do all that needs to be accomplished. Focus your money on priority objectives and seek alternative sources of revenue. Establish an agency account with your business office or bank that enables you to carry unspent or supplemental dollars over from year to year. Fines, book sale proceeds, Friends of the library registrations, and gift monies are often kept in a separate account. This money can accumulate to the point where it is possible to buy a typewriter, file cabinet, or reader/printer. Photocopiers are a source of revenue, usually taking in enough to pay their expenses and provide a profit. Given the right volume and price per copy, they pay for themselves and supply the means to finance other purchases.

Fundraising is a cooperative effort. Get to know your development officers who are always looking for ways to attract donors to the college. A microform reader/printer or microcomputer is not a bad small gift. Unless you can identify needs and have a good working relationship with your development officers, you may never see such gifts. Be careful never to interfere with the operation of the development office by attempting fundraising without its knowledge, lest you both come up empty-handed.

Foundation grants are another source of supplemental funds. Never count on a grant, but be prepared to carry it out if funded. In soliciting grants, work with your development office. Competition is fierce; get all the help you can. Ask the question, "How do our needs coincide with the purposes of the foundation? Will this grant move the library closer towards its goals?" Grants are a lot of hard work and, like gambling, you may lose. However, if you do not write them, you do not get them.

Money is a library's life blood. It is too important to be left solely in the hands of others. On occasion, a library must protect its resources from its own college administration. Identify what the library must have, order, and pay for it early. Prepayment of bills and deposit accounts are effective ways to guarantee protection, but both are very unpopular with small college business managers. If you ask permission, the administration has the opportunity to say no. As with anything, there are certain risks. You can destroy your credibility with the business office if you use these measures on a wholesale basis. Plan purchases to fit the ebb and flow of your institution's cash flow. Purchase orders are more likely to be approved if the administration is not worried about meeting the payroll.

ATTITUDE

The biggest determinant of success is the library director's attitude. The right outlook is what sustains directors in their darkest moments. Because of the nature and size of their task, directors must believe in themselves, their abilities, and their work. Strong self-esteem cushions defeat and allows individuals to wade into the unknown with confidence.

Directors are usually able to control where their library is going. Though there will be forces beyond their control, their responses are a matter of choice. The ability to set a course of action and believe that you can make a difference is important. Faith in your own abilities and goals allows you to begin again. Will power alone will not do it. Balancing an upbeat outlook with perseverance and a realistic assessment of your environment allows you to make tangible improvements and progress. It also allows you to keep a healthy perspective, adapt, and take advantage of unforeseen opportunities.

Contact with other librarians is important for librarians in smaller college libraries. Opportunities to exchange ideas and operational innovations are important sources of new insights, practical advice, and encouragement.

Managing a smaller college library allows you to see close up what library service is all about. Managing the smaller college library is demanding (and not for everyone), but it offers unique rewards and experiences.

References

1. Charles B. Maurer, "Close Encounters of Diverse Kinds: A Management Panorama for the Director of the Small College Library," in *College Librarianship,* ed. by William Miller and D. Stephen Rockwood. (Metuchen, N.J.: The Scarecrow Press, 1981), pp. 97–105.
2. "Library Director," *College & Research Libraries News* 47 (February 1986): 167.
3. Maurer, p. 105.
4. E. F. Schumacher, *Small Is Beautiful: Economics as if People Mattered.* (New York: Harper Colophon Books, 1973).
5. Daniel Sullivan, "Libraries and Liberal Arts Colleges: Tough Times in the Eighties," *College & Research Libraries* 43 (March 1982): 119–123.
6. Evan Ira Farber, "College Librarians and the University Library Syndrome," in *The Academic Library: Essays in Honor of Guy R. Lyle,* edited by Evan Ira Farber and Ruth Walling (Metuchen, N.J.: The Scarecrow Press, 1974), pp. 12–23.
7. *Ibid.,* p. 22.
8. Roger Horn, "The Idea of Academic Library Management," *College & Research Libraries* 36 (November 1975): 464–472.
9. Susan A. Lee, "Conflict and Ambiguity in the Role of the Academic Library Director," *College & Research Libraries* 38 (September 1977): 396–403.
10. Paul Metz, "The Role of the Academic Library Director," *The Journal of Academic Librarianship* 5 (July 1979): 148–152.
11. Lee 1977, p. 398.
12. Metz, p. 151.
13. Lee 1977, pp. 401–02.
14. Charles R. McClure, "Planning for Library Services: Lessons and Opportunities," in *Planning for Library Services: A Guide to Utilizing Planning Methods for Library Management,* ed. by Charles R. McClure. (N.Y.: The Haworth Press, 1982), pp. 7–28.
15. "Standards for College Libraries, 1986," *College & Research Libraries News* 47 (March 1986): 189–200.
16. "An Evaluative Checklist for Reviewing a College Library Program," *College & Research Libraries News* 40 (November 1979): 305–316.
17. "Standards for College Libraries," *College & Research Libraries News* 36 (October 1975): 277–279, 290–301.
18. Jane Robbins-Carter and Douglas L. Zweizig, "Are We There Yet?: Evaluating Library Collections, Reference Services, Programs and Personnel," *American Libraries* 16 (October 1985): 624–627.
19. Susan Lee, "A Modest Management Approach," in *College Librarianship,* ed. by William Miller and D. Stephen Rockwood. (Metuchen, N.J.: The Scarecrow Press, 1981), pp. 65–78.

20. Lee 1977.
21. John P. Kotter, *Power and Influence.* (N.Y.: The Free Press, 1985).
22. William A. Moffett, "What the Academic Librarian Wants from Administrators and Faculty," in *Priorities for Academic Libraries,* ed. by Thomas J. Galvin and Beverly P. Lynch. (San Francisco: Jossey Bass, 1982), pp. 13–23.
23. Gresham Riley, "Myths and Realities: The Academic Viewpoint II," *College & Research Libraries* 45 (September 1984): 367–369.
24. Robert R. Blake and Jane S. Mouton, *The Managerial Grid.* (Houston, Tex.: Gulf Publishing Co., 1964).
25. Isabel B. Myers and Peter B. Myers, *Gifts Differing.* (Palo Alto, Calif.: Consulting Psychologists Press, 1980).
26. John J. Gabarro and John P. Kotter, "Managing Your Boss," *Harvard Business Review* 58 (January/February 1980): 92–100.
27. Kotter, p. 44.
28. Robert J. Merikangas and John F. Harvey, "Negotiation Skills Improvement," in *Austerity Management in Academic Libraries,* ed. by John F. Harvey and Peter Spyers-Duran. (Metuchen, N.J.: The Scarecrow Press, 1984), pp. 135–160.
29. Kotter, p. 59.
30. Robert M. Bramsom, *Coping With Difficult People.* (Garden City, N.Y.: Anchor Press, 1981).
31. "What's A Good Boss?" *Library Administrator's Digest* XXI (February 1986): 14.
32. Robert D. Stueart and John Taylor Eastlick, *Library Management.* (Littleton, Colo.: Libraries Unlimited, 1981).
33. War Manpower Commission, *The Training Within Industry Report.* (Washington, D.C.: Bureau of Training, Training Within Industry Service, War Manpower Commission, 1945).
34. Helen Sheehan, *The Small College Library.* (Westminster, Md.: The Newman Press, 1963).
35. Guy R. Lyle, *The Administration of the College Library.* (N.Y.: The H. W. Wilson Company, 1974).
36. Sheehan, p. 26–27.
37. Lyle, p. 304.
38. "Standards . . . 1986": 199.

The Two-Year College Library

Mark Y. Herring

Two-year institutions are no longer a novelty as they were just two decades ago. In 1960, there were only 521 junior colleges boasting a mere 451,000 students. Twenty-three years later, 1,271 institutions peppered the nation's countryside, and over 4,723,000 students roamed their halls.[1] This is an astonishing growth rate (more than a 500 percent) for what was considered by many as an "experiment" in education. During this same period, community colleges built more than 400 learning resource centers,[2] representing a large capital outlay on the part of their academic communities and testifying to the importance these libraries have to their constituencies.

Two-year colleges, or community colleges, have held their own against four-year institutions; sometimes in spite of themselves, and sometimes because of it. "The community college," wrote Louis B. Shores shortly after it made its first big splash in ocean of learning, "has dared to break some sacred traditions of higher education."[3] More often than not it has been this love of innovation that has caused the four-year college to sit up and take note. Soon after two-year colleges began to burst at the seams with large student enrollments, four-year institutions began offering innovative curricula.

The two-year college also possesses a farrago of students. The four-year institution, in spite of all that has been said and written, is still geared to the young adult population, usually between 18 and 22 years old. The community college, however, shifts gears between that age group and variety of others; and owing to this widespread appeal, it might be thought of as the "prototype of the do-everything college."[4] If this is the case, then the library must be thought of as the archetype of the do-everything library.

The community college often appeals to students with widely disparate socio-economic backgrounds, interests, and needs. Add to this a curriculum that spans the gulf between afternoon Western Civilization courses and night classes in shorthand, and the question of management ceases to be a question and becomes an imbroglio. The picture of management for the junior college librarian is one of a wildly varying student population spanning generations rather than years; a curricu-

Mark Y. Herring is Director, E. W. King Library, King College, Bristol, Tennessee.

lum that touches everything, but covers nothing in detail; and interests and needs that are as different as the colors black and white.

Some people will complain that junior college students are different from four-year college students in that the former are "lower in academic ability and aspirations, older, and from lower sociological levels."[5] Some will say that the job of librarian is really much easier, because junior college students really don't use the library that much. Junior colleges, however, have changed a great deal from the days of William Rainey Harper, their creator.[6] They are more complicated institutions than they were 20 years ago and they require different management approaches.

The good junior college library manager—like any good librarian— is a lover of books. If librarians are *not* bookpersons first, what are they? If they do not make it their business to know about books and the book business, then what is it they are being paid to do? If reading is not the preeminent skill they have honed to a fine art, then what skill do they possess? Would we applaud doctors who had little regard for life, or lawyers who ridiculed obedience to the law? One must never forget that librarians began as bookpersons, and with those who loved books. "Librarianship," wrote Jesse Shera, "began as the highest form of scholarship—the man of all learning, the polyhistor, searching the writings of the past for their meaning."[7] In answer then to the question, What makes a good librarian?, the phrase "love of books" must figure in preeminently.

What else can be said of the good junior college library manager? What are those attributes that make the library reflect the librarian's ingenuity and industriousness? The best way to answer these questions will be to consider how each library operation might be undertaken.

AIMS AND OBJECTIVES

The library processes or implements its information by aims and objectives. Too often librarians overlook this matter, leaving it to the college administration, or more specifically, the president of the institution. They do this at great risk to themselves professionally, and to the great bewilderment of the faculty and students whom they have been hired to serve. The junior college librarian, apart from what students demand the library provide, must know what it is that the academic community requires. The *sine qua non* of good library management is a librarian who knows the directives of the college administration and the faculty of that institution. If these are not clearly spelled out in some document, then the librarian must find out what is expected and know to what extent the administration is willing to fund that expectation. If the expectation and the funding coincide, then the librarian is ready to go to work. If not, then negotiations are in order. No librarian should begin to formulate policy or build a collection without a document of responsibility. Is the librarian to build a collection of books? If so, what kinds and types, and for what purpose? Is the library for research? Then to what extent, and at what level of funding? In a word, what are the librarian's instructions?

Where does such a document originate? Two committees seem likely candidates. If the president of the institution is unwilling, unable, or uninterested in stating something as pragmatic as this document, then the librarian should ask either the Library Committee or the Educational Policies Committee to undertake the responsibility. Whichever committee is used, the librarian should produce the document in writing and have it approved by the faculty and the administration. Some librarians will complain that this is an added step, requiring too much time and effort. Others might argue that such a document is already outlined in the library's acquisitions statement. How is it possible for the junior college librarian to know success, if the imperative is simply to buy books to give to those who ask for them? The acquisitions policy statement should be a subset of this document, not the document itself. The acquisitions policy statement defines what books will be bought in terms defined and explained by the mission of the college. It will serve no one if the librarian buys critical analyses of deconstructionism when the college's mission requires the library to offer the community a hodgepodge of materials on current events and popular ideas.

COLLECTIONS AND THE CLIENTELE

Once the responsibility document is in place, the librarian can construct an acquisitions policy statement limned within these parameters. The statement will be a far more accurate one since its scope, breadth, and depth will have been spelled out. This statement might be thought of as a map or a sextant, telling the librarian where he or she is going, or should be; and if the librarian has sailed off course, showing how to get back on it again.

Knowing the clientele has become proverbial in librarianship. The good junior college librarian will find out just how varied the student body is. One way of doing this is getting to know the students firsthand. The librarian must get out of the office and make the rounds of the college. Ideally, the librarian should also be teaching. Since junior colleges often turn avocations into job descriptions, the librarian will probably get this chance. This exposure to the intellectual milieu of the academic community facilitates wise acquisition judgments.

Asking for suggestions or surveying students is another way of finding out what they want, but this is a less happy way than verbal communication. It is much better to know students from experience, since they will be more likely to seek out and tell the librarian what they want.

The flip side to knowing what patrons want is making sure patrons know what the library has. Making patrons aware of services is an essential part of good librarianship, especially junior college librarianship. Patrons of the junior college library are not unlike patrons of other libraries: they enter the library thinking that such and such will *not* be there, or that they will not be able to find it. If they are better informed, they will be more likely to be satisfied. If the perception of library services is a negative one, all the bibliographic instruction lectures in the world will not change matters.

The approach to this problem should be twofold: first to faculty and then to students. The order is important for community college students' attitudes are most often influenced, if not formed, by the faculty. If the faculty's experience with the library is a good one, then the student's experience will probably follow suit.

HANDBOOKS FOR FACULTY AND STUDENTS

An effectively written faculty library handbook is a most formidable foe against ignorance about the library. Such a handbook should contain: the hours the library is open, what services are available, how those services will be useful to the faculty, special library programs (if any), and an explanation of the library's book budget allocation. The latter is especially important, as it will assuage faculty members' fears about how library money is spent. Lamentably, one of the occupational hazards of the librarian at a junior or community college is the professional jealousy of faculty members about one another's library book allocations. If the budget can be shown to be computed impartially, then some of these fears will be quieted. In preparing this budget statement, the librarian should not fear admitting to an arbitrary assessment of one program over another. No formula has been devised yet that eliminates all hint of subjectivity.

Student library handbooks, on the other hand, should contain a statement on hours and services, along with a statement about library programs. Emphasis in the student handbook should be on an explanation of fines and policies, and any special concerns the library staff has about the collection. Other publications might be single sheet summaries of reference materials in the various disciplines taught at the college, bibliographies on topics of current interest, and even summaries of articles in popular or scholarly journals.

Community college librarians will object that such publications cost too much money and are too time-consuming. Cost considerations can be eliminated in almost any town by comparing the cost between printers for camera-ready copy, or even asking that the printer make this print job a part of the company's donation to the library. If that fails, there is always the mimeograph machine. A publication that is well-written beats no publication; of course, a poorly written publication will beat nothing.

No one denies that such publications are time-consuming, but considering all the time librarians spend on far less profitable ventures, this is a weak argument. A writer needs only two things, other than paper and pencil: an assignment and a deadline. A librarian writing a handbook about library services needs only to adopt these two fundamentals. If this proves too unwieldy, the librarian might call on the English faculty for help. Such a politic motive might be just the ticket to win over another friend for the library.

The publications should include as much humor as the librarian feels comfortable with. Nothing kills the message of a publication more quickly than too much or too little humor. If the librarian feels diffident about it, then all but the barest minimum can be omitted. Libraries are not meant by nature to be places of rip-roaring fun, but not being a "fun" place does not mean the place must be dull. Accentuating what is the strength of the library—its books and services—will camouflage the library's more uninteresting parts.

Publications are a wonderful way of getting the library's message across. There will always be those who will not read them, but there will always be those who will not read anything, a fact that many modern librarians often forget. These people should be left outside of the library's outreach; trying to appeal to them is like a liquor store trying to appeal to the temperance league. It is strange that a profession meant to preserve the art of reading is often the most reluctant to pass along information about itself in a form that can be read. Publications can be used in so many ways to enhance the image of the library. Too much of a good thing will ruin it, but a little leaven leavens the whole lump. "It may be that to meet certain objectives," write two librarians, "publications could be more effective than a librarian talking to a class."[8]

ACQUISITIONS AIDS

The junior college librarian has the same number of library activities—acquisitions, cataloging, reference services, and circulation—to worry about as any other librarian, but the strategy used against these strong opponents must be more general than for the librarian in the larger four-year institution. The community college librarian must make these conquests all at once, rather than individually. Simplicity is the key word.

Acquisitions' bookkeeping in the community college library will take care of itself, if the librarian will leave well enough alone. Librarians are paper-loving people and, if given the chance, will often unnecessarily multiply the amount of paper needed for a task. Junior college library budgets under six figures may need no more bookkeeping than what is being done by the business office. Why is it necessary for the librarian to duplicate what is already being done? Only the government does this, and everyone knows how much money it takes to run the government. If, however, the business office is not keeping records of the library's dollar transactions, then the librarian will find another job added to his or her daily list of tasks.

Librarians, for reasons not readily apparent, require far too many forms for their work. Is it really necessary to keep three, four, or five copies of every acquisitions transaction? Are we not planning to plan in this case? The simpler the process can be kept, the easier it will be to train nonprofessionals to take it over. If a clerical job demands the librarian's daily attention, something is wrong; either the manner in which it is done is far too complicated, or the procedures for doing it are redundant.

In ordering books, the issue is not as easily resolved. No shortcut exists for finding out about books other than reading about them. One of the best ways to do this is to choose as many journals as one has time for and read (or seriously scan) them religiously. The reference here is to *journals,* not to the typical reviewing media journals whose reviews have come under attack in recent years. Well they should, if they ever were the librarian's sole means of acquisitions management.[9] But reading, or skimming, several solid, well-respected journals will serve the librarian in two ways.

First, the journals will bring to mind a number of good books on the market. These will usually be reviewed in depth, more so than the "blown kisses" of, say, *Library Journal* and *Kirkus Reviews.* By briefly looking at these journals, the librarian can determine the merits and defects of the work in question, and better assess its circulation potential in the library. Reviews in these journals are what Robert Dahlin has called "works of reflection"—a critical assessment of the book's merits and defects—as opposed to "works of the moment"—a review that has been dashed off to meet a deadline.[10] Because reviewers of these journals are often paid well (comparatively speaking), their work tends to be a better bench mark of excellence than a review of only one or two paragraphs.

Journals serve community college librarians in another way. The articles apprise librarians of what is happening in the world, what events are being kept before the public, and what events promise to have later historical significance. By scanning these journals weekly or monthly, librarians can be confident that their book choices, and their recommendations to faculty, will be timely and important.

In order to avoid the charge of frivolity and manufactured "news," such journals should *not* include the weekly news magazines that survey the world superficially. Rather, the librarian should choose magazines that canvas the world scene with some intellectual seriousness. Journals such as *National Review, Commentary,* the British magazine *Encounter, New Republic,* and *The American Spectator* have stood the test of modern time, while *Religion and Society Report, The New Criterion,* and *This World* are courageously fighting for their lives following precarious births. No selection of journals is infallible, but those such as the above will give librarians a good start on keeping their collections current in art, music, politics, economics, religion, and theater.

Junior college librarians should bear in mind that the 80/20 rule works in their libraries with as much regularity as it does at the senior college level. About 20 to 30 percent of the collection will satisfy 70 to 80 percent of client need.[11] Because this is true, junior college librarians with limited funds inevitably have to face saying "Not this year, but perhaps next" to faculty members. If they can say no, say why, and then prove it, all the better. Surveys of the circulation activity of the collection can be, with some effort, measured to reveal its use, or lack of it. Circulation is by far the best and easiest way of checking book activity and ascertaining the usefulness of a collection.

Circulation is, of course, not the sole reason for purchasing a book. But what is the difference between a book that has been sitting on the shelf for ten years, and a book that was never purchased? Never mind about the thousands of times faculty and students have *consulted* it, but never took it out of the building. Librarians who want to see the dollar stretched and the collection used should investigate the opportunities afforded by a circulation study, one that can be done by competent student help. As Hardesty points out:

> Given that librarians already know that many students make very little, if any, use of the academic library, it should be no surprise that a large portion of the books in the academic library receive little, if any, use. However, this does not make the continued acquisitions of little used materials acceptable.[12]

Finally, community college librarians can offer their faculty one small but useful bit of assistance by copying the table of contents out of key journals that faculty have identified as ones they'd like to keep up with. This small task will keep the faculty informed, let them know the library cares, and increase periodical usage. Moreover, it is a task anyone in the library can do.

SIMPLIFIED CATALOGING

Cataloging advice to anyone but born catalogers is easy: keep it simple and do as little as is humanly possible and still maintain order. Those with an itch to catalog should look for work in places other than junior colleges. Too much remains for the librarian to do than spend time working on the minutiae of cataloging.[13]

Junior college librarians need to accept as much national cataloging as possible. If the OCLC investment is too much, then in-publication cataloging will have to do. The less time spent checking schedules and cross-referencing tables, the more time the librarian will have for more public-oriented tasks. If original cataloging is avoided, the librarian will have the option of training an intelligent, full-time nonprofessional. If it is true that cataloging systems need to be complex only in so far as the collection is complex,[14] then the cataloging required at a small junior or community college should be easily mastered. Writes one librarian:

> Practical catalogers who produce working catalogs must accept their managerial responsibility. . . . It is time now to conserve the undoubted advances that have been achieved, to eliminate the unnecessary and uneconomical deviations that have arisen, and to identify directions along which change is both desirable and possible.[15]

This advice also applies to the use of subject headings. Librarians at small colleges should not shortchange their patrons, but in a dead heat between numerous subject headings and the book on the shelf ready to read, most patrons will prefer the latter. Main entry, author, and title cards, and one subject card will be sufficient for the vast majority of books.

If the library cannot afford to order cards, then the librarian should look into card duplicating machines. The last thing the librarian needs is a student worker who must count out spaces, line up headings, and take part in other cataloging mysteries. It makes little sense to plan for so much planning, when the librarian and the student worker can spend their time on more profitable things, such as weeding the collection, making more library aids available to students, and studying the use of the collection. This is not to say that cataloging is second-class, but given the state of affairs in which any library job can be made to consume all the time one has, lines of demarcation for *all* staff must be clear ahead of time.

It is a needless waste of time for librarians to spend their or the cataloger's time reassigning Dewey numbers. If the card catalog is meant to be the index to the collection, then so be it. Assigning new numbers, or recataloging classes of books that have already been assigned a Dewey number, serves no one but the fastidious cataloger; it does not serve those for whom the routine was designed. Since many collections will be small ones, it makes little sense to worry about books of a similar content that appear in two different Dewey numbers.

AACR2 and its family of relatives should make cataloging easier, not harder. Librarians who opt to leave an AACR collection in its "pre-2" state should do so without fear of reproof. Those who decide in favor of AACR2 must do so fully cognizant of some of the difficulties involved and should choose it for no other reason than that they are convinced access to the collection will be greatly enhanced by its advent. Whatever the choice, pre-AACR2 cards should be left as is.

Cataloging decisions in the junior college must be made with the function of the library in mind.[16] The decision should be one that will provide the most access with the least amount of effort, or provide the best that can be achieved in the simplest manner.[17] In an age of fast-paced, high-powered technology, patrons will appreciate simplicity wherever they are lucky enough to find it.

REFERENCE STRATEGY

Reference service makes very odd demands on the professional. In cases where the junior college librarian is surrounded by untrained nonprofessionals, reference management often hogs the whole show if the librarian is not careful. Satisfying students with competent reference service is a must, for it is one of the few times that library work and public contact join hand in glove so that both parties know it. But how is the one-person junior college library to satisfy the reference needs of 500, 800, or 1,500 students?

The answer is so obvious that it is nearly always lost on us. Junior college librarians should not hesitate to train nonprofessionals for reference service. The first step is to familiarize the nonprofessional staff with the reference collection, and then outline important reference strategies, such as helping the student or faculty member get to the heart of what they want. This need not involve hours of reference interviewing, as is often recommended, but a few minutes spent with the patron, exchanging guesses (e.g., "So, you want x and not y, or have I got it backwards?"). Lastly, the librarian should train the nonprofessional staff to use general reference sources: almanacs, general and special dictionaries, general and special encyclopedias, and handbooks. By identifying no more than two dozen sources and teaching those sources to the nonprofessional staff, the librarian will be free to establish policy, troubleshoot cataloging, meet with college administrators, and build a solid collection. Depending on the size of the library staff, every staff member should know something about the reference collection.[18]

The circulation of books should not weigh down any one person with the exclusive duty of posting notices, fines, and other extraneous communiques about overdue books and books on hold. Junior college librarians should institute common due dates, and limit the paraphernalia that goes into their books for check-out purposes. Although two cards, one filed by the date due and the other by author, are a nice luxury, a one-card system usually suffices. One-card systems pose problems when a patron wants to know who has a book out, or when a certain book will be back, but library policy can cover these problems.

Fines should be levied and exceptions to them reduced to nearly zero. Notices should be sent out no more than three times. If the matter is still unresolved, the librarian should enlist the help of the college's administration. Fines teach respect for another's property, teach students responsibility, and encourage the right attitude about library books.

Book pockets tend to be a more substantial home for the book card than "diagonals." Unless librarians need some work for a student to do, it isn't necessary for the title and author of the book to be typed on the card *and* the pocket. If the author is to be typed on the card with the title, and again duplicated on the pocket, the student typist can use labels, which are more efficient, can be put on the cards faster, and will easily allow for a more natural work flow.

AUTOMATED SYSTEMS

Online database systems now offer small colleges a chance to renew their academic vigor, if their personnel is daring enough to embark upon the venture. Junior college librarians should not automatically assume that automation is only for the "big" libraries. Online database systems like Dialog and Orbit provide junior college libraries with a chance to eliminate many costly indexes and open up to students research avenues that had been closed to the library. Access over ownership is part of the wave of future. Although it must be admitted that access is inferior to ownership, this wave of tomorrow will either carry those willing to ride on its crest to safety, or drown those who, in the face of its onslaught, refuse to budge. By offering many indexes online, junior college librarians can serve students and faculty in ways they thought impossible only a decade ago. Besides realizing a substantial savings, some of the cost of the reference service can be charged back to the student. Although it has always been thought axiomatic, no one has yet shown why *all* library services must be socialized. In fact, this country's long history of supply and demand leads one to believe that services should be made to pay their own way.

Automated circulation systems are even within reach of some junior colleges and should be investigated, especially the absence file systems, or systems which report only those books that are out.[19] Although the initial cash outlay can be a large one, the rewards of such systems far exceed the disadvantages. Because these systems also offer data that can be molded into a number of statistical designs, the empirical proof needed to justify (or deny) certain acquisitions assumptions is readily available and will prove very useful.

Once the librarian determines that an automated circulation system is right for the library (this can be done by assessing the return on the system against the amount of effort required by the librarian and the amount of money to be spent by the college administration, both of which are considerable), one other thing needs to be done. Campus computer experts (if there are any) and other librarians who have gone through the process should be consulted. If one is going to make a mistake, it may as well be a relatively new one, not one already made by dozens of others.

OCLC and its subsystems are certainly a possibility for junior colleges to consider. Although the level of "return" on the OCLC system is said by many to be at about 5,000 titles a year, many smaller libraries, cataloging slightly less than half that number of titles, have found the system to be a most effective tool. Considering that personnel trained to use the OCLC system do not have to be professionals, and that even students can be taught to competently manipulate much of the routine searching of the system, the potential gains for the library staff are unlimited. The M300 Workstation, a souped-up IBM PC, with its alter idem as a personal computer, has made these prospects all the more attractive to small colleges. The benefits are not staff-oriented only. The industrious junior college librarian will involve his or her faculty in the use of the OCLC systems as often as possible.

MANAGEMENT STYLES

The management of people in the junior college setting is at once the most difficult yet the most important aspect of all library management. Which style is best—authoritarian, participative, a combination of the two? There is no one style that must be used first. Modern management principles all too often make function exceed essence. No one management style appears to work well all the time because people are an amalgamation of experiences, not one-dimensional adumbrations of feelings. It is no wonder that they cannot be "tamed" by a facile approach to managing them.

The literature on management style is abundant, almost superfluous. It is not altogether useless for the junior college librarian, but it should act as a guide, not a commandment. One interesting article contrasted several directors' assessments of themselves against their staffs' more sober views of them.[20] In nearly every case, the power to see ourselves as others see us was lacking. Whatever style of management is adopted will most probably be perceived as something less than what directors desire it to be thought of, and more what they abhor.

The important thing to remember about managing people is that their jobs must be done again and again. Whatever earth-shaking crisis occupies today's worries will be in the penumbra of tomorrow's misfortune. Why panic, and why make an issue out of what will most likely become routine over time? Many people work for ideals, and some are even willing to die for principles, but working for a job—"We must catalog these books before sundown!"—appeals to no one. Management that genuinely seeks a person's happiness is usually the best form of management. It is important for librarians to remember the form of management *they* liked best: that invisible form that encouraged them to work hard, and rewarded them for doing that. It doesn't take a degree in theology or management to know that the way we like to be treated is most often the way we should treat others.

When managing people, nearly all conflicts or confrontations can be warded off by a cool-headed and astute librarian who doesn't need to "prove" anything. Most "grave issues" are of such minuscule importance as to be laughable when considered after the confrontation. The ability to distinguish between confrontations which must be met head on and those which may be defused comes not from adopting this or that style of management, but from making the wrong choice several dozen times.

How does one get to this ideal state of management? How can the librarian reach the point when the staff respond the way they should in order for the library to work effectively? After all is said and done, management that makes decisions, and acts upon them in a fair and consistent manner, produces working conditions encouraging creativity and positive activity. The worst thing the librarian can do is to be afraid to decide, or to be indecisive when the time for a decision has come. This is not meant to be an endorsement of snap decisions or compulsive action, but the luxury of time to study each individual problem almost never comes at the same time as the need for a decision. One must learn to live and die with one's decisions. Some will be complete failures, but the chance for victory is never possible unless one is willing to risk making a decision.

References

1. Bureau of the Census, *Statistical Abstracts of the United States 1986.* 106th ed. (Washington: GPO, 1985), p. 153.
2. D. Joleen Bock, "Two-Year College Library Resource Center Buildings," in *The Bowker Annual of Library and Book Trade Information,* 29th ed. (New York: R. R. Bowker, 1984), p. 406.
3. Louis B. Shores, "The Junior College Impact on Academic Librarianship," *College and Research Libraries* 30 (May 1969): 215.
4. Madison Mosley, "A Profile of the Library Learning Resources Center in the Small Community/Junior College," *College Research Libraries* 45 (September 1984): 392.
5. Pamela Reeves, "Junior Colleges Enter the Seventies," *College and Research Libraries* 34 (January 1973): 7.
6. James O. Wallace, "Newcomer to the Academic Scene: The Two-Year College Library/Learning Center," *College and Research Libraries* 37 (November 1976): 503–13.
7. Jesse Shera, "Apologia, pro Vita Nostra: The Librarian's Search for Identity," *IPLO Quarterly* 14 (July 1972): 10.
8. David Lewis and Allan Forester, "Tuition in Library and Literature Use," in *The College Library: A Collection of Essays* (London: Clive Bingley, 1978), p. 43.
9. Richard Kluger, "Such Good Friends?" *American Libraries* 4 (January 1973): 20–25.
10. Robert Dahlin, "The Book Review Editor and Critic Reflects on Literature and the State of the Art of Reviewing," *Publishers Weekly* 213 (May 1978): 6.
11. Larry Hardesty, "Use of Library Materials at a Small Liberal Arts College," *Library Research* 3 (Fall 1981): 261–82.
12. *Ibid.,* p. 278–79.
13. Michael Gorman, "Osburn Revisited; Or, the Catalog in Crisis; Or, Four Catalogers, Only One of Whom Shall Save Us," *American Libraries* 6 (November 1975): 599–601, and "Fear of Filing. Daunted Librarians Have an Ally in New Rules," *American Libraries* 12 (February 1981): 71–72.
14. Genore Bernard, *How to Organize and Operate a Small Library* (Wisconsin: Highsmith, 1975), 43p.
15. Allen Geoffrey, "Responsibility and the Managerial Challenge for Cataloging in the Computer Age," *Australian College Libraries* 2 (November 1984): 145–50.
16. Geoffrey Allen's "Change in the Catalog in the Contest of Library Management," *Journal of Academic Librarianship* 12 (July 1986): 140–43.
17. David C. Anderson, "Deciding the Future of the Catalog in Small Libraries," *Library Journal* 105 (October 1, 1980): 2034–38.
18. Gordon S. Wade, "Managing Reference Services in the Smaller Public Library," *The Reference Librarian* 3 (Spring 1982): 107–12.
19. Kenneth John Bierman, *Automation and the Small Library* (Chicago: American Library Assn., 1982), 9p.
20. Victoria Kline Musmann, "Managerial Style in the Small Public Library," *California Librarian* (July 1978): 7–20.

The Special Library

Doris Bolef

Special libraries are in the business of providing information to patrons with differing, but exacting, requirements in one or a few highly specialized subject areas. This truism holds for the smallest to the largest special library, even though no two are the same. This service comes at a price and the price is increasingly scrutinized by cost-conscious administrators. It is no longer sufficient to provide resources and services in a general way. Each activity must be examined and justified in the light of its contribution to the organization in which the library functions, taking into account the priorities of the organization and the expectations of the staff. It goes almost without saying that the need for self-examination and feedback is continual and unremitting.

ROLE OF THE LIBRARY

At the outset, it is essential to establish the position and role of the library within the organization's structure. It behooves the manager to obtain the most favorable position possible within the hierarchy, the one that will facilitate quick and easy access to the appropriate executives at the highest possible levels. The manager draws up an organization chart to clarify reporting relationships and then delineates the position of the organization within its larger community or constituency, as it affects the library. Finally, the manager must investigate how the library can best support and promote the goals of the parent institution, which is at the core of the library's activities.

Because of its diminutive size, the small special library is flexible, not necessarily fully structured, given to expediency, not standardized, and capable of responding to rapid change to support its circumscribed clientele with their individualized and changing requirements. The manager enjoys a much closer relationship with patrons than managers in larger libraries. It is to be expected that procedures will not follow those taught in library school. Most strictly library functions, including acquisitions, cataloging, processing, circulation, interlibrary loan, and

Doris Bolef is Director, Library of Rush University, Rush-Presbyterian-St. Luke's Medical Center, Chicago, Illinois.

reference are performed, but probably differently for lack of staff, thus inviting innovation and expediency. The nature of some formats—laboratory notebooks, photographs, newspaper clippings, annual reports—will require wholly different methods of cataloging or listing. The emphasis is on making all information available to all patrons in formats that can be retrieved quickly and efficiently. Circulation may consist of a patron writing his or her name on a book card and dropping it into a box.

ROLE OF THE LIBRARIAN

Life becomes a balancing act. The manager must first learn self-management. Since time is always in short supply, jobs must be listed, and priorities set. As jobs and projects are completed, cross them off the lists. Some routines have to be performed daily at set times with no backlog developing, so the manager has to look about continually for more efficient time-saving ways of performing them all. If a vendor sells a service which has to be performed on a daily or regular basis, buy it. The cost of time taken to do manual, original cataloging must be compared with the cost of buying automated cataloging from OCLC or another service; the results are a foregone conclusion. New, creative, and efficient ways of using telephones, memo pads, computer terminals, etc., must be considered. Perhaps a rule to follow is never to walk more than 25 steps if a telephone call will get you what you need. The manager must be a Renaissance person, performing many different functions requiring differing skills and the creativity and directedness to customize them for particular patrons.

If the library has grown to need more than one staff person, these functions must be divided. The problems of hierarchy and supervision rear their heads, requiring the lines of communication and responsibility to be carefully established and delineated. Whatever the size, the manager and every person on the staff should have a job description which documents all the functions performed and responsibilities held. The job description should be updated to reflect continual changes.

Life is made up of little things—replacing burned out lightbulbs, scheduling cleaning and vacuuming, ordering pencils, dogging the physical plant department to turn down heat and the accounting department to pay a certain portion of a bill. In themselves, each of these trivial pursuits is boring and a waste of valuable time, especially since they will be repeated ad infinitum or ad nauseum. Certainly, they were never taught in library school. Yet, the success of any library program is due in no small measure to the unremitting attention to these and other details.

Above all, confidence in oneself must be cultivated; this will radiate outward to envelop the library. Confidence assumes a style and an approach. The environment we create and our method of working must be thought through with great care. The library and its programs will be inviting and used if the manager makes them so.

No one person can have knowledge of everything about an organization, but a certain level of expertise of the organization's products and services must be learned and absorbed. The manager should never be afraid to ask questions. If carefully phrased, they can be quite flattering and turned to good advantage. Many patrons, especially in corporate entities, enjoy the role of teacher, a role they may not otherwise be able to play. Some may have been professors at one time in their careers; some may conduct workshops, seminars, or classes in their specialties. Seek them out.

RESOURCES

Several elements are key to a successful small special library program. These are the library's resources, the information "locked" therein, the receipt of gifts, archives, some of the newer services provided and the selling of them, the physical facilities, planning, finance, budgets and budgeting. Fortunately, the small special library is capable of changing with ease and with flexibility for the proper mix of elements at any point in its history.

Outside of a small group of dictionaries, directories, indexes, and other reference materials, collections vary as the organization varies. For example, the library in a law firm specializing in labor relations will differ from the one specializing in medical malpractice. Formats also vary. There are few guides and fewer models, and what there is needs to be modified. Few, if any, small special libraries ever attempt self-sufficiency. Collections are built around cores of materials frequently referred to; the rest is borrowed. Perhaps this is why special librarians are considered to be so social, such joiners; it is essential for them to know their counterparts and to set up reciprocal borrowing and service arrangements.

In the building of any organization, the library is often an afterthought and space is at a premium. It is particularly expensive when executive offices occupy space in a city's high-rise. Thus, the collection of books, journals, documents, reports, laboratory notes, slides, tapes, videos, etc., must be kept small but dynamic. The number of items weeded may equal the number of items added. When the circulation of an item slows or stops, that item may become an expensive liability and may be discarded to make way for newer needed materials. It is important to keep an up-to-date collection development policy. It does not have to be elaborate, but it does require constant consultation with the patrons and the organization's administrators.

Because of space constraints, managers depend more and more on microforms and bibliographic and full-text computer databases in place of that information in less-frequently used materials. Managers also cannot overlook the materials generated by their own organizations, which to patrons may be of equal importance to materials from outside. They may be presented in unusual, inconvenient formats that create endless problems in their bibliographic control, calling for ingenuity to deal with handwritten laboratory notes, drafts of proposals, slides of graphs, and so on.

THE INFORMATION CENTER

The collection of books, journals, pamphlets, reprints and reports, and audiovisuals in manual and computer-based formats recedes in importance as the information contained therein takes on greater importance. This change has brought on a shift from strictly library-type operations to information centers, and managers now think of themselves as information managers rather than library managers. In this new era, owning materials is less important than knowing if the information is available, where it can be located, how it can be accessed, and what that access costs. Not only the physical collection, but also the very walls of the library are receding in importance. Selecting what is needed from the increasing body of information takes up a sizable portion of the manager's time. Not even the smallest special library is exempt from the effects of this change and the rate of change is accelerating.

Some special librarians have purchased computer terminals and obtain information through telecommunications systems from databases residing in computers in this country and abroad. Others have purchased microcomputers that can do the same with added capabilities. They perform a variety of functions that increase and enlarge the services the library can provide by increasing the scope of information that can be obtained, the ways it can be presented, and the efficiency of the manager. When automating library functions, go slowly. Keeping up to date with the information available requires some background knowledge, taking continuing education courses, attending database and vendor training sessions, talking to colleagues, experts, and exhibitors at meetings, and reading the literature. One admonition: don't take the word of any computer salesperson unless it is checked with five other salespeople and all the programmers, analysts, and the head of the computer center in your organization.

One of the problems every manager faces is the gracious acceptance of gifts, which is not as easy as it sounds. Gifts can be a blessing or a curse. On the one hand, they may be fugitive materials which add important information not otherwise obtainable since they may not have been published. They may also be materials well-nigh impossible to obtain from the usual book and journal sources. Finally, they may be beyond the library's means. On the other hand, gifts may be duplicates, out of date, or out of scope. Yet, the manager is expected to receive them for political reasons and add them to the collection. The question to be asked is whether the space they take up weighs heavier than the effects of refusal to accept them. Each gift requires a different answer, and taxes the skills of the manager.

Some organizations are so busy that they fail to keep a history of their organization and a trail of its activities. The library can fulfill an important service by taking on this responsibility. The manager can begin only if the administration recognizes the importance of archives and supports the effort, and only if the departments cooperate.

SERVICES

The changes wrought by automation have affected the services provided by the library. Of course, they are as customized as they have ever been, perhaps more so. Documents are obtained for patrons either from the library or on interlibrary loans from other libraries. Printouts from hundreds of databases—bibliographic, full text, and numeric— are made available. Managers no longer sit and wait to serve those who come to the library; they are less reactive and far more proactive. They review the literature in books, journals, pamphlets, and audiovisuals, design and subscribe to SDI's, conduct computer searches, and merge information from several sources for patrons. They seek out relevant information as it becomes available in whatever format and from whatever source.

Patrons may find it is no longer necessary to spend as much time as previously in the library, thanks to the telephone and the terminal with modems and Electronic Mail Service. They can call the manager or the computer, obtain the desired information on their terminal, download if they have a microcomputer, or print it out if they have a printer. Some special libraries can deliver hard copy materials to their patrons.

PHYSICAL FACILITIES

A comfortable, quiet environment with good lighting, heating and air-conditioning, and attractive furnishings conducive to study and library research encourages library use. The services of interior decorators may more than pay for themselves with increased library attendance.

It is important for the library manager to walk into the library from time to time, looking at it through the eyes of the patron. What do they see when they enter? How easy is it to find out what's available? How do they go about getting it? How do they learn about the library's resources and services? Even more basic is the location of the library. During any reorganization, moving of offices, laboratories, conference rooms, etc., it is important to obtain support to move the library to a central location convenient for all patrons. As that center of gravity shifts, so should the library.

PUBLIC RELATIONS

Selling the library takes on several forms. Often a group of patrons form a "belt system" around the library. Usually highly literate and interested in libraries, having used them all their lives, these patrons provide support essential to the library's well-being. They help open the channels of communication both ways, formal and informal. They serve as sources of invaluable information to the manager about the organization and where it is going. At the same time, through them the manager can spread the word about the library's programs, especially new or changed ones. Such patrons should be continually courted and the number increased with no departmental favoritism. It goes without saying that members of this group receive a higher level of service.

It is essential to query patrons from time to time and to set up mechanisms for receiving suggestions, criticisms, and feedback. These serve as sounding boards of user satisfaction, and also as a lever with the administration for improvements and changes. Library news—graphic, clear, and succinct—should be included in all in-house publications. Ways should be found to tell the library story to everyone in the organization; fact sheets and guides should be kept up to date and distributed. Newcomers can be welcomed by letter and custom-designed orientations.

It is also useful to visit patrons in their natural "habitat" to understand their work. These visits may generate ideas of how the library can support them. Listening carefully to patrons' comments on home ground will help identify cores of constructive criticism that can change the face of the library for the common good. The key to a successful public relations program is to give patrons your immediate and undivided attention when they come into the library, letting them know that serving them is the most important thing in the world.

Informing management of all library activities on a regular basis, through some reporting mechanism, is essential. The reporting should not be routine, predictable, and therefore, boring; it won't be read. It can be varied with illustrations, charts, and heartwarming stories. Bookmarks, brochures, and announcements on flyers can be used; slide-tape or videotape orientation programs can be produced. Ask for time to talk at staff meetings. Support garnered from these efforts will help obtain funding for new or different programs. Improvements made possible by the injection of new funding will increase the library's services for the benefit of patrons, and result in greater support.

Libraries must also find ways of directly serving management, particularly the Chief Executive Officer. An example of such a service not directly related to the library's main constituency took place in one organization's library several years ago. As a result of some loans that went bad, this old and venerable institution was close to bankruptcy. The events surrounding this affair caused national and international repercussions and was in the news almost daily for months. The library staff proceeded to check all the wire services for news accounts, reproduced the printouts, and immediately delivered them to the desks of the appropriate managers. When reporters called for their reactions and comments, the administrators were prepared; they knew what they were going to be asked. They weathered the storm, and, perhaps in gratitude, the library continued to be well supported despite a general depression in that industry that caused library layoffs in similar organizations.

Small special libraries often lead precarious existences. If an institution comes upon hard times, the library is one of the first departments to be cut back or, worse still, closed. Matarazzo[1] described the reasons why six corporations closed their libraries. This may not make good bedtime reading, but it deserves careful attention for the survival of the library and its programs. Unlike academic institutions with accrediting agencies that require libraries, nowhere is it written that a corporation must have a library. There will be complaints from some staff if there is none, but they can turn to alternative sources of information in the public or college libraries nearby. Thus, the importance of good and continual communication with patrons at all levels cannot be ignored.

PLANNING

Planning assures logical, predictable development. The first step is the overall strategic plan which takes into account the goals and objectives of the library, the guidelines and mission of the organization as a whole, and the environments and industry of which it is a part. The second step is drawing up detailed tactical plans; and the third is implementing and carrying them out. Finally, the fourth step involves evaluation, monitoring, and feedback. How well is the plan working out? How should it be modified for subsequent planning? Some small special libraries cannot plan for more than one year at a time. For them, planning in six-month or even three-month increments may be the only solution. Some organizations employ planning specialists or consultants and their advice should be sought. The manager may have to follow certain planning procedures. The first attempt at planning is usually frustrating, time-consuming, and discouraging, but subsequent planning becomes easier. When the plan and the updates have been drawn up, they should be submitted to management for approval and incorporated in the organization's master plan.

FINANCES AND BUDGETS

A good deal of respect for, and confidence in, the library will ensue if recordkeeping is accurate, complete, and up to date. Despite commonly held beliefs, it is not difficult to do; it just requires daily persistence and the result is a satisfying sense of control. Alley[2] is one text that can help in setting up records. Often the accounting department can be flattered to assist in creating a system which serves the special needs of the library, yet interfaces with the organization's systems. By cultivating friendships in the accounting and purchasing departments, the library manager can familiarize them with the library's specialized needs and they can assist in bending the organization's regulations accordingly. The manager can then comfortably call upon someone in either department to help when problems arise concerning purchases, invoices, billing, and returns. At the same time, the manager learns the financial mores of the institution as they change.

Many accounting, purchasing, and payroll departments now employ automated systems. The library's printouts, the sine qua non of automation, have to be read. Every line must be understood and checked. Corrections are often necessary and should be made immediately. The day the library's recordkeeping is integrated with the automated system is a day for celebration.

Most organizations understandably require centralized purchasing, relieving the library manager of the time-consuming ordering of equipment, furnishings, and supplies. But it can make the manager's life quite difficult if it is extended to books, journals, audiovisuals, and microforms. The purchasing department's well-meaning procedures are seldom geared for the speed required to order books, claim journal issues, or review audiovisuals before they go out of print or stock. They seldom have staff knowledgeable about the special circumstances surrounding acquisitions. Even the smallest library may find that dealing with book and journal jobbers is worth their handling charges.

Most organizations annually place all their departments on budgets, which must be scrupulously adhered to. They require monitoring throughout the period covered. Reports on their successes or failures should be prepared for administration. Since the departments usually participate in the budgeting process, the library should begin planning for next year's budget right after the previous one takes effect.

THE LIBRARY MANAGER

It is essential to set aside a private place, undisturbed by patrons, to handle the library's routines, such as answering correspondence; ordering supplies; keeping circulation, financial, and other records up to date; cataloging and processing materials; conducting computer searches; and a myriad of other activities. If no office is available, a section can be cordoned off using bookcases. If there is more than one person on the staff, several private areas should be set up and the private time staggered. Every manager needs a diary of what has transpired and what needs to be done. If possible, a project should be completed the first time it is handled.

The time of day chosen to catch up on projects depends, in part, on the manager's internal clock and, in part, the way in which the organization operates. Morning persons find they can accomplish twice as much in half the time in the morning; evening persons do their best work later in the day. Perhaps a slight rearrangement of the library's or the manager's hours may be possible.

Some organizations have fixed hours for everybody; others may have staff that works at various times around the clock. They may expect the library to be open 12, 20, or even 24 hours a day, and library use is dependent on the "honor" system. Although the heaviest use is probably between 9:00a.m. and 5:00p.m., the manager may find it helpful to come in occasionally during the other times to find out how the library is used.

Because the small special library manager often works alone, it is essential to interact with those in other organizations at meetings, workshops, lunch and dinner functions, etc., to share experiences for mutual benefit. Managers can find groups, such as the Small Special Libraries Group (in Chicago) or can form their own networks for sharing resources and services. For example, expensive publications can be union listed and shared; not every library has to purchase them, thereby enlarging the resources available to any one library. Interacting with library managers in similar specialties must also be pursued. Some organizations, such as the American Chemical Society and the American Dental Association, have library or information sections. The Special Libraries Association offers many varied opportunities for interaction with colleagues and for continuing education programs.

Publications, such as *Special Libraries*[3] and the *One Person Library*[4] feature useful articles for the small special library; and the state library publications are often sources of valuable information. It is never a waste to set aside time to read the literature to glean ideas for change and new programs. Keeping abreast of what colleagues are doing with networking and automation is essential. Special library authors are innovative, practical, and hardly ever boring.

Managers should share their own thoughts and innovations with others by writing articles and responding to other articles with letters to the journal editors; volunteering to give talks at workshops, annual meetings, conferences, and seminars; and running for an office in SLA or in other professional associations, locally and nationally. Organizations are pleased when their library managers contribute in such a way since it adds to their stature.

References

1. James M. Matarazzo, *Closing the Corporate Library*. (New York: Special Libraries Assn., 1981).
2. Brian Alley and Jennifer Cargill, *Keeping Track of What You Spend*. (Phoenix: Oryx Press, 1982).
3. *Special Libraries* is available from the Special Libraries Association, 1700 18 St., N.W., Washington, DC 20009.
4. *The One-Person Library* is available from OPL Resources Ltd., Box 948, Murray Hill Station, New York, NY 10156.

2
Administration

Administering the Small Library

Jan Feye-Stukas

What is so good about small libraries? From the user viewpoint, the small library is usually in a small community and is generally accessible to a large percentage of users who live within a short walking or driving distance. There is personalized attention from staff who know their patrons, and the local community and its history; there is easy access to governing authorities and funding bodies; and there frequently are good selections of new titles because there are not as many patrons lined up to borrow them.

From the staff viewpoint, the small library has many advantages: staff are their own boss and set their own agenda; they have community status and the opportunity to represent the library in many arenas. There is opportunity for personal growth and knowledge in all subject areas (staff get to read new books first!); and the ability to be a change agent, influencing people and events because staff know their clientele so well and their patrons know and respect them. Staff are in a position to see and experience directly the results of their work; patrons confide in them and reveal how certain books changed their lives.

What are the not-so-good things? Users frequently feel that the collection is too old, stale, and small, and that there is a limited selection of materials on site; that the staff is untrained and over-worked; that quarters are cramped, with little seating space; that the library is open too few hours; and that there is a lack of privacy in library use.

The library staff feel that there is professional isolation; limited opportunities for staff development and peer exchange; lack of formal professional training and poor initial training; and insufficient guidance. Other disadvantages include too little operating funds for adequate materials and equipment; low pay; poor physical facility with not enough space for collection, equipment, computers, etc.; and finally, not enough staff time to do the myriad tasks that comprise good library

Jan Feye-Stukas is in the Office of Library Development and Services, Minnesota Department of Education, St. Paul, Minnesota.

services. These tasks come under the following rubrics: Reference and Reader's Advisory/Bibliographic Instruction; Collection Development and Maintenance, Circulation, Administration, and Programming. Task by task they include reader/listener/viewer guidance; answering questions in person and on the telephone; assisting patrons in using materials; assembling deposit collections; ready reviews; collecting materials; handling gifts; weeding; inventory; circulation policies; borrower registration; charging/discharging materials; shelving; processing reserves and interlibrary loans, overdues; maintaining communications and attending meetings with staff, board, administrators, faculty, city council; public relations; preparing reports, budgets, and records; training personnel; building arrangement and maintenance; ordering supplies; long-range planning; microcomputer workshops; story hours; seminars.

Despite the limitations that a small library may have, the clientele is much the same as those of large libraries. The small library also gets the same *range* of questions and interests as large libraries, only perhaps fewer in number.

What can be done, if not to solve, at least ameliorate some of the not-so-good factors? How can small libraries respond in the most effective way to users' expectations and improve staff working conditions?

First of all, consider what libraries are here for. What is their mission? All sizes and types of libraries could do a better job of focusing on their primary mission, but this is especially important for very small libraries. Library staff orientation handbooks are usually excellent in covering all the details of where the keys are, who reports to whom, what to do in emergencies, etc., but nowhere is there generally any statement of what libraries are all about. The people who write these handbooks may assume that anyone coming to work for a small library understands its mission. In the real world, this is not true, particularly if a new employee has never been a library user or received any formal education in library science, and is coming to a small library where none of the other staff, if there are any, have any training or library education either.

Then consider what it is that the librarian of a small library should be spending most of her or his time doing. Which of the tasks/responsibilities undertaken by the library staff are really essential; which could be done by someone else; and which may not need to be done at all? The following suggestions will give you more time to spend on the truly essential tasks of your operation.

- Weeding. It is faster and easier for users to find materials and for staff to shelve items when shelves are not totally full.
- Graphics. Help people to help themselves with better signs (commercially

produced, not hand-lettered). Users will feel more comfortable and staff can spend less time giving directions.
- Photocopying. Having a public photocopier that patrons themselves can operate.
- Networking. Acquisitions, cataloging, and processing can be done by vendors or a regional system or network. Order your bestsellers that way too.
- Volunteers. Have job lists ready; repairs and weeding can be done by volunteers.
- Charging. Simplify charging procedures to encourage self check-out.
- Loans. Many small libraries still have only two-week loan periods; lengthening loan periods would result in fewer renewals and overdues.
- Automation. Small libraries should not automate on their own; it is not cost effective. They need to be part of a large system to share the cost of hardware, updates, and maintenance.
- Terminal access. Get a small terminal for dialing into larger library systems for catalog information on an as-needed basis.
- Back issues. Don't waste time, energy, and space on storing back issues of periodicals beyond a year. Borrow these on interlibrary loan.
- Shelving. As books are checked in, have them placed on shelving trucks accessible to your clientele; there will not be as many to shelve.
- Overdues. Don't send overdue notices; after four weeks, send bills.
- Work schedules. Establish an annual calendar and a schedule for various activities: reports, budgets, supply ordering, etc.
- Tasks. Have a daily list of things that must be done.
- Telephone service. Get a telephone answering machine that gives hours and takes requests when the library is not open.

What about solutions to the problems of professional isolation, limited opportunities for staff development and peer exchange, poor training, etc.? A small library librarian can consider these:

- Ask for help from the cooperative library system or multitype type network.
- Ask for help from librarians in nearby small and large libraries.
- Insist on being able to work and spend some learning time in other large and small libraries.
- Rotate subscriptions to basic library literature with other libraries.
- Attend workshops, conferences, multitype networks.
- Always be assertive, recognizing personal strengths and weaknesses, and build on these strengths. Even untrained staff are considered to be the "librarian" by the clientele.

To quote the *One-Person Library Newsletter,*[1] a librarian should at all times "dress the part, speak the part, act the part, and do your job." The librarian represents the library to the community, so it is up to her or him to decide what that image should be.

Solutions to the problem of not enough money, few resources, and low pay—not unique to small libraries—are even more difficult to find. Just remember: when trying for more money, the librarian should at all times operate in a business-like manner. The small library is not your hobby! Here are some possibilities:

- Continually document—and have current numbers ready—your current and long-term needs.
- Produce a brochure that describes how people can include your library in their wills.
- Solicit memorials and publicly thank donors in the newspaper.
- Read library literature and attend workshops on alternative funding.
- Place a jar for donations for a special project (with a picture) at the circulation desk.
- Prepare a "wish book" to circulate, picturing items needed. Have a volunteer prepare the book.
- Use current resources more wisely, such as rotating various collections of mysteries, westerns, romance, gardening books, etc., with other libraries.

The problem of lack of space relates to the funding issue. Librarians need to continually push for larger space. A major weeding project can free up space. Book sales should be ongoing. Current space can be used more wisely by rearranging and limiting work room space. Ask colleagues to come in and give advice; it's easier for someone from the outside to suggest alternative arrangements.

The biggest error librarians working in small libraries make is that they try to do too much of the job alone. There are many resources available to assist them in their development if they can open up and avail themselves of these opportunities, especially from nearby larger libraries, the systems, the state library agencies, and associations. When small libraries cooperate and affiliate with other libraries, they might continue to do more than exist. They might even thrive.

References

1. "But Nobody Takes Me Seriously," *The One-Person Library, A Newsletter for Librarians & Management* (July 1984).

Staff and Personnel

Marlys F. Cresap Davis

Books and other materials may be a library's stock in trade, but when it comes to determining priorities for all its components, the library's staff must be listed as the most important element in its makeup. This is true in libraries of all sizes, but especially so in the small library where the staff are very visible to its clientele.

Think about the way in which the library's budget is divided. According to accepted formulas, from 40 to 60 percent of a library's operating budget should be allocated for salaries—even though most people might expect the largest amount to go for purchase of materials. The reason for this is partly pragmatic. It costs money to support a staff of any size, both for actual salaries and for benefits. However, there is also a less definable reason for expending a major portion of the library's budget on staff. In a word, it is *image*.

The library's image is vitally important to its ability to serve its patrons. Library staff members are what the patrons see when they enter the library. They are able, by their attitudes, appearance, and abilities, to project either an air of capability and the feeling that the library's purpose is to serve the patrons' needs, or the impression that the library exists for no reason except to keep a few people busy puttering around with old books.

No library wants to project the latter image. Therefore, it is in its best interests to see that enthusiastic, pleasant, qualified, and competent staff members are hired and that they receive rewards for maintaining those qualities during their tenure (which, it is to be hoped, will be long and fruitful for all concerned).

DEFINING THE POSITION

The importance of a personnel policy is not diminished by the fact that there may be only a few staff members. Personnel policies should be drafted by the board, with input from the head librarian. Like all policy statements, they should be reviewed on a regular basis and revised as necessary to accommodate changes in attitudes and other variables.

Marlys F. Cresap Davis is a library consultant living in Jefferson City, Missouri.

Some items to include in a personnel policy are criteria for selection, channels for advancement, working conditions, benefits, leaves of absence, compensation for overtime, resignation and dismissal procedures, grievance channels, payment of professional dues, parking privileges, and discount privileges for personal book and materials orders. An example of an outline for a personnel policy follows.

I. *Criteria for selection of personnel*
   A. Education
   B. Experience
   C. Rules regarding employment of relatives of staff
   D. Restrictions on who can be hired (conflict of interest)

II. *Responsibilities and compensation*
   A. Salary schedules (may be included as an appendix)
   B. Channels for advancement
   C. Staff opportunities for participation in management
   D. Staff responsibilities to the library when engaging as citizens in a political or social action
   E. Relationship of staff organizations to management

III. *Limitations, if any, on moonlighting*
   A. Types of activities considered moonlighting
   B. Dispersal of monies received as compensation

IV. *Working conditions*
   A. Hours per week
   B. Schedules (may be a statement indicating that scheduling is done by the librarian and is subject to change as necessary)
   C. Frequency and length of breaks, lunches, etc.
   D. Holidays and free days

V. *Benefits*
   A. Vacations
      1. Annual allowance
      2. Accumulation privileges
      3. Year-round or limited to summer
      4. Responsibility for substitute staffing
   B. Sick leave provisions
      1. Annual allowance
      2. Accumulation privileges
      3. Acceptable reasons for taking sick leave (personal illness, illness of minor child, doctor's appointments, etc.)
   C. Insurance
      1. Hospitalization and medical
      2. Workmen's compensation
      3. Life insurance

    D. Leaves of absence (paid and unpaid)
       1. Study
       2. Travel
       3. Funerals
       4. Maternity
       5. Temporary teaching posts
       6. Military duty
    E. Professional benefits
       1. Payment of professional dues for staff and/or board
       2. Reimbursement for professional conference and workshop expenses
         (including time off with pay)
    F. Other benefits
       1. Released time for voting
       2. Compensation for jury duty
       3. Compensation for overtime
       4. Parking privileges
       5. Perquisites (discount purchase privileges, free use of photocopier,
         etc.)

  VI. *Termination of employment*
    A. Resignation notification requirements
    B. Pension procedures
    C. Dismissal procedures
       1. Severance pay
       2. Payment for accrued vacation, etc.
       3. Channels and procedures for grievance

It is important that each employee has a job description. This document helps staff members to know their duties and responsibilities while on the job. In addition to listing the tasks the employee is responsible for daily, weekly, and less frequently, it may include a statement indicating that the employee is expected to perform "other duties as assigned." This is particularly important in the small library where everyone must pitch in when needed. The library cannot afford to become vulnerable to workers who are uncooperative and who justify such behavior on the basis of "It's not in my job description." The job description for a given position should be shared with each applicant and should be reviewed with the person hired.

The library director should see that enough staff are available to effectively serve the public. When deciding whether more staff should be hired, several factors have to be considered. Money, of course, is an obvious one, but the librarian also needs to consider the stated reasons for adding more staff, and to weigh the possible alternatives to this action.

There are a number of reasons why a librarian might consider hiring additional staff members. A particular program or service may have grown beyond the capabilities of the current staff size to handle it efficiently and effectively; or a new service is being added which no one on the existing staff is qualified to handle. Often new or expanded facilities can dictate a change in staffing patterns resulting in the need for more people in certain departments. For a very small library, it may be just a matter of finding someone to act as a substitute when the librarian is ill or on vacation. (However, in this case the librarian might want to consider hiring an assistant rather than a substitute in order to maintain continuity and allow the person to keep up to date on library operations, policies, etc.)

In any case, the preliminary study of need should be done by the librarian. After the board has authorized hiring additional staff, the librarian should have the responsibility for recruiting and interviewing applicants and making the final hiring decision (and then reporting that decision to the board).

THE RIGHT PEOPLE FOR THE RIGHT JOBS

When beginning the process of recruiting good potential library employees, it is important to consider the qualities needed for the job— not only the necessary skills, but also the candidates' enthusiasm, willingness to work, ability to cooperate, and personality traits which might either help or hinder them in providing service.

The qualifications which a library board or higher administration may feel are important for a head librarian to have are many and varied. Generally they fall into three major categories: personal, administrative, and professional.[1]

Personal qualifications include health, appearance, memory and intelligence, judgment, social qualities, work habits, and job responsibility.

Administrative skills—leadership, the ability to plan and evaluate, personnel administration skills, financial acumen, legal knowledge, public relations and communication, and general administrative traits— are abilities which are applied to the use of resources, including personnel, in order to fulfill the library's mission.[2]

Professional competencies are usually developed through education and experience, particularly via library training. They are attitudes, abilities, and practices which are considered unique to librarianship. Included in this category are commitment to, and involvement in, the profession; possession of professional knowledge and the ability to apply that knowledge to the job; an appreciation of the role of library boards; and professional versatility.[3]

Many of these qualifications for a head librarian would also be applicable to candidates for other staff positions. Personal qualities in particular are fairly universal. Depending on the position, some administrative and professional skills may also be needed.

Finally, the reasons why a person applies for a job at the library should be considered. Is it just to have a job or is there some more compelling reason? During the interview process, try to get a handle on the applicants' view of the library. Do they use the library? How would they handle a given situation (such as a censorship threat)? Above all, call the references each applicant lists. These people may be able to add something to your impression of the candidate which they were unable to convey in a written recommendation—either good or bad.

TRAINING NEW STAFF MEMBERS

Once a person has been hired to work at the library, whether full-time or part-time and regardless of the position, there should be some kind of orientation to the job and to the library in general. Even the most ardent library-user-turned-employee cannot know all there is to know about the library's purpose, operations, etc.

First of all, the director, perhaps with the help of his or her secretary, should review the personnel policies and job description with the new employee. This may have been gone over lightly in the interview, but it should be explained in more depth and any questions cleared up at the very beginning. Now is the time to make sure that all necessary employment forms get properly filled out and that the new staff member understands the requirements and benefits of Social Security, the public retirement plan, the library's benefits package, etc. A tour of the library is also in order, especially the workrooms and staff-only areas. In the case of a new director, responsibility for this orientation falls to the library board.

On-the-job training is the best kind there is. It takes time, and everyone on the staff has to get involved in the process, but it's really the only way for new employees to learn their jobs.

The basics of the job must be learned quickly when you're training on the job. If this does not seem to be happening, perhaps some special help after hours is needed. In any case, those who are helping the new staff member to learn must be sure to stress that it's all right to ask questions—even dumb ones. In fact, encourage this by stopping at the conclusion of each newly learned process to ask if everything is clear to the learner.

It may be helpful to structure the training in layers, so that as the new employee learns each task a new one is added to the list of duties. This not only allows reinforcement of the parts already learned, but keeps the job from seeming to be overwhelming.

A procedures manual is an invaluable tool for both new and old staff members. Everyone forgets how things are handled sometimes. Coming back from vacations or illness is hard enough to handle without having to relearn the entire job. It takes some time to compile a complete procedures manual and it probably will never be really complete, but it's worth the effort. (See pages 132–140 for a discussion on writing such a manual.)

One mark of a good personnel manager is the ability to match people to jobs and vice-versa. Try to pick up on any particular interests or talents that the new employee demonstrates and capitalize on them. For instance, if the person you just hired to be a desk clerk expresses interest in making bulletin board displays (and nobody else on staff can draw a straight line with a ruler), let the new employee try taking over that responsibility. If she or he turns out to be any good at it, add it to the job description. Of course, this must be handled carefully in order not to step on anyone's toes, but it can prove to be of great benefit to the director, the staff, and the library as a whole—ensuring that each job is being done by the best person available for that particular duty.

Library directors may forget that continuing education is as important for their employees as it is for themselves. Even clerical staff benefit from getting out of their usual environment, meeting new people, and learning new techniques. Half the benefit of going to meetings and workshops is discovering that other people have the same problems and questions. Theory is an important part of librarianship too, and through continuing education, nonprofessional librarians and staff members can acquire the theoretical background which professionals get in library school.

STAFF MEETINGS

For any library with two or more employees, staff meetings are almost an imperative. Staff members need to meet with the director and with other employees. No matter how small the library, there is always a need for collaboration. If nothing else, the opportunity to bounce ideas around and get reactions is valuable. Staff meetings are also good for coordinating activities, doing long- and short-range planning, airing problems and finding solutions, and simply letting the staff members know how each one's work is progressing, as well as their schedule of work and activities for the following period. This last allows each employee to schedule—and receive—uninterrupted time when clerical duties or other nonpublic activities can take place.

Staff meetings should occur on a regular basis, preferably weekly or monthly. They need not be terribly formal, although there probably should be an agenda to follow so that the meetings don't degenerate into social circles or complaint sessions. Even when there are no major projects in the works, staff meetings should continue, if for no other reason than to allow employees to touch base with each other. This is particularly important in the small library where staff members may not see each other every day and may lose track of what each one is doing.

HANDLING STICKY SITUATIONS

There are any number of "sticky situations" which can arise in the library. Dealing with recalcitrant staff members is one. There will always be some employees who feel that their personal convenience is more important than that of others or of the library itself. Employees who repeatedly ask for special consideration in work schedules, vacation, sick leave, etc., can cause more than just headaches for the librarian. Other employees, seeing such special treatment occur, can become disillusioned with the supervisor's ability to be fair. Or they may begin to ask for special treatment also. It should be made clear from the outset (or at least from the time when it becomes apparent that this behavior is habitual) that special treatment for certain employees is not company policy.

This extends to the supervisor as well. Certain benefits may accrue to the position of manager, but they should not be abused or flouted. The supervisor should expect to follow the same rules as the employees under his or her management. For instance, if evening and weekend hours are a regular part of the staff's responsibilities, the librarian or supervisor should be expected to take a turn at working those hours as well. It is never fair for one or two people to have to work all the "drudge" hours while others never do. The exception to this is when an employee specifically asks to be assigned only to those hours and when this request does not interfere with library service or the rights of other employees.

When scheduling and assigning duties, the librarian should attempt to be as fair as possible and to accommodate staff members' needs to the greatest extent possible without jeopardizing the library's interests. When special consideration is warranted by circumstance, it should be granted if possible. When it becomes habitual, it should be nipped in the bud.

Intra-staff tensions can also become a problem. Sometimes personalities clash, or mannerisms or habits grate on nerves. If the problem becomes too noticeable, it can cause a decline in the quality of work as well as a loss of image for the library. The library director or supervisor needs to keep an eye out for this sort of trouble and move quickly to alleviate it in order to maintain a satisfied staff and a smoothly running library.

Talking to the "combatants" individually is the most likely place to start and may provide insight into the problem which can then be used to solve it without resorting to confrontation. Rescheduling or reassigning employees to other departments may prove an easy solution. However, if both of the parties involved are already assigned to areas and duties for which they are best suited, the library's services—and, by extension, its image—may be damaged by moving them to other departments. The rights of other employees must be considered as well. It is up to you to decide whether rescheduling or reassignment is a compromise or a cop-out.

Depending on the situation and the people involved, you may find it necessary to bring all the parties together for a joint discussion of the problem and alternative solutions. Confrontation may not always be the best course and its use should be judicious. However, if all else fails (particularly if part of the problem seems to be lack of communication between the staff members and/or between them and you), this may be a viable way of handling the situation.

Occasionally problems may arise between staff members and patrons. These may be isolated incidents, but watch for any recurrence which might indicate undesirable traits in an employee. In general (and in public), the patron is always right. The exception might be "problem" patrons. However, even the most problematic patron has rights—among them, the right to be treated as courteously and fairly as possible in the given circumstances. As part of their training, staff members should receive instruction in dealing with such people in a way that will not damage either the patron's self-respect, the employee's reputation, or the library's image.

PERSONNEL EVALUATIONS

Personnel evaluations are a valuable tool for both the employee and the employer. In larger libraries, merit pay is often tied to employee evaluations. This may not be the case in small libraries, but that does not render the evaluation process any less important. Not only do staff evaluations examine what has happened in the past, but they provide a springboard for the future. The purpose of evaluating staff members is not to find out what they're doing wrong, but to discover how to make things even better.[4]

Personnel evaluation should take place at all levels. The library board evaluates the director; the director in turn evaluates the other staff members. Employees need to know whether, and in what ways, they are doing a good job (or not). It may be that staff members feel that they are performing satisfactorily when in fact your expectations are higher than staff realize. Or staff members, not receiving any concrete evidence of good performance, may feel that they are unable to do the job well, or that you do not appreciate their efforts. Equally important is the need to create an opportunity for staff members to air complaints or problems with their jobs as well as to let you know what is good about it.

There are several methods used for evaluating personnel. The accepted format calls for the evaluator (director or supervisor) to prepare a written evaluation of the employee's performance based on observation. The employee is asked to read and sign this document (though the employee need not necessarily agree with the evaluator's assessment). This ensures that a public record is kept of the fact that the employee was evaluated and knew of the evaluation). Usually, an oral evaluation session is also conducted, allowing employee and supervisor to discuss the points covered in the written evaluation, to bring up any problems arising from the job, and to discuss ways of improving performance and/or give recognition for a job well done.

Each library manager will want to devise evaluation forms that will reflect the unique characteristics of his or her institution. Often librarians are evaluated on the basis of predetermined traits or qualities which are considered to be important for their effective performance. The following section of the Performance Evaluation Form from Southeastern Library Services, Iowa, is an example of this:[5]

EMPLOYEE TRAIT RATING

The statement checked in each of the following groups was selected as the most descriptive of your general work habits, relationships with people, resourcefulness, work interest, productivity, and work quality.

1. ( ) frequently adapts projects resulting in improvements over original assignments
   ( ) work often fails to meet expectations
   ( ) finished product usually conforms to department expectations
2. ( ) consistently presents work of impeccable quality
   ( ) makes numerous errors
   ( ) work is usually done correctly
3. ( ) work is apt to be completed carelessly
   ( ) is highly observant of work details and uses good judgment in completing projects
   ( ) completed work shows care in its preparation

Some evaluation forms include a section that rates the performance of certain tasks or duties according to a grading system (see Figure 1).

FIGURE 1   Performance Evaluation[6]

Evaluation Elements	Rating 1	2	3	4	5	Comments:
Quantity of Work: Does the employee consistently accomplish a satisfactory amount of work or does work output fluctuate from day-to-day?						
Quality of Work: Does the employee turn out a satisfactorily finished product or must much of the work be carefully checked or occasionally redone?						
Dependability: Is it necessary to follow up on the employee's work to a greater extent than normal or can the employee be relied upon to keep commitments?						
Cooperation: Does the employee get along well with fellow workers and does the employee accept correction or supervision?						
Attendance: This reflects absences from duty for any reason, however legitimate, and includes punctuality.						
Overall evaluation: This is a summary evaluation of an employee's performance.						

Others may weight the importance of various duties in relation to the overall responsibilities of the job. Management by objectives (MBO) requires that evaluations include setting job-related objectives for each employee and basing performance evaluation on how well those objectives are met before the next scheduled evaluation (see Figure 2).

When designing evaluation forms for use in the library, many library managers choose a combination of two or more of these approaches. Evaluation of an employee's performance based on personal traits or on how well certain tasks are accomplished is probably the easiest method. Using the MBO method of defining objectives takes much more time but may be a more realistic way of determining whether an employee is capable of doing the job.

No matter what method is used to evaluate library personnel, the process must be done on a regular basis. It's the same principle as weeding and assessing the collection or reviewing policies: as soon as the process is done once, you go back to the beginning and start all over again. The job doesn't necessarily get any more pleasant, but with

Figure 2   Management by Objectives[7]

<table>
<tr><td colspan="3">PLANNING AND PERFORMANCE REVIEW</td></tr>
</table>

Name _____   Department _____   Period of Review:
Title _____   Division _____   _____
                                        to _____

OBJECTIVES (Planning Session)	EXPECTED RESULTS (Planning Session)	ACTUAL RESULTS (Performance Review)

Job-Related
Development Goals

Employee Career
Goals and Comments

Date of 1st Session _____   Date of Results
Employee's Signature _____   Review Session _____
Evaluator's Signature _____   Employee's Signature _____
                                        Evaluator's Signature _____

practice, it may get easier, and the benefits are worth the time and energy expended.

THE EXIT INTERVIEW

When an employee leaves his or her position, for whatever reason, often there is no process in place by which you can use this departure to benefit the library. This may not be the case when an employee is fired; presumably there was a specific reason for dismissal which was discussed previously. Staff members who quit their jobs, however, may be able to give you some insight into their reasons for leaving which could be translated into the ability to hire the right person to fill the vacancy.

Let's consider first the firing (dismissal is a nicer word) of unsatisfactory employees. You must make sure that all the proper channels (as defined in the personnel policy) have been followed when deciding on whether to retain or dismiss an employee. If there has not been prior discussion of whatever problem exists, either in a regular evaluation session or in a special interview with the employee, grave legal problems could result for you and the library. Due process must be a part of the personnel policy and must be followed to the letter in order to avoid nasty lawsuits. A cardinal rule is that employees must be told the reason for their dismissal and must understand that reason.

It is in everyone's best interests to attempt as congenial a parting as possible. The library does not need an enemy on the streets; former employees who hold grudges against those who dismissed them can spread particularly nasty rumors about the library and those who work there. Needless to say, this will not enhance the library's image in the community. Likewise, the employee may very well need to be on good terms with a former supervisor. The fact that an employee wasn't satisfactory for the library may not mean he or she would not do well in some other setting. Getting another job could be difficult if you refused to give a recommendation on the basis of personal dislike or disgruntlement against the employee for leaving.

Losing a good employee, for whatever reason, can be as traumatic as having to fire someone. The thought of having to conduct a search for someone to replace an "irreplaceable" staff member strikes terror in the hearts of most managers. However, no one is irreplaceable, and the experience need not be a complete loss. The library may be able to benefit from the experience of a good staff member, if the opportunity is taken. Conducting an exit interview is a way of discovering information which may be of use when hiring a replacement. Try to find out what the staff member liked (or didn't) about the job, and why. The employee's opinion on possible improvements in the job description or procedures could be invaluable for the future. It might even prove beneficial to ask if the employee knows of anyone who would make a good replacement candidate. This should not be the entire basis for hiring the replacement, but people often have friends or acquaintances with similar interests and talents who might be qualified and appropriate for the job.

NO EASY TASK

Personnel management is not an easy job. In fact, it is probably one of the more difficult tasks a librarian has to perform. Needless to say, it is essential to the smooth operation of the library and as such should receive the utmost care and attention.

References

1. Robert R. McClarren, "The Marks of a 'Competent' and 'Qualified' Head Librarian," *Illinois Libraries*, 66, No. 8 (October 1984): 415–19.

2. Ibid.
3. Ibid.
4. Jane Robbins-Carter and Douglas L. Zweizig, "Are We There Yet?" *American Libraries* 17, No. 2 (February 1986): 108+.
5. "Performance Evaluation Form." Southeastern Library Services, Davenport, IA (1981).
6. Robbins-Carter, p. 110.
7. "Employee Performance Evaluation." City of Sioux City, IA (1979).

Budget Preparation

Alan Hall

In small libraries, the librarian often must do at least a portion of the financial accounting work; in some cases, all of it. A school, academic or special library's budget is part of the budget of the larger organization with which the library is associated. The librarian should learn about the library's legal organization and how it fits into the broader picture. Is the library a departmental branch of city government, or does it operate independently? Most public libraries have a board which is directly responsible for the operation of the library. Is that board responsible to another local government and if so, how does that relate to the finances? School and academic librarians should determine the chain of command between the library and administration of the parent institution.

Locate the board's minutes or journal. It may be a lot of work, but reviewing the written journal of the board and doing a simple index of the minutes for the last ten years is an excellent way to establish a library's background, and to have pertinent information at hand. As time permits, review the earlier minutes. In many cases, it will be helpful to know that information, as well as to glean a general history of the library from those minutes. Written policies, by-laws, or constitutions which relate to the library are essential as developed by the library board, school board, or college administration.

Previous library budgets are vital in determining where the library has been. The last two years are the most important, but five years may reveal patterns and trends. You'll need these documents when preparing future budgets. In gathering this information, the librarian can determine the basis of support for the library: What are the tax sources and how are they collected and distributed? Does the library have endowments and trusts, and how can they be used? Are there levies for library support? Are they voted by the general public, and when do they expire? Is there a capital improvement levy or bond issue funding improvements to the building?

After developing a feeling for the library as it financially exists on the local level, it is time to find the state laws which relate to your

Alan Hall is Director, Public Library of Steubenville and Jefferson County, Steubenville, Ohio.

library. Compilations of these laws are commonly published by the state library agency or state library association. The local library may own that publication or others on a related topic, such as trustee handbooks and manuals for financial officers. In addition to the valuable financial information in these publications, the introduction often contains an overview and background to the state's financing of libraries, and a history of library development in your state.

To whom do you look for further assistance? The library world is full of willing resource persons. State library agencies have consultants who can offer help in a vast array of problems as well as supply referrals to the proper authorities. The state library association and its employees all stand ready to aid its members. Many states contain cooperatives of libraries that provide an invaluable source of professional expertise from the area librarians. A phone call to a neighboring library's professional may bring a quick response with tips and guidance. Other libraries within the system or institution will be willing to assist with budget problems. City and county officials can help with financial matters and may provide an important local link.

From earlier investigations, you will have determined the fiscal year of your library. The most common fiscal years are a calendar fiscal year (January 1–December 31) or the fiscal year from July 31 to June 30. You will also need a calendar of events and dates relating to the timetable for budget preparation of the library. Some state handbooks already have this calendar of dates available. And school administrators have calendars developed for the departments or at least the dates from which a calendar can be formulated. Becoming familiar with the dates will prevent rushing to meet a deadline, or missing an important date.

THE BUDGET PROCESS

The budget—the library's plan for operation—can be produced in a timely manner. It is developed by the librarian and the board jointly in public libraries. In the case of a school or academic library, the budget is prepared by the librarian and submitted to the administration of the school. All budgets are based on a long-range plan for development. Any type of library must be guided by a map of the services. What are the plans for the next five years? The plan for a public library is developed after studying the community and its needs, and making a plan to meet those needs for library services. A school library's plans relate to the needs of the school for library services, and may be a part of the larger document for the entire school system. Once that plan has been developed and approved, the budget becomes the means for reaching those goals and objectives within a specified year. The librarian selects the amount of progress desired toward meeting the goals of the long-range plan based on available resources within that fiscal year.

Many librarians try to operate year-to-year, adding a little for added costs, and with no visible plan. This method of operation results in a lack of justification to taxpayers, and little foresight and growth in library service. Small libraries need long-range planning just as much as larger libraries. The hunch of the librarian can not be the guiding force behind a library's planning.

The politics of the budget situation require a decision about the kind of budget request to be made to local officials or administration. Do they want the librarian to submit a budget that requests funds totaling exactly the estimates, or do they want a "wish budget" that includes everything the librarian would like to have and do for that fiscal year? This important question may be answered by the board or those involved in earlier budgets. One type of budget request can anger local officials; the other can short the library of possible funds by being too conservative. The best allows the librarian to present the library's needs with knowledge of the possible funding levels.

Some librarians think their budgets should be simple in nature; rather, a small library budget should be complex enough to meet the needs of that library. Most librarians working in small libraries use a line-item budget which breaks down the budget into lines illustrating each category of receipts and expenditures. The terms may vary based on individual need, but are similar in nature from one budget to the nest. In the box on page 87 is an example of a line-item budget, using the basic expenditure groupings found in any budget.[1] In some situations, the board may be required by law to utilize specific budget formats.

Personnel costs include all salaries paid to library employees, usually divided into categories of employees. In addition to actual salary costs, this section should include library payments for retirement benefits and employee insurance costs. Other employee benefits are included in this section in order to show the actual complete cost of the library staff.

Operating expenses cover the cost of operating the library facility, including various supplies, services, and repairs. Utility costs also are found within this account, and are divided into each different utility so as to better track those costs.

Library materials are the purchases near to the heart of most librarians and, indeed, are the reason for a library's existence. Unfortunately, it is the category which has the greatest flexibility within a library budget, and is usually the first to be cut when needed to balance a budget. The cost of new book purchases and shipping costs are included here, as well as all other formats of library materials, including computer services. Maintenance and repair of library materials is also a

LINE-ITEM BUDGET CATEGORIES

RECEIPTS

Taxes (subdivide for each different type of tax received; establish a line-item for each subdivision)

Government Grants (specific federal, state, or local grants)

Patron Fines and Fees (overdue fines and other fees; sources of fees can be divided, such as copy machine fees)

Earnings on Investments

Contributions, Gifts, and Donations

Miscellaneous

EXPENDITURES

Personnel

Employee salaries (subdivide by category of employee)

Retirement benefits (employer's share paid to retirement systems)

Insurance benefits (employer's share paid for health insurance, life insurance, etc.)

Operating Expenses

General administrative supplies

Property maintenance/repair supplies

Travel expenses

Printing and publicity

Property maintenance/repair services

Insurance (property, liability, etc.)

Rents and leases

Utilities

Library Materials

Books (can be subdivided many ways: children and adult, standing orders, etc.)

Pamphlets

Periodicals

Audiovisual

Computer Services

Rebinding and repair

Capital Outlay

Land

Buildings

Building improvements

Furniture and equipment

Other

Dues and memberships

Refunds

Contingency

line item here since they are part of the cost of providing materials to library users. A school library's budget is likely to contain expenditures mainly in this category; personnel costs are a part of the overall operation of the school system as well as the operating costs of the physical space which the library uses.

Capital outlay refers to replacement equipment and furnishings in many budgets. (Major building renovations or completely new buildings and their equipment and furnishings are usually funded by different means than the annual operating budget, and are then placed in a separate account.) If you are planning to budget monies each year to transfer into a building fund, that money could be placed here for transfer. Should the local taxing authority grant the library funds (other than a bond issue) within one fiscal year to construct a new building, that money could be budgeted here.

If a library has expenditures which do not fit into any of the previous accounts, they can be placed in an "other" category which might include dues and memberships to library organizations, refunds made to patrons, or a contingency account, if permitted. Budget accounts should be flexible—add more if that helps the accountability of the financial system, but have only as many as are necessary.

Librarians are forever trying to assign percentages to their budget categories to see if their library is "normal" compared to the budgets of other libraries of the same type. No such percentage breakdown exists which can be applied as a norm. The only general conclusion that can be made is that personnel costs will be the largest portion of the budget. The percentage breakdown within budget categories, and within the line items, should reflect the needs of the library, and the goals and objectives as set forth in the long-range plan.

DEVELOPING BUDGET FIGURES

When doing the actual budget, the librarian should take a leadership role with the board or administration. Board members, or a board's finance committee, will look for a preliminary document from which discussion can begin. Keeping in mind that next year's budget is being developed early in the prior year, the librarian should prepare a statement of actual and estimated revenues. This document should contain all receipts and expenditures used in the library's budget, listed in order down the left side of the sheet, with five headings across the top extending to the right which read:

ACTUAL—19X5
ACTUAL—first six months of 19X6
ESTIMATED—remainder of 19X6
TOTAL ACTUAL AND ESTIMATED—19X6
ESTIMATED AND REQUESTED—19X7

The budget for the upcoming fiscal year (19X7) is the place to examine the budget for 19X5 and 19X6 to determine how well the budgeted amount covered the expenses. In combination with the plan for 19X7, a decision is made as to what to place in the 19X7 column as a request.

In completing the 19X7 column, the librarian should have in hand the statistics, studies, and justification that explain the expenditures. This information can either be attached to the budget or presented as a supplemental document. The board or administration probably have definite ideas regarding the total amount of funds requested from the local taxing authority, but the long-range plans and data from the documentation will be the overall leader in the request.[2]

Once the budget is submitted to the authority, the procedure varies widely from one state to the next. A public hearing may be required to accept public comment on the budget, or the budget will be included in a larger document submitted. The documentation presented with the budget form should be clear and concise. Local officials and administrators are flooded with budgets, and will not read lengthy, complicated documents. The "bulk" should be saved for further questioning or a second meeting.

Since local officials may not be aware of library terminology, the librarian should be careful using words like "serials" and "circulation" in the information. Surveys and data can be presented, but the conclusions from that data must be shown. Input from board members as well as the public is helpful in budget support.

Once the budget is accepted by the authority (that acceptance is often termed "certification"), the librarian must continue to monitor the current year's budget for any miscalculation that might arise as the remainder of the fiscal year passes. Near or after the beginning of the new fiscal year, the board approves appropriations; the budget is then formally accepted and readied for the new fiscal year. Remember that "appropriations" only means that amounts of money have been assigned to categories; the actual flow of cash into the budget depends on distribution of funds by officials to the library. The flow of funds into the budget must be studied to determine when purchases can actually be made.

ACCOUNTING FOR THE BUDGET

It is important to observe basic accounting procedures and practices in the library's bookkeeping. As a consumer of funds, the library is expected to account for them to the general public or higher administration. That accountability begins with the use of purchase orders. As an assurance that an order is valid, a purchase order is issued by the library to encumber the needed funds to cover the total cost of the purchase from the proper account. When funds are encumbered, the cost of the purchase has been set aside so the fund balance will not reflect the monies already committed to another purchase. A copy of the purchase order is attached to the payment record to assure proper accounting for later reference.

The overall accounting system is mandated by a local or state agency in the public and school library; others will follow the rules and procedures of their parent organization. Those agencies often have guidelines which can help in improving accounting; many sponsor workshops.

Fundraising and donations are a final budget item that must be considered. Many small libraries depend on donations for their survival, but if officials feel that the library can operate sufficiently on donations, the chance of growing and improving with public funds is lessened. Donations should be used as a way of purchasing special items to supplement the library; buildings and additions are funded often by donations. Librarians should be careful not to donate their library out of existence by making it appear their library does not need steady, predictable support.

COMMON BUDGETING TERMS AND DEFINITIONS

Appropriations funds set aside into various budget accounts for expenditure.

Budget a plan for operation from the financial perspective.

Capital outlay the cost of construction, remodeling, furniture and equipment.

Cash flow the receipt of monies throughout the fiscal year, examined to determine the pattern and expectation of such funds.

Certification the act of an authority setting the budget for a fiscal year.

Encumbrance funds set aside within a category to cover the cost of an order; made to reflect clearly the funds remaining for future orders.

Line-item budget a budget form commonly used in libraries, in which the budget is divided into "lines" of accounts, each one covering a general or specific expense.

Operating expenses the cost of operations including such items as supplies, utilities, property/liability insurance, services, and repairs.

Personnel costs the salaries and all employer-paid benefits, such as retirement and medical/life insurance.

Purchase order an order issued for the purchase of a specific item or items, with the order allowing sufficient funds to be set aside for that purchase.

References

1. Thomas E. Ferguson, *State of Ohio Chart of Accounts for Public Libraries* (Columbus, Ohio: Bureau of Inspection and Supervision of Public Offices, 1984), pp. 2–14.
2. Edward S. Lynn and Robert J. Freeman, *Fund Accounting: Theory and Practice,* 2d ed. (Englewood Cliffs, N.J.: Prentice-Hall, Inc., 1983), p. 79ff.

The Physical Plant

Ruth Fraley

A library's atmosphere is the product of several interacting variables; the staff's attitude and approach to their work and to their patrons, the quality and extent of the library's collections, and the state of the library's physical facilities. Library patrons tend to make quick judgments of the library atmosphere, and these opinions are often influenced by its physical plant more than any other variable. Patrons who spend a long time working in the library notice their surroundings first; their subsequent opinion of the facilities will be based on prolonged observation and use. Those patrons who do not spend such long periods of time in the library may form a long-lasting opinion based solely on the atmosphere they encounter walking through it.

The atmosphere and general condition of the library can be self-perpetuating. Many people react to their environment by changing their actions to reflect it: they will add debris to a dirty environment, noise to a noisy one, and so on. Thus, the dominant factors in the environment are reinforced, and the cycle of negatives grows in magnitude. Many ways of improving the library atmosphere involve improving the physical plant, and if this also creates a more positive atmosphere, every effort should be made to do so.

Even though facilities have a significant impact on library support and operations, librarians do not always have the power to change major practices or policies. For example, libraries in a corporate setting may be considered solely as another room or series of rooms that have to be maintained in the same way and using the same techniques and materials as other parts of the organization. A school district may assign the same custodian to clean classrooms, hallways, and the library—and the policies or cleaning guidelines set by the school board for all district facilities will apply. If the floors get washed once a month, this will be the case in the library too. If restrooms are cleaned weekly, this is when the library's rest rooms will be cleaned. If there is no maintenance staff member on duty on weekends, there will be no one available to maintain the library, even if it is open on Saturdays and Sundays, often the busiest days. If there is a policy against dusting or touching the surfaces

Ruth Fraley is Chief Librarian, New York State Unified Court System, Albany, New York.

of desks or counters, the circulation desk may never be touched by the cleaning crew. A similar situation can exist for libraries located in public buildings maintained by the town, county, state, or federal government.

INFLUENCING LIBRARY POLICIES

Support for library activities, plans, and programs is influenced by the perceptions of those members of the organization or community who vote or have the authority to fund library activities. Although there appear to be occasions when policies and conditions are beyond the influence of library personnel, librarians are in a good position to point out the pros and cons of decisions affecting them, and they should make every effort to inform, enlighten, and explain library operations to those responsible for decisions—poor decisions are most often a product of ignorance. Librarians must be able to look at all of the elements of library operations and understand the short- and long-term impact of any proposed facilities project, as well as routine policies and practices. The potential impact must be explained before the policy is set in place and should be backed by facts and illustrations.

The fiscal impact of any proposed policy is one of the most important and convincing considerations. When a facility policy is made to decrease the library security system, for example, and the projected loss rate for the collection will rise above three percent as a result, a dollar estimate of the impact of the policy can easily be presented and understood. Librarians can be particularly influential in pointing out the consequences of proposed facilities policies because they are intimately acquainted with the details of library operations of which decision makers are often totally unaware. For instance, although deferred equipment replacement saves an organization money in the short term, the long-term deleterious effect on library collections can cost more than the initial saving.

THE LIBRARIAN'S ROLE IN FACILITIES PLANNING

While it may be relatively easy for librarians to apply their expertise to influence specific budget decisions, it is considerably more difficult for them to provide meaningful input when a decision involves major facility changes and improvements, especially if they are not familiar with facilities planning procedures and options.

New construction or renovation is a special project, and when the construction is underway, librarians often work with individuals they have not worked with in the past. This type of project calls for different skills and timetables than those which typify day-to-day library operations.

In setting goals for proposed facilities changes, librarians in charge of small libraries face a major obstacle: it is difficult to focus on the goals and long-range plans of the operation when the library is staffed by only one or two individuals who do everything: charge out materials, repair the copy machine, plan the menu for a large reception, respond to reference questions, conduct complicated online database searches, and make sure supplies are adequate. But these goals and plans are particularly important since these individuals, overburdened by the details of daily operations, can find themselves left out of the decision-making process.

It is possible for the plans for facility improvements to be drawn and the construction started with either no input or token input from the librarian. But major facility changes and improvements undertaken without timely input from the librarian will create more problems for the library than they solve. The librarian must be familiar with the primary objective of a project, tentative timetable, and floor plans before the project goes out for bid.

THE VALUE OF STANDARDS IN FACILITIES PLANNING

Standards have a great deal of potential value in the process of creating a persuasive document to convey facility requirements to decision makers. National and international standards can be effectively used in presenting a convincing case for change. In addition to outlining and explaining operational needs, it is sometimes even more convincing to relate conditions in the library to standards, especially those which support a primary goal of the library.

Assuming library goals have been articulated, and reviewed, the standards can be used to support specific objectives, and perhaps bring the library closer to reaching a goal.

Standards are also useful in developing the facilities plan. For example, the librarian may know just by observation that there are not enough seats in the library; just how many should exist can be determined by using a standard. But although standards are useful as guidelines to facilities planning, their strict application is problematic: often the only feasible physical arrangements, given the space and budget constraints faced by most small libraries, violate all of the published rules and guidelines available in the literature and most of those determined by common practice. For example, what college or university library is able to seat one-third of its student body? How about one-tenth? What public library has .7 square feet per capita?

Because of the difficulty of meeting facilities standards as they appear in the literature, particularly at a time when resources are scarce, there is a dichotomy of views regarding how to interpret and apply them. According to one school of thought, facilities standards should be general enough so that a librarian can set in motion and succeed with a plan for meeting them within a reasonable period of time and with a reasonable fiscal commitment. One example of this general approach is: "Colleges and universities should have adequate seating for the student body."[3] One could argue that the general standard can precipitate endless discussions about adequate and inadequate without moving to a stage where actual plans are drawn. But a specific standard such as "a college library should be able to seat one-tenth of the student body" is not flexible enough to accommodate different types of colleges and the variations in their curriculums. For example, a community college library serving commuting students has different facility needs than a graduate liberal arts institution.

However, general statements provide little or no guidance for individual librarians trying to persuasively justify a budget or convince an architect committed to a different perspective to change his or her views. When a standard contains general statements, comparative information is the only source of data to use in a report. Telephone calls or visits to libraries of a similar size and mission can yield valuable information, it is true, and occasionally it is possible to compile a base of comparison by working with a group of colleagues in similar situations. But the relatively isolated position of librarians, and the amount of time and effort involved in explaining the library operation to decision makers who do not have a grasp of the complexities involved, may actually weaken the library's position.

Standards created and adopted by national agencies and organizations are well established and provide a goal easily understood and accepted by nonlibrarians whose main interest is to balance the needs and goals of the library with the needs and goals of other segments of the organization also making demands on scarce resources. When it is not possible to bring in consultants whose expertise is universally accepted by everyone involved in planning and operating the library, these standards serve as "consultants" in the sense that they are the collective, considered opinion of experts in the field.

A library may develop for a period of time under the general "good service" goal, but as limited resources makes it more difficult to select options, specific standards and goal statements will be increasingly important. Otherwise, the library's development may reflect the preferences of decision makers who may not understand library operations.

FACILITIES MAINTENANCE

There are no standards for library facilities maintenance procedures, and perhaps there should be. Preserving facilities and keeping
the library attractive is an important part of administration and operations; library functions are largely dependent on the physical plant, and
the tasks involved in properly maintaining library facilities require
special procedures.

The library often has a higher rate of traffic than any other area in an
institution, making it more difficult to keep clean and to maintain.
Multiple corners, aisles, shelves and other flat services, and several
pieces of furniture add to the duties of the custodial staff. An office
where the typical traffic flow during each day averages ten people, all of
them coming from other places within the building, will not get as dirty
as a library which is open to the public 12 to 14 hours a day and where
the traffic involves many individuals coming in from the outdoors, and
where the flow of people tends to be dispersed rather than concentrated
around desks.

Working and Cleaning Personnel

If librarians have no direct control over maintenance personnel, they
should attempt to arrange an agreement with those in charge whereby
special provisions are outlined for library cleaning procedures. They
might even get involved in evaluating and suggesting appropriate
salary increases for cleaning staff. Since library hours often differ from
other segments within organizations, the cleaning staff may have to
work on a different schedule. This is an area where union contracts
could intervene unless special provisions are added for library maintenance. Librarians should work with the cleaning crew to establish
mutually convenient schedules.

Those librarians able to hire a cleaning crew that works for the
library are fortunate, as they can provide on-the-spot training and set
up procedures. The library staff should monitor facilities and collections
cleaning as part of its overall responsibility. The process consumes a
surprisingly large amount of time.

Bookstock and Shelving

A small library might not house rare books or an extensive "special"
collection, but the material it does contain must be preserved and
protected. The bookstock should be vacuumed or dusted with a feather
duster at least weekly. If this is done routinely in a systematic manner,
the collection will remain in good condition. The type of cleaning

equipment and cleaning agents used must be carefully selected. Shelving, especially black and brown metal, is difficult to clean; oily furniture polish will only impart a temporary shine. Dust removal with a vacuum or a dry cloth should be the first step. No shelves should be washed with anything other than mild water if they are metal, and a clean cloth if they are wood. Consult the manufacturer if you are uncertain about how a cleaning agent will affect the books.

Also be sure the cleaning crew understands the importance of keeping dust and strong chemicals away from books and the other library materials. In addition, when tables and counters are polished with an oil-based liquid, the polish must be rubbed in thoroughly or the library materials in use the next day will soak up the polish.

Care of Computer Equipment

Equipment will fail unless it is properly cared for; in fact, some equipment warranties are void if climactic conditions are not maintained or improper chemicals are used in cleaning. The library staff is responsible for running head-cleaning programs, replacing dust covers, and caring for lenses and other small pieces. Both staff and cleaning crew must constantly monitor temperature control systems and inspect the library for leaks.

Although CRTs look like household television sets, they are specially constructed units. Therefore, the use of glass-cleaning chemicals may generate more destruction than they prevent. Care and cleaning instructions usually arrive with a unit and these should be provided to the cleaning crew.

It is often necessary to leave computers up and running during the night in order to preserve information, back up systems, or otherwise carry out the recordkeeping tasks generated by daily operations. If there is an electrical outlet problem, library staff and cleaning crew must reach an agreement about what is to be plugged into each outlet and which plugs can be pulled. If computers are in operation during the hours the cleaning staff is in the library, processing could be interrupted by a surge or drop in electrical current caused by operation of cleaning equipment.

BUILDING SYSTEMS

Building systems are a major component of the physical plant and form the framework of all library operations. These systems include air handling, temperature control, wiring and electrical outlets, waste disposal, plumbing, security, and fire prevention. Many building systems can be handled by experts only; others are very simple and can be carried out by the library staff. The procedures and precautions for each system should be explained as soon as a staff member begins work. The operational impact of failed waste disposal, electricity, plumbing, security, and fire protection systems is obvious. These systems are the basic substructure of any building and librarians must become familiar with their idiosyncracies and allocate space in a way that will not interfere with their proper operation.

Many of the systems in buildings subsequently converted into libraries were designed for offices or living—not for library use. If there is an opportunity for input prior to renovation or construction, the librarian must use every available avenue to insure that minimally adequate systems are provided. The systems must be able to handle the flow of people and materials considered routine for a small library. Any system testing should be done using the maximum flow as a model.

Air Circulation and Temperature Control

Temperature systems can be controlled by thermostats on the wall, by an outside temperature sensor, or by master panels and elaborate computerized temperature control mechanisms. Whatever the setup, most temperature systems are not designed to handle the continuous opening and closing of entrance doors inherent in heavy library use, and so they can fail easily.

When library collections are located in buildings originally designed for another function the air system will work differently than originally intended, as books absorb air and serve as sound and light barriers. Even if shelving is designed to maximize air flow, stack sections up to seven feet in height are certainly different from wall dividers that are only forty inches high.

How furniture is placed can prevent or enhance air circulation. Buildings constructed without windows that open usually handle air through a system of ducts. Consequently, improperly placing furniture or work stations can have a major impact on the system. Try to consult an HVAC (heating, ventilating and air conditioning) engineer before furniture is arranged to see if some of the ducts can be directed to change the temperature and air flow.

Since adding or removing walls also affects air circulation and temperature, library configurations must be planned so that people— patrons and staff—do not have to work in an airless, unhealthy environment. Again, if it is possible, consulting an expert is advisable. Custodial staff who have worked in the building are also an excellent resource.

FACILITIES REQUIREMENTS FOR TECHNOLOGY SYSTEMS

The characteristics of the physical plant are a major determining factor as to the extent to which technology can be incorporated into library operations. Computers may be desirable—even necessary—but they cannot be installed without adequate space and the proper telephone and electrical facilities. Microcomputer programs for cataloging and for small library operations can save employees several hours of clerical work. However, if the library uses one desk in its public service area for administration, processing, and reference, additional space will be needed for the microcomputer and for the information required to produce catalog cards. This usually involves little more than a number of electrical outlets and a secure location for material not yet processed. But small facilities, especially those in older buildings, may not even meet this basic need. Extension cords covered with protective rubber caps to keep people from tripping over them become the order of the day. The best solution is to add electrical service to the building and include requests for additional outlets with each equipment request.

A rule of thumb: purchase no new equipment without first assessing its impact on the building systems. If the systems are inadequate and cannot be modified to meet the requirements of a new computer or electronic system, then the purchase will have to be postponed or the budget increased to include the cost of modification. Your library will appear in a very poor light if the equipment is ordered and cannot be installed and made operational.

SPACE ALLOCATION

Balancing library space between the needs of patrons, collections, and staff is critical to the library's atmosphere and operation, and it is one area in which there is usually more local control. Most libraries show a deficit in at least one of the three areas. For instance, if the primary library goal is to provide good service to patrons, and the majority of space is committed to collections, then the service goal will change as the space decreases. It may then be necessary to add service staff because circulation will increase as seating decreases and so will demands for help in service areas.

Because of the magnitude of operations in large libraries, it is necessary to delineate specific areas of the building for certain parts of the operation. In a smaller setting, the trick is to select and combine appropriate elements from the larger departmental arrangement to enable a combination of functions to be carried out in one location. For example, circulating nonprint materials may involve a separate circulation desk in a large library, whereas small libraries must circulate everything from one service point.

Collection Space and User Space

Very few small libraries have adequate space for users. The problem is especially acute in older libraries, in which the actual growth rate of their collections was usually vastly underestimated during the planning stage. They were built to house the collection in existence—often two or three years removed from construction—providing inadequate allowance for collection growth and no plans for nonprint materials and information.

The space allotted for collections will usually overtake user space first. Since the process is gradual, it is easy to overlook the situation until the problem has become significant. Under these circumstances, a zero-growth collection policy would seem to be the only feasible strategy to preserve user space. Actually, this policy is extremely difficult to implement given the ever-increasing amount of information available; its usual result is a slowdown in the collection growth rate.

When the space given to collections grows slowly, the problem simply becomes more subtle—stack ranges are expanded one section at a time, aisle space is reduced, and more creative ways to handle the collection are introduced, such as free-standing display units. Since user space often includes free space surrounding the unit, there is a tendency to devote some of that free space to the collection, or to use it for some new form of material, such as a cabinet for disks. For example, an individual carrel for research may be replaced by a small table housing a microcomputer and printer.

Seating Arrangement

Given the limitations on both space and resources in small libraries, the selection and arrangement of patron seating must be considered carefully. Versatility is a key element in the choice and layout of furniture; the configuration of the building and the needs of library users will largely determine the choices made.

Seating capacity figures are deceptive. A table designed to seat four is often effectively used by two who like to spread out. Large lounge chairs may be tempting, but they are space eaters and they rarely survive in a library setting for more than a few years. Types of seating range from locked private carrels for researchers, to small beanbags for preschool story hours. They may include wet- and dry-auditorium seating, lounge chairs, sofas, and the ubiquitous tables and chairs. Often, furniture labeled for library use is actually suited only for a library in a private home. If librarians have the option of purchasing furniture, it is best to order from a library supplier, whose furnishings have the durability to withstand heavy use.

Workspace

When library users have been crowded out of every possible area with potential for use as collection space, staff workspace is next to go—the collection will be stacked in offices, and the librarian's office may serve as a closed reserve area, a home for problem processing, and a resting place for items on their way out the door. This piecemeal arrangement can lead to inconvenient and distressing conditions for library staff.

The amount of space allocated to library work stations differs from that in a typical business office, even for staff whose positions might be similar. For example, a typist in an office may need space for a typewriter and little else. However, a library typist needs space for a booktruck to circle around the desk. Filing in a traditional office setting requires space around legal- or letter-sized file cabinets, while library filing includes the card catalog and shelf list in addition to office files.

Staff in small libraries usually perform several functions, and space must be allocated for each of them. The same person may work circulation, reserve, and interlibrary loan—each of which involves different segments of the collection. Instead of one work station, space must be arranged for each segment of the collection involved in these functions. The space for each requires a different set of characteristics.

Reserve collections must be in a controlled access area where staff members have access but patrons do not. The circulation desk must be near the door; for control purposes, as much of the library as possible should be visible from the circulation desk. The circulation desk should also be within sight of the reference desk, since the reference librarian needs to keep an eye on the reference collection and, in addition, frequently refers to the collection. It is also important to be able to see some if not all of the patron seating.

Staff work areas generally consist of offices with large desks, or three-by-five tables surrounded by book trucks. The workspace usually requires electrical and telephone lines in addition to the dual requirements of visibility and privacy.

Occasionally, plans for small libraries are drawn which do not include an office for the librarian. This is an example of exceptionally poor planning and a lack of understanding of library operations. These offices are necessary to protect the confidentiality of patron inquiries and to allow librarians to concentrate without interruption on reports, documents, budgets, and other items involved in running library operations.

Security Systems

A security system also requires space and constant attendance. The system will be effective only if a staff member is able to quickly respond to alarms. When manual security is in effect, a work station must be set up near the door with a flat surface to use for checking bags and cases.

Shipping and Receiving Space

While providing adequate space for patrons and staff is a major element in a library's atmosphere and operations, it is equally important that enough space is allotted for shipping and receiving. New library materials are constantly unpacked and checked. Invoices and vouchers must be prepaid, and fiscal records maintained. The public cannot be allowed routine access to this area, especially since the shipping-receiving phase of operations is particularly susceptible to theft. Ideally, a freight elevator will open into this room so that mail and packages can be easily delivered. The room should also contain the raw materials required to wrap and ship library materials. In a very small operation, the librarian's office may serve as a shipping/receiving area. This will be successful only if the room can be secured and a minimal amount of furniture can be added and committed to the shipping function.

The proportional allocation or balance of library space between patrons, collections, and staff is an important consideration in how the physical plant contributes to the atmosphere and how the library actually operates. The allocation decisions for space allocations are just as significant as the allocation of money to departments. The optimal balance will be defined by the library's goals and its primary clientele, and will be achieved once the particular characteristics of the facility and the systems to operate it are understood.

References

1. *Z39.7 Library Data Collection Standard* (New York: American National Standards Institute, 1984).
2. *Interim Standards for Small Public Libraries* (Chicago: American Library Association, Public Library Association, 1962). Also in *A Public Library Space Needs Outline; Draft.* (Madison, Wisconsin: Division for Library Services, Department of Public Instruction, State of Wisconsin, October 1985).
3. "Standards for University Libraries," *ACRL News,* June 1979.

Library Boards

Gordon S. Wade

Library boards are an important part of any library operation and dealing with them effectively is critical in the development of a good library. This subject, however, is frequently neglected in a librarian's education and rarely are seminars or meetings devoted to the topic. This is unfortunate since the proper "care and feeding of a library board" can offer great rewards to a library and its director.

MAKE-UP OF THE BOARD

Library boards come in all sizes from the very small to the very large, with the usual range between seven and twelve members.[1] The size is something which cannot be controlled since it is usually set by local ordinance. The geographical area and the population served by the library are also determining factors in who is appointed or elected to the board. Any board can become too large to be effective. In larger boards, members may not have the opportunity to express their viewpoints on every matter being considered. A disadvantage of a smaller board is that when a member finishes his or her term and is replaced by someone new, the character of the board may make a sudden shift in personality. When the board is small, it is also easier for one or two members to dominate the thinking and thereby control the direction of library policy. This can work in the library's favor, or it can have the opposite effect.

How representative is the library board of the community it serves? Not very representative in most instances. Library board members are chosen mainly from the professional ranks. How many factory workers or waitresses can be found on a library board? Rarely do blue collar or pink collar workers serve. The sad truth is that most people appointed to library boards come from a homogeneous group, mainly college graduates. Does the board have a good representation of all ages in the community or is it skewed to middle-aged and older people? Are different races and religions represented? Probably not. It is unfortunate that the typical library board is not representative of the

Gordon S. Wade is Director, The Carroll Public Library, Carroll, Iowa.

community it serves since this deprives the library of a wide diversity of viewpoints.[2]

SELECTING TRUSTEES

Some trustees are chosen because they have expressed a genuine desire to be on the library board; others are appointed because they have complained about the library; some are put on for a specific reason (e.g., to keep taxes down); others because it is considered to be an honor; and still others are elected to the board. When appointing a new member to the library board, government officials often have no specific criteria in mind. The resulting group is a mixture of people with conflicting motives and interests. It is the library director's job to mold these individuals into an effective board that will push for the best quality library for the community.

The library director who has a say in the selection of library board members, as sometimes happens, must use caution in exercising this power. The director should, however, attempt to secure an evenly representative group, one that reflects as many facets of the community as possible. Qualifications for serving effectively on a library board are difficult to determine at best; people considered good prospects as trustees sometimes don't work out that way. If the library has a Friends support group, a good way to find capable trustees is to observe that group, paying particular attention to the interaction of personalities and the actual effective progress made by individual members. Library boards consisting of trustees who are active users of the library may *not* be effective in terms of real accomplishments. Sometimes the most effective boards are composed of men and women who only enter the library on nights when the board meets. They are effective because they are powerful within the community and use that power to promote and expand the library. Frequently, boards made up of avid readers and users of the library are weak. They have the desire to improve the library, but are lacking in any real power to do so.

One way to help eliminate poor appointments to the library board is for the current board to submit a list of potential candidates to the person or persons who make the appointments. The library director and the board also should discuss the qualities they feel are needed in board members and then make a list of possible candidates. Current board members undoubtedly have worked with people on other boards and committees and know the names of those who would have the interest and ability to serve on the library board. The list may or may not be used for the next appointment, but often it is used or retained for future reference.

REMOVING TRUSTEES

Removing negative trustees from the board is a delicate matter. The board's by-laws list the grounds for removal; local ordinances may also do this. Generally there are only two grounds for removal: moving from the district or nonattendance at a given number of board meetings. In some communities, members of the library board are reappointed year after year and must actually die in order to get off the board. Such a situation may lead to a stagnation of ideas. One solution is to have the appointing agency adopt an ordinance limiting individuals serving on any government board to two consecutive terms. The results of such a change are often mixed. The board loses some of its most supportive members, but it also gains new blood and new ideas.

TRUSTEE FUNCTIONS

The powers of the library board fall into six broad areas: providing for a building to facilitate library service; deciding on regulations for the use of the library; securing money for the operation of the library; contracting; creating financial operations; and establishing personnel policies and wage scales.[3] The board hires the library director who is responsible for the administration of the library. Problems can arise when the roles of the director and the library board are confused, especially when there is an overlap of functions in the minds of the two, so it is important to distinguish them. The distinction should be made clear that the board *makes* policies and the librarian *implements* those policies. For example, the board may decide that the library should rent original art to its patrons. It would establish a policy governing the loan period and the rental fees. The board would authorize the librarian to purchase the items in the collection and would provide the money for the purchases. The librarian would select the art works within the budget limitations set by the board, and establish the rules and procedures for adding the material to the collection and renting it out to the library users.

An excellent discussion of the functions of the library board and the library director appears in Virginia Young's *The Trustee of a Small Public Library*.[4] The section entitled "Duties and Responsibilities" could be read in a board meeting. Each new trustee should also receive a copy after being appointed to the board.

LIBRARY BOARD STRUCTURE

By-laws, a necessity for every library board, provide the structure for the board's effective operation. The by-laws state by whose authority the board exists; its powers and duties according to both local and state law; the officers of the board; the meetings—how often they will be held and the order of business; standing and special committees; and the provisions for hiring the library director and the director's duties. By-laws should be written during the first meeting of a newly organized board and should be reviewed and revised frequently. For an already established board, writing the by-laws should receive first priority.

Board officers differ from library to library. Some boards function with a president and secretary; others have a vice-president and treasurer as well. One very good way to involve trustees in the work of the board is to assign them to standing committees. A typical board may have three committees: By-Laws/Goals, concerning itself with general library objectives, specific library goals, the by-laws, materials selection policies, acceptance of gifts and memorials, and relations with library support organizations; Ways and Means, dealing with the annual budget, salaries and wages of library personnel, probation, promotion, and retirement of employees, holidays, vacations, and sick leave of staff members, professional meetings, and payment of dues and fringe benefits; and Operations, consisting of policies on hours of service, overdue materials, registration and circulation, services to special groups, nonresidents, cooperation with other libraries, extension of services, building and grounds, and public relations and publicity.

The standing committees meet at least once each year, review library board policies in their respective areas, and make recommendations to the board. Functioning committees are important to any library board because they give individual trustees the opportunity to speak out in a particular area of policy that interests them. Trustees who are silent in a board meeting may be less so in a small committee meeting. Committees also serve to integrate new trustees into the ebb and flow of the board. The committee should always meet with the library director in attendance. As the qualified expert, the director usually prepares the groundwork for the committee. Past policies and current practices are examined. Recommendations by the committee to the library board do not always pass without change, but the chances are much improved if the matter is thoroughly discussed first in committee.

Special committees may be appointed by the board to deal with particular situations. For instance, the need to replace the library director is addressed by the Search Committee, which meets on a continuing basis while seeking a replacement and then ceases to function when a new director has been successfully employed by the library. Occasionally, a special committee will involve trustees and individuals from the community who have expertise not available in current library trustees. One example of such a committee is a Fine Arts Committee that was created in a library to bring art shows by local artists to the adult reading room. A trustee interested in the project served as chair and three members of the committee were appointed from outside the board. The committee followed the guidelines established by the library board.

MEETINGS

An important factor affecting the operation of the library board is the frequency of its meetings. Some libraries have so much business to discuss that they need to meet monthly; for others, bi-monthly or quarterly meetings suffice. It is important to have meaningful business for the board to act upon. If the library director cannot come up with truly important matters to discuss, the board is probably meeting too frequently. On the other hand, if board meetings are stretching out and becoming marathons, the board should consider meeting more frequently.

Too frequent meetings with too little business may create a situation in which trustees cross the line from policy-making to library administration. This has negative consequences for both the director and the board. There is a fine line between the functions of the trustee and the library director; when there is a crossover by either side, problems develop.

Since trustees are often uninformed about library operations, it is the library director's job to educate them. Reports are a good way to do that. The more information the board receives, the better the chances are that they will make intelligent decisions on library policy. Making reports to the trustees is one way of filling the time and educating the board. The director can let trustees know what the library is doing with the summer reading program; report on magazine circulation and which issues are borrowed the most; tell what other staff members are doing, how the book sale went, why the fine policy isn't working; explain how the director selects, orders, and catalogs materials for inclusion in the collections; describe how the library's hours of opening compare to other libraries, etc.

Library board meetings should be open to the public even though, in many communities, attendance by the public is negligible or nonexistent. The agenda should be sent out to the trustees before the meeting as well as posted in the library. The meeting should start on time and end within a reasonable period—two hours or less, if it can be managed. The order of business is determined by the board's by-laws, but again, it is important to have enough business to fill the allotted time. Trustees are not paid for their attendance at meetings and all of them have other places they could be.

The library director's report should be presented early in the meeting. It informs the board about the results of changes initiated at the previous board meeting, significant day-to-day happenings at the library, the financial condition of the library, and statistics on such areas as circulation and materials added to the collections.

When proposing a change in library policy, the director should be absolutely certain that the "homework" has been accomplished prior to the meeting. Research pays off with a better chance of board approval of the change. The director should try to anticipate questions the trustees will ask, remembering that they have a different perspective and are usually not as well-informed about library practices. The director should also be prepared for all arguments against the proposed change. It's a good idea to do a mental run-through of the items on the agenda before actually meeting with the board.

Too often, the library director and the library board develop an adversary relationship.[5] One way to reduce potential conflict is to promote an informal atmosphere during the meeting, for instance, serving coffee and cookies. This not only gives the board a feeling of solidarity, but serves as a small thank-you to the trustees for giving their time; this simple courtesy can have lasting effects for both the library director and the trustees.

No one likes surprises at board meetings. It is better to warn the board ahead of time about a possible change than to spring it on them at the meeting. A hint can be skillfully dropped in the library director's report at one meeting and the problem brought up for a discussion at a later one. Changes in hours and the purchase of expensive furniture or equipment are two areas where some groundwork may be needed to prepare the trustees in advance of the actual proposal.

When proposing a major change in library operation, the director should ask the board to authorize a study of the problem at a meeting prior to the one at which it is hoped the change will be approved. Although board approval may not be necessary to make the study, authorization alerts the board to the problem. It gives the board time, before the actual discussion takes place, to think about alternatives and the effects the change will have on the library. Making a careful study of the possible change also increases chances that passage will occur.

COMMUNICATION

Communication between board and director is a must. Problems library directors encounter on a daily basis can be discussed and solved at board meetings. Board meetings also serve as a sounding board for trustees who, as representatives of the members of the community, often bring complaints they have heard from library users to the meetings to resolve.

Since all trustees do not attend all meetings it is important to keep the members informed. After each board meeting a copy of the minutes must be sent to each member of the board whether they attended the meeting or not. In addition, copies of all reports and proposals presented at the meeting are sent to those trustees who did not attend. It is very important that all board members feel that they are a vital part of that board. Occasionally something occurs between meetings which should be called to the trustees' attention. In this case, a memo or letter should be sent to all trustees informing them and alerting them to possible action. For instance, when the library's budget is approved by the various governing bodies, all trustees should be informed about its passage. Even though it is sometimes tempting to tell just one or two trustees who seem more interested in the library than others, this must be avoided.

AN OPEN FORUM

Each trustee has ideas which may alter the thinking of other members of the board. It is better to hear these opinions at the time set aside for discussion than to have them expressed outside the meeting or not expressed at all. They can become the basis for a negative vote. A skillful president of the board will elicit opinions from everyone, but too often the president does not have this skill. The library director should not hesitate to ask the nonparticipants for their ideas. Some trustees need to be encouraged to speak out, while others seek to dominate the discussion. An effective board is one where everyone states his or her mind. In any disagreement occurring between trustees, the library director should try to remain neutral and give only factual information. While keeping the good of the library in mind, the library director must also remain neutral and look for the good points made by either side.

Since the library director is more knowledgeable about library concerns than the board members in most instances, it is easy to fall into the trap of dominating the meetings. During the meeting, the library director should remember to be quiet and let the trustees discuss each problem. Meetings will go better if the director doesn't appear to have all the answers. In the end, the trustees will want to know the director's feelings on the matter.

Trustees do not wish to agree with library directors on every matter that comes before the board. If they did, they would serve no useful function. It is not a good idea to have only items on the agenda which are critical to the success or failure of the library program. Some items should be included which, if rejected by the board, will have little significance in the long run. If board rejection of an important item seems imminent, the director can seek to have it tabled or referred to committee for further study. In that way the idea is kept alive and may be brought up at a future meeting when passage is more likely.

USING PSYCHOLOGY

The spirit of competitiveness can be used to the library's advantage. After sifting through the data and pulling out all of the statistics for those libraries serving similar populations within a range of one thousand, the library director can rank them, including his or her own library, using all the different yardsticks provided by the data. These yardsticks include total budget; book and other materials budget; square feet of usable building space; linear feet of shelving; magazine subscriptions; funds per capita; circulation; and any other useful measurement. The director and the board will know exactly how the library compares with others in the state serving approximately the same population. The director can present the comparisons at a regular board meeting and call for a discussion. Trustees do not want their library to be poor or average! Using these comparisons may have a miraculous effect on the board, not only in improving the library's rank on each of the measurements, but also in maintaining the level of adequacy once it has been achieved. Comparing one library to another is one of the best ways to initiate changes that will improve the library's collections and program.

Appreciation of the library board should come from the library director. Being a library trustee is, for the most part, an unrewarding job. Even when the library program receives excellent ratings from the community, the board rarely receives the credit. The trustees should be thanked for coming to the board meetings; they should be kept informed about the library; and they should be praised in the library's publicity for improvements in the library and its programs. The director might call a library trustee's attention to a special book for his or her personal reading pleasure; or take a trustee to a meeting. Once or twice a year when sending out the minutes of the board meeting, the director might take the time to write a personal note to each trustee, making a positive comment on some aspect of the meeting or letting them know that their stand on a particular topic was appreciated. This personalizes an otherwise formal contact with trustees and conveys appreciation for their input and support.

CITY MANAGERS AND OTHER IMPOSSIBILITIES

Library boards can act as a buffer between a seemingly hostile city management and the library. Trustees can often convince government agencies of the need for more library funds where library directors acting alone would fail. It is one of the stated functions of the trustees to procure the needed monies for the library. In this respect, trustees in small communities are at a distinct advantage over their larger city counterparts. In nearly all instances, small community library trustees know the elected government officials personally, a fact which frequently lowers the barriers for the library. Library directors should acknowledge this function of the board and encourage trustees to fulfill their obligation.

In some communities, the city manager has replaced the library board. In that situation, the library director becomes a department head. Instead of reporting to a board with the power to make the decisions about the library, the library director is at the mercy of another administrator. If the city manager is favorable to libraries, the local library may flourish; if not, the library may languish. When a library director reports to a city manager, an advisory library board is sometimes appointed. The success of advisory boards is limited because the actual decision-making process has been denied them.

Hostility from local government officials, both elected and appointed, may be inevitable. When the library is governed by a citizen board of trustees, the city may feel that it does not have control over what it considers to be just another city department. The small library may receive funding from various sources, but the bulk of the operating budget is contributed by the local municipality.

The strength of any public library lies in its library board, which should be protected at all costs. The library board must continue to act as an independent group charged with the responsibility of producing the best library the community can afford. In doing so, it often has to go its own way and ignore some of the negative attitudes found in city government. At the same time, the board must cooperate with the city and keep members of the governing body informed about the library's goals, objectives, and priorities.

In order to keep the agencies that fund the library aware of library board actions and policies, an abbreviated copy of the board's minutes and annual library reports should be sent to major contributors of tax monies. Communication with the city manager is important. Comparisons of the library with others its size should be sent to the city council. A well-informed council is important, particularly around budget time.

THE GOOD TRUSTEE

Good trustees are individuals who are interested in having the best possible library for their community and are willing to work toward that seemingly impossible goal. Good trustees are at the meetings of governing bodies at budget time. They are creative and have interesting ideas for improving and promoting the library. Good trustees listen to all arguments and make their own decision, always bearing in mind their goal to have a quality library. It is possible to improve the quality of a library trustee, to reverse the negative attitude sometimes seen in a library board member. In fact, trustees have been known to blossom overnight after receiving proper cultivation.

References

1. Donald J. Sager, *Managing the Public Library* (White Plains, N.Y.: Knowledge Industry Publications, 1984), p. 38.
2. Carol Emerson, ed., *Iowa Trustees' Library Guide,* 2d ed. (Des Moines, State Library of Iowa, 1985), p. 3.
3. Sager, p. 38.
4. Virginia G. Young, *The Trustee of a Small Public Library* (Chicago: American Library Assn., 1978).
5. Sager, p. 40.

Library Cooperation

Nicky Stanke

Service to the user is the end towards which all library activities are aimed. We open our doors at hours that are most convenient to the people we serve; we arrange the furniture and the collection with ease of use in mind; cataloging, processing, display, and circulation systems are all designed toward the same end—efficient and effective library service.

How does cooperation among libraries help us towards accomplishing that ultimate goal? Libraries have been cooperating for years on many different levels and for many different reasons. Cooperation is, in fact, a multifaceted concept that exists under a variety of names. Below is a working vocabulary for exploring this concept of cooperation.

DEFINITIONS

Cooperation is the broadest of the various terms used to name the relationship between libraries, describing a loose affiliation to which each participant contributes and through which each participant benefits. Libraries may cooperate simply because they are neighbors—by exchanging paperbacks or lists of periodicals subscribed to, for instance. Plans and publicity for National Library Week are further examples of possible cooperative activities.

Networking is a more formal and precise relationship, generally with specific interlibrary loan or resource-sharing goals. Libraries in a network may subscribe to an electronic mail system and/or have their holdings published in a shared database. Formal procedures and protocols are usually established to standardize communication.

Resource sharing is an activity between or among libraries that results in the users of one library accessing the materials of another. Occasionally, *human* resources are shared for reasons of their expertise. To one degree or another, almost all libraries are involved in resource-sharing. Reciprocal borrowing, which allows a cardholder in one library

Nicky Stanke is the Administrator of the East Central Regional Library, Cedar Rapids, Iowa.

to borrow materials from another, is probably the most economical resource-sharing.

Cooperative library system is a legally established entity, often with its own governing board, whose primary purpose is coordinating and sponsoring interlibrary loan, reference support, and often library development. Systems may comprise groups of libraries within a specified area of a state or they may be multistate entities. Libraries of the same type, e.g., public, health science, or academic, may form systems without regard to political boundaries.

DECISIONS

When confronted with the option (or reality) of system membership, a local library administrator may well ask him- or herself a number of important questions. If membership is not an option but a de facto situation, the administrator needs answers that will enable the agency to become an effective participant. Obviously, if membership is an option, the administrator wants answers that will affect the decision.

Quite often, the first question asked is "What will happen to us?" Phrased more defensively, the question is frequently "Will the system ultimately take over local rights and responsibilities?"

The pattern of cooperative service in many states is such that the local library retains administrative autonomy and can partake of cooperative services without submitting to superimposed requirements of staffing, programming, collection, facilities, etc. The library board of trustees (in the case of public libraries) is still appointed locally according to ordinance and remains responsible for hiring the director and establishing policy. Some states do have a minimum local funding requirement based on the taxable valuation or a per capita support level. Reciprocity among the libraries participating in the system is often a requirement for membership. The Association of Specialized and Cooperative Library Agencies (ASCLA), a division of the American Library Association, has published a checklist titled *Multitype Library Cooperation State Laws and Regulations*. While this publication does not deal with systems that have been created exclusively for public libraries, it does reveal the variety of responses at the state level to the concept of multitype library legislation.

Reading the statutes and/or articles of incorporation and/or constitution and by-laws of one's own particular cooperative system is a must for the director of a small library. What restrictions there are, if any, on local library administration would surely be spelled out in those documents.

Those of us who work with small libraries, and not necessarily in small libraries, have heard the refrain so often: "We're just a SMALL library. . . ." Usually the speaker is excusing his or her agency from participating in something that could, for its users' purposes, make the library larger. *A cooperative system helps a small library become larger by joining with other (small) libraries.* Because libraries gear collection development plans to their immediate, local audience, the nature of each collection is unique and will have some unique items. These unique materials form the very heart of resource sharing, since it is impossible to buy everything and to anticipate the patrons' every need. Although libraries survey and study collection use patterns, requests for materials not owned by the institution do occur. If a member, the first search for requested materials will take place at the cooperative system level. The strength of a system lies in the participation of all its members; their willingness to share their resources, no matter how small the collection, is crucial.

Some system protocols allow for a hierarchical search order so that the largest libraries in the system are not always searched first. The requests are stair-stepped up to the next size of collection. In cases where a union catalog exists—whether online, on fiche or film, or on cards—requests may be deliberately spread among the members so that no one agency bears the load of interlibrary loan. All libraries benefit because no library can provide all of its patrons' wants.

WHAT IS INVOLVED IN A PRODUCTIVE SYSTEM MEMBERSHIP?

Knowing how to become involved with the system requires a knowledge of the purpose, plans, and goals of the system. A library director who wishes to become an active system member must understand what it is that the system is about. He or she must be willing to participate in system design, to offer suggestions for system improvement, and to accept the protocols that facilitate cooperation. It takes time and patience—and the ability to listen to the needs of other participants in the system.

The director must attend system meetings, respond to system surveys and other inquiries, and read system mail. Just as a director keeps up with developments in the local community, so must he or she keep up with system-wide developments. What other systems are doing is a valid, and often enlightening, path to explore. Talk to your neighbors and your neighbor's neighbors at every opportunity; ask them about system activities. Your cooperative system will grow at the rate of creative energy that you put into it.

WHAT SERVICES CAN BE EXPECTED OR EXPLORED?

Listed below are some activities that cooperative library systems have been involved in:

Resource sharing. Union lists of all items, of serials, of special subject or format collections, of professional materials, etc. Some systems—as well as individual libraries—subscribe to OCLC, a national bibliographic database, for resource-sharing purposes. The cost of that service may prohibit some libraries from joining. A cooperative system with a large pool of funds and with the express purpose of facilitating resource sharing may be a more likely interface with the OCLC system. Magnetic tapes from OCLC can be used to create a local database, either online or COM (Computer Output on Microform), allowing the system to search OCLC for materials not found within its boundaries. Using OCLC, a library seeking materials must be a member and subscribe to the ILL module. Both propositions incur costs to the local library that, in the case of a small library, may not pass a benefit analysis. When considering the costs borne by a local library to participate in interlibrary loan, a library director must look at what percentage of its circulation is generated by interlibrary loan. Frequently it is less than two percent. The figure deserves close scrutiny.

Public service. Supportive reference service, system-wide library cards, reciprocal borrowing, programs—both for adults and for children, referral systems, etc. Many systems have established resource or reference centers that serve the rest of the system members as reference back-up. In some cases this service is available through the state library; in others, it is available at both a system (substate) and state level. Procedures and protocols are established for members to access the system for services such as subject searching, photocopy and/or periodical searching, and information/referral service.

Library service. Centralized cataloging and/or processing, cooperative purchase of materials, and equipment or supplies, etc. Systems will often enter into agreements with vendors guaranteeing a volume purchasing level in exchange for favorable discounts. A system may offer catalog card production and other processing activities at a savings, done either inhouse by the system or contracted out.

Public relations. Brochures, bookmarks, news releases, radio and TV spots, graphics services, public-speaking engagements, signs, buttons, newsletters, shared exhibits, etc. A cooperative library system may have a print shop or a print shop contract through which the local library can get these promotional materials produced at moderate prices.

Library development. Workshops, staff development training sessions, consultant services, professional collections, etc. Because development of local libraries is often a stated priority of a cooperative system, training sessions may be offered that are on a calibre above the local library means. For a small, or no, registration fee, local library staff can have access to programs presented at national conferences that may be otherwise unattainable. One-on-one consultation provides local library directors (and trustees and staff, for that matter) with the opportunity to discuss specific problems and discover new solutions. Access to a collection of materials relating to library operations may be yet another benefit of a cooperative library system.

Supplemental collections. Films, videos, program kits, library tools, large type materials, books-on-tape, rental books, foreign language materials, etc. Often materials such as these are best shared on a cooperative basis as the local audience may be limited for these relatively expensive items.

WHAT IS THE SOURCE OF FUNDING FOR A COOPERATIVE SYSTEM?

The funds necessary to operate a cooperative system may be derived from one or a combination of several sources. In some areas, systems have their own taxing authorities and can go to their voters for an increased millage rate. In other places, systems are funded by the participating jurisdictions—cities, counties, etc. In yet others, systems may be financed entirely through state funds, with special grants of federal funds coming from the state library agencies.

Membership costs vary in proportion to the services provided to members. A full-blown online network may have steep initial membership charges; these must be weighed against the long-term benefits. If over a period of time the library would spend that amount on a less efficient system, it may be wise to give serious consideration to funding the long-term returns. What is important to remember is that system activity does *not* reduce the cost of running the local agency but assists the agency by making dollars go further.

As system members, a librarian and possibly trustees may be called upon to lobby the funding authority on behalf of the system; it is important to emphasize what the system activities have meant to the local user—how he or she has access to a wider range of materials and expertise that would otherwise be unavailable. Ask to see your system's budget proposals so that you can speak with familiarity about its operation.

The local library's contribution to the system often is not more than time and energy—a small price to pay for large returns. Typically, a system may have a specific service to sell—training courses, catalog card production, perhaps online database searches. Because of the spirit in which most library cooperative systems are established, costs of any services rarely exceed the actual system expenditure.

WHAT ARE THE CONSEQUENCES OF NONAFFILIATION?

The benefits to the users are clearly the rewards of cooperation. Conversely, a library that has chosen not to participate or to affiliate with the system or systems available to it may well be short-changing its users in terms of access to materials and to broader expertise.

In an information-based society the small library can be viewed as an access point to the world of information. As such, it cannot afford to reject its networking function. Necessity, they say, is the mother of invention: as the library world watched, the information base grew beyond the capacity of even the largest libraries, and the need for cooperation became obvious. A library cannot claim to provide even adequate service if it does not provide the interface with other resources.

IS COOPERATION BY TYPE MORE IMPORTANT THAN COOPERATION BY AREA?

A library may have the opportunity to cooperate with libraries of the same type or to cooperate with libraries in the same geographical area regardless of type. Both of these configurations work to the advantage of the participants.

A system with libraries of all one type may be more likely to supplement its members' resources and specialized requests. However, it may be unable to fill requests that diverge dramatically from the standard collection.

A system within a geographic area may be able to arrange reciprocity so that users can travel to the other libraries within that area, regardless of type, for materials. If there are no links with other systems beyond that geographical area, users are limited to the resources and types of libraries that happen to be there.

Assuming there is nothing to preclude activity in both types of systems, participation in both is the best-chosen route. Even informal cooperative arrangements can provide users with better library service.

Small libraries must take the initiative to cooperate among themselves and with other, larger libraries as the concept of the global village becomes more of a reality. Small libraries must interact in a cooperative manner—willing to share as well as to borrow—to stay a vital part of the modern world.

The Planning Process

Nancy M. Bolt

Planning is deciding what's going to happen over the next year or few years at the library. Since it is the library director (with the board or other authority) doing the deciding, planning is taking charge of the library's future and creating it the way the planners think is most responsive to what the community needs and the library can deliver.

The director of a small library may be thinking, "Why bother? I don't have the time or the money to do all I want to do now. Why spend precious time on planning for what might happen a year from now when I haven't solved last week's crisis yet." This is precisely why planning can be most helpful. Planning helps predict which crisis might occur so that preparations can be made. Planning provides information to library leaders about the community and the library. Planning generates discussion and usually enthusiasm about the library and things it might do differently or better. Most importantly, planning forces decision makers to set priorities about who will receive what service with what efficiency. At its best, planning provides information to use in decision making and can be a blueprint for future library direction.

STEPS IN THE PLANNING PROCESS

The planning process is designed to get planning underway when time and funds are limited. It includes six steps: 1) determining the role of the library in its particular community; 2) collecting information about that community and the library; 3) writing a mission statement for the library; 4) writing goals and objectives for the library; 5) implementing the plan; and 6) evaluating the plan implementation.

It should take about six months to complete the first four steps of this planning process, depending on how much time is spent collecting information about the library and its community. The plan can be written to cover any period of time, but the further in the future library leaders try to plan, the fuzzier the crystal ball becomes. The usual long-range plan covers three to five years. Once an annual plan is written, plans that designate areas for a year's focus can be written.

Nancy M. Bolt is president of JNF Associates, Milford, Ohio.

WHO DOES THE PLANNING

Plans often are written by a planning committee. There are several options for the composition of this committee. Most include a combination of the library director and representatives of the library board or other governing authority, the library staff, and the community.

It is critical that the planning committee includes the library director and some trustees as members. These are the people who will ultimately be responsible for the policies and activities necessary to implement the plan. These are the people who will determine which objectives are most important and should be implemented first. Their input must be available throughout the planning process. Depending on the size of the library staff, some staff members might also serve on the committee, for instance, the head of a branch (or one representative of all the branches), the head of major library services (children, reference, etc.), or an assistant director.

Some libraries also choose to include representatives from the community such as members of a library Friends' group, the League of Women Voters, businesspeople, school representatives, people from different age groups, local government officials, etc.

If additional staff and community representatives are not included on the committee, their input can be gained when information about the library and the community is gathered. Including staff and community people either on the committee or in the information gathering provides an important support group when it is time to implement the plan's goals and objectives.

Normally, the library director or a member of the board chairs the planning committee once it is formed. The committee should meet monthly to work through the steps in the planning process; the library director or library staff usually does the work of collecting information and presents it to the committee.

DETERMINING THE LIBRARY'S ROLE IN THE COMMUNITY

More and more library decision makers are realizing that they cannot be all things to all people. There are limits to staff time, money, resources, and knowledge that prevent the library from meeting every need that exists in the community. How do library leaders make a choice about what the library should do?

In 1985, a group of librarians from small Massachusetts libraries (serving populations under 10,000) applied for and received LSCA funds from the Massachusetts Board of Library Commissioners to conduct the Options for Small Libraries Project. This author served as consultant to the effort and as part of the project, a Role Prioritization Exercise was developed (the complete Exercise can be found at the end of this chapter). This Exercise is designed to help trustees and the library director clarify their opinions about the roles the library should play in the community. Nine roles are presented for consideration. For each role there is a brief description; a list of community needs that this role might fill; and a list of some services that a library might offer if this role were chosen.

The nine roles are: interlibrary access point, recreational reading and viewing for adults, information agency and adult independent learning center, children's reading and viewing center, young adult reading and viewing center, student auxiliary, community center, local history and genealogy center, and outreach to special groups.

The Role Prioritization Exercise is a starting point for a discussion of the library's mission. It focuses attention on what the library *should* do rather than on what the library is now doing. The Exercise is only the starting point for library planning. It allows library planners to state their beginning assumptions and opinions about library service. Once these have been made, the library can challenge them during the information gathering stage and then determine the library's mission.

COLLECTING INFORMATION

Information gathering is a stage in the planning process where library directors and planning committees often get bogged down. It is not necessary or even desirable to collect everything that exists about the library and its community. It *is* necessary to narrow the focus of the data collection. Information gathering usually includes: a review of the existing literature about the community; a review of the library's current performance; and surveys of community residents, library users, staff, and/or students. Planning is gap-filling. Once library decision makers know what is most needed in the community and how well the library is currently performing, plans can be made to fill the gap between what is and what is needed.

A simplified information gathering process might consist of the following:

Interviews with community leaders. Community leaders often have a perspective about the needs of town residents, particularly client groups with which they deal most often. Such interviews also call the library to the attention of the leaders and demonstrate the library's commitment to planning and improvement. The following are examples of people who could be interviewed: town officials; chamber of commerce or other business leaders; school principals and superintendents; local aging commission; directors of nursing homes and senior centers; leaders of youth groups (or the group itself); club presidents; chair of the historical society; and other community leaders.

Comparing census data. It is particularly useful to compare the 1970 to the 1980 census. Just browsing through the data on social character-istics can give helpful insights into the community. What are the general trends in population? Is the town gaining or losing people? Where are new residents coming from and what do they expect for library service? What is the location and type of occupation of the workforce?

Locating local studies already prepared by other agencies. Many community governments have prepared long-range or developmental plans. Many community agencies or organizations have conducted studies or completed analyses of the needs of their constituencies.

Reviewing current library performance. Libraries may already col-lect data for the state's annual statistical report form that can be useful in decision making, particularly comparing the library's performance over the past several years. Other information can be gathered for two or three weeks and projected for a year. In *Output Measures for Public Libraries,* Zweizig and Rodger describe 12 measures that can be used to measure the performance of the library.

Conducting surveys. Blane Dessy has written another chapter in this book on citizen surveys. Special surveys can also be constructed to discover the needs of children and young adults. These can be most effectively administered through cooperation with the local schools. Staff should also be asked their opinion about the library's present and potential future services. *A Planning Process for Public Libraries* by Palmour offers examples of both student and staff surveys.

The planning committee should consider for each role: what infor-mation already exists about the community in relation to this role; where this information can be obtained; how well the library is already performing this role; and what people should be interviewed about the community's need for this role. The committee should collect at least minimal information in all roles, including those roles that did not score highly in the Role Prioritization Exercise. This will help the committee challenge its own assumptions about the community and the library.

CRITICAL FACTORS

As part of the Massachusetts Options for Small Libraries Project, the Steering Committee identified ten factors that were considered critical to the success of any library. In gathering data, local planning committees might consider the degree to which their library achieves these critical factors.

1. *A place for library purposes.* Even if small, there should be a place

devoted solely to library purposes, where people can go for their library services. There should also be sufficient space to house a current collection and for library users to sit and work.

2. *Adequate hours.* The library should be open hours that fit the needs of the community. In towns where most of the people work during the day, the library should be open evening and weekend hours. In libraries with heavy study use, the library should be open in the late afternoons, evenings, and on weekends.

3. *Friendly, knowledgeable staff.* In addition to being pleasant, staff must also be knowledgeable about the community's needs, the collection, and ways to obtain information and material not immediately available in the library. This implies a continuing staff training program in the areas in which the library concentrates its efforts and a thorough knowledge of regional and state back-up services.

4. *Current and adequate materials.* A library must have a current collection in whatever areas library planners choose for the library to concentrate. People want current information without undue delay. Large collections of primarily outdated material are useless and should be weeded.

5. *Written policies.* Every library should have certain policies that relate to library service in general (such as a collection development policy, a personnel policy, policies on hours and fines, a meeting room policy, etc.). In addition, there are issues of local concern that require policies.

6. *Telephone.* There are still libraries without telephones. Telephones are a necessity in today's world; without a phone, local librarians cannot call other libraries or regional/state libraries for information and back-up services. Without a phone, people cannot call the library for information.

7. *Informed and supportive trustees.* It is difficult for change to occur in a library unless trustees are knowledgeable about local library service and about improvements that can be made. Trustees should participate in the planning process and be willing to support full implementation of the approved plan.

8. *Adequate funding.* Libraries cannot accomplish basic services without adequate funding. Trustees and library directors must be willing to request and lobby for funds. Competition for funds is often brisk and the library must be able to establish and present its case for an increased share of limited dollars.

9. *Publicity about the library.* People will not use nor support what they do not know about. Regardless of the roles chosen by the library, the community needs to be informed about library activities and resources and about the library's ability to interact with other libraries to fill needs.

10. *Evaluation of performance or use.* Part of planning is predicting the level of public use. Planning also involves preparation and encouragement of that use and allowing for evaluation of the services. *Output Measures for Public Libraries* is a useful tool to accomplish this evaluation.

MISSION STATEMENT, GOALS, AND OBJECTIVES

At this stage, the library planners have: completed the Role Prioritization Exercise once to determine their beginning assumptions and preconceptions; collected basic data on all the roles that are remotely related to the community (not just the top point-getters); and examined critical success factors for a library. With these tasks done, the library is ready to write a mission statement, goals, and objectives. Some definitions might be helpful at this point. A *mission statement* is a broad statement of the purpose of the library, specifying the fundamental reasons for the library's existence. It establishes the scope of the library's activities and provides overall direction for the library. The mission statement acts as a foundation for the development of general and specific objectives as well as program plans. The library's mission should be related to the major roles chosen.

A *goal* is a broad, general, timeless set of directions. Goals outline what the people should receive from the library or what the library should have, or be able to do, to accomplish its mission. *Objectives* are statements of specific programs of action to be taken or measurable results to be achieved within a specified period of time which, if accomplished, will move the library closer to the goal.

Mission statements typically include the following: who will be served, to meet what needs, with what resources, under what philosophical concepts. At the top of page 124 is a "Chinese menu" approach to writing a mission statement. Library planners can combine the elements in any way that is appropriate for the local situation or add other statements. Beware of writing a mission statement that is too broad and general.

Two sample mission statements are:

The Longmont Public Library shall function as the central access point to information media for the education, enlightenment, and enjoyment of all the people of the community.

The purpose of the West Allis Public Library is to provide the members of its community with access to materials which can improve their minds, broaden their lives, and fulfill their cultural, civic, intellectual, educational, and recreational needs.

WHO
people in the community
children
young adults
adults
senior citizens
people eligible for service
library users
library nonusers
students

NEEDS
recreational
leisure
informational
educational
cultural
historical
social
civic
intellectual

RESOURCE
books
AV materials
nonprint materials
print materials
popular materials
reference books
library resources
library materials
technology
facilities
local history
genealogy
business materials
programming

CONCEPTS
access to all information
meet user needs
interlibrary cooperation
freedom of information
community center
participation in the region

Once the library has a mission statement, library planners can begin work on goals. Goals depend on the mission of the library and can be related to any aspect of library service. For example, a library might choose from among the following areas in establishing goals. No library would have a goal in all areas below. Each set of goals would be tailored to the local community, the library's mission, and the roles chosen in the Role Prioritization Exercise:

adult services
children's services
young adult services
senior citizens
students and/or cooperation with
  schools
services to other special groups
reference
collection development

intellectual freedom
public relations
facility improvement
staff development
interlibrary cooperation
automation for resource sharing
automation for public and staff use
audiovisual collection and services
finances

After the library planners have decided upon goals, objectives should be written for each goal. Objectives should include a date by which the objective will have been completed; what will be accomplished by the date indicated; and how the accomplishment of the objective will be measured.

Two examples of goals and objectives are:

Goal: The public will have access to information and recreation through library programming.
    Objective: Maintaining children's programming at current level of an average attendance of 50 children per week.

Goal: Service to the public will be improved as a result of the library's participation in library networks.
    Objective: By December 198x, the library will have negotiated and signed the revised regional cooperation contract.

In the first objective, the date is a weekly occurrence; the result is children's programming maintained at a set level; and the measurement is the average of 50 children per week. One purpose of gathering information about the library's current performance is so that objectives can be made measurable. In this case, the library had kept records of attendance at children's programs; was able to determine the average attendance; and decided that maintaining that level was sufficient. Without collecting that information, they would not have been able to make that decision. In the second objective, the date is clearly specified, the result is the revised contract, and the measurement is whether or not it has been done by the date specified.

IMPLEMENTING THE PLAN

With mission, goals, and objectives written, the plan is usually presented to the Board of Trustees for approval. Although the committee will have prepared the plan, it usually endorses it as a recommendation to the Board of Trustees for final approval. In most libraries, it is only the Board that has the authority to approve and thus implement the plan.

After approval by the Board of Trustees or other appropriate governing authority, action plans can be written to implement the plan's objectives. Not all objectives will be targets for implementation every year. At the beginning of each year, the library director can propose to the trustees, or the director and trustees can decide together, which objectives will receive emphasis in a given year.

Action plans to implement the objectives are usually written by the library director or staff. They include: tasks to be done to reach an objective; who is responsible for completing each task; when each task should be completed; and resources needed to complete the tasks.

EVALUATING THE LONG-RANGE PLAN

There are two kinds of evaluation. The first is the library director's evaluation of the process used to write the long-range plan. Did the process go smoothly? Was too much or too little information gathered about the library and the community? Was the information available to make the objectives measurable? Would the planning committee have functioned better with a different composition?

The second kind of evaluation judges the success of the library in meeting objectives. If the objectives are measurable, the evaluation should determine whether the desired result was obtained at the indicated level by the date specified. How many of the objectives were met? Why weren't all the objectives met? This information can be used on an annual basis to revise annual objectives and after the long-range plan has run its course.

REWARDING RESULTS

Long-range planning is an exciting process for those who go through it. Most librarians find that the experience is rewarding and results in increased interest in the library by the community.

LIBRARY ROLES IN YOUR COMMUNITY
A Role Prioritization Exercise
by Nancy Bolt and Corinne Johnson

It is difficult to imagine a library having sufficient funds to do everything it wants in its community. Decisions about the allocation of resources must be made and priorities must be set.

On the following pages are listed some possible roles that a public library might play in its community. This exercise should help you decide which roles are the most appropriate for your public library.

Roles are listed below. For each role there is a brief description, a list of community needs this role might fill, and a list of some services that a library *might* offer if this role were chosen.

DIRECTIONS

1. Read the descriptions of all nine roles. Do this as an individual without talking to others.
2. As you read the role descriptions, ask yourself these questions:

   - Do many people in my community have these needs?
   - Are there other agencies/institutions in the community that already fill these needs?
   - Can we realistically fill this role?

3. You have 100 points to divide among the roles you consider appropriate for your library. These are roles you feel your library *should* play in your community. Obviously, some roles should not receive any points at all because they are inappropriate for your library. Try to divide the 100 points among the roles you feel are most important for your library.
4. Once each individual has assigned his/her points, at a meeting, combine everyone's points for each role. To see if this is really how the group feels, discuss the roles receiving the top votes to make sure that the "gut" feeling about the role of the library in the community matches the top vote getters. For example, compare the top roles with services currently offered by the library.
5. You can use this concept of roles to organize the collection of information about the library and the community.

IN SUMMARY

- Read role descriptions without talking to other group members
- Divide 100 points

• Compare choices and combine points
• Discuss to see if point count matches "gut" feeling about the library

ROLE PRIORITIZATION EXERCISE

Please read the role descriptions before assigning points.

1._____ Interlibrary Access Point
2._____ Recreational Reading and Viewing Center for Adults
3._____ Information Agency and Adult Independent Learning Center
4._____ Children's Reading and Viewing Center
5._____ Young Adult Reading and Viewing Center
6._____ Student's Auxiliary
7._____ Community Center
8._____ Local History and Genealogy Center
9._____ Outreach to Special Groups

ROLE DESCRIPTIONS

1. *Interlibrary Access Center.* The library participates in a regional or state network to fill many community needs. Similar in concept to a small Penney's or Sears store with limited goods available immediately, but the "full catalog" available within a few days.

   Need for this role in the community:
      to provide information and materials that the library does not have
   Some library activities:
      active participation in and the development of the regional and state network
      frequent use of interlibrary loan for books, periodicals, and AV materials
      participation in an automated network if possible
      use of back-up telephone reference for adults

2. *Recreational Reading and Viewing Center for Adults.* The library serves as a free or inexpensive source of recreational reading, listening, and viewing.

   Need for this role in the community:
      for inexpensive, convenient recreational reading and viewing
   Some library activities:
      continuous purchase of best seller and popular reading (may be in the form of paperbacks) such as mysteries, romance, popular authors, westerns, science fiction, light nonfiction

development of an audiovisual collection such as records, tapes, and videocassettes (either through purchase or participation in a regional program that allows the library to have these collections for extended loan), family film programs, subscriptions to popular magazines.

3. *Information Agency and Adult Independent Learning Center.* The library collects and dispenses information essential for daily living. The library serves as an agency for self-education and enrichment.

Need for this role in the community:
    to satisfy curiosity
    for consumer information and product evaluation
    for self-help such as cookbooks, automobile repair, do-it-yourself manuals, physical fitness and health
    for information to solve problems
    for information on current events and topics
    for information on personal finances
    to be an informed citizen
    to learn legal rights and processes
    for basic self-education
    for career selection and job hunting information
    for continuing education beyond formal schooling
    for cultural programming
    for spiritual and philosophical exploration
    to understand cultural identity
    to develop competency in English or a foreign language
    to learn to read (literacy training)
Some library activities:
    development of a ready reference collection and services
    subscription to consumer publications
    collection development and regular updating in self-help areas such as popular legal material, personal finances and investment, politics, etc.
    access to electronic data bases
    subscriptions to periodicals and journals
    development of a well-rounded balanced collection of nonfiction: history, literature, science, social studies
    development of collection on career and job hunting
    information programs in music, art, history, etc.
    exhibits in the library

4. *Children's Reading and Viewing Center.* The library offers programs and services for children entering the world of reading and learning. This includes both independent learning and recreational uses of the library.

Need for this role in the community:
    to learn that reading is fun

to satisfy curiosity

for inexpensive materials to read, view, and listen to

Some library activities:

friendly librarian who has experience with children's story hours and other recreational programs

current, updated collection of popular children's materials, fiction and nonfiction

subscription to children's magazines

cassette and record collection (either owned or borrowed from a regional library for extended loan)

5. *Young Adult Reading and Viewing Center.* The library offers programs, services, and materials specifically for young adults. This includes both independent learning and recreational uses of the library.

Need for this role in the community:

to learn the enjoyment of reading

to satisfy curiosity

for inexpensive materials to read, view, and listen to

Some library activities:

friendly librarian who relates to young adults

recreational and informational programs to meet young adult needs

current updated collection of popular young adult materials, fiction and nonfiction

cassette and record collection (either owned or borrowed from a regional library for extended loan)

6. *Student's Auxiliary.* The library assists children and adults in formal elementary, secondary, and college programs.

Need for this role in the community:

for materials and information to help with homework

when the school library is closed or nonexistent

when the school library (if existent) is unable to provide sufficient materials and information

Some library activities:

cooperative, friendly librarian

close cooperation of library staff with school administrators, teachers, and library media specialists

development of curriculum support materials (much can be done with inexpensive pamphlet materials and newspaper/magazine clipped articles)

guidance and assistance in assignment completion

development of basic collections to augment textbooks and other curriculum materials

7. *Community Center.* The library serves as a meeting place for people and groups in the community. Includes provision of information about services and resources available in the community:

> Need for this role in the community:
>> for a community meeting place
>> for information about community services and agencies
>
> Some library activities:
>> meeting room for public use
>> collection and organization of information about the community, where services can be obtained
>> file of community agencies and services
>> exhibits, performances, and presentations by local individuals or agencies

8. *Local History and Genealogy Center.* The library serves as an access point for community and family history.

> Need for this role in the community:
>> to have access to community history
>> to document family history
>
> Some library activities:
>> collect and maintain records of community history
>> develop a genealogy resource collection or develop cooperative ties with a genealogy resource collection

9. *Outreach to Special Groups.* The library reaches out to nonuser groups. This role should only be chosen if such a group can be identified and the library wishes to single it out for service.

> Need for this role in the community:
>> depends on community—could include senior citizens in nursing homes, homebound, illiterates, pre-schoolers in day care centers, institutionalized, incarcerated
>
> Some library activities:
>> taking library services out of the library to the target group
>> developing resources and services within the library for the target group

The Procedure Manual

Kathleen Ryan and Peggy Royster

What is a procedure manual? For our purposes, it is a collection of instructions covering the operation of a library. It is analogous to a manual covering the operation of a new food processor and should, similarly, tell you everything you ever wanted to know (and maybe more) about the item.

To begin, let us distinguish between policy and procedure. In spite of the importance and interrelationship of policy and procedure, we are concerned here with the creation of procedures. A policy, according to the *American Heritage Dictionary,* is: "Any plan or course of action adopted by a government, political party, business organization, or the like, designed to influence and determine decisions, actions, and other matters: American Foreign Policy, the company's personnel policy."[1] A procedure, according to the dictionary, is: "An act composed of steps; course of action."[2]

A library will have a set of policy statements, for instance, for circulation and for acquisitions, which will serve as general guidelines. The procedures of the same library will include specific, how-to information. While a library's circulation policy might include statements on who may borrow books, penalties for overdues, etc., the circulation procedure will include such details as when and how to prepare date due cards, exact steps in checking out books, and who to call when the charging equipment is broken. Policy is written with public dissemination in view; procedures are created for staff use inside the library.

WHY A MANUAL?

Why does a library need a procedure manual? In writing on the importance of a *Reference Policy and Procedure Manual,* Geraldine King states: "Such a manual is needed for staff training and everyday referral and as a record for the next person in the job; it is also useful when patrons question specific practices."[3]

A procedure manual is invaluable in staff training. With the manual

Kathleen Ryan is Director at the Seminole Public Library, Seminole, Oklahoma.
Peggy Royster is Director at the Guthrie Public Library, Guthrie, Oklahoma.

serving as a guide, the instructor (in a small library, probably you) knows when the task has been covered in all of its multitudinous details. No facet is forgotten if listed in the manual. New employees have the manual available for reference when in doubt or when they have forgotten everything they learned their first day on the job. Other employees (if you are so blessed as to have others) may also refer to the manual, possibly when filling in for others during vacation time.

Providing valuable assistance to one's successor, a procedure manual helps bridge the gap between administrators. For a new librarian becoming familiar with an institution, the procedure manual provides an accurate record of the past. This is particularly important in a one-person library, and also critical for the small library with only a few staff members.

Finally, the manual is an aid in the constant battle for consistency. It ensures that a task is done the same way each time. This is crucial in some areas, such as when maintaining statistical reports.

The procedure manual is always subject to change and should never be considered "engraved in stone." It should be kept in an easily revised format such as a looseleaf notebook and should be reviewed periodically.

WRITING THE MANUAL

One of the first decisions to be made is what to include. A good way to approach this is to begin keeping a list of procedures that should be included. Some recommended procedures are opening and closing the library; circulation; statistics; interlibrary loan; ordering; processing of materials; and check-in of periodicals.[4] As these procedures are written and put into the manual, more will come to mind. Think about including various other materials along with the procedures; it is convenient to have all relevant information available in one notebook. Such items may include job descriptions, an organizational chart, the library's mission statement, a history of the institution, and pertinent policies governing the library. You should also include a review schedule in the manual. Instead of tying yourself to wholesale revision of the manual, establish a schedule for reviewing sections of the manual on an annual basis. This won't put too much strain on your time. Complete revision of the manual is assured perhaps every three to five years using this method.

The very first step in preparing a manual is to gather all possible pre-existing information. If a public library, check with city officials for any current city manuals or policies affecting library operation. If an academic or school library, check with your administration for similar guidelines. For a special library similar action should be taken with those in the corporate structure. This saves time-consuming duplication of effort and the confusion of conflicting information. Next, comb the library for pre-existing written documents. They may be found mixed in with old board meeting minutes or stashed in long-untouched file drawers. After locating all the documents that you can, an appropriate decision can be made regarding whether to include them in the manual as is, to change them, or to eliminate them.

At the same time that you are searching for previously written information, begin researching sample manuals for examples of possible formats and details. The state library may be able to provide examples. Other area libraries may have already prepared a procedure manual; it pays to ask. A brief search of *Library Literature* should turn up information that you may be able to borrow via interlibrary loan.

After having embarked upon all of these preliminaries, it is now time to sail into the nitty gritty of writing your library's own manual. Three methods of gathering the required information prove the most helpful: observation, task performance, and log-keeping by the staff member performing the task.

Information Gathering

Observation is a particularly useful technique if you are new to the library. You will, in this case, need to learn how tasks are performed locally before even considering changes in procedures. Observation helps you learn the system. The main disadvantage of observation is the possibility of staff discomfort. If staff members are not yet acquainted with you, they may become uneasy. In any case, a clear explanation of your purpose in observing them will help and should be offered.

The most difficult aspect of learning by observation is to keep the blinders on, and to observe only one procedure at a time, in all of its minor details. Decide ahead of time what is going to be the "procedure of the day" and stick to observing that. For example, while at the circulation desk there is much activity (reserves, books being checked in and out, questions), but if you are working on writing a procedure for issuing new library cards, pay close attention to this process only. Although you may have a general idea of what issuing a card involves, look for the details, especially those unique to your particular library. Pick the task apart into separate functions (patron fills out registration card, clerk enters information into borrower's register, etc.) and write these down in order of performance, creating a rough draft of the procedure. Listening to how a staff member explains a task to a new worker is another "observation method"—you might learn a new approach to a familiar activity.

Job analysis, a second avenue, is simply a more immediate form of observation: do the job yourself. This method is best if you have worked for the library long enough to be intimately acquainted with its operations; otherwise, it may be very easy to miss local idiosyncrasies. It is important when using this method to perform the task you are observing more than once, at various times, and in various circumstances so that you become aware of possible variations in the routines. For example, if you only issue library cards in the middle of the day, you may not be aware of any differences in the procedure when issuing them to children (which requires a parent's signature). As you did with direct observation, write down the separate segments of the operation in the order in which they are performed in order to produce a rough draft of the procedure.

Finally, it may be helpful to ask the person who regularly performs a given task to keep a log. This has the advantage of staff participation and also ensures that the person writing down the information is closely acquainted with the task. This approach does have some disadvantages. First, whatever is written is in another person's "language" and something may be lost in the translation as you interpret it. Second, unless you are very careful in defining the parameters, you may receive a list of everything that goes on during that person's work day. Whether or not you decide to try this method should depend on the individual who performs the task. Can she or he define the task in an organized manner or is it performed unthinkingly, by rote, and in the same manner for the last twenty years? After the log is completed sit down and discuss it with the preparer. Question any terms or activities that are not clear and put the functions in order of performance. You will, once again, have completed a rough draft of your task.

Polishing the Rough Draft

If you have not done so already, solicit staff input. Go over the rough draft with those performing the tasks and ask them: Is this really how it is done? and, Are there any other variations or comments? After reviewing this information with your staff, you have to decide whether or not to divide the responsibility of writing the manual among your employees. You should question this long and hard before reaching a decision. Do staff members have the free time, on a routine basis, to devote to this process? The problems multiply when you consider that in the small library, to avoid political problems, all staff should have the chance to work on the manual. Does your staff have the critical skills necessary to complete this task? It might well be that your staff can make comments concerning the creation of procedures, but is not interested in or able to write such a document. Their views are beneficial to your work, so don't ignore their criticism or ideas.

You should take responsibility for producing the manual, but your strength as a manager will be increased by including the ideas of your staff in the manual. Don't, however, become so caught up in democratic methods that you undermine your document by having too many writers.

As you prepare to complete the manual, look at what you have documented carefully in order to determine whether the procedures require changes. If any procedure is not ideal, or if you see a way to streamline it, this is the time to make a change—before adding it to the manual. Any changes must be thoroughly reviewed with those performing the task.

CREATING A FORMAT

Should your procedures be presented in standard essay format, outline form, or as flowcharts? The decision has to be based on your needs and the needs of those who will be using the manual regularly. Ease of referral and quick accessibility are two of the criteria that you should use to decide. An outline form prevents verboseness. When you use flowcharts to describe procedures, actions interrelating in activities and decision points in activities are clearly shown. Since the rough draft is in a semi-outline form already, polishing it into a final product, whether chart or outline, is relatively easy.

It is a simple matter to graphically outline the sequential steps of library procedures. The flowchart, while demonstrating the exact steps of a procedure, also allows the integration of subprocedures that affect the main procedure. As you begin to diagram, remember to use the basic points of your outline to follow down through the procedure. It may be necessary to teach staff members the meaning of a few symbols used in charting: circles or ovals to indicate start/stop; rectangles to input information; diamonds to indicate yes/no decisions. After mastering the basics of chart reading, one can quickly glance through and understand the meaning of the chart.

As you diagram the various procedures which you have already outlined, consider creating general charts to explain graphically the various systems in your library. Some useful charts might be a chart of a good reference question, covering what a staff member should say when approached with a question and when the staff member should refer the question to the librarian; a chart of the movements of a patron through a complete library visit, covering what should happen between the time the patron enters the building and leaves, and what are correct staff responses, helping patterns, and interactions; and a chart of the daily routine of activities during the workday, covering what exceptions in routine there are for holidays and weekends and when procedures vary.

This same information can be conveyed using the outline form. When outlining, strive to eliminate any unnecessary details or editorial comment. You simply want a person to know how to issue a library card—not how it was done before, or any other superfluous information. The more unnecessary detail, the less likely the manual is to be used.

Consideration of format should also extend to the physical appearance of the manual. Choose an easy-to-use format—looseleaf binders provide the easiest method of production unless you have access to a microcomputer. Plan to add and delete from the procedure manual as needed. As soon as you have completed the first procedure, put it in a notebook, label it, date it, and announce that the rest of the work is "in process and will be arriving soon."

Illustrations are also important. Even for those who have limited resources available, the copying machine, scissors, and Scotch tape can help produce useful illustrations. Include these in the manual to make it more interesting reading and to reinforce your text. We are all a more sophisticated audience these days; graphic elements give credibility to your document.

Another mechanical note: each procedure should begin a new page. This simple step will eliminate much revision work in the future. Another useful detail is to date each procedure as it is written. This helps in determining when a procedure is in desperate need of review.

EVALUATING AND TESTING

Writing this manual is an on-going process, not neatly packaged into the months that it takes to actually produce the document. Just as you should decide what to include in your manual, you should decide how to judge its contribution to your workplace.

Remember why you decided to write a procedure manual in the first place. You believed, realistically, "that a Procedures Manual will increase the efficiency of your organization. . . . Procedures can save time and wasted effort and thus reduce the cost of labor and even materials. Procedures are particularly useful for efficiency objectives when the procedure is repeatedly utilized by several workers. When many people do the same job over and over again, the opportunity for savings using an efficient procedure is significant."[5]

Efficiency in training new employees probably is another benefit of having a procedure manual, a written guide for new employees to refer to, reducing the amount of time that you or other staff members need to take away from tasks to help the new employee. Not only are the difficulties and tensions associated with the supervision and training of new employees lessened, but trainees can learn on a more independent basis after minimal instruction.[6]

Savings in effort, reduction in waste, and learning new tasks quickly are three projected outcomes from using a procedures manual. Your evaluation of the manual should be based on these criteria, and all others that you used to justify creating the manual. During the process of writing the procedures, formulate the tests that you will use to evaluate its usefulness. Do you want to evaluate the time between hiring a new circulation worker and leaving him or her alone at the circulation desk? Observe how long this currently takes and, in the future, routinely measure the amount of time that elapses between hiring and completed training. Will the procedure manual shorten the length of training? Only through testing current performance and comparing it with future performance, across the range of activities described in the manual, will you be able to ascertain this. It is not difficult to create test situations. Evaluate your organization as it is currently so that you will be able to track increases in performance that may occur as the manual comes into common use.

Test the usefulness of the draft procedures by distributing copies to the person involved in each activity you document and asking for comments on your work. As previously mentioned, this will provide the benefit of having staff members "own" a part of the manual, decreasing the amount of convincing you will have to accomplish to win worker acceptance of it.

Another excellent in-process evaluation method is to test the clarity of your writing by having someone use your procedures to work through the process described. As well-informed as you are about what you have written, it is intended to be used as a guide for others. To be effective, your procedures must give good direction and there is no substitute for applying your procedures to everyday use in order to test their clarity. Observe the person following your instructions. You may observe some surprising gaps in the sequence of instructions. Try to find someone who has minimal involvement in the process to participate in this evaluation.

Introduce and demonstrate the use of the manual to your staff once it has been made "public." Referring to the manual yourself will provide a useful example when the manual is still new. During a typical week, count the number of referrals to the manual. Over the course of a year, with different staffing and staff scheduling, this measure should reflect whether or not your workers are using the manual. At the beginning of the manual's use, select the weeks that you will measure manual usage and announce the dates. This will again aid in staff acceptance of the process.

The impact the manual has had on your organization should also be part of the evaluation. Develop a check system to determine whether the manual is being used, create a quick-and-dirty questionnaire for the staff to complete, and monitor the staff activities to see if there are additional procedures that need to be included in the manual.

A questionnaire distributed to the staff is a very useful evaluation tool. It can pinpoint specific problems the staff may be having and can allow the staff member to suggest other procedures to be included in future editions. You can also find out who refers to the manual most frequently and why. You created the manual for staff benefit; find out if they are actually deriving those benefits.

By monitoring staff activities on several typical days you can observe whether activities have been added or deleted from their schedule of daily activities. Has a procedure been totally deleted? This monitoring proves that the manual is organic—change is inevitable in a viable organization.

UPKEEP AND RE-EVALUATION

Re-evaluation of procedures should also take place when you add or delete equipment from your library. Red-flag the sections of the manual that include references to the procedures that mention a particular machine or process, and establish a date to present a rewritten edition of the procedures. In the case of a new piece of equipment, don't be too hurried in writing its procedure. In time you will be familiar enough with reactions to it and actions around the equipment to begin documentation of its use. Incorporating and deleting procedures as items are added or discarded from the library decreases the amount of time needed to rework your manual at the annual evaluation points.

It is not enough to glibly state "this manual will be reviewed on an annual basis." After struggling to create a document to use as an integral part of your training and organization, whether or not it remains a vital part of your workplace depends on the document's relevance. Testing the document's accuracy is an important part of the annual review process. As you observed your staff while writing the document and testing the current practices of the library, now observe whether the procedures that you created are still accurately reflecting the work of your staff. Do the same steps still follow in an activity? Has some part of a system altered? Intent observation will be necessary to pick up on slightly different nuances in procedures. Alter the procedures to reflect the reality of the current situation.

THE DOCUMENT'S WORTH

Creating a procedure manual requires a lot of time and effort. Processes are not measured, observed, and recorded quickly. The energy that is expended during its writing is directly related to the worth of the document; one must be willing to record accurately the procedures as they occur, studying them to separate multiple tasks and identify unique situations. But the time invested in writing the manual will be offset in the future by the time saved as new employees learn tasks more quickly and by the improved efficiency of completing tasks and procedures as staff members refer to a single source to guide their actions.

References

1. *The American Heritage Dictionary of the English Language* (Boston: American Heritage Publishing Co., Inc. and Houghton Mifflin Co., 1969).
2. Ibid.
3. Geraldine Kind, *Reference Service in the Small Library* (Chicago: American Library Assn., 1985), p. 9.
4. A. Kolb, "Happiness Is (A Procedure Manual in Every Library)," *Sourdough* 18 (October 1981): 9.
5. John R. Rizzo, *Management for Librarians: Fundamentals and Issues* (Westport, Conn.: Greenwood Press, 1980).
6. Ibid., p. 82.

Using National Standards

James O. Wallace

All librarians should have available a copy of the national library standards applicable to the type of library in which they are employed. The standards should be utilized to evaluate the condition of services, to develop planning goals and objectives, and to communicate the results to the institution in which the librarian serves. Standards alone do not improve library services, but they do provide a focus and direction for the actions which will bring about the improvement. National library standards provide significant guidance for libraries of all sizes, but they are especially valuable for small libraries. Where else can you find expertise so inexpensively available in easily accessible format?

National standards are the criteria for the measurement of library programs and services that have been approved by the American Library Association (ALA) or one of its divisions. By comparing what exists in a specific library to national standards, specific areas in which the library needs to develop can be pinpointed; these, in turn, become the base for the development of goals and objectives, both long-range and immediate.

A standing or special committee charged with responsibility for reviewing or drafting the national standards or guidelines examines previous standards or guidelines, identifies strengths or weaknesses, holds hearings, prepares and distributes drafts for review, and, ultimately, when the final draft is acceptable to all concerned, obtains official approval from the ALA division. The process can be very extensive; some standards have required over five years from appointment of the committee to ultimate approval. Committee members provide their expertise without charge.

National standards have been developed which are applicable to small public libraries, elementary and secondary school libraries, and to two- and four-year colleges. In the case of colleges, there are also standards relating to off-campus centers and to branch libraries. The resulting documents are the best source of current information about practices that should be followed. For any professional to disregard such competencies in planning services in any library is inconceivable.

James O. Wallace lives in San Antonio, Texas.

FUNCTION OF STANDARDS

An understanding of national standards includes an awareness of what they cannot and will not do. They can be used in the accreditation process for schools and colleges, but they are not accreditation standards such as are issued by the regional accreditation associations or state departments for schools and colleges. These groups can require that the institution meet the standards. Any national library standard can assess where a library has strengths and weaknesses, but the national library standards and guidelines do not compel an institution to make any correction. Failure to meet the standards expresses a negative evaluation of the quality of services and resources, but constitutes no punitive threat to an institution. Ignoring them, however, shows an insensitivity to professional advice. The function of the national library standards can suggest a professional level of service, but they cannot insure that the level is reached. On the other hand, they can be an incentive to improvement of service in any type of library without the implication that all libraries of that type are near to meeting the standard.

National standards in themselves provide incentive to improvement. At a forum in 1961 at the American Association of Junior Colleges Convention, many junior college presidents questioned the then new library standard requirement that a junior college have a minimum collection of 20,000 volumes. There were probably less than a dozen two-year colleges in the country at that time with a collection of that size or larger, and regional accrediting associations required less than half that amount. A decade later most two-year college collections exceeded 20,000 volumes, and today many two-year college collections are larger than 100,000 volumes. National library standards deserve at least partial credit for the way American libraries have improved over a period of time.

STANDARDS IN PLANNING AND EVALUATION

Accreditation standards or criteria of the regional accrediting associations differ from national library standards in that the accrediting association can and does require compliance as a condition of membership, although the ultimate decision as to accreditation is based on the institution as a whole and not just on the acceptable condition of the library. This does not mean that the national library standards should not be part of the accreditation process; they are useful in the self-study and planning and evaluation process required in the accreditation process as a supplement to the specific requirements of the accreditation standards or criteria. They often identify other aspects of library services that should be considered.

The emphasis in recent years has been on the planning and evaluation process at each institution. This consists of a regular cycle involving formulation of institutional and library goals, development of specific objectives for the budgetary year, tailoring the budget to those objectives, and evaluation of achievement in the course of development of goals and objectives for the following year. National standards can be used effectively in the determination of these goals and objectives. The standards for public libraries, in fact, are based on the planning process,[1] supplemented by output measures.[2]

The status of the public library standards highlights one factor that must be considered when using national library standards—obsolescence. Since standards can become out of date, regular revision is necessary. The public library standards were published in 1980 after several years of work; the output measures were published in 1982. The school standards were published in 1975,[3] and the university library standards in 1979.[4] The revised two-year college standards were approved in 1981.[5] All of them are being considered for revision; only the 1986 college library standards can be considered up-to-date.[6]

Should the other standards be disregarded because they are several years old? By no means. Until replaced, such standards continue to serve as a basis for formulating programmatic and budgetary requirements and for evaluation purposes.

USE OF STANDARDS

Since the most recently approved national standards are for college libraries, they will be used to illustrate how standards can be utilized in the planning and evaluation process.

Standard 1 deals with objectives: "The college library shall develop an explicit statement of objectives in accordance with the goals and purposes of the college." Does such a statement exist? If the answer is yes, is it current? If that answer is affirmative as well, was it developed by the library staff in consultation with others in the college community as suggested? If that answer is also positive, nothing further is necessary; if any of the questions are answered negatively, then a goal is provided: "Develop (or revise) a statement of objectives for the library in accordance with the goals and purposes of the college."

The next step is to relate the established goal to the objectives for the next budgetary year and to a time period. Obviously, this specific goal is not conditioned by the availability of funds, and its implementation will not have to be determined by final budget allocations as will be the case with some other goals. The time period will depend upon the complexity of the communication process with the remainder of the college community, but for a small institution, it should not require an extensive period of time if the goals and purposes of the college have already been developed. An objective might then be: "During the fall semester the library staff will prepare and obtain approval of a statement of library objectives based on the goals and purposes of the college after input from faculty, students, and college administrators."

Standard 2 relates to the collection and provides a quantitative formula for the library holdings which includes audiovisual and other nonprint items as well as physical volumes. Applying this formula requires information about the size of the present collection, full-time equivalency of faculty and students, number of undergraduate and graduate majors and minors offered in the curriculum, and number of doctoral fields. The small college will be limited to undergraduate programs with only a few master's fields, if any.

Let us assume that there is a college of 500 FTE students, 50 FTE faculty, 15 major, and 20 minor undergraduate fields, no graduate program, and an existing collection of 50,000 volumes. Under the formula, the desired collection would be 109,750 volumes as a goal (double the present collection). This represents a basic collection of 85,000 items, plus 5,000 volumes additional for faculty (50x100), plus 7,500 additional for students (500x15), plus 12,250 additional for curricular fields (35x350). To double the size of the collection in a single year is not within the realm of probability at any college even when funds present no problem. Other factors are involved: size of staff available to process the additions, physical space to house the collection, time to select and purchase the items desired, and processing time. Some of these factors are addressed in other standards. By the grading system, the current collection rates only a "D" in this example; the evaluation expressed reflects a need for improvement.

The formula must not be disregarded even when it is not immediately possible to make changes. It identifies the existing collection as inadequate for the educational program of the college—in the opinion of the leading librarians in the nation—in a way that supersedes any subjective evaluation by the college; improving the size of the holdings must become a long-range goal. In terms of goals, this can be expressed: "To increase the size of the collection to provide adequate holdings to meet instructional and student needs."

For objectives based on this goal to be used during the budget year, several types would be possible. Examples could be very specific: "Increase the number of books by 5,000 additional during the year" or "Add 100 videotapes during the year." Objectives might also relate to specific subject areas: "Develop the collection needed for Sociology 415" or

"Improve the holdings on applications of computers to education." Each of these examples would be appropriate to the goal involved.

Quality of the collection as well as quantity is a matter of concern in the standards. The commentary sections of this standard document refer to such matters as resource sharing and borrowing and lending to other libraries, utilizing the expertise of faculty members in checking holdings, and checking the collection against standard bibliographies. Each of these topics could be developed into objectives for the next budgetary year.

Standard 3 relates to the organization of the collection. As with all the national standards, each aspect can be formulated into a question to be answered, a possible goal to be sought, and objectives. In some libraries, the goal might be to integrate all holdings into a catalog; in others, it might be to discontinue a card catalog in favor of one on microfiche or utilizing an online computer system. The library may be so well organized that no action is necessary, but for most small libraries there is likely to be some action which should be taken, including mundane matters such as eliminating backlogs of filing in the central catalog or other catalog maintenance needs.

Standard 4 relates to the provision for staff. For the small library, this may be the least useful in terms of staff size. There is no specific formula for support staff other than that they should be no less than 65 percent of the total staff. The formula for librarians is one for each 500 FTE. This implies that only one full-time person (or 65 percent part-time) is enough. This conclusion should be checked against opening hours, other services provided, and availability of student assistants before eliminating other options. The standards for school libraries are better here; for a school of 500 students, the requirements include one head librarian, up to one additional professional, one to two technicians, and two to three aides. For the college, there are saving statements that relate to the services provided which could be used to justify staff. If the collection is to be doubled, a second professional librarian for this purpose might be justified along with other personnel objectives: "Add one additional library faculty member to develop the collection" or "Augment library services by a library faculty member to provide audiovisual and microcomputer expertise to the campus" or "Add a technician to supervise the use of the microcomputer and audiovisual learning laboratory" or "Add a clerk to provide additional night and weekend hours to meet student needs."

Standard 5 relates to services. Some of the more specific aspects can easily be turned into goals and objectives, for instance, bibliographic instruction is a specific requirement of services. The college library must assess what information and instruction methods are currently followed and determine what additional should be used. Standard 6 relates to facilities and has a formula for space based on space for users, books, and staff. Standard 7 relates to administration, and Standard 8 to budget. The process for the development of goals and objectives would be similar for these two standards.

SUPPLEMENTARY STANDARDS

National library standards are often supplemented by state library standards for schools, public libraries, and colleges and universities. At times, state standards are higher than national library standards. This is true of the accreditation standards for public schools in Texas where several items, including size of the print collection and the number of books and audiovisual items added yearly, are higher than the national standards.[7] The library is fortunate indeed when this occurs because the higher figures can be appropriately substituted. The national library standards can be used in connection with other standards effectively in such cases.

References

1. Vernon E. Palmour, Marcia C. Bellassai, and Nancy V. Dewath, *A Planning Process for Public Libraries* (Chicago: American Library Assn., 1980).
2. Douglas Zweizig and Eleanor Jo Rodger, *Output Measures for Public Libraries* (Chicago: American Library Assn., 1982).
3. American Association of School Librarians and the Association for Educational Communications and Technology, *Media Programs District and School* (Chicago: American Library Assn., 1975).
4. *Standards for University Libraries* (Chicago: Association of College and Research Libraries and the Association of Research Libraries, 1978).
5. *Guidelines for Two-year College Learning Resources Programs* (Chicago: Association of College and Research Libraries and Association for Educational Communications and Technology, 1981). This was supplemented by *Statement on Quantitative Standards for Two-year College Learning Resources Programs* (Chicago: Association of College and Research Libraries, 1979).
6. *Standards for College Libraries* (Chicago: Association of College and Research Libraries, 1986).
7. *School Library Media Centers,* TAC Chapter 81, Sub-chapter F (Austin: Texas Education Agency, 1985).

Evaluation

Ron Norman

This is a modest proposal for evaluation. Over the years, a variety of documents addressing the subject of library standards and evaluation have been published by professional library associations, state and local agencies, institutions, and other governing authorities. Some of these documents are quite elaborate—almost to the point of being unusable, while others are more basic. Whatever the case, it is evident that these documents reflect the need for tools offering direction and goals so that librarians can provide their particular publics with the best library and services.

The tool presented below is deliberately general. It covers eleven areas for evaluation, but does not attempt to say how something *should* be done. Rather, it asks only if something *is* being done. The purpose of the evaluation is to identify and recognize areas of both excellence and weakness.

Although the evaluation can be self-administered, it would be most beneficial to the library if an outside individual or team of two were invited to conduct it. This would not only bring greater objectivity but provide a variety of viewpoints to apply to the evaluation.

AREAS FOR EVALUATION

Budget. Using salaries/benefits, books, and operations as the three basic categories of the library's budget, how is money allocated among the three? What is the desirable allocation and how close does the library come to meeting it?

Collection. Some of the questions to be considered in collection development are: How are materials selected and are there sufficient selection tools? How are materials ordered and how much time elapses from when materials are selected and they are ordered? How are materials processed and how much time elapses from when materials are received and they are ready for the public? What materials are available to the public and is there an ongoing or periodic check to see

Ron Norman is Director of the Kearney Public Library and Information Center, Kearney, Nebraska.

what areas need additional materials and what materials need updating? Are efforts made to select the place to order materials which offers good service at the best price?

In maintaining the collection, are efforts made to keep existing materials in the best possible condition through relabeling, mending, rebinding, new dust jacket covers, cleaning, etc., and through periodic ongoing checks of the collection to determine which materials need attention? Is easy access for the patron and staff provided by checking frequently to make sure that materials are in the proper order on the shelves?

Card Catalog. Is the card catalog maintained in a neat, clean, and orderly manner? Is filing kept current and done accurately? Are efforts made to resolve card catalog discrepancies in a manner to best serve patrons and staff?

Written Policies. Does the library have a written policy statement covering the following people and tasks: trustees, staff, job descriptions, selection, weeding, complaints, and gifts and donations?

Communications with Trustees, Higher Administration, Local Authorities. Are these groups regularly informed of library activities? Are they periodically briefed on the functions of various departments within the library?

Internal Communications. Does the staff have easy access to the director? Are they regularly informed of library policies? Is there adequate communications between departments?

External Communications. Does the library maintain a cohesive communications program using media, friends groups, user's surveys, handouts, and displays?

Intragovernmental Communications. Is there communication between library and city administrators and communication and cooperation between the library and other departments of city government?

Cooperation with Other Libraries. Does the library work with libraries both within and outside the community?

Ongoing Programs. Does the library maintain such ongoing programs as storytime and summer reading programs? What others are there?

Physical Facilities. Is the library interior bright, attractive, and inviting? Are the exterior grounds well maintained?

STATISTICS AND EVALUATION

Statistics have been described as the science of classifying and manipulating data in order to draw inferences. If the library manager's inferences are right, he or she is a genius, a master tactician; if the inferences are wrong, he or she is a fool; and if the inferences are wrong too often, the manager will probably be unemployed—this, too, is an inference from available data.

Librarians work with statistics constantly. We know how many adult materials and children's materials are circulated each day, month, year. We know how many fiction titles circulate, and how many nonfiction. We know how many items we receive on interlibrary loan, how many we send. We know how many and what kinds of materials we accession and withdraw. We know how much we spend for which materials. *To what degree, however, do we use the statistics available to us to better understand what we are doing*—to evaluate our services?

A case in point: the circulation statistics for the Kearney Public Library and Information Center were reviewed for the years 1971–1972 and 1976–1977 successively through 1984–1985. In 1971–1972, the library was in a small, inadequate Carnegie building. In November 1972, there was a successful bond campaign. From June 1973 to June 1975, the library was in temporary quarters. After opening for business in the new building, we experienced a sharp increase in circulation.

As a result of this data collection effort, we were able to evaluate some collective development objectives and draw an interesting observation on use patterns:

1. The strengthening of the nonfiction collection had been a major library objective since the early 1970s. The success of the objective was reflected in our statistical review of circulation, which showed a 227 percent increase in circulation of nonfiction materials in the Adult Department and 165 percent increase in the Children's Department.
2. The library cautiously but steadily expanded its collection of audiovisual related materials, especially in the Children's Department. Our circulation review revealed a 2,134 percent increase in circulation in the Children's Department during the statistical period.
3. Also, during the statistical review period, general circulation in the Adult Department increased from 50,871 to 128,252 (152%); and circulation in the Children's Department increased from 36,531 to 97,091 (166%).
4. The most interesting observation about the ratios concerns constancy. There was, it would seem, one use pattern in the old library. In many instances, with the opening of the new library, this pattern changed—to the positive. And now a new pattern appears to be established—and constant: for every adult fiction title circulated, approximately one and one-half adult nonfiction titles circulate. For every three juvenile fiction titles circulated, approximately one juvenile nonfiction title circulates. For every fiction title circulated, approximately three-fourths of a nonfiction title circulates. For every item circulated in the Children's Department, approximately one and one-half items circulates in the Adult Department.

IMPLICATIONS FOR THE LIBRARY

The statistics collected at Kearney would seem to indicate that once a pattern is established, it does not seem to vary significantly—until a new and significant variable is introduced. The significant variable for the Kearney Public Library and Information Center was a new building. Because of the new building, old patterns changed and new patterns emerged. Since the emergence of these new patterns, however, there has been very little change. It is probably safe to say that, unless a new, significant variable is introduced, circulation could increase ten-fold and the patterns would remain relatively the same. It should be noted that even the new library building did not change the ratio of juvenile nonfiction to fiction, and adult circulation to juvenile circulation.

Why keep statistics if they are not going to be used? If statistics are kept, they can be analyzed, used to evaluate services, and inferences drawn from them that can be applied to new directions in the library's services. If we are satisfied with the way things are going, then we make as few changes as possible and don't rock the boat. If we aren't satisfied, then armed with the data we can decide what significant variables to introduce so that the changes we want can be channeled in the direction we want, to achieve the results we want.

3
Collection Development and Technical Services

Censorship and Access

Connie Miller

BUILDING THE COLLECTION

A morally injured and irate patron demanding the withdrawal of a book or magazine from a library collection springs immediately to most librarians' minds when the word censorship is mentioned. While other, more subtle forms of censorship exist which are no less destructive, external pressures on a library to prevent or promote access to certain materials constitute a difficult and dangerous threat to intellectual freedom, a threat with which librarians must be prepared to deal. Intellectual freedom means freedom of expression and freedom of access. Whenever any individual, group, or organization acts to limit access to or to label controversial or objectionable materials, intellectual freedom is attacked. The American Library Association's (ALA) Council drew up the Library Bill of Rights to affirm the library's position in society as an institutional advocate for diversity. Censors oppose diversity by wanting to mandate, on the basis of their own moral or ideological preferences, the information available to everyone.

While in some ways they seem conceptually distant, a patron's objection to the material included in, or excluded from, a library's collection and the library's materials selection policy form two sides of the same coin: both actions—objecting and selecting—represent a decision on behalf of others that not all information can be available. The close relationship between these two actions makes librarians vulnerable to the accusation of controlling access but, if the closeness is understood, it can also provide libraries with a source of defense and protection.

Because it involves choosing to make some items and not others available in a collection some authors believe that the selection in which librarians must rigorously engage is a form of censorship. "Every time I decide to buy this book and not that book," says Hole,[1] "I censor the reading material available to the public. And I do it on the basis of moral judgment . . . by what seems good . . . at the time. . . . [W]hat we *buy* demonstrates that we know perfectly well freedom of speech is not an

---

Connie Miller is Science Librarian, University of Illinois at Chicago, Chicago, Illinois.

absolute right." Swan[2] feels that the Library Bill of Rights is a guiding principle rather than a law and that its purism should be replaced by realism. Since librarians, he says, are inescapably censors as well as disseminators of knowledge, they "must be doubly aware of the danger which [their] acts of censorship pose to the intellectual freedom of those whom [they] serve."

This approach, which views librarians as inevitably culpable in the practice of sins that they oppose in theory, has its passionate opponents. Ficociello[3] stresses that censorship is an action while reading is not. Librarians who decide to include or exclude items from collections on the basis of their potentially good or harmful ideas, or on the basis of their potential to upset members of the community, rather than on the basis of predetermined selection guidelines (e.g., author's reputation, library size and budget, reading interests of the community), are making moral decisions about the ideas readers have the responsibility to encounter. Broderick[4] insists that librarians cannot be censors; they can only be "good or bad selectors." A library decision not to purchase a book says only that to purchase it would not be a legitimate use of funds. "Interested parties can still buy the book if they wish."

Concerns like Hole's and Swan's cannot be dismissed lightly, but emotion surrounding the distinction (or lack of it) between censorship and selection can serve to obscure the practical reality. Librarians, especially in small libraries, must continue to develop their collections selectively. Asheim[5] distinguishes censorship from selection in a way which is perhaps the most practically applicable. "The selector says, if there is anything good in this book let us try to keep it; the censor says, if there is anything bad in this book, let us reject it and since there is seldom a flawless work in any form, the censor's approach can destroy much that is worth saving." The collection that a selector develops reflects, not the selector's likes, dislikes, or insecurities, but rather the selector's view of what the readers want and need.[6]

Preparing a clear and detailed written Materials Selection Policy is the best first step a librarian can take to guide the selectors in finding reasons to keep, instead of justifications to reject, items for the collection. This document not only helps guard against internal censorship, but also provides an effective and certainly essential defense against the external censor. A written Materials Selection Policy should include a statement defining and advocating intellectual freedom, a discussion of general selection guidelines, and specific definitions of the depth, breadth, and formats in which each subject area is to be collected. The appropriate governing authority, whether it be a library board, a board of education, a company administrator, or a church council, should be familiar with, and supportive of, the selection policy and should have given it formal approval.

In *Book Selection and Intellectual Freedom,* Merritt[7] supplies excellent examples of actual selection policies appropriate for a variety of audiences and subject areas. While his sample policies are derived specifically from larger public libraries, the basic principles can be applied to small and special library collections. The application of principles rather than particulars is vitally important because no selection policy developed by one library should be adopted by another wholesale, a fact which gave Merritt reservations about even including sample policies in his book. Specifications simply cannot be provided for the creation of a document which is valuable only to the extent that it reflects individual conditions. "The selection policy," Merritt warns, "is intended as a tool to enable a library staff to provide a good library collection, tailor-made to the needs, interests, and dreams of the community the library serves. It should be well balanced, yes; but balanced in the sense of a mobile rather than a teeter-totter. Specifications for making a teeter-totter undoubtedly exist, but who ever heard of specifications for a mobile?"

All small libraries should have on hand the most current edition of the *Intellectual Freedom Manual,* published by ALA's Office of Intellectual Freedom. Not only does this practical *Manual* provide advice on the development of a Materials Selection Policy, it also provides copies and interpretations of, and policies related to, the Library Bill of Rights and the Freedom to Read Statement. It includes a discussion of intellectual freedom as an "all-embracing concept" in relation to all types of libraries and discusses its legal implications. Perhaps the most helpful parts of the *Manual* are the sections detailing the essential preparations a library should make before a censor comes and the deliberative steps that should be taken afterwards.

THE CENSOR COMETH

The *Manual* recommends that, in addition to writing a detailed Materials Selection Policy, libraries make the following preparations in anticipation of a censor's arrival:

1. Prepare and maintain an up-to-date, written Library Service Policy. The policy should cover programming and all issues related to access. It would be useful to include with the policy such documents as Free Access to Libraries for Minors, Exhibit Spaces and Meeting Rooms, and/or the Statement on Labeling, copies of which appear in the *Manual.*
2. Prepare and maintain a written Procedure for Handling Complaints. Central to this procedure is the requirement that all complaints about library materials or services be filed in writing on a standard form and that the complainant be formally identified. The Statement of Concern About

Library/Media Center Resources, prepared by ALA's Intellectual Freedom Committee, can be used as is or adapted by libraries to suit their local situations. The Procedure to Handle Complaints should also include a reevaluation of the item to which the complainant objects by the original selectors in light of the library's written Materials Selection Policy; a written response to the complainant about the results of the reevaluation including instructions on how to pursue the complaint further if necessary; and an appeal to the head administrator of the library.

3. Provide on-going in-service training for staff, administrators, and the library governing authority to reinforce intellectual freedom and to describe the Materials Selection Policy, the Service Policy, and the Procedure for Handling Complaints.

4. Maintain an active public relations program. Utilize corporate or institutional newsletters or community newspapers, radio, and television stations to publicize library programs and policies, particularly as they relate to intellectual freedom. Communicate with local civic, religious, educational, and political groups or institutional committees, emphasizing the library's role in serving the diverse needs of its community.

A library cannot be sure, however thoroughly it prepares, that an individual or group from outside—or even inside—the library will not insist that access to materials be limited by the termination of a subscription, the removal of an offensive item, the labeling of certain items, etc. In the event of a complaint, the *Intellectual Freedom Manual* recommends the following:

1. Recognize the complainant's right to complain by responding calmly and politely. It is always possible that, upon reevaluation in light of the Materials Selection Policy, an item will prove to have been inappropriately selected.

2. Make sure that the complainant records the complaint in writing on a formal Statement of Concern; receives a written response as quickly as possible; and is informed continuously about the next step in the complaint procedure.

3. Notify, in writing, the library administration and the governing authority about the nature and source of the complaint and the procedure being followed.

4. Enlist the support of local media, organizations, and committees when appropriate.

5. Do not remove or restrict access to any library materials until a court determination rules that such action is necessary.

6. Contact ALA's Office of Intellectual Freedom, the state intellectual freedom committee, the American Civil Liberties Union, and other organizations to enlist their support and advice.

Complaints which librarians receive may focus, not on the removal of materials from the collection, but rather on their addition. Individuals or groups—anyone from Phyllis Schlafly to a gay and lesbian support group, from Mothers Against Drunk Driving to Creationists, from an organic chemist to a committed believer in Unidentified Flying Objects—may insist that a library balance its collection by including items that represent a certain point of view. Since it is the librarian's responsibility to provide access to a diversity of ideas, these complaints must be given very serious consideration. If books, films, journals, tapes, pamphlets, etc., which represent a certain viewpoint and which fall within a library's Materials Selection Policy, are not available in the collection, the imbalance should be rectified.

The idea of balance, however, must be viewed qualitatively rather than quantitatively, according to Landor.[8] A collection, for example, which includes fewer books on communism than on democracy, or on homosexuality than heterosexuality, may be well-balanced in spite of numerical discrepancies. Broderick believes that the notion that library collections should represent all sides of all questions is unrealistic. In actuality, the issue becomes "how many sides of what questions?" Preoccupation with balance, says Landor, necessitates at least some degree of labeling, some tendency to judge rather than to respond to a diversity of ideas.

As with complaints aimed at the removal of library materials, those aimed at the addition of materials to the collection can be handled best by a library which has examined its own conscience in respect to intellectual freedom by preparing a written Materials Selection Policy, a Library Service Policy, and a Procedure for Handling Complaints. At the heart of the library's institutional commitment to diversity lies not only the librarian's freedom to disseminate ideas but also, and more importantly, the public's freedom to receive them.[9]

ACCESS TO COLLECTIONS

"Is it possible for an index to be a tool of censorship? Unfortunately, the answer is yes: it is possible and it happens all the time that indexes effectively bury materials."[10]

Essentially, librarians and censors disagree about access. The former attempt to promote it and the latter believe it should be mandated. Promoting access and selectively developing library collections resembles sailing a small boat through dangerous waters. It is possible, with care and attention, to get a boat safely to land. Like skillful sailors, librarians have developed the particular care and attention necessary to balance collection building and intellectual freedom without capsizing on the hidden shoals and reefs of censorship. They have had a great deal of practice; external complaints which librarians receive have almost always focused on the presence or absence of undesirable or desirable materials in a collection. Librarians, however, have not been forced to confront censorship in *finding* materials in library collections the way they have in building these collections. Perhaps this is because patrons usually find what they need; perhaps it is because they usually don't know what it is they didn't find. Whether confrontation has occurred or not, the fact remains that if library catalogs and indexes do not provide adequate access to some or all of the materials in a collection, regardless of how skillfully the collection has been developed, librarians, like censors, are mandating access and their responsibilities in promoting and fostering diversity will remain only partially fulfilled.

For years, a relatively small but outspoken group of librarians have been protesting the failure of existing subject heading lists (e.g., Library of Congress Subject Headings, the Sears list) and classification lists (Library of Congress Classification, Dewey Decimal Classification, Universal Classification) to provide adequate access to information in general, but especially to alternative materials and information about minorities. While improvements in these authority files and classification schemes have been and are constantly being made, Berman[11] warns against the all-too-common practice of simply accepting outside cataloging copy from LC or through national cataloging consortia like OCLC, which may not be adequate for local purposes.

What cataloging copy often seems to lack is an appreciation for diversity, a characteristic which the very existence of libraries is supposed to defend. Behind cataloging principles and practice lurks what Marshall has called the "hypothetical reader."[12] Harris and Clack point out that "it was almost an article of faith in librarianship that subject analysis was objective; that is, the subject cataloger, on the basis of literary warrant and usage, devised subject terms and classification notations to fit the works being cataloged."[13] Unfortunately, in spite of societal multiplicity, it was for the benefit of a particular reader that "objective" subject headings and classification notations were established—a very subjectively defined reader who can be identified as American/Western European, Christian, white, heterosexual, and male. When such a narrow conception of experience forms the entire basis for locating information in libraries, either through finding terms in a catalog or through browsing the shelves, it is questionable, says Marshall, whether spotty revision in established vocabularies or classification structures can ever correct the fundamental bias toward serving some and disserving or underserving many.

Those who protest a lack of fairness in the treatment of women and minorities tend to be labelled—often dismissively—as radicals. It is important to point out, therefore, that problems with access through library catalogs have been a vital concern not only to so-called radicals but also to moderates, and that access problems affect all subject areas and are not restricted to materials sometimes viewed as fringe.[14] In addition to research which indicates that subject headings and classification systems inadequately provide access to many subject areas, groups of people, or points of view, some studies suggest that users would appreciate and benefit from enhanced cataloging.

The record left by patrons who search online public access catalogs has made possible the examination of their information-seeking behaviors to an extent not possible with the physical card catalog. Studies of this behavior have shown that "subject searching is the most frequent user activity and the area of most user problems"; and the results of these studies have been taken to heart by the profession, as witnessed by a six-part symposium in *American Libraries* designed to "help professionals understand the present state of subject access and identify and address its problems."[15] McClure[16] found that articles in periodical indexes receive almost five times the number of subject headings (an average of 4.5 headings per seven-page article) as books in catalogs, giving library patrons "at least a five times better chance of finding more subject-related information through [indexes] than through the subject headings in a typical card catalog." Users of library catalogs have expressed the belief that additional access points—standard practice assigns about 1.5 LC subject headings per book—would help them locate information.[17]

The simple reality of smaller numbers of items to control, combined with their more narrowly defined reasons for existing, suggests that small libraries have both the ability and the obligation to devote significant time and resources to the accessibility of the materials they collect. Depth of analysis, i.e., the number of access points assigned to individual works, has been directly linked to collection size.[18] On the assumption that "the large library is more likely to have whole books devoted to subjects that may only be chapters of more general works in small libraries," works in the latter libraries require many access points while those in the former need few. When a relatively small number of records is involved, it has been demonstrated that the addition of descriptive terms taken from books themselves to standard catalog records makes the retrieval of materials both more effective and more efficient.[19]

In spite of user studies, research, and environmental characteristics which make small libraries seem appropriate—even ideal—places for making enhanced catalog access a priority, these institutions may feel restricted by inadequate budgets or limited personnel. There is not consensus among experts in librarianship concerning the purpose of catalogs or the benefits of their enhancement.[20] Card catalogs, in the opinion of some, exist to provide the location of books as bibliographical units rather than to index book content. Wiberley cautions against increasing the number of access points since information overload already causes problems for a significant proportion of catalog users.[21] In a study correlating catalog record access points with circulation, Knutson found "that increasing the number of Library of Congress subject headings [incrementally, i.e., from one or two to three or four,] may have little or no effect on book retrieval."[22]

Depending on its unique circumstances (e.g., budget, personnel, user characteristics, subject matter of the collection, etc.), each small library must ascertain the degree to which its catalog offers, obscures, or impedes access to its collection and what action needs to be taken to improve this access. While "a rich entry vocabulary is not inexpensive to maintain, it has been demonstrated to be cost-effective because it greatly reduces the intellectual burden on both the cataloger and the searcher," according to Mandel and Herschman. Good quality, locally specific cataloging which promotes the use of carefully and expensively selected, labelled, and shelved materials cannot be viewed, says Berman, as uneconomical. Different subject areas and user groups affect catalog use enormously, states Knutson, implying that catalogs should be designed according to specific institutional situations [and diversities] rather than according to traditional expectations.

CATALOGING PRINCIPLES

Small libraries which decide to enhance users' access to their collections through their catalogs can turn for guidance to work done in the past. On the basis of six principles she identified for establishing subject headings relating to people and peoples, Marshall developed a thesaurus for nonsexist indexing and cataloging. Her six principles, which have enough general applicability that all catalogers will want to keep them in mind, include:

1. The authentic name of ethnic, national, religious, social, or sexual groups should be established if such a name is determinable. If a group does not have an authentic name, the name preferred by the group should be established. The determination of the preferred or authentic name should be based upon the literature of the people themselves (not upon outside sources or experts), upon organizational self-identification, and/or upon group member experts.

2. In establishing subdivisions for use with the names of people or peoples, consider the connotation, in addition to the denotation, of the wording and structure of the subdivision. Avoid words which connote inferiority or peculiarity. In establishing subdivisions for concepts applicable to all

classes of people, avoid variations in the structure of the subdivision under certain people or peoples. Avoid American/Western European ethnocentrism. Avoid value-loaded words; aim for neutrality.

3. The wording and structure of headings for minority or other groups should not differ from headings for the majority. Avoid all *as* and *in* constructions to describe practitioners of an activity.

4. Be specific and current. Do not use previously established terms to cover new topics.

5. Do not use subsuming terminology. Do not establish headings for some, but not all, classes of people or peoples.

6. Do not allow huge files of undifferentiated cards to accumulate under a heading. One inch of cards represents approximately 100 titles; it takes quite some time and patience on the part of a user to examine that many titles in order to select those wanted.

In the introduction to her thesaurus, Marshall provides detailed explanations of each principle and elaborates with numerous examples.

At Hennepin County Public Library, extensive local cataloging has dramatically increased the number of access points to a wide range of information and altered the classification to encourage serendipitous discovery through browsing. In *The Joy of Cataloging,* Berman offers the following guidelines to catalogers interested in improving access:

1. Make added entries for sponsoring, producing, or otherwise closely associated presses, groups, and agencies; and, for informational purposes, provide *public* notes in the catalog that briefly identify such producers and organizations.

2. Make added entries for subtitles and catch-titles that catalog users may remember and seek.

3. Impose no upper limit on subject tracings, applying as many as necessary to substantially and accurately reflect the content of each work.

4. Assign subject tracings to novels, short stories, poetry, and other literary genres on the same basis as subject tracings are assigned to nonfiction.

5. Reform biased, imprecise, clumsy, or antique subject descriptors that misrepresent, defame, or obscure the topics they ostensibly denote.

6. Establish new descriptors to represent subjects not currently "legitimized" nor recognized in the LC thesaurus.

7. Compose notes to clarify contents, indicate special features, and show relationships to other works, persons, or groups.

8. Extend classification notation when too much material falls under a single, over-crowded number to avoid intermixing disparate books and other media.

Clack discusses specificity as it relates to subject headings assigned to black literature resources, and defines and provides examples of six levels of heading adequacy.[23] Almost a decade ago, Pauline Cochrane completed the Subject Access Project (SAP). This project involved the creation of a database in which about 30 terms carefully selected from a book's index and table of contents were added to each Machine Readable Cataloging (MARC) record. Use of the database demonstrated that adding "inherent attributes of a publication . . . [that is,] those attributes which essentially are provided by the author or publisher, instead of so called 'assigned' attributes which are added by librarians,"[24] increased the number of relevant documents found and decreased the search time per useful document.[25] An explanation of an efficient method for selecting descriptive terms from indexes and tables of contents can be found in Cochrane's report of the Subject Access Project.[26]

References

1. Carol Hole, "Who Me, Censor?," *Top of the News* 40 (Winter 1984): 147–53.
2. John C. Swan, "Librarianship Is Censorship," *Library Journal* 104 (October 1979): 2040–43.
3. Tony Ficociello, "Censorship, Book Selection, and the Marketplace of Ideas," *Top of the News* 41 (Fall 1984): 33–39.
4. Dorothy M. Broderick, "I May, I Might, I Must," in *Book Selection and Censorship in the Sixties,* ed. Eric Moon (New York: R. R. Bowker, 1969), pp. 28–32.
5. Lester Asheim, "The Librarian's Responsibility: Not Censorship But Selection," in *Freedom of Book Selection,* ed. F. Mosher (Chicago: American Library Assn., 1954), pp. 95–96.
6. Lester Asheim, "Selection and Censorship: A Reappraisal," *Wilson Library Bulletin* 58 (November 1983): 180–84.
7. LeRoy C. Merritt, *Book Selection and Intellectual Freedom* (New York: Wilson, 1970), pp. 32–54.
8. Ronald A. Landor, "The Fallacy of 'Balance' in Public Library Book Selection," in *Book Selection and Censorship in the Sixties,* ed. Eric Moon (New York: R. R. Bowker, 1969): 37–40.
9. Asheim, "Selection and Censorship: A Reappraisal."
10. Sheila S. Intner, "Censorship in Indexing," *The Indexer* 14 (October 1984): 105–08.
11. Sanford Berman, *Prejudices and Antipathies: Tract on the LC Subject Headings Concerning People* (Metuchen, N.J.: Scarecrow, 1971); Sanford Berman, *Joy of Cataloging: Essays, Letters, Reviews, and Other Explosions* (Phoenix: Oryx Press, 1981); Sanford Berman, "Cataloging for Public Libraries," in *The Nature and Future of the Catalog,* ed. M. J. Freedman and S. M. Malinconico (Phoenix: Oryx Press, 1979): 225–39.
12. Joan K. Marshall, *On Equal Terms: A Thesaurus for Nonsexist Indexing and Cataloging* (New York: Neal-Schuman Publishers, 1977).
13. Jessica L. M. Harris and D. H. Clack, "Treatment of People and Peoples in Subject Analysis," *Library Resources & Technical Services* 23 (Fall 1979): 374–90.
14. K. W. Russell, ed., *Subject Access: Report of a Meeting Sponsored by the*

Council on Library Resources, Dublin, Ohio, June 7–9, 1982 (Washington, D.C.: Council on Library Resources, 1982).

15. Pauline A. Cochrane, "Modern Subject Access in the Online Age," *American Libraries* 15 (February-July/August 1984): 80–83, 145–50, 250–55, 336–39, 438–43, 527–29.

16. Charles R. McClure, "Subject and Added Entries As Access to Information," *Journal of Academic Librarianship* 2 (March 1976): 9–14.

17. Neal K. Kaske and Nancy P. Sanders, "On-Line Subject Access: the Human Side of the Problem," *RQ* 20 (Fall 1980): 52–58.

18. Mary D. Pietris and Lucia J. Rather, "Comments from the Library of Congress," in "Modern Subject Access in the Online Age," ed. Pauline A. Cochrane, *American Libraries* (May 1984): 336–39.

19. Carol A. Mandel and Judith Herschman, "Online Subject Access—Enhancing the Library Catalog," *Journal of Academic Librarianship* 9 (July 1983): 148–55.

20. See Cochrane, "Modern Subject Access in the Online Age," and Carol A. Mandel, "Enriching the Library Catalog Record for Subject Access," *Library Resources & Technical Services* 29 (January-March 1985): 5–15.

21. Stephen E. Wiberley, Jr., "Reducing Search Results a High Priority," in "Modern Subject Access in the Online Age," ed. Pauline A. Cochrane, *American Libraries* (April 1984): 250–55.

22. Gunnar Knutson, "Access Points and Book Use: Does the Catalog Record Make a Difference?" Paper presented at the 1986 Association of College and Research Libraries meeting in Baltimore.

23. Doris H. Clack, "The Adequacy of Library of Congress Subject Headings for Black Literature Resources," *Library Resources & Technical Services* 22 (Spring 1978): 137–44.

24. Irene Wormell, "SAP—A New Way to Produce Subject Descriptions of Books," *Journal of Information Science Principles & Practice* 3 (February 1981): 39–43.

25. Mandel and Herschman, "Online Subject Access. . . ."

26. Pauline A. Cochrane, *Books Are for Use: Final Report of the Subject Access Project to the Council on Library Resources* (Syracuse, NY: Syracuse University School of Information Studies, 1978).

Collection Development

Jerry Pennington

The future of the small public library is expanding. Social trends and changing technology could increase further the need and importance of the small library collection. Increased pressure upon individuals for use of their time, emerging patterns of families in which both parents work full-time, and families with one single parent can make the neighborhood library more important in the future. And, as the world grows smaller through improved communication and technology, the small neighborhood library can provide an improved access point for the informational needs of a community. In fact, there already is evidence of an increased use of community libraries, probably spurred by greater interest in—and need for—technical information, consumer information, cultural heritage, and recreational reading.

Using output measures to indicate success of public libraries challenges the assumption that bigger is better. For collections smaller than 50,000 items, it is common to observe a clear increase in use as volumes are added. For collections greater than 100,000 items, the increase in circulation is significantly less by comparison. While it is no longer considered valid to compare circulation, volumes, and expenditures of one library with another without clearly understanding the communities and the goals of the individual libraries, some small public libraries can exceed two volumes per capita, a periodical title per 10 people, circulation of 1.5 per volume, circulation of 5 per capita, or patron visits of 3 per capita. These are listed as a measure of quality, not as a standard. Since individual items of a collection of 50,000 or less will be used more heavily than items in collections of 100,000 or greater, the selection of items in a small collection is important to the library's success.

GENERAL GUIDELINES

Collection development requires careful planning. Just as a careful shopper would not do the marketing without a shopping list and some

Jerry Pennington is at the Appleton Public Library, Appleton, Wisconsin.

planning before buying, a selector for library materials should never buy from a review journal until careful planning has been made. Economic realities demand that librarians spend wisely and not shop for books without a shopping list. Principles of librarianship demand that library employees understand the needs of users and of a specific collection, and the desired additions to the collection.

While the small library may not develop collections with relative strengths compared to identical areas in larger collections, areas of emphasis have to be established, determined in part by the community's needs and how those needs are being met. The librarian should maintain a profile of the existing collection, write and have approved a selection policy guarding against censorship, and have a clear understanding of the role of newsprint, periodicals, and nonprint media in meeting collection goals.

Selection of library materials should be made according to the requests of present library users and in order to broaden the base of information for those users according to anticipated need—as well as to attract those not using the library. If the library has limited funds, and the collection is not enormous in size—as is true in most small libraries—the librarian may well hesitate before attempting to build a well-rounded collection at the expense of not meeting present demand. This conflict must be addressed to determine the level of demand that will be met and the depth of the collection that will be maintained.

Another set of principles is concerned more with the quality of the books selected than the group who will use them. Will some standard of excellence be applied in selection, or will anything requested be purchased? Librarians committed to the view that materials acquired should meet high standards of quality in content and format would emphasize authoritativeness, factual accuracy, effective expression, significance of subject, sincerity of purpose, and responsibility of opinion. These librarians might resist buying a book which fails to meet these standards, even if the book were in heavy demand. The opposing view would not hesitate to purchase a mediocre book which will be read in preference to a superior book that will not. Facts seem to indicate that two libraries of similar size and environment can be two very different institutions, reflecting choices of selection and services.

The collection development process is a collective process that uses the expertise of as many individuals as possible. In the small library, this usually includes most employees. A growing trend is to enlist the expertise of individuals from neighboring libraries. This process provides the mechanism for stronger collections but requires greater coordination.

FREEDOM OF SPEECH AND ACCESS TO COLLECTIONS

It is important for librarians to study the issue of the right to read before conflict arises so that they can best express themselves to the public. During times of nonconflict, librarians should continually endeavor to raise citizen consciousness about freedom of speech and the right to read; in times of conflict, it is difficult to change anyone's ideas.

Some matters to consider include: 1) The necessity to assist citizens in understanding that if they wish to have their rights respected, they must respect the rights of those who hold opposing views; 2) Since the media are usually privately owned and edited, public libraries have increased responsibility for the protection of freedom of expression and the freedom to read; 3) Good librarians leave their personal values outside the library and select and circulate materials without regard to library employees' personal views on issues; 4) Actions that are illegal when exercised are not illegal when read.

No goal of the public library provides more interesting discussion than a study of "recreational" reading. A film or a book that does nothing more than delight a viewer/reader is sometimes deemed less worthy than those materials which address crisis concerns of the time. Recreational reading is sometimes made to seem less important than nonfiction. Novels are lumped together, ignoring differences among the writings of James Baldwin, Barbara Cartland, A. J. Cronin, Stephen King, Norah Lofts, Arthur Mailing, Jean Plaidy, Mary Stewart, Irving Stone, Leo Tolstoy, and Morris L. West. Judging the importance of content by the medium is a mark of an untrained librarian. If librarians accept the idea that tax-supported libraries provide the views of society today and yesterday, popular and unpopular expressions of those views will be seen as appropriate and necessary. Throughout history, fiction has shared with nonfiction the role of presenting ideas in the expression of different points of view. Recreational reading is an important part of a public library collection.

Questions of access to information have special importance today since increased skills are needed to participate effectively in the economy. The nation's basic policies and institutions for disseminating information were formed in an era of the printed page. Today the printed book shares the responsibility for dissemination of information with the television screen, the computer terminal, the microfilm reader, satellites, and elaborate communication systems. These information media are managed by large institutions, controlled by elaborate laws and regulations, operated by complex technologies, and guided by varying and sometimes contradictory public policies that do not always promote the widest accessibility of information, but rather lead to limitations and constraint.

Public libraries have always collected nonbook material—pamphlets, maps, periodicals, and clippings. Over the last three decades, nonbook has come to include phonodiscs, films, artwork, audiotapes, microfiche, video, and computer software and hardware. The major problems involved in collecting nonbook materials occur in financing, selecting, and administering the collections. Some librarians have boggled at the tasks involved in checking film for damage; splicing broken film; operating projectors; cataloging, storing and preserving records; and purchasing equipment. These difficulties must not weaken the resolve to purchase information, regardless of media or format.

COLLECTION STUDIES

Collection analysis employs varying methodology to determine use patterns and to anticipate growth. Although such studies have not been used extensively within the community of small libraries, much can be learned from studies completed by larger libraries.

Most collection studies develop profiles of existing collections; evaluate use of the existing collection, including circulation and inhouse use; study users and their needs; evaluate interloan use by area; and show the relationships of these studies to each other. A large part of these tasks includes statistical gathering, which requires professional decisions in the interpretation and combining of statistical areas. And adequate staff time is required to collect, arrange, and interpret data.

Profiles of existing collections should be developed for as many parts of the collection as possible, dividing broad areas such as history into many areas. Circulation statistics are the most important, but other aspects of the collection, for instance copyright date, can be used to determine use of older materials. For example, if an area has five titles and the oldest title circulated four times in a given period, a decision can be made about the need for additional materials in that area. The process is extremely labor intensive, but rewards are great. Ideally, the collection profile for an area should be done by the individual responsible for developing that collection. But one individual should coordinate all the profiles so that the process is coordinated and the results recorded properly.

User studies are a part of the profiles but go beyond to include information about unanswered questions, searching for materials not found in the collection (including lost or unavailable), and special interests. User studies (body counts) have traditionally been considered the most clerical of the studies; they should be the most professional. By having users respond to a questionnaire about areas of interest, and their ability to satisfy that interest, important information will be gained.

No single area has been more often overlooked in gathering information about library use than interlibrary loan statistics, yet few areas offer greater information about an individual collection. Continuing interlibrary loan requests for material in a specific area are a profound indication of the need for collection development.

Another useful tool for determining depth in a collection area is the use of citation indexing. Using bibliographies and citations from journal articles for a specific area, the librarian can determine the ownership of these materials within the collection. If authors consistently cite books that are not present in the collection, the need for expanding the material in that area becomes evident. This process, which is not an integral part of user profiles and interlibrary loan studies, requires untiring effort, but provides a system of checks-and-balances for use against the result of these studies.

SELECTION TOOLS

Librarians depend upon certain selection tools for reviews and information about new titles, print and nonprint. Studies have revealed that most reviews tend to be favorable, perhaps because only those books considered worthwhile are chosen for review. And, many books in the total publishing output are not reviewed. It should be remembered that the reviewer is not thinking of an individual library collection; the need to balance current and retrospective collection development should be kept in mind.

Some basic selection/review tools are:

Library Journal. New York, Bowker, 1876– (Semi-monthly, 20 issues).

The book review section is arranged by broad subject areas, containing signed reviews written by librarians and educators, giving practical evaluations, both negative and positive, of current titles. Many of the reviews appear prior to the date of publication. Approximately 4,500 adult books are reviewed annually. Special features include spring and fall announcement issues and special issues on business (including "Best Business Books"), technical, medical, and scientific books, reference books ("Best Reference Books"), small presses, and AV materials. A Reviews-on-Cards service supplies reviews reprinted from every issue on 3x5 cards.

School Library Journal. New York, Bowker, 1947– (Monthly, 10 issues).

Supplies review coverage of juvenile books similar to that given adult books in *Library Journal*. Total number of signed reviews appearing in a year usually exceeds that of any other single reviewing service covering books published for children and young adults. Special features include semiannual "best books" lists. Also offers a Reviews-on-Cards service.

New York Times Book Review, 1896– (Weekly).

This is published weekly as part of the Sunday edition, but is also available as a separate subscription. Daily editions also carry reviews of books, but not by the Book Review staff. Also includes information reviews, some written by authorities in the subject field, others written by staff members. Has an annual "Best Books of the Year" feature.

Booklist. Chicago, American Library Association, 1905– (Semimonthly).

Each issue contains longer reviews of 10 to 20 reference books (prepared by ALA's Reference and Subscription Books Review Committee), 100 to 130 shorter reviews of adult fiction and nonfiction, as well as books for children and young adults, films and other nonbook media, and selected government publications. All items listed are recommended for library purchase and are intended to represent the best judgment of library subject specialists, who are familiar with the new books in their respective fields.

Horn Book Magazine. Boston, 1924– (Bi-monthly).

Provides detailed, signed reviews of children's books and audiovisuals, along with many articles by and about authors and illustrators.

Invaluable though they may be to the selection process, extensive reliance on a few general review sources can stifle opportunities for creative collection development. The small library may be able to subscribe to only a small percentage of the book review media, but a wide range of collection development aids is available at no additional cost through publications which the library already acquires for general interest purposes, for instance, *Art News, Poetry Magazine, The New Yorker,* and *The Nation.* These are not primarily review journals, but the reviews included are of particular value because they represent the perspectives of leaders in a given field.

Other tools which might be used if funding is available include:

Publishers Weekly. New York, Bowker, 1872– (Weekly).

A standard American book trade journal, carrying "forecasts," a section of descriptive annotations of nonfiction, fiction, children's books, and paperbacks (originals and reprints) to be published. *PW* also has special issues on children's books, religious books, etc.

Bulletin of the Center for Children's Books. University of Chicago, 1947– (Monthly).

Each issue contains 60 to 80 reviews of current trade books for children and early teens. Unsigned reviews by specialists are critical, and grade levels, reading level difficulty, and literary quality are always evaluated. The *Bulletin* is noted for its coding system and reviews of not recommended titles.

Book Review Digest. New York, Wilson, 1905– .

Recent books published or distributed in the U.S. may have reviews cited here if enough reviews (generally, two or more for nonfiction and four or more for fiction) appear in selected periodicals within 18 months after publication of the book. Coverage per year now runs around 6,000 titles. Each book is entered under author, with full bibliographic data, followed by a brief descriptive note.

A visit to a larger library periodically could give access to:

Kirkus Reviews. New York, Kirkus Service, 1933– (Semi-monthly).

Informal and informative reviews of books including children's books, with particular emphasis on coverage of fiction, appear about six weeks before date of publication. This is a feature which many librarians have found very useful since they can order and receive books by the time they are published and before reviews for them appear in the general reviewing media, leading to a demand by patrons for the books.

Choice. Chicago, American Library Association, Association of College and Research Libraries, 1964– (Monthly).

Evaluates current books of a scholarly or academic nature considered to be of interest to an undergraduate library. Signed reviews of about 500 to 600 titles are provided in each issue. These are prepared by the editor and a large roster of subject specialists. Although intended to assist in the selection of books for college libraries, this tool is useful in public, junior college, secondary school, special, and foreign libraries. Special features include the "Opening Day Collection" which began in July 1965 and is now in its third edition (separately published in 1974) and regular subject-centered bibliographic articles. There is also a "reviews-on-card" service supplying the reviews reprinted individually on 3x5 cards.

Tools for retrospective collecting are:

Books for Public Libraries. 3d ed. Chicago, American Library Association, 1981. 374p.

This is an unannotated Dewey Decimal arrangement of recommended titles. Includes an author-title index.

Children's Catalog. New York, Wilson, 1909– .

The fourteenth edition of this work appeared in 1980, containing over 5,000 titles selected for their usefulness in school libraries and public library work with children. The book is arranged in classified order and supplemented annually, adding approximately 600 titles per year. Each entry gives full bibliographic data, including subject headings and aids to cataloging, with an evaluative annotation quoted from reviews.

Fiction Catalog. New York, Wilson 1908– .

A guide to adult fiction found most useful in public libraries, this is published periodically, with an annual supplement. The tenth edition, containing more than 5,000 titles in the basic volume, with 2,000 more covered in the four annual supplements, was published in 1980. Arrangement is alphabetical by author, with full bibliographic information and annotations.

Public Library Catalog. New York, Wilson, 1934– .

The seventh edition of this work was published in 1978. It is a selected, classified list of over 8,500 nonfiction titles which have been suggested because of their usefulness in public library collections. Annual supplements update the work with approximately 3,200 additional titles.

Elementary School Library Collection. Greensboro, N.C., Dart Foundation, 1965– .

The fourteenth edition of this regularly updated tool appeared in 1984 and included more than 10,000 recommended books, periodicals, filmstrips, transparencies, etc. Annotations are included and indications of which titles are considered most basic to a beginning collection.

Junior High School Library Catalog. New York, Wilson, 1965– .

The 1980 edition includes 3,775 titles selected for grades seven through nine. Annual supplements add approximately 500 titles each year.

Senior High School Library Catalog. New York, Wilson, 1926– .

Formerly the *Standard Catalog for High School Libraries,* this list emphasizes material for students in the tenth through twelfth grades. The twelfth edition, published in 1982, includes over 5,000 titles.

Other specialized tools include:

Katz, William. *Introduction to Reference Works.* 2 vols. 5th ed. New York, McGraw-Hill, 1987.

Provides comprehensive reference selection sources, as well as reference works.

Wynar, Christine L. *Guide to Reference Books for School Media Centers.* Littleton, Colo., Libraries Unlimited, 1981. 377p.

Annotates more than 3,000 titles. Selections are chosen on the basis of suitability for grades K-12 and junior college.

Katz, William and Linda Sternberg Katz. *Magazines for Libraries*. 5th ed. New York, Bowker, 1986. 1,057p.

This is an annotated list of approximately 6,500 periodicals considered suitable for the general reader. Comments on the value of each periodical for a particular type of library are usually included. Updated regularly.

VERIFICATION

Suggestions for selection may originate from staff and users. Titles selected from standard library review periodicals will most always have pertinent order information including the author's name, title, publisher, edition, series, and International Standard Book or Serial Number (ISBN or ISSN). Requests from patrons may be less complete. In searching a trade publication, *Books in Print, Cumulative Book Index,* or *Publisher's Trade List Annual* are most helpful in establishing clear order information.

CHOOSING THE DEALER

Choosing a dealer is second in importance to the selection of the books themselves. Libraries have three primary sources to purchase current books: publishers, bookstores, and wholesalers (also called jobbers). Factors to consider in deciding where it is most advantageous to buy include: discount, speed, billing, and accuracy in filling orders and promptness in correcting mistakes. These factors do not always reside in any one of the three sources. In some cases, speed may be more important than discount; accounting procedures may take precedence; accuracy may be more important than speed or cost. A given library might, therefore, order from all three sources, although this greatly increases the paperwork. Savings effected by shopping around and placing smaller orders at more favorable discounts may well be swallowed up by increased bookkeeping costs. Where speed in acquiring a title is the primary consideration, nothing could be faster than walking across the street to the local bookstore and picking the book off the shelf. But as the library moves out of the area of currently popular titles, success in finding the less popular items in the stock of the ordinary bookstore diminishes.

Wholesalers receive a sizable percentage of library orders. The advantage of dealing with the wholesaler is clear: the librarian places one order, receives one package, pays one bill, and has only one person to deal with on service problems. The services offered to libraries by wholesalers have steadily expanded: special catalogs and lists have been compiled; prebound books will be supplied; and notification on the status of a book is made quickly.

A sampling of library jobbers includes:

BAKER & TAYLOR COMPANY
652 E. Main St.
Bridgewater, NJ 08807

BLACKWELL NORTH AMERICA
1001 Fries Mill Rd.
Blackwood, NJ 08012

BRODART COMPANY
500 Arch St.
Williamsport, PA 17705

F.W. FAXON COMPANY
15 Southwest Park
Westwood, MA 02090

FOLLET COLLEGE BOOK CO.
1000 W. Washington Blvd.
Chicago, IL 60607

KEY BOOK SERVICE
425 Asylum St.
Bridgeport, CT 06610

MIDWEST LIBRARY SERVICE
11443 St. Charles Rock Rd.
Bridgeton, MO 63044

SCHOOL BOOK SERVICE CO.
2030 SW 71st Terrace Bay C9
Davie, FL 33317

TAYLOR-CARLISLE BOOK CO.
245 Seventh Ave.
New York, NY 10001

YANKEE BOOK PEDDLER
Maple St.
Contoocook, NH 03229

Periodicals

Al Tweedy

Periodicals and serials are materials that must be considered by looking at the various users of different types of libraries. To a great extent, users and library budgets determine the types and number of periodicals a library will buy.

PUBLIC LIBRARIES

In very small public libraries, periodical use is almost entirely recreational. Limited library resources in terms of both funds to purchase periodicals and number of hours open usually preclude the use of the library for anything but the most basic research by the public, including students. In a way, this places the least number of restrictions on what is subscribed to and leaves the most room for selection. However, if the librarian is looking to the future and expects to expand at some later date, starting to subscribe to and store the most used research magazines such as *Time* and *Newsweek* (which your patrons will enjoy anyway) is a wise step.

Periodical purchases should fit the library's users—be they farmers, predominately of one race or ethnic group, housewives, or workers in a particular industry; their needs, not what the librarian wishes their needs were, must be met. A regional magazine from the area and/or the periodical from a large city nearby will be used by library patrons who shop there. If the library's budget is very small, an arrangement could be made with some library users to subscribe to selected periodicals which they would donate to the library once finished with them. Entering into such an arrangement should be determined by the usefulness of the material to the library.

Most small public libraries are open enough days and hours to serve not only the adult and preschool needs of the public, but also some of the reference needs of adults and students in the community. Of continued debate is whether public libraries should spend their limited resources

Al Tweedy is at the Springfield-Greene County Library District, Springfield, Missouri.

to serve the needs of students in their community, but like it or not, most do.

Selection Tools

When the library reaches this plateau of service, it is faced with two distinct groups of periodical users with very different needs. Both need reference or research help and both depend on indexes to locate information. What does the librarian collect? Only those periodicals that are indexed? Having a magazine that is indexed is more valuable and a better use of limited funds than one which is not indexed, at least for the group of users doing research. Indexed periodicals are not as important for recreational users. They read magazines to "keep up with things" or "to see what's new," and seldom need or want to go back to previous issues.

There are two basic guides which annotate and indicate the quality of periodicals. Linda and Bill Katz's *Magazines for Libraries, 5th ed.* (New York: R. R. Bowker, 1986), is an annotated listing of over 6,500 periodicals arranged within some 130 subject headings. Each section is prepared by an expert in the field and is preceded by a select list of titles for that subject. It is to this list that the librarian should turn first.

The second guide, Linda and Bill Katz's *Magazines for School Libraries* (New York: R. R. Bowker, 1987) is a "spinoff" of the first title. It is limited to about 1,400 magazines suitable for consideration by school libraries, but most of the titles will be of equal interest to those in small public libraries as well.

In addition to these two sources, current information on new periodicals can be found in the "Magazine" column, edited by Bill Katz, in *Library Journal,* and in *Choice*'s monthly column on new titles for academic libraries. For keeping track of serials—and guidance in selecting them—refer to *Serials for Libraries: An Annotated Guide to Continuations, Annuals, Yearbooks, Almanacs, Transactions, Proceedings, Directories, Services* (New York: Neal-Schuman Publishers, 1985).

The librarian has to make far-reaching and long-range decisions about whether or not to circulate magazines, and if so, which ones. Some patrons will only use the magazine collection if they can take the magazines home. This presents the interesting problem of formulating a policy which preserves the back issues needed for research and reference and still allows sufficient circulation of magazines to make the time spent creating a procedure and training the staff worthwhile.

If the library circulates magazines, it can count on losing some issues. A good source for missing issues is the Friends of the Library book sale. If the community is in the habit of bringing donations, magazines are standard fare. The library should take whatever magazines it can get and fill in the missing back issues.

Since periodicals are expensive, someone on the library board is almost certain to question the amount of money spent on them in comparison to the amount spent on books. Be prepared to defend this area of public usage with facts and figures by keeping records of use, including back issues. Keep the figures for magazine circulation separate from book circulation so that they can be added to the back issue use for total periodical circulation.

The most difficult figures to obtain are those for inhouse use of the current magazines on display—usually the highest area of use. The most common way to compile these figures is by the procedure presented in the handbook, *Output Measures,* from the American Library Association. Although these figures are usually compiled only twice a year, they do give some indication of usage.

The one group of periodicals that probably should not circulate under any circumstances are the consumer reporting magazines. These should be treated as reference tools. But since the charts and articles are usually not more than a few pages long, copies can be made so that patrons can take the information outside the library.

Newspapers are a problem for the small library. The only ones worth retaining are those from the local town or county, but keeping them means that they will be looked on as reference and research sources. However, there will almost certainly be no index to them. The answer may lie in selecting a certain number of general topics (births, deaths, schools, the library, city and county governments, business, and industries), buying two copies of the local paper (some articles will appear back to back), and having the circulation staff, when they are not busy, or volunteers, to clip the articles in these few areas.

A further problem arises—storage. Even if the newspaper clippings are stored in acid free folders in as cool a place as possible, their shelf life is only a few years. Given this fact, the librarian must weigh the usefulness of this service against the time it takes to remove the articles and file them.

SCHOOL LIBRARIES

Periodicals in school libraries exist to support the curriculum. Small school libraries are tied to Wilson's *Abridged Readers' Guide to Periodical Literature,* although many are hard pressed to afford all of the magazines in this abbreviated index, in addition to purchasing a few education magazines for the teachers and a local newspaper or two. However, with the advent of several groups that index regional publications, the possibility may present itself to widen the collection's scope a bit, probably at the expense of some of the *ARGTPL* titles. If this kind of index is available in the library's area, funds should be sought to take advantage of it. Many titles can be used for course work and it will provide diversity.

If the budget is a little fat, the librarian should try to provide a title or two in areas of interest or hobbies that the kids themselves may not be able to afford. Model airplanes or cars, hairdos, TV and movie stars, hot rods, or other areas of interest are possibilities. Titles should be selected to reflect students' interests rather than to meet school assignments. These titles are an extra, however; supporting school assignments is the first priority.

Serials in school libraries, like public libraries, are for the most part attached to the reference needs of the library. However, if the library is really strapped, and unless it orders books on interlibrary loan, there may be less need for *Books in Print* than at a public library.

SMALL COLLEGE LIBRARIES

Like the school library, the small college library ties its selection of periodicals and serials to the curriculum offered by the college. But where the school library should cover the needs of the assignments given by the teachers, the small college almost always "must" meet these needs. College students rely on periodicals for the most current findings and discoveries in all fields. They also rely on them for a diversity of subjects that are not of sufficient length to have a book published about them. Therefore, college libraries are tied closely to indexes because of the wider range of information sought and the fact that this diversity simply is not covered in any other media.

The average small college library does have a greater budget line to meet these needs. This greater funding also allows it to at least consider supplementing paper indexes with electronic ones. Although online services can provide bibliographies of magazine articles on given subjects as well as book titles, the introduction of CD-ROM (Compact Disk—Read Only Memory) into the marketplace is placing electronic indexes of periodicals at the library's disposal—for a price.

The CD-ROM index is not only helpful to the librarian (updates do not need to be cataloged), but the students really seem to like using the units. A unit can be obtained with a bank of microfilms of the periodicals it indexes; by merely inserting the proper cartridge, the student can obtain a copy of the article without the library staff having to retrieve the magazine. Since the cartridge will not work anywhere else, it should also cut down on theft. This means that any article desired by a student from that index will be available when they want it. A real plus.

On the negative side is the fact that only one person can use this index at a time, and the cost of such a system is as much as $15,000. When evaluating its cost effectiveness, it is important to include the cost of staff time to retrieve and replace the periodical if those shelves are closed, or the cost of replacing missing or mutilated issues if the shelves are kept open for browsing. Always having the article when it is needed is an intangible, but it should be figured in. The positive reception of the students cannot be measured in dollars and cents, but it is a valuable part of the equation nevertheless.

In the college library, as in the other libraries, the bulk of serials is in the reference area. However, the findings of learned societies, various other annuals, plus the odd series which is to be a set of volumes published over a period of several years are important additions to the collection.

Some annual or biannual reports can be placed on standing order; those that cannot must have a system that triggers an order at the proper time. This can be done with a card file divided into months, or a personal computer that can print out, by the month, those items to be ordered. If the serial cannot be placed on standing order or subscribed to, but is not an annual either, a list should be checked against *Books in Print* each time a new edition appears.

SPECIAL LIBRARIES

Whereas college libraries *can* make use of electronic indexes and databases, in special libraries it is almost a necessity. The present is dominated by online databases; the future lies in CD-ROM. Usually the needs of these users are so specialized that only the most general of specialized periodicals are carried inhouse. Currently, it is probably cheaper to access and retrieve articles online, especially if full text is available in that form. CD-ROM has the potential for providing indexing to a vast amount of knowledge, such as Medline provides.

Although these services are expensive, and promise to continue being so, most special libraries have little choice but to move in this direction. The librarian must become aware of what is on the market, keep abreast of new developments, and be prepared to demonstrate the impossibility of maintaining sufficient materials to answer the specialized needs of his or her clientele. The costs involved in the electronic indexes can be justified as the only means of meeting the needs of the users, and thus the company or institution in general.

Some serials can already be accessed online, and will eventually be available on disk. The need to present findings to users in a timely fashion will become ongoing, rather than an annual process, and many serials, especially in the business and scientific areas, will slowly be phased out. Because of the rapidity with which these areas are changing, one-a-year information will be out of date before it is presented. This will force many learned societies to become clearinghouses for online services.

ORDERING PERIODICALS

In ordering periodicals, the library, no matter how small, will be time and money ahead by using a jobber. The two largest companies are Faxon and Ebsco, but small, local jobbers should not be overlooked. A jobber should be selected on the basis of who will do the best job, not who is the biggest. Personal service and a willingness to follow up on problems by phone with the vendor, not just spit out notices to them, are important attributes in a jobber.

Most libraries can benefit from being part of a network. Small public and school libraries benefit from access to monographs, serials, periodicals, equipment, expertise, and staff which usually they cannot afford individually. College libraries benefit from generalized monographs and serials which do not directly support their curriculum but are useful in research papers. If the network offers automation services, the librarian should request that periodical circulation be kept separate. This information will be needed to support periodical purchases. Joining a mixed network of school, public, and other libraries makes increased services to users possible. Once the library joins a network it should not be afraid to use it.

Local Materials and Donations

Al Tweedy

Since in smaller localities, the local library may be the only place where a safe and sheltered environment can be provided for local literary and historical materials, it does become the logical place for people to bring their requests to accept materials about the community and bequests.

The librarian can be prepared to deal with these requests and bequests by planning—through discussions with the board of trustees or administration—what the library policy will be. You will have to consider where the materials are to be stored, how much room is available, the types of materials to be accepted, and the costs involved (staff time, acid free containers, etc.).

In addition to the materials which you may feel are of value to the collection or may enhance service to patrons or students, the question of who is doing the giving will have to be weighed. Since politics are often involved in gifts, the responsibility for the decision should be shared with the library's board or administrator.

The types of materials that may be offered are various: books by a local author, or by the author's family who live locally even though the author lives elsewhere; books that are quite old or are first editions; sets of books collected by a local person either on a specific subject or that are "just a collection"; photographs of historic interest locally; local high school and college yearbooks; back issues of local or regional magazines or newspapers; local memorabilia; and scrapbooks containing newspaper clippings.

BOOKS BY A LOCAL AUTHOR

This is probably the most important type of material to keep, and is one area in book selection that the librarian will be able to acquire

Al Tweedy is at the Springfield-Greene County Library District, Springfield, Missouri.

indiscriminately. Information about local authors is usually the first information passed on to a librarian new to the community. The librarian who has lived in the community all his or her life knows how proud people are of these authors and is probably proud of them too.

All books by local authors—regardless of their quality or value to the collection—should be available in the library. You may find that some have to be kept in the librarian's office or another secure area so that they do not "walk off." Also, be aware of attempted censorship if the author is not politically popular. Books by a person who grew up in the community but no longer lives there should also be given strong consideration. Again, the pride of the community is involved, which is a legitimate reason to acquire the books. This philosophy should be stated in the book selection policy.

OLD BOOKS

Old books not of local interest and not suitable for the collection, are, along with old periodicals, likely to be pressed upon the library at some point. The least desirable of gifts, they are possibly the most politically volatile items to be received. If there is space in the library, first editions or books that might be sold could be culled from the donations, to be appraised later. Those items which are sufficiently valuable can then be given space.

In screening a donation, there is one cardinal rule to remember: If it is not in "like new" condition, it probably has no value. The value lies only in what the library would receive if it sold the item, so what the marketplace says must become the selection criterion, regardless of the librarian's personal feelings. Although it is not too difficult to acquire the expertise to do the original screening, since books of "like new" quality and of sufficient value are few and far between, unless there is a good deal of room for all the library's other materials, a collection of old books is probably best avoided.

SETS OF BOOKS

Decisions to keep sizable donations of books on a specific subject are best shared with the library board or supervisor since, again, a significant amount of space and sometimes a politically sensitive reply are involved. This type of collection should be kept only if it meets the following criteria: 1) Is the material of sufficient value and current enough that it would add to the collection? 2) Are the books in good enough condition to hold up under library use? 3) Are there any special stipulations that come with the books (e.g., they must be placed together in a separate area; the collection must be given a special name)?

The main consideration in estimating the value of the books to the small library collection is the currency of the information. For instance, a collection of turn-of-the-century religious books is unlikely to be of value to a small library. The donor may have an elevated estimate of its worth and politically it may be difficult to turn down the offer, but everything should be done, tactfully of course, to see that it is not accepted.

Confronted with a collection of books of marginal value to the library but in good shape, the librarian must question whether they are worth the cost of cataloging; given a collection not in great shape, its value must be weighed not only against the cost of cataloging, but also the cost of rebinding. Books in a "collection" not on a specific subject are usually of even less value—especially if any stipulations are attached—and should be avoided if possible. In general, if there are any stipulations besides a bookplate for the front of the book, don't accept the item.

HISTORIC PHOTOGRAPHS

Pictures of historic interest to the community should be considered for storage, especially by the public library, but the cost of doing so must be taken into account. If the subjects are unknown, however, the items are usually of little value. Getting older people in the community to help identify the pictures could be the basis for a program by the local historian, and could justify keeping a great many more pictures.

Preserving older photographs may require additional funds if they are deteriorating or are on glass negatives and so have to be copied onto newer materials. The state archives, or a large college archives, might provide assistance by storing the original materials and providing copies which are easier for the local library to store and maintain.

HIGH SCHOOL YEARBOOKS

Yearbooks are useful to local historians and genealogists and so are worth storing unless space is extremely limited. Whether or not to keep high school yearbooks is a decision which will vary by type of library. College and special libraries will probably not consider them and school libraries may maintain complete collections of them. Public libraries could make a case to go either way, but even if the high school has a collection, it is available only when the school is open—part of the day, and not all of the year. The public library could provide greater access.

LOCAL NEWSPAPERS

If someone brings the library a newspaper which is of such local historical importance that a decision is made to keep it in its original form, it should be encapsulated as soon as possible. The local school may have a laminating machine large enough to do the job, or the library system may be able to help. If only a small laminator is available, the item can be cut to fit the machine; if the material is valuable enough to encapsulate, it is better to preserve it in two or more pieces than to do nothing at all. If the cost to laminate an entire piece is too high, consider preserving only the first page (but photocopy the original intact).

LOCAL MEMORABILIA AND REALIA

Memorabilia is one of the most rewarding areas to collect. Here too, however, decisions on what to keep because of costs and storage must be made. But, such objects as tickets, programs, invitations and announcements, pamphlets, award ribbons, and buttons are easily stored separately in acid-free files in acid-free boxes.

SCRAPBOOKS OF NEWSPAPER CLIPPINGS

The only thing that deteriorates faster than newsprint by itself is newsprint attached to cheap acidic scrapbook paper. Since usually they cannot be separated from each other without damage to the newsprint, and it is essential that the information be kept, reproduce it on a copy machine on good quality (preferably acid-free) paper and throw the original away.

STAFF TIME, STORAGE CONSIDERATIONS, AND LIBRARY POLICY

Collecting local materials and accepting donations is possible by even the smallest of libraries, but certain things must be taken into consideration: the staff time needed to care for and catalog the materials, whether there is room on the shelves to store the materials, and security. These all are cost-driven factors; the storage is perhaps the most crucial. Storage space on the library shelf costs money in terms of lighting, heating, and cooling; cleaning; reshelving; as well as the normal library overhead of staying open. These costs can amount to $20 per linear foot, with special environmentally controlled storage units costing even more.

If there is sufficient interest on the part of the librarian and the institution's board or administration to make the commitment necessary to accept at least some donations, they can add a lot to the value of the collection, as well as interest and support for the library. But whatever decision is made, the library must have a written policy. It will make for more consistency in what materials are selected and will protect the library if challenges should ever arise.

The Vertical File Collection

Nancy M. Bolt

The vertical file collection is an inexpensive way to supplement the small library's circulating and reference collections. Vertical file material consists of pamphlets, brochures, newspaper clippings, magazine articles, pictures, and similar material. These materials are usually filed in folders and stored in a file cabinet; libraries not able to afford file cabinets sometimes use sturdy cardboard boxes.

Vertical file materials can be on any topic—and are often on narrow, specific aspects of a topic. They are particularly useful in the areas of local history, careers, health, local businesses, and consumer information. Vertical files really shine in the area of current events. Much information is published in newspapers and magazines before it ever shows up in a book, and sometimes important bits of information, like the details of local seat belt laws, never appear in books at all.

"Teasers" are often included in the vertical file to encourage people to look for more information elsewhere. A teaser might be a photocopy of the table of contents of a particularly helpful reference book. Reference librarians who have spent hours searching for citations on a topic (such as all the references in *Readers' Guide* on a particular subject) may file these in the appropriate vertical file so the same search does not need to be done again.

The library staff is a major user of the vertical file. One librarian has said that she goes to the Big 3 in a search: the card catalog, *Readers' Guide,* and then the vertical file. A carefully constructed vertical file can be the source of information not existing elsewhere and as a "last resort" after all other sources have been checked out.

Students, new adult readers, and travelers are other major users of vertical file information. Young people often look for a small amount of very specific information to complete an assignment at the last minute or to support one side of a debate topic. New adult readers find vertical file information easier to read than books. Travelers find the condensed, specific nature of travel brochures helpful in planning a trip.

Nancy M. Bolt is president of JNF Associates, Milford, Ohio.

ACQUIRING MATERIALS

Building a vertical file collection is largely a matter of keeping one's eyes open for interesting information. Materials can be found just about anywhere and much of it is free or very inexpensive, sometimes requiring only the cost of a postcard or letter. Libraries with local history vertical files clip local newspapers regularly. Magazine articles are another fruitful source since they often suggest additional places. While much of this information is also available by searching *Readers' Guide,* having it easily accessible in the vertical file saves time for both the librarian and the patron and fills a need when the magazine is missing.

Community agencies and organizations are rich sources of vertical file materials. A quick note or visit to local hospitals, service and travel agencies, and other community groups can yield a massive amount of current information. Library staff and trustees who travel should be asked to bring back whatever free information is available. Additional travel information can get found by combing directories for addresses of chambers of commerce, state tourist bureaus, and foreign embassies. Information about area histories, maps, lists of upcoming tourist events, tourist attractions, and motel/camping facilities can be requested as well by asking to be put on a permanent mailing list for new information each year.

Career information is available from professional and trade associations. A perusal of the *Encyclopedia of Associations* provides the addresses of these groups and other organizations that provide free information on a wide range of topics. Local businesses are usually quite willing to supply information about their industry and services, their annual reports, and other useful information—information frequently used by job hunters. Some libraries keep this information for five years to show industry growth or decline.

When writing for free information be sure to specify FREE to avoid an unexpected invoice later. Many librarians ask that the free information be sent with an order catalog for any materials for which there is a charge. A decision can be made later about spending the money for these items.

There are a great number of tools from which to select pamphlets. The *Vertical File Index,* the standard selection tool, is available by subscription from the H. W. Wilson Company. Arranged by subject like the other Wilson indexes, it describes some free but mostly for-a-charge publications. Some of the "pamphlets" are more in the nature of paperback books.

The federal government publishes two helpful selection guides. The *Selected U.S. Government Publications* is a smaller version of the *U.S. Monthly Catalog,* which is used primarily by larger libraries and is available by subscription. The *Selected* list is available for free. Another useful government publication is the *Consumer Information Catalog.* This Pueblo, Colorado, operation is well known for its fast-paced, tongue-in-cheek commercials. Many pamphlets included are available for free.

The professional library journals are also valuable selection tools. Both *Library Journal* and *School Library Journal* publish annotated listings of free and inexpensive materials in their "checklist" columns in each issue. The *Wilson Library Bulletin* carries a "Marketplace" column and Neal-Schuman publishes *Collection Building,* which has a column entitled "Free and Inexpensive Materials," and *Information America,* a serial published three times a year which describes the information services of 1,500 different organizations each year, and which includes an index to free and inexpensive materials.

ORGANIZING THE FILE

There are four major tasks related to managing vertical files: 1) ordering and collecting material; 2) organizing the material and assigning subject headings; 3) filing the material; and 4) keeping the material current through weeding. The task of ordering can be simplified through form letters and postcards; your staff can contribute by picking up pamphlets through their travels, visits to the doctor, errands to community agencies, etc. Just because something is free, however, does not mean that it should be included in the file. If an item is outdated when it is received, or not useful or suitable for the community, file it in the wastebasket. To be most useful, the vertical file must be lean and current.

Organizing the material and assigning subject headings is a critical task. Use a standard guide to subject headings, either *Sears* or *Library of Congress,* or the *Readers' Guide.* One possibility is to use the same subject heading guide used for the card catalog.

Whichever guide is used, it is necessary to keep track of the actual headings in the file. Most people use a separate card file with one subject heading on each card. Some librarians put the library's vertical file subject headings on a word processor for easy revision. A computerized list has the advantage of being easily duplicated for branches or other library desks. The list should include not only the subject headings chosen, but the "see" and "see also" references that refer people from one subject heading to another.

When a subject heading is assigned, it should be written on the item so that it is always filed in the same subject folder after use. If the subject heading is always put in the same place on all items, it will decrease filing time, since the filer will not have to search the document for the heading. Write the subject heading either directly on the item (using ink since pencil smudges), or put on a label that is applied to the item. Dark covers always require a label. It is also helpful to date the item to indicate when it was received and filed. This is useful information when it is time to weed. Some material will have a publication date, but this can be quite different from the date it was obtained.

The next task is filing, which requires a file cabinet or sturdy boxes, file folders (either the traditional manila or accordion files that hold more), and labels for the items and the folders. The biggest danger in filing is not keeping up with it. An item not in a folder and thus not accessible is useless.

The final critical task is weeding. Files can quickly become outdated, and it is frustrating for staff and patrons to sort through old, tattered, outdated material trying to find the relevant information. Old material also takes up space needed for new, more current information. Weeding is not only a necessity but a constant task. Reviewing one file a day or, at least, three a week on a continuing basis is an example of one schedule which ensures regular updating of the material.

There are a number of likely candidates who might manage the vertical file. Some work requires judgment—deciding what to order and what to clip from newspapers or magazines, assigning subject headings, and weeding. Other tasks which are more routine and can be done by pages or high school volunteers include sending the form letters and post cards to an assigned list and filing items once subject headings are assigned. The work requiring judgment can be done by the library director, assigned to a library staff member, or assumed by a library volunteer. Some libraries use volunteers quite successfully in this area. Managing the vertical file can be a fun task and keep a volunteer involved and dedicated. If a volunteer is assigned the responsibility, he or she needs to have a clear understanding of the kinds of material to be selected, the budget that has been assigned, the subject heading authority to be used, and guidelines for weeding.

PROMOTION AND CIRCULATION

The best way to alert people to the information in the vertical file is to put cards for each vertical file subject heading in the card catalog with the appropriate cross references, so that when people look up subjects in the card catalog, they will be led to the information in the vertical file as well. It is helpful if all library staff are aware of the vertical file and its contents and are encouraged to use it. Some vertical file material can also be used as attractive additions to displays or useful additions to bibliographies—a more subtle form of advertising their existence.

Depending on the library's circulation system, vertical file materials can be checked out using the same process as other material, or by hand. Some librarians consider vertical file materials an extension of reference and do not let them circulate; others try to maintain the integrity of the folder and check out the whole folder only. Most, however, use the vertical file collection to fill gaps when other material is checked out and will circulate individual items. If the topic is a popular one (which often happens with student assignments), some librarians limit the number of items that can be taken. To protect the items while they are being circulated—increase the chances of getting small clippings and pamphlets back—many librarians insert them into large envelopes either specially purchased for the purpose or saved from postal mailings received.

One librarian devised an innovative way to meet multiple patron requests on the same topic and build the vertical file at the same time. When a patron requested information and there was only one copy of a pamphlet left, the librarian duplicated the needed material. The item was then circulated to the patron instead of given to him or her as would have been the case if the patron had paid for the copying. When the patron returned it, the item was placed in the vertical file, thus building up multiple copies of popular items.

Nonprint Materials

Eugene T. Fischer

No other area of library service within the framework of a small public library deserves more scrutiny, thought, and planning than the collection and circulation of nonprint materials. While even large libraries have difficulty meeting the varying needs and wants of their clientele for audiorecordings and videocassettes, it is much more difficult for the small library to start and maintain successful nonprint collections, especially if there is no access to a regional library's resources.

Four factors should be considered before starting or expanding an existing nonprint collection: commitment, ability, community response, and community need.

Commitment is the determination by the director and, more especially, by the board of trustees or other governing authority that it is in the best community interest for the library to offer nonprint materials. Without a firm commitment both in policy and in the allocation of financial resources, the nonprint collection will be started and then languish—victim to disinterest and little development.

Ability is the capacity for the librarian to start, develop, and maintain the nonprint collection. The library must be sufficiently funded to support both a print and nonprint budget year after year: space will be needed to house the new collection; equipment will have to be purchased to check the materials, circulate, and, in some cases, repair and clean them; and personnel will have to be trained in acquisition, circulation, and maintenance procedures.

Community response is no less important than commitment and ability. Library patrons should express a positive attitude toward a nonprint collection; it may surprise some librarians to learn that many patrons still feel that the library should contain only books. Demographics will play a large role in community response. For example, an aging community might express a great deal less enthusiasm for a collection of microcomputer software than would patrons found in a community where there are a large number of school-age children using microcomputers in the classroom.

Community need must be present; the library should fill a definite gap in the resources available to residents. It should not attempt to

Eugene T. Fischer is at the East Chicago Public Library, East Chicago, Illinois.

duplicate—in most instances, badly—resources already available to community residents at or near the cost the library would have to charge in taxes or fees.

TYPES OF NONPRINT

Nonprint collections can consist of a number of different types of items, depending upon the goals and objectives of the plan for service.

Audiorecordings include music, spoken word, books on cassette, sound effects, or any other of a great variety of materials suitable to the audiorecording medium. The formats for audiorecordings are phonograph records, cassettes, and compact disks. Eight-track tapes and open-reel tapes are commercially obsolete and should be avoided. While phonograph records were, until recently, the most common format, the cassette has replaced the record as the medium of choice. Experts in the recording industry now feel that the compact disk will ultimately replace both phonograph records and cassettes.

All of these formats have advantages and disadvantages: the phonograph record is fragile for public use but is most common; the cassette is compact and requires less care than the record but is subject to erasure; the compact disk has the highest technical quality and is generally impervious to fingerprints and dust, but is expensive and in somewhat short supply at present.

In selecting a format for an audiorecording collection, community demographics should be studied. An all-compact disk collection might be appropriate for an affluent community because the hardware for that format has entered that type of community. Less affluent communities might react more favorably to cassettes. Discussing the situation with local stores selling recordings might help to determine the popularity of the different formats and to highlight future trends in recording purchases. There are also a number of periodicals which discuss the differences between the formats and feature extensive reviews.

Video recordings are available in a variety of formats. The 1/2-inch VHS and 1/2-inch BETA are the only videocassettes considered here. It is important to note that the players and recorders for these two formats are incompatible, both in size and the method of recording. A standard television will display either VHS or BETA tapes, depending upon the type of player/recorder used, but the VHS system is the most widely owned and much more material is available in this format.

The small library should not attempt to duplicate the services of a video store. Videocassettes are very expensive compared to books and some other nonprint materials and the small library will not have the resources for a full-blown video collection. In fact, the library director must decide whether to let the video stores continue their role in the community and not to start a library collection which could be inadequate from the very start due to financial considerations.

Multi-media kits are combinations of two or more types of media in one package to serve a specific purpose. Examples of these are language-lesson recordings in which a book and cassette or record are housed in one package; neither is complete or even usable without the other. Other examples are sound filmstrips, computer-program learning packages, children's books with narration on cassette, and seminars on tape with an accompanying text. A collection of these kits should have a definite goal in the library's service program; individual kits should not be purchased in a random fashion. It must be decided whether these kit materials can accomplish their stated purpose better than print media alone.

Since *films* are expensive, replacement footage very costly or not available, and special equipment is needed to clean and inspect films when they are returned by patrons, the library director of a small public library should think twice before starting a 16mm or 8mm film collection. Many film titles are available on videocassettes at a fraction of the cost of the film.

Slides are useful for particular subject areas, but are available for only a limited range of topics. In addition, some sort of narration or accompanying literature is necessary to put the slides in perspective. In general, it is best to avoid these materials unless there is definite use for them in the presentation of a specific topic.

Filmstrips—a series of slides on one strip of film—are available in sound or silent versions. Sound filmstrips have either an accompanying cassette or phonograph record with narration and cues for the projectionist to change to the next photograph. While filmstrips are used in schools, unless there is a definite use for them in the library, they should be avoided. Not only are they expensive, but they also require special projectors.

Computer software will be collected, needless to say, if the small public library has a computer. Some software for public use with the library's computer might be purchased. Since software is expensive and the types of personal computers are numerous, libraries without a microcomputer should not consider purchasing the software.

Framed art and sculpture are usually museum replicas that patrons can check out and hang in their homes or offices. Both art prints and sculpture are expensive and the amount of use usually does not justify the purchase price for the very small library.

Toys and games are available in many libraries for children and adults to use in the library or to check out. The librarian choosing to have such items must contend with missing pieces from puzzles and games and items which come back soiled and have to be cleaned. Most of these materials are not expensive and some libraries build good public relations with them. Conversely, it should be asked if the distribution of toys and games is necessary or even wanted in a small library with a restricted materials budget and collection.

Sewing patterns are donated to some libraries to set up an exchange collection. Other than the space required, the cost is minimal. However, a small library with a small number of patrons is not likely to have a large or useful collection unless a number of persons in the community are avid sewers and are willing to donate their used patterns.

Realia include items which are not printed, nor do they fit into any of the categories already described. For example, a patron may donate a seashell collection which the library then makes available for children or adults to inspect or take home. In combination with other library materials, realia might serve a very useful purpose. Other types of collections in this category are stamps, coins, arrowheads, dried leaves, flowers, etc. If there is a use for such material and the space to house it properly, it might be appropriate for the small public library.

SELECTING NONPRINT MATERIALS

The need for a good selection policy for nonprint materials cannot be overstated. The policy should state what materials will be collected, the format, what purposes the materials will serve and for what age groups, and the selection guides that are used.

It must be decided from the very beginning what types of recorded music will be purchased. This is not as clearcut as it sounds. The different types can be roughly divided into popular, rock, soul, musicals/ soundtracks, classical, and spoken word. It is best to realize from the start that the small library will never have a comprehensive collection of any of these groups: there are simply too many recordings produced in the past and coming onto the market each week. Input from the community, both library users and nonusers, is extremely important in deciding which types will be purchased. If this input cannot be obtained, only trial and error will determine what types of materials will be *used* by patrons.

The small library cannot collect all of Haydn's symphonies by three different orchestras and conductors and have these sit on the shelf for the one or two persons who may use them. The small library is not a research library and must concentrate on those items which the community will use and enjoy. Conversely, the library cannot afford to spend public funds on flash-in-the-pan rock groups simply because those recordings will result in high circulation for the four or five months before they are replaced in popularity by another rock group. Perhaps the best approach is to buy only current recordings of all types which have gotten good reviews by critics.

It may be advantageous to buy recordings from local record stores if the prices are competitive with mail order dealers such as Rose Records and Chambers. It is always good for public relations to buy materials locally, as well as helping the library's tax base.

After deciding what types of recordings to buy, a decision must be made about format—records, cassettes, compact disks. For videocassettes, either the VHS or BETA format can be chosen, although VHS significantly outsells BETA, possibly due to the greater availability of compatible VHS home machines. Community input is necessary to determine which type of format dominates any particular locality. Since there is little one can do about the quality of the reproduction on a videocassette, the primary decision is the movies themselves. Standard film guides like Leslie Halliwell's *Halliwell's Film Guide* (New York: Scribner, 1985) rate and give a brief synopsis for older films. Most larger newspapers review current films which will later become available on videocassette.

As with audiorecordings, a decision must be made as to the content, aims, and objectives of the collection. Since small libraries cannot compete successfully with a local video store in the breadth and number of copies of each title available, the library should concentrate on providing titles that are not normally available in the video store—while not totally excluding the purchase of exceptional new films. Emphasis could be placed on classics, Academy Award winning films, children's films, foreign films, and nonfiction.

Several book jobbers, such as Baker and Taylor and Ingram, sell videocassettes. In addition, there are a number of video dealers who will sell at large discount. It is wise to purchase locally if the prices are competitive.

A number of audiovisual vendors will be more than happy to provide the library with catalogs of *multi-media kits, filmstrips, and slides*. In addition, NICEM indexes provide reviews of pertinent educational materials. The majority of materials in this category must be purchased from the producers since there are no general jobbers.

Computer software is best purchased from the same dealer who sold the computer to the library. Although available through mail order, sometimes at quite a substantial savings, the accompanying how-to-use manuals can be very confusing. It is advantageous to have a dealer who knows the library's computer system and who will stand behind the software if something goes wrong. Software that is purchased for use in the library obviously must be compatible with the library's computer, and should be relatively easy to use and of practical value to the community. Computer buffs in the community should be able to suggest which programs would be of use locally. Library public relations materials announcing that a software collection is being started will also elicit suggestions from the community. If local schools use a particular type of computer, the librarian should try to find compatible software.

Art prints and sculpture are sold by a number of dealers, among them Gaylord Bros., Alva Museum Replicas, and the New York Graphic Society. Selecting art prints and sculpture is difficult because it is so subjective. As with other selection procedures, the person selecting these items will have to put aside personal preferences to determine which types of art will be most used in the community. Since these materials are relatively expensive, high anticipated use is of great importance.

CATALOGING AND PROCESSING

Cataloging nonprint materials can be complex or extremely simple. The complexity will depend upon whether the small library belongs to a system, where system rules have to be followed. For the library involved in machine-readable cataloging, there are formats for all of these materials which must be followed with consistency. If the library is not part of a system nor involved in machine-readable cataloging data, cataloging can be extremely simple. Since the collection of audiorecordings will probably not grow very large, the following is an example of cataloging for the recording "Pearl" by Janis Joplin:

```
PR

Jop     Joplin, Janis

           Pearl.   Columbia,  C-4902,  1970




           I. Title.    I. Rock Music
```

The PR indicates a phonograph record (CA would be used for cassette and CD for compact disk); "Jop" represents the first three letters of the artist's last name; Columbia is the record company; C-4092, the record number; 1970, the date of the recording. Tracings are made for the title and for a locally used subject heading "Rock Music." Although this example will probably cause the purist cataloger to cringe, it serves the purpose of letting the patron know what records the library has by the artist, the titles, and in what genre and format—in a simple and efficient manner.

Videocassettes, sculpture, art prints, etc., would have a title main entry:

```
VC

Gon      Gone with the wind.  Clark Gable,

              Vivien Leigh, MGM, 1939.  Color, 186m.




         1. Gable, Clark.   2. Leigh, Vivien.
```

More could be added such as a subject heading, notes, etc., but it is doubtful that the collection would grow large enough to require that information. The VC stands for videocassette (other call number/location indicators could be SCU, AP, KIT for sculpture, art prints, and multi-media kits); "Gon" for the first three letters of the title; and the "m" in 186m stands for the running time or the length of the movie. A classification number could be added under these indicators.

Cards for the nonprint collection can either be kept in separate files by category of materials or, if the collection is larger, interfiled in the main catalog. Interfiling gives a multimedia approach to the catalog. For example, if the library owns the movie *Gone with the Wind* and "Songs of the North and South" by the Mormon Tabernacle Choir, they would appear in the catalog along with books about the Civil War. In addition, the shelflist could be used to gather all of the particular types of material in one file, thereby offering the benefits not only of the separate file method, but also of the multimedia approach.

HOUSING AND CIRCULATION

Record bins, special locking cabinets for video- and audiocassettes, and other special items to house nonprint materials are available from library suppliers such as Gaylord, Brodart, Demco, and Highsmith. If it is not feasible to buy these items, empty cassette boxes can be left out for patrons to peruse while the actual cassettes are kept in a secure place. All nonprint materials can either be housed on regular book shelves or, in the case of art prints, hung on the library's walls.

There is no reason why nonprint materials cannot be circulated. Special items may have to be purchased, such as jackets for records and plastic cases for videocassettes, but it requires only a little ingenuity to label containers and attach pockets for date-due cards or slips. Many libraries circulate nonprint items (with the exception of art prints and sculpture, for which a longer loan period is the norm) for a shorter period than books. The reason given is usually that there are fewer of these items and a shorter turn-around time is desirable. The loan period is a matter of individual library preference.

Videocassettes can be "booked" by keeping a block style calendar page for each videocassette to record names and other circulation information. However, the "first come, first served" method results in less clerical work and fewer telephone calls to notify patrons that materials are available.

All nonprint items should undergo a careful visual inspection when they are returned. Most damage to these materials seems to be apparent to the eye except for deliberate sabotage of tapes and computer software.

CARE AND REPAIR OF MATERIALS

All nonprint materials require basic care. They should be kept away from dust, excessive heat, and direct sunlight, and should be touched as little as possible. If phonograph records or compact disks become dirty, they should be cleaned with a soft, lint-free cloth or with a special cleaner. Cassettes and computer software should be kept away from magnetic fields which can erase them. Computer diskettes should only be touched on the cardboard or plastic portion.

Patrons should be educated to take proper care of their own machines. Bad phonograph styli, dirty tape heads and rollers can easily destroy phonograph records and audiocassettes. Faulty mechanisms in a tape or videocassette player can scratch, twist, or break cassettes. Before nonprint items are circulated, it is a good idea to have patrons undergo a brief orientation as to proper care of the materials. In addition, slips with care instructions can be attached to the containers.

Phonograph records cannot be repaired. If they are scratched, chipped, or warped, they should be discarded and the patron charged accordingly. The collection should not deteriorate into a mass of barely listenable recordings; it is better to have a smaller collection in good shape. Records should be cleaned each time they are circulated.

Audiocassettes can be spliced and the mangled parts removed, if the ruined section is not too long; they do not have to be cleaned. Videocassettes should be checked for three things: a broken cassette shell, and broken or twisted tape. Any other damage will not be apparent without playing the tape. The shell should not be opened nor the tape spliced unless the librarian is prepared to risk damaging a patron's VCR. If, for example, some adhesive from the tape seeps through to the other side, it could tear or break the video heads. If not reassembled properly, the tape could twist in the machine and create a mess. If a tape is repaired, it is best to play it all the way through on the library's machine to insure that the repair has been done properly.

If the library collects nonprint materials, equipment will have to be purchased to check them. A patron may complain about the quality of a particular item and the only way to verify that complaint is to use the item on the library's own equipment. Consequently, at least one piece of hardware for the different types of nonprint materials is required and should be budgeted for at the start of the collection. The staff must become thoroughly familiar with its use. Whether the hardware is used by patrons in the library and/or checked out is a policy matter for each individual library. For in-library use of audio materials, headphones can be supplied to the patron.

COPYRIGHT CONSIDERATIONS

It is extremely important to recognize that nearly all nonprint materials are copyrighted: it is illegal to copy audio and videocassettes. Consequently, the materials may only be used in the manner for which the copyright owner has given permission. Feature film videocassettes are sold for home use only. This does not give the right to show it to a large group in the library, even if admission is not charged. In order to do this, a public performance right would have to be obtained. Patrons should be informed that they do not have the right to show the videocassettes that they have borrowed to large groups, even if the group is a nonprofit organization such as scouts, religious groups, or senior citizen groups.

Weeding and Keeping Collections Current

David Ashcraft

The *American College Dictionary* defines a weed as "a plant occurring obtrusively in cultivated ground to the exclusion of the desired crop." Just as in a garden where a constant battle is waged to keep weeds from crowding out the desired crop, in a library the collection must be continually evaluated and materials eliminated from areas where they are taking space that is needed for new and more useful materials. The process used to accomplish this is known as weeding.

All libraries, regardless of size, sooner or later find that the shelves are becoming crowded and that room must be made for new materials. Since expanding the facility to make room for more shelf space is out of the question for most libraries, it is necessary to establish a policy of constantly monitoring the collection to eliminate materials that are no longer useful. Small libraries may encounter this problem sooner and more frequently, but a smaller collection is also often easier to work with when this problem occurs.

Unfortunately, because of the many decisions that have to be made, most of the job has to be done by the librarian. Volunteers can help by finding and pulling materials that need to be repaired, but most of the time spent weeding involves making decisions based on the value of the materials to the collection.

GETTING STARTED

To do a good job of weeding, a librarian must consider the needs of the community served, exercise good professional judgment, and approach the task with an iron will and a firm determination to do the best job possible.

Weeding is *not* one of the easier tasks in running a library. The first step is to put yourself in the correct frame of mind and rid yourself of any doubts you may have about disposing of "public property." Librarians,

David Ashcraft is at the Franklin Avenue Library, Des Moines, Iowa.

by nature, tend to be "pack rats" and often find that parting with library materials is a task postponed until there simply isn't any space left on a shelf or in a section. There tends to be a nagging feeling that if something is weeded out, there will almost certainly be a need for that very item sometime in the future. Unfortunately, the librarian cannot allow the luxury of this feeling, particularly in a small library.

Once you are in the proper frame of mind and before you begin the actual weeding process, take some time to develop a written policy concerning weeding in your library. Since you will be disposing of "public property," a written policy which has been approved by the library board will help to avoid any possible future misunderstandings with members of the community. The policy should include a statement of purpose, criteria to be considered in weeding, and a section on methods used for disposing of the library materials.

WHERE TO BEGIN

An excellent place to begin weeding is at the circulation desk. As materials are returned to the library and before they are returned to the shelves, take some time to evaluate their condition and value to the overall collection. Keep a box on hand in which to put the materials to be discarded, and another for materials that need to be mended.

Before you actually begin to weed the materials on the shelves, take plenty of time to examine the collection and look for areas that are especially crowded. These are priority areas. Keep a record and start working on them first. Less crowded areas can wait until later.

Wherever you decide to begin, continue with that section until it is completed. Although you will be following some general criteria that apply to all sections of the library collection, each section will require some unique considerations. Within sections, finish the area in which you started. If you have an area of "easy books," and begin in that area, finish the "easy books" before going on to another area in the fiction section. As you continue in this manner through the collection, keep a record of where you have weeded so that you avoid duplicating your efforts.

CRITERIA

There are a number of criteria to be followed in weeding a library collection. Some of these are quite simple and involve only the use of a little common sense. Others require careful evaluation, professional judgment, and a good knowledge of your collection and the needs of the community it serves.

Damaged Materials

One of the simplest and most obvious criteria used in weeding is the condition of the material. Check for books with damaged spines and corners, look for torn or missing pages, pages which have been written or scribbled on, and pictures which have been cut out. Nonprint materials such as records and tapes should be checked for breakage, scratches, warping, and missing pieces. Damaged materials should be pulled from the shelves and a decision made as to their value to the overall collection. If an item is of questionable value or definitely has outlived its usefulness, the decision is simple. Don't hesitate or procrastinate: Get rid of it. If, however, you feel that the item is still useful, a decision must then be made as to whether it should be mended, rebound, or replaced.

When deciding what to do with damaged but useful materials, take into consideration the severity of the damage and the amount of time that would be required for repairs. Materials that can be repaired relatively easily should be kept together, as should books that are to be rebound. If the material is so badly damaged that an excessive amount of time would be required to repair it, replacement is usually the only solution.

If an item is in such bad condition that replacement is required, reconsider its usefulness and value to the collection. Many items, particularly books, go out of print quickly due to the fact that publishers can be taxed on inventory in their warehouses. Locating a replacement may take quite a bit of time and effort. Even if a replacement copy can be found, the item may now cost considerably more than it did when it was originally purchased. The money necessary to replace it might well be spent on other materials.

Old and Fragile Materials

Many librarians may find themselves hesitant to get rid of a book simply because it is "so old." When they see a copyright date, they get a queasy feeling about parting with the book. If you find yourself in such a quandary, then you need to get over this feeling quickly: most old books are simply that—old. Such books have no place in the collection. Even old "classics" aren't useful to the circulating collection if the pages are yellowed and brittle.

Books that you feel may have some value due to age, author, edition, or because of their historical information could be kept in a special collection. However, since such special collections are better left to larger libraries with more space, it is best to pull the books from the collection. Donate the books to a local historical society or study group, or set them aside for appraisal by an expert on rare books. If any books of value are found, they could be sold (with the library board's permission) to raise money for the library.

Frequency of Use

How often has the item been used? In most cases, an item that isn't being used is only taking up valuable space. Small libraries often have an advantage over larger ones in determining usage because many use a circulation system that requires patrons to sign a card for the book when it is checked out. By checking the card, you can see how frequently an item is used and when it last circulated. If you are using a system which doesn't give you this information, you can start a simple system. Put a slash or "hash" mark on the pocket each time it circulates. By using a different colored pencil or marker each year, you can see when it was last used.

You will want to establish some guidelines (and these should be in the policy statement) for your library in using this criterion, and decide how often and how recently an item should be circulated to justify being kept as part of your collection. For example, you may decide to pull all items that haven't circulated at least five times in the last five years. Consider factors such as where the item is located. Does it have adequate visibility? Is it in an area easily accessible to patrons? Would it circulate better if placed in another area? Whatever guidelines you decide upon should be based on your library's particular collection, how severely crowded it has become, and the use patterns of your community.

Multiple Copies

Many times you may find multiple copies of an item on the shelves. Perhaps numerous copies were donated to the library, or maybe a subject has been extremely popular in past years. In the case of fiction, multiple copies of a title are often purchased to meet the need for a popular new title. Whatever the reason, unless the item is still in demand and circulates frequently, in most cases these items can be weeded down to no more than two copies at the most. If you have storage room and really feel that you might have future need of additional copies of an item, you might store these items for a while and weed them out later if they still haven't been needed.

Currency of Information

One of the most important tasks facing any librarian is that of keeping the collection current and relevant. This is of particular importance in the nonfiction area. Many materials such as travel guides, atlases, and books on countries and on elected officials quickly go out-of-date. It is very important to the overall strength of the collection that these items be weeded out and replaced with new, up-to-date materials. If your library only has a few items in a subject area, even if they are dated, you may want to make note of these items and keep them until new materials can be purchased. In the case of materials on elected officials, you can temporarily update them by writing in names of new officials until new materials are acquired.

SPECIFIC CRITERIA FOR NONFICTION

Certain areas of nonfiction become dated more quickly than others. These areas are:

000S   *Encyclopedias*
Those in the reference area should be updated with a yearbook each year, and at least one set should be replaced every five years. Older sets can be allowed to circulate.

100S   *Philosophy, Ethics, Psychology*
Many books are published in this area, particularly in popular psychology. Such books are extremely popular for a period but rapidly go out of fashion.

200S   *Religion*
New books constantly appear as written by popular religious personalities. Weed out any that are no longer used.

300S   *Social Sciences*
This area includes almanacs, law, government, and education. Almanacs should be replaced in the reference collection yearly with older copies placed in the circulating collection to be kept no more than five years. Materials in the areas of law, government, and education are frequently published and quickly become dated. Materials in this area are often needed for debate and reports. Keep a balanced collection with materials on both sides of an issue represented.

400S   *Languages*
Keep a good basic collection and replace as items become worn.

500S   *Pure Science*
New discoveries and information cause materials to become dated quickly.

600S   *Applied Sciences*
This area requires constant attention. It includes medicine, diets, physical fitness, business, clothing, hairstyles, and cosmetics. All of these areas involve new discoveries, fads, or styles, and become dated very quickly.

700S   *Music, Art, and Sports*
Within this area are found biographies and autobiographies on actors, musicians, and sports figures. Watch for multiple copies and books which are no longer being used.

800S   *Literature, Plays, and Poetry*
Keep a good, basic collection, and watch for multiple copies of titles which are no longer popular.

900S   *Travel, Geography, and History*
Many changes take place in these areas, and information frequently becomes obsolete. Constant weeding and purchasing is required.

Biographies
Keep only those biographies on important people with enduring interest. Replace as new works are published.

Magazines and Newspapers
These can create a problem because of the space required. Keep local newspapers at least a year if possible. Magazines which have research value should be kept at least five years, and can be bound.

Vertical File Material
Keep as current as possible. Weed out files that aren't being used.

STANDARD AIDS

All books, particularly in the area of fiction, should be checked against a standard booklist before being withdrawn from the collection. Booklists frequently used are: *Children's Books: Awards and Prizes*, Children's Book Council; *Children's Catalog*, Wilson (contains both fiction and nonfiction); *Public Library Catalog*, Wilson (nonfiction only); *Fiction Catalog*, Wilson (adult fiction only).

Also useful to libraries involved in a weeding project is *Books in*

Print, published by Bowker. With its comprehensive list of titles in print, *BIP* helps in reordering and in deciding whether to withdraw, repair, or rebind a title.

WITHDRAWING MATERIALS

This is a very important topic to consider when engaging in a weeding project. The public in all sizes of communities can be very sensitive to what it may see as misuse of its tax dollars. This is especially true in small communities, and where a written policy which has the approval of the library board will be useful.

In 1977, I conducted a survey of school librarians in Northwest Missouri. One of the questions asked about their policy for disposing of withdrawn materials. One of the most common methods was that of burning or hauling away discards. If this method is used—and it may be the best method for damaged or out-of-date materials—it is best that it be done as quietly as possible. The public can be unreasonable if, after hearing librarians talk about the lack of money for materials, they find library materials on the trash heap.

Another disposal method which, although not widely used among the school librarians that I surveyed, is often used by public libraries. This involves establishing a sale table in the library on which discarded materials are placed to be sold at a reduced price. This is probably the best method of disposing of materials which are still usable, and it frequently meets with the approval of the public. Instead of merely destroying library materials, you are "recycling" them. You generate income for the library, and give the public an opportunity for a bargain at the same time. You may still hear complaints about disposing of someone's "favorite" book, but at least you have given them a chance to buy it. The biggest problem in maintaining a sale table is finding storage space for the materials to be sold. There is also the time involved in keeping the sale table looking attractive and continually stocked with new selections while removing items that don't sell.

A third method of disposing of materials is to give them to community organizations such as churches and synagogues; to nonprofit organizations such as Planned Parenthood or Goodwill; or even possibly to a library in another community. Before doing so, you may decide to allow interested members of the public to take what they want. This method is also preferable to burning or destroying materials because once again it "recycles" them and extends their usefulness.

A library is a business providing for the informational and recreational needs of the citizens of a community. As a business, it can no more afford to keep old, unattractive, and unpopular merchandise on its shelves than can the department store down the street. A careful and continuous program of weeding will not only create space, but will point out strengths and weaknesses in the collection and, in this way, help with collection development. Weeding helps to ensure that the library has the materials and selection that meet the needs of its community. Instead of stagnating, the library will be a vital, growing, and useful part of the community.

Cataloging

Deborah J. Karpuk

Cataloging in the 1980s offers options for automating library files which were affordable only by the largest or wealthiest of libraries during the 1960s and 1970s. New and viable options for automating library catalogs are now available to small libraries of all types. Size rather than type of library governs decisions regarding technical services operations. Sheila S. Intner illuminates this view in "A Giant Step Backward for Technical Services."[1] Professionally established international standards for cataloging and classification have been developed to promote uniformity in the cataloging record. These standards can be adapted or simplified to smaller library environments.

The *Anglo-American Cataloging Rules* (2d ed.) present more options for the description of library materials and for distinguishing between materials available in several formats. The philosophy behind *AACR2* is to use forms of entry more consistent with patron thinking. A simplified version of standard cataloging can be taught to library staff at all levels which will ultimately aid in cataloging consistency.

THE CATALOG

The catalog serves as a concise index to materials in the library collection. No matter its format—card catalog, microfiche catalog, public access online catalog—the fundamental principles of cataloging remain the same. Librarians working in small libraries, despite limited staffing resources, are in the enviable position of knowing the library collection in detail. The size of the collection is limited, but for this precise reason, the librarian can establish cataloging policies that are designed to meet current cataloging needs, paying close attention to changing community size, clientele interests, projected organizational plans for growth of the library, and possible future computerization of the catalog. Consistency in adapting and simplifying cataloging and classification to maximize the service to library clientele can double for good longer-range planning.

Deborah J. Karpuk is Associate Library Director, Haltom City Public Library, in Haltom City, Texas.

The card catalog provides multiple access points offering the library patron access to the collection using several approaches—author, title or subject. Consistency and uniformity are required and standard formats for bibliographic description have been developed for cataloging consistency. Most libraries follow the Library of Congress system because of familiarity with LC cards, but "original" cataloging is devised in a similar format. Data elements are recorded in a specified order and formatted in paragraph form. Where MARC (machine-readable cataloging) tagging is used, the computer will format a properly tagged record in the desired order on catalog cards, in book or in COM catalogs, or on a computer terminal screen, and include: heading, body of entry, physical description area, series area, note area, standard number, terms of availability area, tracing, and call number (see Figure 1). The spacing holds for catalog card typing or whether the record is input online in MARC format.

Experience with manual catalogs, and conversion of card catalogs into machine-readable form for either COM (computer output microfiche) catalog production or as part of building an online public access catalog, has emphasized that consistency is critical in all catalog formats. For this reason, efforts at following standardized cataloging methods should be seriously considered. The development of the MARC record, ISBD (international standard bibliographic description) punctuation, and the evolution of *AACR2* all provide opportunities for following a standard consistent with that employed by libraries throughout the world. This consistency provides patrons with a learning aid which will serve them well through a lifetime of using libraries and aid in constructing a standardized card catalog which could be computerized with minimal difficulties.

PHYSICAL DESCRIPTION

The *AACR2* provides three levels of description of library materials, of which the first level will probably suffice for small libraries, depending on the clientele served, and the nature of the library collection. The first level of description constitutes the minimal level of cataloging; the second level is that used for input into OCLC; the third level of description is the LC level. The cataloger may choose the level which provides the necessary amount of detail and follow standards in international cataloging rules at the same time. Less emphasis has been placed on the "main" entry under *AACR2*. Multiple access points in a complete bibliographical description eliminates the need to designate the "main" entry. Under *AACR2*, forms of names used in cataloging are those used by the authors themselves—often better known to library

FIGURE 1   Data Elements and Order on Author and Title Cards

```
Call      Author.
Number      Title : subtitle / first statement of
          responsibility ; each subsequent statement of
          responsibility. -- edition statement. --
          First place of publication, etc. : first
          publisher, etc., date of publication.
            Extent of item : other physical details ;
          dimensions. -- (Series)


            Note.
            Standard number.

            Tracing.
                                O



Call      Title : subtitle / first statement of
Number    responsibility ; each subsequent statement
          of responsibility. -- edition statement.
          --First place of publication, etc. :
          first publisher, etc., date of publication.
          Extent of item : other physical details ;
          dimensions. -- (Series)

            Note.
            Standard number.

            Tracing.


                          O
```

users as well. Corporate bodies are no longer treated as authors under *AACR2*.

The first level of description includes at least the elements below:

Title proper / first statement of responsibility, if different from main entry heading in form or number or if there is no main entry heading.—Edition statement.—Material (or type of publication) specific details.—First publisher, etc., date of publication, etc., date of publication, etc.—Extent of item.—Note(s).—Standard number.

The second level of description includes at least the elements below:

Title proper [general material designation] = parallel title: other title information / first statement of responsibility: each subsequent statement of responsibility.—Edition statement / first statement of responsibility relating to the edition.—Material (or type of publication) specific details.—First place of publication, etc.: first publisher, etc., date of publication, etc.—Extent of item: other physical details; dimensions.—(Title proper of series / statement of responsibility relating to series, ISSN of series; numbering within the series. Title of numbering within subseries).—Note(s).—Standard number.

The third level of description (LC) follows the rules applicable in the *AACR2* and subsequent revisions.[2]

GENERAL MATERIAL DESIGNATIONS

To assist in distinguishing between materials with the same title but in different formats, a general material designation has been offered in *AACR2* for North American and British catalogers:

American	*British*
map	cartographic material
globe	graphic
art original	machine-readable data file
chart	manuscript
filmstrip	microform
flash card	motion picture
picture	multimedia
slide	music
technical drawing	object
transparency	sound recording
machine-readable data file	text
manuscript	videorecording
microform	
motion picture	
kit	
music	
diorama	
game	
microscope slide	
model	
realia	
sound recording	
text	
videorecording	

DESCRIPTIVE CATALOGING

Descriptive cataloging is the part of the cataloging process concerned with the identification and description of an item, and then translating this information into the cataloging record, determining and formatting the access points. Selecting subject access points is a separate part of the process. Chief sources of information usually provide the most complete bibliographic information about an item in all the elements cited above. If other titles exist, the cataloger must note whether the additional titles vary significantly from the title proper. Examples include the following for books: cover title (on the cover), binder's title (on the original spine of the book), running title (repeated on top of each page or alternate page of the book); sound recordings, motion pictures, and graphic materials may have titles on containers that differ from the chief source of information. Serials may have additional titles on the cover and on an added title page. Chief sources of information vary according to the type of material. *AACR2* provides an integrated approach to the description of library materials whereby all materials are described according to the same set of principles.

The title page and verso of the title page provide chief sources of information for book materials. Nonbook materials are not often handled in the same way as monographic materials. A policy decision within each library determines whether to catalog and/or classify special materials. The physical dimensions of these materials make it difficult to shelve nonbook materials with books and influence the location of the materials in the library collection. Classification of nonbook materials diminishes in importance while the physical description becomes more important.

Cartographic materials (*AACR2,* Chap. 3) such as atlases use the title page as the chief source of information; cartographic materials other than atlases use the item itself, or the container/case or cradle/stand if the item itself cannot be used. Manuscripts (*AACR2,* Chap. 4) use the title page if there is one and it was originally part of the manuscript. The colophon, caption, heading, and the text itself are also used. If this information is not available, the following should be used in priority order: 1. another manuscript copy of the item; 2. a published edition of the item; 3. reference sources or other sources.

Published music (*AACR2,* Chap. 5) uses the title page, cover, or caption—whichever furnishes the fullest information—as the chief sources of information. If information cannot be taken from the title page, the following can be used in priority order: 1. caption; 2. cover; 3. colophon; 4. other preliminaries, other sources.

Sound recordings (*AACR2,* Chap. 6) fall into several formats with varying sources of information: disc use the disc label; tape cassette use the cassette and the label; tape cartridge use the cartridge and label; roll use the label; sound recording on film use the container and label.

Two or more labels are treated as one chief source of information. If a collective title is used in accompanying textual material and the chief sources above do not, then the collective title may be treated as a chief source. If chief sources of information are not available, follow this priority: 1. accompanying textual material; 2. a container; 3. other sources with preference to printed over sound data.

Motion pictures and video recordings (*AACR2,* Chap. 7) use the title frames from the film itself as the chief source of information. If a permanent container accompanies the material, the container and label may be used. The established priority for other sources of information are: 1. accompanying textual material; 2. container that is not an integral part of the piece; 3. other sources.

Graphic materials (*AACR2,* Chap. 8) use the item itself including permanently affixed labels or containers. If two or more parts comprise the item, use a container which provides a collective title if the item does not. The established priority for other sources of information is: 1. nonintegral; 2. accompanying textual material; 3. other sources.

Machine-readable data files (*AACR2,* Chap. 9) use internal user labels as the chief source of information. If two or more parts comprise the item, use a container that provides a collective title if the items do not. The established priority for other sources of information is: 1. label on the storage medium itself (disc, cassette); 2. label on nonintegral container; 3. accompanying documentation; 4. other sources.

Three-dimensional artifacts and realia (*AACR2,* Chap. 10) use the object itself along with accompanying textual material and the container issued with the item. Information permanently affixed to the item is a preferred source of information.

SERIALS

A clear distinction should be made between serials and monographs. A monograph represents a complete bibliographic unit and may be issued in successive parts and regular or irregular intervals. A monograph is not intended to continue indefinitely. Serials include both periodicals and nonperiodicals. Periodicals have distinctive titles and are issued more frequently than once a year. Yearbooks, memoirs, proceedings, annuals, etc., and series cataloged together rather than separately are serials. Pseudoserials, and frequently issued and revised publications (editions), may be treated as a monograph first, but treated as a serial after numerous edition changes.

The principles for cataloging serials are generally the same as for cataloging books. Changes in title and in bibliographic descriptions necessitate changes with minimum modifications to the bibliographic record.

Examples of numbering complexities are:

[Vol. 1] (July 1950)–v. 8 (Spring 1977) = no. 1–38
Vol. 1 (1962)–v. 26 (1975) ; 1976-
Vol. 5 (1938)–v. 22 (1955) ; New ser., v. 1 (1956)–v. 23 (1978)

Frequency notes are used in *AACR2* unless the frequency is apparent from the title or statement of responsibility or is unknown; a note on frequency is needed if apparent from the rest of the publication.

Title changes are recorded when a serial changes title and a note is made for the preceding title, or a subsequent title. Common linking notes include:

Continuation = Continues: Society
Continued by = Continued by: Modern society

Mergers, splits, and absorptions will occur occasionally in periodicals and serials.

The note area is especially important for serials. The order in which common notes for serials appear are:

1. Frequency
2. Additional information about the language or title
3. Classification or the statement of responsibility or if important, the name of the editor
4. Linking notes denoting relationships with other serials
5. Irregularities in numbering or temporary suspension
6. Library holdings, if not complete
7. ISSN (International Standard Serial Number)[3]

Classification and subject headings for serials are usually more general although physical description is more complex than for books. Small libraries may elect an alphabetic arrangement for periodicals. Serials may be briefly cataloged as in Figure 2.

FORM OF ENTRY

AACR2 has introduced changes in form of entry which should aid the librarian working in a small library. The name by which a writer is known is preferred over a legal name. Although small libraries can be

FIGURE 2   Sample Serial Catalog Card

```
        Society. -- Vol. 9, no. 4-    = no. 74-
          (Feb. 1972)-    . -- New Brunswick, N.J. :
          Transaction, 1972-
          v. ; ill. ; 23 cm.

          Monthly (except July/Aug. and Nov./Dec.)
          Continues: Trans-action
          ISSN 0147-2011


          1. Social sciences -- Periodicals.


                           ◯
```

more flexible in local practices, decisions should be documented in policy statements. A file should be maintained documenting which headings are used and the "see" references from headings not used to headings in the catalog. The LC name authority file is available through microfiche or through an online bibliographic utility.

AACR2 and revisions serve as the basic cataloging authority for form of entry, which designates the title page or its substitute to determine how a name is to be entered in the catalog. Where an author's name appears in many forms, the form used most frequently on the title page is preferred. When commercial card services are used, it would be more cost effective to use the form of name used on the commercial cards. Corporate names, as with personal names, can be complex in nature and *AACR2* should be consulted before determining the catalog form of entry. The most general guide concerning corporate entries is to enter the name directly under the most predominantly known form of name which represents the distinct identity. Sources provided in the references section will detail specifics of corporate complexities and forms of personal name entry.

SUBJECT HEADINGS

A book can have only one classification number and be shelved in only one place. Subject headings assigned to the material provide catalog access to several topics covered. Entering material in the catalog under subjects involves a knowledge of the terms people use, and selection of as specific a term as the subject warrants. Subject headings should be determined and assigned at the same time the classification number is assigned in order to avoid examining the book twice. Selecting appropriate subject headings involves examining the title page, table of contents, scanning the preface or introduction, and reading brief sections of the book. The content of the book as well as the author's purpose for writing should be determined. *The Library of Congress Subject Headings* and *Sears List of Subject Headings* are standard subject lists and provide instructions for use and forms of subject headings.

POINTS OF ACCESS

The term access point has become popular with *AACR2* and the advent of computers as a bibliographic tool. Prior to the online environment, headings were the terms used to reflect the manual form in which names appeared in the card catalog. Each item in the library collection may merit more than one access point in the catalog. Only the main entry card need contain the complete cataloging information.

Based on the descriptive cataloging for any given material, the number and detail of points of access will vary (see Figure 3). A policy decision by the library will determine whether subjects, author, and title cards will be interfiled or organized into a divided catalog. Primary access points would include a joint author, editor, compiler (if used), collective titles, portion of the title in the catalog record, full title in the catalog record if not a title main entry, subject heading access points, series titles, corporate bodies responsible for publications, and for a translated work, the original title. For points of access, except for subject headings, the information used as access must appear in the body of the bibliographic description as justification for the added entry and used as a heading on the catalog card. Expansion of access points to entries in an online catalog has introduced a level of search and retrieval flexibility not found in card, book, or COM catalogs.

CLASSIFICATION

The primary classification problem faced by the cataloger is determining the dominant focus of the book and locating the material properly in relation to other books in the library collection. After the main subject of the book has been determined, the classification sched-

FIGURE 3   Points of Access

```
523.1    Greenstein, George, 1940-
G            Frozen star / George Greenstein. --
         New York : Freundlich Books, c1983.
            274 p. : ill. ; 24 cm.

            ISBN 0-88191-011-2


            1. Astronomy.   2. Pulsars.   3. Black holes
         (Astronomy)   4. Universe.   I. Title.

                                        83-25459
```

```
             Frozen star.
523.1    Greenstein, George, 1940-
G            Frozen star / George Greenstein. --
         New York : Freundlich Books, c1983.
            274 p. : ill. ; 24 cm.

            ISBN 0-88191-011-2
```

```
             ASTRONOMY.
523.1    Greenstein, George, 1940-
G            Frozen star / George Greenstein. --
         New York : Freundlich Books, c1983.
            274 p. : ill. ; 24 cm.

            ISBN 0-88191-011-2


            1. Astronomy;   2. Pulsars.   3. Black holes
         (Astronomy)   4. Universe.   I. Title.
```

ule (Dewey Decimal System, LC Classification) is consulted to determine the classification number. Like materials on a subject should be shelved together for easy location by the library patron. The librarian should employ a system conducive to prompt and effective service with concern to the smaller section of the classification scheme as well as the main classification divisions. The shelf arrangement should be flexible and permit insertion of new titles and the shifting of materials without destroying the logical order.

The shorter and simpler the notation can be—as long as it indicates all the necessary differences in the grouping—the more it adds to the usefulness of the scheme. The librarian working in a small library may elect to shorten the numbers for relatively small collections. Whereas the logic behind this practice is clear, it is suggested that the numbers used in the Cataloging in Publication (CIP) or by the LC or Dewey Decimal Classification be preferred over a local number unless a special classification scheme is employed. The philosophy outlined earlier concerning consistency with national standards is a preference in classification schemes. With CIP (Cataloging in Publication data) readily available, the need for determining numbers "from scratch" is reduced. If numbers are shortened to only major class divisions, it may be necessary to reclassify portions of the collection as the library grows.

References

1. S. S. Intner. "A Giant Step Backward for Technical Services," *Library Journal* 110 (April 15, 1985): 43–45.
2. *Anglo-American Cataloging Rules*. 2d ed. Prepared by the American Library Association, the British Library, the Canadian Committee on Cataloguing, The Library Association, the Library of Congress. Michael Gorman and Paul W. Winkler, eds. (Chicago: American Library Assn., 1978), p. 15.
3. Susan Grey Akers. *Aker's Simple Library Cataloging*. Completely revised and rewritten by Arthur Curley and Jana Varlejs. (Metuchen, N.J.: The Scarecrow Press, 1984), p. 118.

Bibliographic Utilities

Liz Bishoff

Whenever a bibliographic utility is mentioned—either in generic terms or by individual names such as OCLC, WLN, or RLIN—the initial reaction of the librarian in a small library is frequently "We're too small to use a bibliographic utility" or "It's too costly; we can do it cheaper ourselves," or "Our materials are so specialized we won't benefit from the utility," etc. Certainly, in some situations, all these statements are true; however, many librarians working in small libraries can find the use of a bibliographic utility cost effective, while enhancing their existing service with a higher quality product. Today, in excess of 7,000[1] libraries—school, public, academic, research, and special—use one of the major bibliographic utilities in the United States. The number of items added to collections annually ranges from tens of thousands at such institutions as the University of California–Los Angeles to the Harvard School Library in the Los Angeles area, which adds 600 titles per year.[2]

BIBLIOGRAPHIC UTILITY BACKGROUND

A bibliographic utility is a commercial or not-for-profit organization that provides to customers or members a variety of services including cataloging, interlibrary loan, acquisition programs, authority control, retrospective conversion services, archival tapes, access to specialized collections, etc. Bibliographic utilities began in the late 1960s, when small groups of libraries began experimenting with MARC (Machine-Readable Cataloging) records supplied by the Library of Congress (LC). In 1967, a group of academic libraries in Ohio developed a cooperative, time-sharing system, which provided access to a MARC database and collected the input cataloging of all member libraries.[3]

This early cooperative was called the Ohio College Library Center, later renamed OCLC. MARC records from LC were added on a regular basis, with more libraries joining the cooperative, expanding beyond Ohio academic libraries to include public, school, and special libraries

Liz Bishoff is Principal Librarian for Support Services, Pasadena Public Library, Pasadena, California.

from throughout the United States. Today United Kingdom MARC (UKMARC) records are also added to the OCLC database. By June 1986, 7,413 OCLC terminals had been installed in U.S. libraries, with 6,579 libraries using one or more subsystems.[4] The OCLC services are offered through one of 19 state or regional networks, which are responsible for preparing orders, handling local telecommunication matters, and training local library staff.

An alternative to OCLC, BALLOTS (Bibliographic Automation of Large Library Operations), was introduced by Stanford University in 1972, and offered sophisticated searching of a MARC database, including subject access to the online system.[5] BALLOTS offered libraries the ability to search by subject; search terms in the title, subtitle, and series statements; and allowed libraries to retain and retrieve their own cataloging records. In 1978, BALLOTS became the basis for RLIN (Research Libraries Network), a bibliographic database offered nationwide for research libraries. By 1986, RLIN had 1,130 installed terminals in approximately 600 research and nonresearch libraries.[6] In addition to the bibliographic database, RLIN users can also access AVERY, an online index to architectural periodicals, and SCIPIO, an art sales catalog database.

In addition to the nationwide databases of OCLC and RLIN, a regional bibliographic utility—the Washington Library Network, later the Western Library Network (WLN)—was established by the Washington State Library in 1967. By 1986, WLN supported 270 installed terminals, and provided services for 315 libraries in the Pacific Northwest.[7] The primary goals were to serve as a resource sharing network for libraries in Washington and to provide multistate computer services. A union list was produced in book format in 1972 and online in 1975. One unique service of WLN is the marketing of its software to individual libraries, library systems, and other organizations, allowing a replication of the WLN bibliographic processing functions. Organizations such as the National Library of Australia, University of Illinois-Urbana, and SOLINET (the OCLC network serving libraries in the southeastern United States) have purchased a WLN software license to be used in creating local online catalogs.

Networks generally coordinate bibliographic access services on a state or regional basis, but some networks provide additional services such as electronic mail, microcomputer training, cooperative purchasing programs, authority control, and tape processing services. Major networks include NELINET, SOLINET, AMIGOS, BSR, and CLASS.

A shared cataloging system was also developed in Canada in 1973 by the University of Toronto. Utlas, the University of Toronto Library Automation system, offers online access to both cataloging and authority records. The Utlas database includes LC, Canadian, and United

Kingdom MARC records, the MARC file from the Bibliotheque Nationale du Québec, and member-contributed records. In 1985, the Utlas system was sold to International Thomson, and its services are now marketed in the United States and Japan in combination with other Thomson services.

Similar bibliographic databases have been developed by commercial vendors, such as Autographic's Agile system. Like OCLC and RLIN, Agile is based on LC's MARC format records and contributed cataloging by participating libraries. Many commercial vendors provide retrospective conversion and Computer Output Microform (COM) services.

Mention should be made of Dialog and how it differs from a bibliographic utility. Dialog is an online reference service of the Lockhead Co., composed of over 200 individually produced databases. The databases contain either bibliographic citations and abstracts; statistical, financial, and demographic information; and directory type information.

Although cataloging was, and still is, the foundation of the bibliographic utility's service, one of the earliest by-products was the identification and verification of the item, including the libraries owning the item. This knowledge of ownership was based on their creation of the bibliographic record, or use of the bibliographic record for the production of catalog cards, or a machine-readable cataloging record. Gradually OCLC, RLIN, WLN, and Autographics developed online interlibrary loan subsystems to facilitate the interlibrary loaning of materials. During 1986, the ten millionth item was loaned via the OCLC ILL subsystem by the University of Kentucky Library to the University of Vermont Library.[8]

CATALOGING AND UNION LISTING SERVICES

When the bibliographic utilities began offering cataloging services to libraries, the primary purpose was the production of catalog cards. The library was able to customize the catalog card to meet local requirements, including classification numbers, form of name and subject headings, special notes, etc., while not having to originally catalog the item. Cards arrived at the library in filing order, requiring no additional typing or sorting. As the databases grew in size, libraries found the utilities provided a high percentage of their cataloging copy, reducing their original cataloging requirements. "By 1973, member cataloging represented almost half of the online records [in OCLC] . . . and [by] the early 1980's MARC-generated records constituted only about 25 percent of the more than 7.75 million records in the OCLC database."[9]

A 1986 study done by the Riverside City County Library in California found that 74 percent of the cataloging records used by the library during a six-week period were LC MARC records, while 26 percent were contributed by member libraries. On further analysis, of the 2,300 books cataloged, 74 percent used LC MARC records, 25 percent were member-contributed MARC, and 1 percent required original cataloging. In contrast, of the 173 audiovisual items cataloged, including sound recordings, LC cataloging was found for 15 percent of the items; OCLC member libraries supplied 51 percent of the cataloging records; and 34 percent of the items added required original cataloging.[10]

A by-product of the use of the database for cataloging copy was the creation of a nationwide union list. Each participating library is assigned a code that identifies that library. In the case of an OCLC library, a three-letter institution code is assigned. When the library uses a record for card production, its code is attached to that bibliographic record. Libraries, through the process of cataloging, were creating a nationwide union list.

Coincident to the development of the databases was the introduction of computer output microform (COM) techniques as an alternative to the card catalog. Various vendors could produce microfiche or microfilm copies of the catalog cards, based on the machine-readable bibliographic records used by the library during the cataloging process. Libraries began receiving, in addition to catalog cards, a copy of their cataloging activity on a magnetic tape, which could be read by a computer. In turn, a microfiche or microfilm listing of catalog cards with all the desired library access points—author, title, and subject—as well as holdings information was created. Many large public library systems adopted these COM catalogs, replacing the card catalogs in their branches and departments. The COM catalogs provided each library with the card catalog and holdings information for the entire library system.

Many regional library systems produced union lists of holdings based on the machine-readable cataloging records of their member libraries. One of the largest of these union lists is the California CATALIST, which reflects the holdings of the 169 California public libraries. Tapes from four bibliographic utilities—OCLC, RLIN, Brodart, and Autographics—were merged into one file and distributed to the public and academic libraries throughout the state. In 1983, the California State Library signed a contract with OCLC to provide union catalog services to the public libraries in the state. OCLC loaded the machine-readable copy of CATALIST into the OCLC online system, making the holdings of all California public libraries available online via OCLC. Current cataloging by the public libraries participating in the program is added online for OCLC participating libraries or tapeloaded quarterly for RLIN, Agile, and Brodart users.

Table 1 compares the content of the database of the major bibliographic vendors. Each of the utilities is capable of handling all the

MARC formats, books, serials, sound recordings, audiovisual materials, machine-readable data files, and authority formats. When selecting a bibliographic utility, it is important to consider the composition of the database, special collections that have been added, and search strategies, as well as cost.

TABLE 1   Database Comparisons

	OCLC[11]	RLIN[12]	WLN[13]
Books	11,633,400	18,055,834	3,103,000
Serials	883,200	1,994,157	350,000
Maps	175,260	112,783	In devel.
Sound recordings	400,200	142,903	42,000
Machine-readable data files	8,280	1,179	In devel.
Audiovisual materials	343,620	95,068	98,000
Scores	284,280	281,559	*
Archival materials	55,200	69,767	In devel.
Authority records	1,630,000	2,000,000	4,288,451**

*Reported with sound recordings.
**Includes author, series, and subject headings.

INTERLIBRARY LOAN SERVICES

Interlibrary loan (ILL) has always been a small but highly valued library service, regardless of the size of the library. The creation of a union catalog as a result of the cataloging activity leads libraries to search the bibliographic utilities to identify an item and the owning library. These systems provided a more timely and accurate reflection of a library's holdings than did the *National Union Catalog* and other printed lists. Until 1979, libraries utilized traditional methods, such as the American Library Association's interlibrary loan form or TWX transmission systems to request materials. In 1979, OCLC introduced their ILL subsystem with its name/address directory containing borrowing and lending requirements of the participating libraries, and the names and addresses of ILL personnel; an online ILL form, with the ability to move data from the bibliographic record to the ILL form; and the ability to list up to five holding libraries. The introduction of the ILL subsystem allowed a library to combine the verification of the existence of an item, identification of holding libraries, and the transmission of a request in a single continuous step at one terminal. Significant reductions in turnaround time were noted, reducing the time between the initial request and receipt of the item. Studies of OCLC ILL activity in

Illinois and New York showed a 30 percent reduction in turnaround time, from 15.9 to 10.8 days and 27.4 to 17.0 days, respectively.[14] Similar ILL systems have been implemented by RLIN, WLN, and Agile.

OTHER SERVICES

Bibliographic utilities offer other services to libraries, including serial control systems, acquisition modules, retrospective conversion services, and local circulation and online catalog systems. The retrospective conversion services and options are many and varied, including sending the library's shelf list to the utility where the library's cards are matched against the utility's database; using a microcomputer to collect standard numbers (LCCN and ISBN), brief author, title, and publishing data; and sending an existing non-MARC or brief record database to be matched against the utility's MARC database. Many of the vendors offer authority file services to update subject headings and personal and corporate names.

The match, or hit rate, and cost for these services vary from vendor to vendor ranging from $.25 to $1 per title. Generally, the closer the vendor comes to converting 100 percent of the catalog records, the higher the cost. Before undertaking a conversion project the librarian should have a test match done by potential vendors to determine the likely hit rate and identify problems. A minimum of 1,000 titles representing all areas of the library's collection should be tested. Most libraries can expect a 50–75 percent hit rate when matching with standard numbers. Collections of technical materials or highly specialized collections are likely to experience a lower hit rate. Collections with sizable numbers of audiovisual materials also find a lower hit rate, particularly when the database is primarily composed of LC MARC records.

The acquisition, serial control, and local system modules offered by the various bibliographic utilities can be operated as part of the host computer, but current trends see these highly localized services being moved to micro- and minicomputers in the local library. While designed and maintained by the utility, the inhouse systems are operated by local library staff. The bibliographic services such as cataloging, retrospective conversion, and authority control are compatible with the local system providing a single source automation package.

OPTIONS FOR PARTICIPATION

A variety of options exist for libraries wishing to participate in a bibliographic utility. The options for membership and use vary from utility to utility; however, the most popular include full membership, tapeload membership, or search-only membership. Libraries can use a dedicated or dial-access terminal, printer terminal, or microcomputer, participate in shared or cooperative use, or utilize the services through a processing center. With these options, even the smallest of special, school, or public libraries can use a bibliographic utility.

Most libraries access the bibliographic utility's computer with a dedicated terminal, designed to meet the specific requirements of the individual utility and the library application, such as cataloging, searching authority files, and card production. Connected via phone lines to the computer, the dedicated terminal is always able to access the host computer. The current generation of terminals, first introduced in early 1984, are modified microcomputers, particularly IBM-PC's. Still in use at many libraries are the specially designed terminals with their only purpose providing access to the utility's computer. Both of these terminals are supplied, installed, and maintained by the bibliographic utility.

In addition to the utility-supplied terminals, libraries can use many off-the-shelf microcomputers and printer terminals. To use one of these terminals, the library staff must determine the protocol and equipment needed to use the specialized features of the utility's host computer. The utilities are generally able to provide the necessary information to use the most commonly available printer terminals and microcomputers. If this option is selected, the library must access the host computer in dial access mode, requiring a modem and phone line in addition to the computer. Modems are supplied by the utility for dedicated terminals; however for dial access, the customer must supply the modem.

Regardless of the terminal used, the library can either purchase a terminal for its own use or participate in a cooperative with other libraries and share a terminal. There are many examples of shared use. As early as 1979, five[15] special libraries in one office building in downtown Chicago shared a printer terminal to access OCLC for cataloging purposes. Each library used the terminal on its scheduled day, picking it up from one user and delivering it to the next. A 1981 project at the North Suburban Library System in Wheeling, Illinois, included five small libraries using a dedicated OCLC terminal located at the system headquarters. The five libraries developed the plan for use, did a cost-benefit study, and set up a schedule for use of the terminal. They searched for cataloging copy, edited records, produced cards, and responded to interlibrary loan requests. This project served to demonstrate the shared use of the terminal, while introducing OCLC to these public libraries. Several of the libraries eventually purchased their own terminal, two purchased IBM-PC's to be used in dial access, while several continued to use the system's terminal. Over a period of three years, ten libraries used the terminal for their cataloging and interlibrary loan requirements. Other shared projects involved several libraries using a terminal located in one of the libraries.

In California, with a two-year $150,000 private foundation grant, 12 private schools are using OCLC in a shared arrangement. The objectives of the project are to bring state of the art cataloging and computer access to the schools; to create a union catalog of school library holdings and provide a machine-readable record of these holdings to be used for individual online catalogs; and to provide each school with equipment, training, and staff assistance to improve other aspects of library service and to teach computer access as a research skill.[16] A professional cataloger was hired to implement the project and train staff in OCLC cataloging. Each library purchased an OCLC M300 terminal, printer, and modem. OCLC is used in dial-access mode by all project libraries. Each library has its own holding symbol for identification and each library receives its own cards. Simultaneously, the libraries are creating a machine-readable record of their holdings, providing the participating libraries with a bibliographic database for individual or shared local circulation or online catalog system.

The major demonstration of use of a bibliographic utility by small- and medium-size libraries was undertaken by the Illinois Valley Library System in Pekin, Illinois. From January 1980 to December 1982, 33 public and nonpublic libraries participated in a Library Services and Construction Act funded project on OCLC use. "The purpose was to examine the costs and benefits of using OCLC. . . ."[17] Each library was given an introduction to OCLC and provided with hands-on experience with the system, at a minimal cost. Following the project period, each library was given the option of continuing to use OCLC at its own expense or returning to its earlier method of cataloging.

The Illinois Valley project addressed the full range of issues associated with use of OCLC, including implementation, cost studies, attitudes about OCLC, use by library clusters, OCLC public access terminals, and interlibrary loan before and after OCLC. An important indirect result of this three-year project was the creation of a machine-readable record of the holdings of the 33 system libraries, as the libraries cataloged both their current purchases, as well as their existing collections. This database was eventually loaded into the Illinois Valley Library System's local circulation system, providing a regional online union catalog. The report of the three-year project can be found in the eight-volume report published by the System, *Illinois Valley Library System OCLC Experimental Project*.

A final common way for a small library to use a bibliographic utility is through the services of a state or regional processing center or contracting with a larger library for cataloging. The Riverside City County Public Library has contracted with several smaller libraries in the county providing catalog cards for the materials those libraries acquire. Working from an order slip prepared by the contracting library, the staff at Riverside catalogs the materials and produces cards and labels, which are shipped directly to the local library from OCLC and Riverside, respectively. Unlike a processing center, Riverside does not receive the materials ordered by the contracting library.

The member libraries of the Westchester Library System in Elmsford, New York, can use the services of Utlas via the System processing center. Libraries submit order slips and the center handles acquisition, cataloging, and processing, with an average turnaround time following receipt of the book of five to eight days. Utlas provides the System with a complete package including catalog cards for the local library and a regional union catalog on COM. At this writing, the system only processes books, due to concerns about delivering audiovisual materials on the System's van delivery system.[18]

Another shared use of bibliographic utilities involves several local libraries sharing an automated circulation system. Libraries in the North Suburban and Suburban Library Systems in Illinois use OCLC for their cataloging. The bibliographic record is transferred into the Systems' CLSI circulation system via an Innovative Interface, Inc. interface unit. In a single process, the item is cataloged, the bibliographic record is transferred to the circulation system, catalog cards are produced, and the local library holding information is created. Development of a single OCLC profile, and assignment of one holding symbol for all the participating libraries, can further facilitate the local cataloging and streamline resource sharing activities.

COST-EFFECTIVE CONSIDERATIONS

Before signing a contract to use a bibliographic utility, the librarian should undertake a cost benefit study, comparing the cost of the current method of cataloging and cost associated with using the bibliographic utility. The study should include staff costs, including fringe benefits; the cost of catalog cards; cost of card sorting; the cost to correct catalog cards that have errors. In considering staff costs, the appropriate level of staff to perform the work must also be compared. The local library using the catalog card service of a book jobber can expect to receive cards for 75 percent of the items ordered if they require standard information, including LC cataloging. If the library is willing to accept original cataloging prepared by the vendor's staff, a higher hit rate can be expected. For the remaining 25 percent and for all audiovisual materials, the library will have to do its own cataloging. While the receiving and sorting of catalog cards can be done by a clerk or technician, original cataloging requires the skills of a librarian. With catalog cards from a book jobber, the cost of correcting errors, erasing incorrect or lengthy classification numbers and subject headings, the cost of typing new numbers or subject headings, as well as the cost of entirely retyping card sets with major errors, must be calculated. One member of the North Suburban Library System project discovered that 25 percent of the card sets received from the jobber had errors significant enough to require complete retyping. The library had paid the vendor for the card set and then had to originally catalog and prepare the new set of cards. Clearly the most costly aspect of cataloging is personnel.

The report of the Riverside City County Public Library experience[19] demonstrates the cost savings when using a bibliographic utility. The Hemet Public Library's per title cost for Fiscal Year 1986 using the services of the Riverside Public Library was $2.57 per title or $4,321 per year. Hemet realized important personnel savings, including reduction in librarian time allocated to cataloging from 30 hours per week to three hours, and a clerical time reduction of 50 percent, for a total staff time reduction from 45 hours weekly to eight to ten hours. The Hemet staff was not reduced, but reassigned to public service functions.

More difficult to apply a cost to, but equally important, is the additional delay in receiving new materials when cards are ordered from the book jobber. For books in stock, many jobbers report a seven to ten day shipping period. When cards are required, shipment can delay receipt of new materials by the local library by four to six weeks. When using a bibliographic utility, the library can search for the cataloging record, edit the record to meet local requirements, and produce cards in one process taking several minutes. The book can then be sent for processing and finally to circulation. It does not have to wait for catalog cards to be typed or corrected, but becomes more quickly available for patrons and staff.

A library with specialized or technical materials not acquired through a book jobber will have to consider an alternate source of cataloging information or do more original cataloging. An annual subscription to such cataloging sources as *National Union Catalog* is costly and can add further delays in making materials available due to publishing time requirements. Analysis of the bibliographic utility's membership may identify libraries with similar or related areas of interest, increasing the likelihood that one of these organizations has cataloged the item.

COST OF THE UTILITY

The costs will vary from utility to utility and in the case of OCLC from network to network. Initial costs include hardware—both terminal and printer, staff training, supplies, and membership fees, where applicable. For the library wishing to use the system in dial access and already owning a microcomputer and printer, the costs are minimal, having to cover only a 1200 or 2400 baud modem, communication software, and membership and training costs. Ongoing monthly costs for a dedicated terminal generally include terminal maintenance fees, modem fees, telecommunication fees, as well as fees for using the system—searching the union catalog, producing cards, requesting an item on interlibrary loan.

Dial access is cost effective for libraries cataloging less than 2,000 titles annually. The library has greater control over costs, as dial access charges are billed based on minutes online, rather than a monthly fee. For example, at this writing the OCLC dial access charge is $9.60 per connect hour, plus a $4 per month password fee. For OCLC PACNET libraries, the monthly telecommunication charges are $175 per terminal plus $65 modem fee per modem. The dial access user can be online 26.5 hours per month before equalling the monthly telecommunications and modem charges. If the library does not use a utility-supplied terminal, costs for terminal maintenance are also eliminated, further reducing the charges by $36–$43 per month.

Current RLIN search only fees include a $225 one-time start-up charge. Recurring charges include $15.50 per hour Tymnet connect charges, $4.20 per month Tymnet account fee, and $63 per connect hour fee to search the database. OCLC PACNET dial access charges include $9.60 per hour Tymnet connect charge or $25 per hour Telenet fee, $4 per month Tymnet or Telenet password fee, and $200 per year dial access authorization fee. Neither utility has minimum per month search charges.

Before a librarian decides what avenue to select—dial access versus dedicated terminal, purchasing a vendor supplied and modified terminal versus using off-the-shelf equipment—the library needs to calculate the true cost of each option. Due to the methods used in dial access, it takes longer to edit and produce a record than on a dedicated terminal. Whereas a search and produce on a dedicated terminal may take three minutes, a search and produce on a dial access terminal may be double the time. Since the library is paying for each minute online, telecommunication costs can rapidly exceed those of the dedicated terminal. Purchasing a terminal specifically modified for use with the utility, from the vendor, will result in improved staff performance and reduced staff cost. This issue is rapidly becoming moot since many vendors are now using modified IBM-PC's which allow the library to use the utility's terminal for online reference searching, word processing, and other library and office automation applications. The next step for the utilities is development of software that will allow off-the-shelf microcomputers to emulate the modified terminals, further removing the library's dependence on a specialized terminal.

References

1. The number of libraries reported by OCLC, RLIN, WLN, and Utlas, July 30, 1986.
2. DiAnn Iverson, Coordinator OCLC PACNET, Claremont, California, phone interview July 28, 1986.
3. James Rice, *Introduction to Library Automation.* (Littleton, Co.: Libraries Unlimited, 1984), p. 55.
4. Phil Schreiber, OCLC, Inc., Dublin, Ohio, phone interview, July 25, 1986.
5. Rice, p. 57.
6. Kathleen Bales, Manager Systems Analysis and Design, Research Libraries Group, Stanford, California, phone interview July 28, 1986.
7. Bruce Ziegman, Coordinator, Western Library Network, Seattle, Washington, phone interview, July 29, 1986.
8. "10 millionth OCLC ILL," *LJ Hotline* (June 23, 1986): 2.
9. William Saffady, *Introduction to Automation for Librarians.* (Chicago: American Library Assn., 1983), p. 188.
10. Thomas L. Johnson, memo to Administration, Riverside City County Public Library, Riverside, California, regarding survey results on source of bibliographic records, November 26, 1985, p. 1.
11. Schreiber.
12. The RLIN database totals reflect individual member copies of bibliography records.
13. Ziegman.
14. Saffady, p. 200.
15. Arlene Schwartz, former ILLINET network manager, Illinois State Library, Springfield, Illinois, phone interview, July 25, 1986.
16. John Shaloiko, "Independent School Network Joins OCLC," *OCLC Newsletter* (June 1986): 10.
17. Linda Bills, *Illinois Valley Library System OCLC Experimental Project Report, No. 1.* (Pekin, Ill.: Illinois Valley Library System, 1982), p. 1.
18. Mitch Freedman, Director, Westchester Library System, Elmsford, New York, phone interview, July 29, 1986.
19. Thomas L. Johnson, "Cataloging Service Contracts: the Riverside Experience," *Technicalities* (June 1986): 14.

Circulation Procedures

Carl O. Heffington

"You certainly seem to be asking for a lot of money. Just how many books do you check out anyway?" Sound familiar? When librarians say that they need more money, the first thing elected officials and citizens usually want to know is how many books the library checks out. Of course, librarians know that circulation is only one aspect of the entire library operation, but many "outsiders" seem not to realize this. As a result, circulation has probably assumed a far greater importance than it should to public and staff alike. Circulation of books is something that most people readily comprehend; books are the most visible and perhaps the most often used service. Today's library, however, circulates computers, computer software, records, audiocassettes, videocassettes, art works, audiovisual equipment, and interlibrary loan (ILL) materials. Some even have expanded their holdings to tools and toys.

POLICY AND PROCEDURES

No matter what a library plans to circulate, there are questions which first must be answered: What items may be checked out? Who will be able to check out items—resident, nonresident, children? How long can an item stay out? Will some items stay out longer than others? Will fines be charged, and if so, how much—and will all fines be the same? Will a patron be able to check an item out if a fine is owed? How long will a fine continue on a particular item? The librarian also needs to ask how the library will keep track of those materials checked out.

Policies are similar to by-laws and constitutions and are generally made by the governing authority. Every library has a group of people who govern that library's operation. Public libraries generally have a board, whether elected or appointed; colleges and schools have boards plus principals and superintendents; and special libraries in businesses, hospitals, etc. all have some governing authority. It is imperative that all policies be approved by the governing body. The librarian should draft the policy and explain its ramifications to that body. When a policy has not been approved, problems can be expected. Guidelines for

---

Carl O. Heffington is the Director of the Fitzgerald-Ben Hill County Library, Fitzgerald, Georgia.

developing policies vary, but one rule should always be followed: be flexible so that the governing body does not need to be constantly redefining what it means.

In writing a policy, look at what other libraries have done and/or see what the professional library associations have come up with. Know the community and determine what will work best. Keep the policy brief and succinct. Remember that it can be changed, but if it is general enough, the librarian won't have to go back to the drawing board. Policies cannot be the same for all libraries. Some libraries may not circulate any items; some may circulate only to the staff of their institution or organization. But regardless of the library, a policy statement should be general enough to allow the librarian some flexibility. Policies set general guidelines for the administration of the library and protect that administration by the power/authority the board gives it. A policy also enables the administration *not* to have to go to its board each time for a procedural/regulation change.

Many libraries do not have a circulation policy, but a set of procedures which may or may not have been approved by their boards throughout the years. Boards do not need to be involved with day-to-day decisions, but they should be given an opportunity to review proposed procedural changes. While the librarian is not asking for approval, the board is being kept informed. If the board objects, then it has the opportunity to express itself.

Once a policy is in place, procedures can be enacted to implement it. Procedures can be divided into two categories: mechanical and philosophical. Procedures are specific, e.g., "books may be checked out for two weeks and may (or may not) be renewed." In procedures, the library can require identification, a library card, and anything else it feels is necessary. As circulation methods change, the rules may also need to be changed. The following is an example of how one library combined both circulation policies and procedures. (At the end of this chapter are additional examples of library procedures.)

Circulation Policies of "x" Library
Books

1. No limit to the number of books that a person can check out.
2. Unless otherwise stated circulation period is two weeks.
3. Reference collection does not circulate except at the discretion of the director and then only overnight.
4. Current magazines circulate overnight; other magazines circulate for two weeks.
5. Classroom loans to teachers circulate indefinitely, but are renewed every two weeks.
6. Children 14 years old and younger are encouraged to use the Children's

and Young Adult Section. It is felt that these books are best suited for their reading level. Children needing adult books are encouraged and helped.

7. Fines are a nickel per day per hardback books and magazines. Paperback book fines shall not exceed 25 cents per paperback (all paperback books are donations).

Video Tapes

1. Limit of two tapes per household.
2. Tapes circulate till closing time of the next day.
3. No one under 18 can check out tapes. (Done in conformance with the Georgia Obscenity Law of 1982.)
4. The day before closing for a holiday, the library circulates four tapes per household. (Done to disperse collection in case something happens to building.)
5. Fines are two dollars per tape per day for overdue tapes. (Done to prevent overdues.)

What circulation system is the library going to use? Should it be manual, semi-automated, or fully computerized? If the library is going to cost-efficient, the choice should be based upon the size of the population to be served. If cost is not a problem and the numbers justify it, or the library wants to be up with the "big boys," a fully computerized/automated system can be chosen. There are essentially two phases in setting up a circulation system.

Phase One: In the most basic and frequently used circulation system, the name or number of the patron is entered on the circulation card next to the date due. The only equipment required is a date stamp. This time-honored method still fills the needs of hundreds of libraries and requires little or no staff training. Next upgrade is semi-automation, with probably the Gaylord Model C Charger—about as semi- as one can get. This machine is much like the mousetrap—basic, functional, and practically unchanged over the years. It allows the flexibility of being able to use four different check-out periods and lasts a long time. Gaylord will also do "tune-ups" on the machine.

The big time is a fully automated system. Many opinions abound as to how the amount of circulation and size of the library system justify being fully automated. Both are important factors. There are many different systems; more will be evolving and some will fall by the wayside. Just look down that yellow brick road and plan. Don't box yourself in. If you are building, but aren't now planning to automate, plan the building so that automation will be no problem in the future. While it may not be feasible to automate now because of size, in ten or twenty years, even if the size has not changed, advances in computerization plus a lowering of costs will probably make it practical.

There are two approaches for the librarian to consider when automating: a turn-key operation or a system individually developed. A turn-key operation requires adapting to the available program(s). This can result in a major restructuring, not only of procedures, but also of staff thinking. These systems can also be very expensive. In a small system miles from a large area with computer support, there may be a downtime problem while waiting for assistance or repairs.

Or you can choose to do it yourself. The librarian can identify several people in the community who have expertise in programming and pick one to train staff on the computers and to write programs for the library. There are many advantages to having a local expert who can tailor a program for the library's specific needs; is close by for emergencies; is usually less expensive; and is easy to deal with.

Phase Two: After the method of circulation has been chosen, filing and recording must be considered next. The computer can do both, theoretically eliminating the worry, and saving many steps and lots of paperwork. It can generate reports from circulation activity which can be invaluable in determining what is really happening.

But, for most small libraries, filing and recording will be done manually. There are many variations. As an example, in Conway (Horry County), South Carolina two due dates were used for regular and short loans. All regular loan items were due back on the same day of the week, Friday. Items which could go out for a shorter period were also due back on Friday.

Horry County's system has been in use for several years and seems to work well for very small and medium size systems. The county serves a spread out population of 100,000 people with no large cities, and consists primarily of two very small libraries and three other slightly larger ones. Circulation at the small ones runs between 20,000 and 35,000 a year with just one full-time staff person and occasional part-time help. The drawbacks of this system include: 1) each day's circulation has to be interfiled in the correct date-due file; 2) people using the library initially have some difficulty thinking about the length of the loan, which varies depending on the day of the week the book is checked out; and 3) due dates tend to have a large number of returns resulting in increased workload at the desk. The advantages are: 1) fewer alphabets to search for reserves; 2) better scheduling of overdue notices; 3) date stamps changing only once a week; and 4) a certain mnemonic assist in having all due dates on same day of the week.

After the "due-back" method has been chosen, exceptions must be considered. While circulation is fairly straightforward and uncomplicated, there are usually deviations in any library. Many libraries have different checkout periods for bestsellers, art prints, videocassettes, and reference material. These differences will not cause much of a problem, if any, to an automated system although it may cost the library more for more complicated programming. The Gaylord Charger has four different due dates which allow some flexibility, but also limit it. To make up for what the charger can't do, a date stamp can be used or after using the charger, the due date can be marked through and the correct one written in. With this latter method, the library still has the imprint of the library card and the patron's ID number. If the patron's number or name is written in, the library immediately has problems; human error in writing the number and the time it takes to do the writing.

Another problem may develop is a library checks out periodicals. If several issues of a periodical are checked out at a time, there are basically two choices; have a card for each issue or check out all the issues on one card. While this method is a tremendous timesaver and easy to do, there is a major drawback: since the date of the periodical and the patron's name or ID number have to be written in they could be recorded incorrectly.

In many libraries, videorecordings have become one of the chief factors in circulation; in some, they account for nearly half of all circulation. The kinds of videos the library acquires—popular movies, children's movies, educational/instructional films—all have an effect upon circulation procedures. There should be a policy concerning acquiring videos, especially because of the copyright law. The director and/or staff should then determine the length of time items can be checked out plus the amount of the fine. Here are some samples of actual policies:

Library "A"

I. Video Cassette Tapes
A. Patrons must be registered library users and can only use their card.
B. Patrons must be 18 years or older.
C. Overnight circulation only except for tapes otherwise marked. Tapes must be returned one hour before closing the following day. Tapes checked out on Saturdays are due the following Monday, one hour before closing.
D. There is a $5 per day late charge on each tape checked out. Days closed also count as there is an outdoor book drop.
E. Tapes must be rewound.
F. There is no limit on the number of tapes that can be checked out.

II. Video Equipment
A. Equipment circulates to organizations and businesses.
B. Equipment may be used in the library by registered patrons 18 or older.
C. Circulation is usually for one day only. Check with director if more time is needed.

Library "B"

The library has motion pictures on VHS video tape which may be checked out for home use. They can be checked out on a regular patron card by anyone 18 years old or older. One or two titles may be checked out per family for a 24-hour period. There is a $1 per title, nonresident fee for use outside the six Georgia counties which are served by the library system. Overdues are charged when the materials are not returned on time; they are $1 overnight and 25 cents per hour that the library is open, per title. The person checking out the videos is responsible for their safe return, and all pertinent copyright laws do apply.

The library staff should review all policies and procedures on an ongoing basis. New policies such as those concerning videos can be reviewed at regular staff meetings to see if they are meeting the patron's and the library's needs, keeping in mind what is best for the patron and not necessarily the staff.

Art works seem to be less of a problem because not as many are checked out and most libraries check them out for fairly extended periods of time and are generous with renewals.

Cassette recordings may create special problems in circulation. Placement for patron's browsing has a direct bearing on the manner in which these materials are checked out. For example, a library may keep the cassettes in their cases with the circulation card and house them with records in a bin. This will work out fine until lack of space and difficulty in keeping them in order require another solution. Revolving cassette carousels are fine except that cassettes in their cases with circulation cards will not fit into the slot in the carousel. The solution to this problem is to keep the circulation cards in a separate place in Dewey order. When a patron checks out a cassette, the card is retrieved. The empty cases can be kept on a shelf close by the circulation area. The cassette can then be placed in a case, with a date due slip.

Automation becomes more attractive if a library has a huge circulation in video- and/or audiocassettes. If that is not feasible, either more staff is needed or another look taken at the need for circulating these items. This is the time to reconsider the need for such items in light of the expense involved and a reevaluation of the library's *policy* concerning videos. In most communities, videos can be rented for as little as $1. Is there a need for the library to have the same material when it is so cheap elsewhere? It is time to consider cost efficiency over cost effectiveness. If a library decides to discontinue video- and audiocassette material, a Catch-22 situation arises. Circulation is lowered and political and governmental authorities will conclude that citizens do not need the library as much, and therefore not as much money needs to be allocated. The catch is that audio- and videocassettes and records usually bring in a great number of people who would not otherwise use the library, and these people will cease to be exposed to what else the library has to offer if this service is discontinued.

Many libraries check out various types of equipment such as slide projectors, 16mm projectors, cameras, and opaque and overhead projectors. Generally, circulation of these items is best limited to groups, businesses, and civic clubs. Even with groups, the policy should require that the person checking out the item be registered; or the library might issue company/business library cards, making the organization responsible for the library materials. Exceptions can be made, but in the long run everyone is saved a lot of grief if the library is strict. Businesses have to abide by rules and they will have greater respect for the library if they know it is run in the same manner.

Another problem for the small library is checking every record and cassette that is returned to see if it is warped, broken, etc. Some libraries have stopped circulating these items altogether because of staff cost. Others believe that the hassle is worth the trouble: if nothing else, popular records will bring in those young people between the ages of 13 and 20 who tend to forget the library.

At the time of registration, or when a library card is given, the patron should be given information concerning the procedures for checking out materials plus the user's responsibility for returning these materials. If the library is not automated for circulation, certain steps need to be done manually when a patron checks out an item. Someone must see if the patron is in good standing. This necessitates looking at the patron's registration card, which can be tagged in some manner to alert staff that the patron has overdue material or owes fines. One of the more effective means of tagging cards is with a color-coded plastic shield (cover).

THE THREE R'S

Renewals, Reference, and Reserves—libraries can't do without them but many find it difficult to work with them.

Renewals. If the library allows renewals, several questions must be answered beforehand. What items may be renewed and will there be any exceptions? There should be a definite policy which is made clear to library personnel. Exceptions are generally left up to the director. How many times may an item be renewed? This is again up to each individual library system, but should be a written part of either the library's policy or procedure. Renewals of bestsellers should also be in writing, but probably not as a part of policy; what determines a "bestseller" may vary. May an item be renewed if someone else has requested it? It is hoped that the answer is no. Most patrons will understand and know that when they want an item they will have a better chance of getting it. When may an item be renewed? In general, most libraries do not allow books to be renewed more than three or four days in advance of the due date. If an item is overdue, it probably should not be renewed. If the public knows that the library is impartial and will enforce their rules, then few problems should result.

In addition to policy/procedural problems, there are also some "mechanical" questions to be resolved. How should the circulation card be marked to let the staff know that someone wants an item and how will they know who wants it? Some libraries write the patron's name or number on the circulation card itself. This has obvious drawbacks: it is extremely messy and there may not be enough room to write all the names. A computer can automatically produce a signal, but for those not automated, the best way may very well be to place a color-coded plastic slip on the circulation card. The staff person should then refer to where the information on requests are kept (usually behind the circulation desk). Some libraries use an index card box, with the cards arranged alphabetically by author, or title, or both. The patron's full name, telephone number, and address should be written on the card, especially if notices are to be mailed.

When patrons are contacted, they should be told how long the item will be held (which should not be indefinitely!). After the patron is notified, the date of notification plus the patron's name and/or number should be written down on the item in such a way as to let the rest of the staff know when the notification transpired. If the item is not picked up, the library should move on to the next person on the list or put the item back on the shelf. If all procedures are followed, the patron knows what is expected and the staff has protection and guidance.

Reference. The director generally determines what constitutes reference materials. Most small libraries do not have a professional staff reference person, but if they do, then the decision should be made jointly. Whether a reference item may or should be circulated depends upon the philosophical question, How *restrictive* should a library be? A public library ought to be as unrestricted as possible, but in actual practice this is not always the case. Some libraries permit their patrons to take out reference materials, even though it might be only for overnight, but this policy has many pitfalls. It will only work if the patron doesn't forget; doesn't have car trouble; doesn't have his/her car or house burn; doesn't have the material stolen; or doesn't die! Any librarian can vouch for one of these things happening, and when it does, another patron invariably wants that particular item, and expect the same privilege. Another unfortunate result is lost or unreturned items that are irreplaceable or very expensive. Librarians must use common sense and good judgment and should beware of making exceptions.

Reserves. "Would you please not let anyone check out books on American constitutional law for the next six weeks? My students will be working in this area and will need this material." How familiar this is!

What about the garden club that wants their material set aside or the NAACP wanting special materials set aside for Black History Month? The library could allow these items to go out for "x" number of days or not at all. While the former is good for community relations, it does cause special recordkeeping headaches and other problems such as where to find space for all these special collections the library has suddenly acquired. Usually no one is satisfied.

INTERLIBRARY LOANS

Many of the procedures concerning interlibrary loan (ILL) are already determined by state and national ILL policies and procedures. There are several books which can be of help: *Interlibrary Loan* by the Association of Research Libraries, Systems and Procedures Exchange Center; *Interlibrary Loan,* Vol. 6, edited by James E. Rush; and *Interlibrary Loan Practices Handbook* by Virginia Butcher. While the cost effectiveness of ILL may be questioned, its effect as promotional tool cannot. ILL allows any library to say *yes* instead of *no*. The positive response may take longer, but it keeps the library's reference and loan procedure in a positive mode. Negatives should never be a part of a library's standard vocabulary.

FINES AND FEES

Since charging, collecting, and recording fines and fees are usually the function of the circulation staff, the duties of bookkeeping and cashiering should be added to their job description. Fines and fees can have a negative impact on circulation since the person who owes will not be able to check anything out. Some libraries carry this a step further by denying any of the person's family the right to check out materials, although this is usually done when the delinquent patron is young and is not considered responsible because of age. In effect, this keeps the family from checking out materials for that person on another family member's card. This procedure has its pros and cons, but if applied fairly, works well.

OVERDUES

When patrons are informed of overdues at the circulation desk, they may become upset, especially if they claim that they did not know and/or they never checked out that item, and/or they returned the item and it wasn't late, and/or if they ask why they are just being told. To avoid this situation, libraries have devised a variety of methods to notify the patron of an overdue. In small libraries, the circulation personnel are usually responsible for this notification.

Some libraries send out notices every two to four weeks. The notice contains the number of items outstanding plus the amount of fines owed. If there is a state or local ordinance (a necessity if the procedure is to have any teeth), it should be included. Since sending out overdues and even charging fines can be an expensive procedure, some libraries have quit sending notices and some have even quit the fine business. Probably the greatest block to quit charging fines is a moral one. Many people seem to feel that those who don't obey should pay, even if it costs the taxpayer money in the long run. The principle of the issue becomes dominant.

RECORDKEEPING

Recordkeeping is frequently considered nothing more than additional paperwork which the small library has neither the staff nor the time to do. Yet it is very important. A recordkeeping system should reflect accurately what has transpired by day and month in the library. Two basic sheets can be used to record circulation statistics. One is a daily log and the other a monthly recap.

For the daily log, a count is taken two to three times a day (counts should not wait until the end of the day or the library will never catch up). At the end of the day, the information is transferred to the monthly recap sheet. This system doesn't take long, even when done manually, and the information is invaluable. Looking at a library's recordkeeping, however, does make a computerized system seem more inviting and less expensive.

There is practically nothing that goes on in a library, especially a small one, which doesn't affect circulation. Acquisitions, fines, fees, reference, programs, publicity, displays, etc., all have an effect upon items circulated by the library. All personnel should be cognizant of the fact that what they do affects other parts of the library's operation. Circulation personnel should be made aware of special library programs and activities which will probably result in an upsurge of items being checked out and the need for more personnel at the circulation desk. Good communication is essential.

SAMPLE CIRCULATION DESK PROCEDURES

Books Returned to Desk
When a book is returned to desk, check pocket for transaction card.

Books Not Overdue
Check library stamp on pocket.
1. If book belongs to another library:
   a. Leave transaction card in book pocket.
   b. Place book in the delivery box for pickup.
   c. If transaction card is missing, insert a Returned Without Transaction Slip (Form ____) in the pocket and charge the patron $.25 for loss of card.
2. If book has been returned to owning library:
   a. Pull transaction card and separate into designated order by 100s or 1000s ready to be sent to Record Control Unit.
   b. Check the reserve list and if the title is not on the list, book is ready to be placed on book truck and shelved.

Overdue Books
1. Determine amount of fine by reading date due on transaction card and using fine computer. (Fines are computed at the rate of five (5) cents per day per book that the Library is open. Maximum fine for one book is $2, or the price of the book, whichever is smaller.)
2. Collect money and deposit in desk drawer and enter amount on Daily Cash Report (Form ____).
3. Give patron a receipt if amount received is $5 or more or if patron requests receipt for lesser amount. Retain duplicate in library receipt book and give patron original copy.

Damaged Books
1. When a patron returns a book damaged beyond repair:
   a. Check *Books in Print.* If the book is listed, collect the amount shown. (This is also to be done with any books having the price on the book pocket.)
   b. If the price is *not* in *Books in Print,* charge the patron the average price for that category as listed in the *Bowker Annual.*
   c. Once the book has been paid for, the patron may keep it, but all library identification *must be removed at that time.*
2. If the book can be rebound:
   a. Consult the bindery price list for the amount to be charged.
   b. Charge the patron only the cost for rebinding and not the price of the book.

3. The amount paid is entered on Form ____. Give the patron a receipt (original copy) and retain the duplicate copy in the Library. The receipt should include the patron's name, book title and author, accession number, and the name of the owning library. It should also have "DAMAGED BOOK" indicated.
4. When applicable, overdue records should be cleared and any fines paid at the time the damaged book is returned.

Lost and Paid-For Books
1. When a patron comes in and wants to pay for lost material *before* he or she receives a notice from Record Control Unit:
   a. Tell patron to delay payment for lost materials until he or she receives a notice from Record Control Unit. In the meanwhile, the patron should check thoroughly and so will the library.
   b. Please make a note of the patron's name, book title, and date he or she offered to pay for the lost materials. Fines will be suspended from that point.
2. When a patron has been notified of the prices of the materials checked out and is ready to pay for the lost materials:
   a. Collect price of the lost materials (books, prints, etc.) and record on proper form.
   b. A receipt must be given for amount of money received and should include patron's name, book title, author, accession number, and branch ownership. The original copy is for the patron and the duplicate to be retained in Library receipt book. Indicate "LOST BOOK" on the receipt.
   c. Advise patron that should the lost materials be found, he or she may receive a refund upon surrender of the material and a copy of the receipt or cancelled check.
   d. Follow standard delete procedures.
   e. Send notice to Record Control Unit so that they can clear their records. Clearly mark "PAID" on the notice.

Lost and Damaged State and Inter-Library Loan Material
When state or interlibrary loan material is damaged by a patron, the amount to be charged will be determined by the lending agency. Notify the Reserve Librarian, who will contact the lending agency and advise you of the amount to be paid by the patron.

Refund for Payment of Lost Book
If patron returns book that has been paid for, with either a cancelled check or a library receipt, fill out Patron Refund Slip, Form ____, and the check will be mailed to patron from the Comptroller's Office. UNDER

NO CIRCUMSTANCES GIVE THE PATRON MONEY FROM THE CASH DRAWER.

Claims Returned Overdue Book
When a patron claims he or she has returned an overdue book:
1. Check the shelf. If book is on shelf, write on the overdue notice "On Shelf" and send to Record Control Unit.
2. If patron does not have notice or if patron phones in, write down the following information and send to Record Control Unit:
   a. Library checked out from.
   b. Library returned to.
   c. Date Due Number on Notice.
   d. Patron's name.

Renewals
When a patron returns a book to the desk for renewal:
1. Check transaction card. If book is overdue, collect fine according to the procedure for overdue books.
2. Check Hot Sheet or Reserve Cards held in your library. If it is on reserve, the book cannot be renewed. Place it with other reserves to be notified, or send it to the Reserve Librarian, whichever is appropriate.
3. If the book belongs to another library, and is not on the Hot Sheet, telephone the owning library to determine if it has a reserve on the book. If on reserve, the book cannot be renewed and must be returned to the owning library.
4. If the book is not on reserve, pull the transaction card for return to the Record Control Unit. Charge out the book using regular checkout procedure.

Delete Procedures
To delete a book from the computer records:
1. Fill out a loss on a Book Inventory Update form (____).
2. If a book is being reordered, write reorder on the bottom of this sheet.
3. Send the completed forms to the Catalog Unit on Tuesdays.

Audiovisual Materials (Films, Cassettes, Recordings, Filmstrips, Art Prints, Audiovisual Equipment)
See Audiovisual section for circulation policy and procedure.

Paperback Books
Paperback books are handled by two different methods within the system, with each library electing which of the two methods it will follow. Paperback collections in each of these libraries are comprised of either donated paperbacks or of ones which are purchased.

1. Libraries having collections of donated paperbacks use the following check-out and circulation count procedures:
   a. Paperbacks are not charged out on the Recordak. They are instead date stamped only on the inside back cover.
   b. No overdue fines are charged for these books.
   c. The circulation count is hand tallied on the Weekly Circulation Report.
   d. These paperback books will all be clearly marked as donated materials. Libraries holding an all-donated paperback collection have the option at any time of changing to a collection of purchased paperbacks.
2. Libraries with a collection of purchased paperbacks use the below listed check-out and circulation count procedures:
   a. Paperbacks are charged out on the Recordak. Their author, title, and identification as a paperback are entered on the book pocket placed on the inside back cover so that this information can be photographed. Transaction cards are used with these paperbacks, just as with hardbound books.
   b. Overdue fines are levied at the rate of $.05 per day, with a maximum fine of $2 or the price of the book, whichever is *less*.
   c. The circulation count is automatically included with other filmed transactions on the Weekly Circulation Report (Form ____).

Libraries holding a collection of purchased paperbacks will accept donations of these materials but will treat them as purchased paperbacks once they become part of the collection.

Children's paperback books are considered as purchased paperbacks and are to be treated as under Number 2 above.

Recordak Procedure
1. Do not move cards or place your hands over cards until the Recordak has completed its entire filming transaction.
2. Center and arrange book pocket, transaction card, and patron's card as close together as possible when filming on Recordak.
3. The following should be clearly visible when filming transactions:
   a. Transaction cards—transaction card number, branch number, and date due number.
   b. Bookpocket or white card—author's name, title, accession number, call number.
   c. Patron's library card—patron's name, address, telephone number, and library card number.
4. Exposed Recordak films *must* be sealed in the blue plastic containers, *not* in paper envelopes or boxes. These containers should be taped shut, with the proper form (____) applied to the front of the box. Send to Record Control Unit for processing.

Payment by Check

When a patron pays for a fine, lost book, nonresident library card, etc., with a check, the following information should be either printed or written on the check legibly:

1. Correct name and address.
2. Telephone number.

All checks should be made payable to the ____ County Public Library System.

AUDIOVISUAL POLICY AND PROCEDURES

All audiovisual equipment and material will be checked out as follows:

1. Juvenile card holders will not be permitted to check out framed prints (excepting mini prints), 16mm films, videorecording tapes, or audiovisual equipment. They may check out audiovisual materials.
2. Nonresident and transient card holders will not be permitted to check out audiovisual materials, framed prints, 16mm films, videorecording tapes, or audiovisual equipment.
3. All audiovisual equipment, framed prints, 16mm films, and videorecording tapes must be checked out on a free, *permanent* card only (one which has been mailed to patron by the Record Control Unit).
4. Up to two items of audiovisual material may be checked out on a New Registration Check Out Slip (Form ____).
5. All audiovisual material and equipment will be checked out at and returned to the circulation desk.
   a. Audiovisual materials are charged out through the Recordak. Book pockets and cards are provided for this purpose.
   b. Framed prints and mini prints, 16mm films, videorecording tapes, and audiovisual equipment are *not* charged out on the Recordak. Special forms are available for maintaining check-out records on these items. (Framed prints and mini prints: Framed Prints— Form ____; 16mm films, videorecording tapes, and audiovisual equipment: Audiovisual Equipment and State Films— Form ____.)

Cassettes

1. Cassettes may be checked out for two weeks, or less time due to supply.
2. Requests for cassettes follow the same procedure as books.
3. Overdue fines are $.25 a day, per cassette. Maximum fine $10.

Filmstrips

1. Filmstrips are checked out for two weeks or less time due to limited supply.

2. Limit five filmstrips or limit two for holiday or demand material.
3. Overdue fines are $.25 a day, per filmstrip. Maximum fine $10.

Phonograph Records
1. Records are checked out for two weeks.
2. Overdue fines are $.05 a day, per record. Maximum fine $2.

Slides
1. Slides are checked out for two weeks.
2. Overdue fines are $.25 a day, per set. Maximum fine is $10.

Video Recording Tapes
1. Video recording tapes are checked out for two weeks.
2. Overdue fines are $1. per day, per tape. No maximum fine.

Framed Prints
High quality framed prints will be purchased for circulation as the budget allows.

Print Check-Out
1. Check Framed Print file to see if patron has other prints checked out.
2. If patron owes a fine from a previous loan, fine should be cleared before any further check-out.
3. A patron may check out two (2) prints at a time but may have no more than two prints in his or her possession at any one time—with the exception of mini prints when the number becomes four (4).
4. Fill out Framed Prints form (___) from Framed Print file. Have patron read and sign. Verify signature from patron's library card.
5. Damage due to negligence on the part of the patron will be charged to the patron—this may include cost of reframing or replacing print.
6. Prints will be loaned for one month and may be renewed one time if there is no other request for the title on file.

Print Returns
All prints must be returned to or renewed at the library from which they were checked out.
1. Pull Framed Prints form and verify item returned.
2. If all items are returned and not overdue:
   a. Initial and date form and place in returned file.
   b. Check weekly for overdue.
3. If print is overdue:
   a. Collect fine of $1 per day, per print. No maximum. Mini print $.25 per day, per print. $10 maximum.

   b. Indicate amount of fine on Fees and Fines Daily Cash Report
      (Form ____).
4. Check for damage.
   a. If damage is found, note damage on Framed Prints form and send
      print to Processing.
   b. If no damage is found, display print for circulation.

Circulation Count
So that there will be no double counting on visual aids, keep your count
for the monthly Circulation Report as follows: in addition to recording
those audiovisual materials that are transacted on the Recordak, you
must also keep an accurate count by hand. At the end of the day subtract
each audiovisual transaction from the Recordak total for that day.
   Example: If a patron checks out a box of filmstrips (with 5 filmstrips)
and two cassettes you have two transactions. For your hand count you
will have five filmstrips and two cassettes but you will subtract two
transactions from the Recordak total. Framed prints are counted by
hand only. This will give you an accurate count for filmed circulation
and an accurate account under Audiovisuals.

16mm Film Service
1. Films are ordered from the State Department of Education, Public
   Library Division, with the following requirements:
   a. The Library cannot provide film service to public or private
      schools or kindergartens connected with a public or private school.
      Eligible schools can register for their own film service with the
      State Department of Education.
   b. The patron is required to present evidence that the film will be
      shown by a qualified projectionist. Payment for damage to the film
      will be charged to the patron at the rate established by the State
      Department of Education.
   c. Films are ordered the 1st of the month for the last 15 days of the
      month and the 15th of the month for the first 15 days of the
      following month.
   d. Libraries that have a subscription to this film service are
      _____.
   e. Film orders may be placed at any agency but all films will be
      coordinated geographically as follows:
      Library and patron orders are sent from:

   f. State films and equipment must be returned to the branch from
      which it was checked out unless prior arrangement is made.

    g. Include use of films and equipment for Story Time on your weekly report for inclusion in the monthly report.

2. The Library Board has established the following priorities in the use of films:
   a. The main use of films shall be for library-sponsored programs.
   b. Individual patrons may use the film service for home, group, or business use, but the person to whom it is checked out (whose name is on the library card) will be responsible for damage and any fine incurred.
3. Overdue fine is $1 a day, no maximum.

Audiovisual Equipment
The Library requires that audiovisual equipment be checked out only to those who are of any age of legal responsibility—18 or older, and are residents of the county.

    The following equipment is available to the public by request for a limited amount of time—overdue fines will be $1 a day, no maximum.

cassette player	super 8mm projector
filmstrip sound projector	screens
slide projector	Porta-Sound P.A. equipment
16mm projector	

Audiovisual Loans to Schools (see also School Loan Policy)
Teachers may borrow filmstrips, cassettes, records, video recording tapes, and study prints from the ____ County Public Library. Due to severe limitations of this collection, the check-out period varies but the maximum of time for a loan is two weeks with limited renewal.

    Delivery Service to ____ County Schools: Audiovisual materials will be delivered to the Board of Education or, at the discretion of the Audiovisual Coordinator, to the school.

    Delivery Service to City of _____ Schools and private schools: audiovisual materials will be delivered to the school on Wednesday afternoon. Pick-ups and deliveries to the library nearest the school will be made only at the discretion of the Audiovisual Coordinator.

Fines and Fees
Fines will be the same as for regular loans, due to limited size of the collection. School loans are not to be checked out on the Recordak.

4
Public Services

Reader Services

Janet R. Baker

The traditional or conventional definition of reader—or guidance—service casts the librarian in a somewhat formal educational and inspirational role, helping users educate themselves, become purposeful readers, extend their frontiers of knowledge, expand their powers of discrimination, appreciation, and judgment, and develop sound, lasting reading habits.

Arguing with that definition is difficult. To be very practical, however, reader service is perhaps better described as helping users find the materials they want, for whatever reason they want them. When looking at all the ways libraries use to bring books and readers together, we recognize that what is called "reader service" is an integral part of everyday library service.

The reader service program emphasizes the importance of the library's users and their needs and interests; it dispels the idea of the library as an elite, reference-oriented place just for people who have to "look something up." In practice, the reader service program ranges from book displays to booklists; from talk about books in the stacks to book talks to groups; from reserving a specific title to service to special groups.

The importance of staff commitment to a reader service program cannot be overemphasized. A combination of a helping, nonjudgmental attitude, wide book knowledge, and familiarity with the collection are essential staff requirements. The librarian's attitude contributes to the user's perception of satisfaction. What the request is doesn't matter. The request for a "good book" is not less important than a request for the causes of the French Revolution; the user's request should not be judged by its seriousness. Each person should leave the library feeling that he or she was helped, whether or not the specific request was satisfied.

READER ADVISORY SERVICE VS. REFERENCE

Larger libraries often divide service to users by function, with separate reference, circulation, information areas. This, plus more staff

Janet R. Baker is Director of the Gale Free Library, Holden, Massachusetts.

anonymity, may require a conscious commitment to the provision of the reader advisory service because there is no single place a user can go for assistance. In the small library, however, there is often only one service point, making it difficult to distinguish reader advisory service from all the other services provided. The same interaction may move smoothly from picking up a reserved book to a discussion of the bestseller list to actual advice on "something good to read" to finding an article on a particular subject.

In general, the reader advisory service is more casual or informal than reference service. It follows questions such as "I like to read about _____, what can you recommend?" "Is there another author like _____?" "What's a good book on _____?" "Has this author written any other books?" or statements such as "They're not writing books like they used to," "I'm tired of historical novels," "I haven't read anything for a long time," and "I've read everything you have."

STAFF/USER INTERACTION

If librarians are to be of service to users, they must let the user know that they are there to help. The librarian who is busy reading book reviews, filing catalog cards, writing a report, or working at any one of the hundreds of tasks in a small library must guard against sending the message "I am too 'busy' to help." The right message can be conveyed by: assigning responsibility for reader service; scheduling work that can be done in a public area; looking up, smiling, saying "hello"; being visible and accessible; using signs with messages: "Bother me, I'm here to help," "Advice on reading," "Looking for something good to read?"; being aware of the user's—and the librarian's—body language; saying: "I'm here if you need me." "Did you find what you were looking for?"; moving around, being approachable; wearing a name tag or a button with a library message; calling attention to displays of materials by tending them (straightening, adding, rearranging). The message sent is more important than the methods used, but the librarian should be comfortable with the method, so that the message "I can help" gets across. Librarians should use techniques that suit them personally, but should do something.

PREFERENCE INTERVIEW

When users seek advice, there are several possible steps which may be taken first, depending on what is asked for and the resources of the library. The most crucial to success is the preference interview which, like the reference interview, seeks to establish the user's needs. The simplest form of this interview consists of a conversation between librarian and user, in which the user answers such questions as: What do you like? What did you used to read? Who are your favorite authors? Do you like paperbacks? Are you familiar with large print? What don't you like?

The librarian uses this information to identify taste, interest, and perhaps reading level, and takes the user to the shelf where individual titles can be shown. Through the user's statements and body language, the librarian should be able to narrow the choices to those most suitable. Several selections might be pulled for the reader to choose from, or the user may be left to browse in an appropriate area. If a user asks for recommendations of mystery writers who feature women as detectives, but says, "Nothing that takes place in England—can't stand them," the librarian might point out shelf locations of several authors and leave the user to browse.

A more elaborate form of preference interview results in the personal preference file. This file keeps track of the reading choices of individuals; it can be kept either manually on file cards or on computer. Such files can be arranged by broad subjects, with the names of interested readers noted, or they can be arranged by user's name, with subject interests noted.

Some ways to acquire information about readers for such files are: request the information when registering new borrowers, either by personal interview or questionnaire; advertise the service and either conduct personal interviews with interested users or have users fill in printed questionnaires; make note of people's interests in special subjects as learned from newspaper articles and other sources.

Many small libraries give a casual kind of personal service to frequent users because the staff gets to know each person's tastes and interests or particular needs. While this is definitely a bonus which probably should not be taken away from those frequent users, the librarian should examine whether the necessary time can be given to create a formal personal preference service to meet all users' needs. Not only must each user's preferences be surveyed, but also a system of notifying them of the availability of appropriate material must be devised. This is not a one-time effort; it is a planned and periodic service. The preference file must be kept up-to-date; the notification process is ongoing. The small special library with a limited clientele is perhaps more likely to find a preference file worth the effort for its users because their needs and interests are often specialized and job-related.

DEVELOPING READER ADVISORY KNOWLEDGE

The process of matching library materials with users requires a thorough knowledge of books and their authors and the collection as a whole, as well as specialized reference tools. Although reader advisory is most often associated with public library service, the function exists in every kind of library. The librarian needs to know both the collection and the library's users, and be able to bring them together. When the librarian responsible for reader advisory is also responsible for collection development, as is often the case in small libraries, knowing the collection is simpler.

Some of the many ways librarians can increase their knowledge of the collection and their users' potential needs are to: shelf read from time to time to stay familiar with the collection; weed regularly, not only to withdraw and replace, but also to stay familiar with the collection; read book reviews, professional literature, the literature of the special library's field; be aware of TV and movie tie-ins, local and national newspaper and magazine coverage of books and authors (*Get Ready Sheet*); utilize resources such as lists of prize winners (Pulitzer Prize, American Book Awards, Notable Books); become familiar with the specialized guides to reading available at regional and system libraries; know who the popular authors are and were; know authors by genres; read widely.

BEYOND THE SHELF: RESERVES

When requested materials are owned but not on the shelf, the librarian should offer to reserve the missing items and let the user know when they are available. Though libraries may consider reserves routine, this service is a very important one from the user's point of view. There is now one less item on his or her list of things to do, get, or remember.

When talking about reserves, however, we are talking about popularity. It may be the blockbuster bestseller, the latest scoop on a highly technical process, the most popular book on the school reading list, or research for a local phenomenon such as a bicentennial celebration, but the library is being asked to provide it, over and over again.

If the library does not have a book selection policy or if the policy does not cover the handling of popular requests, this must be addressed first. No library should be without written policies for operation and collection development. They help ensure consistent, responsive service. When such policies are developed, they should be based on established user needs, both individual needs and the needs of the community of users. For example, a policy which provides an additional copy of a bestseller for each five reserves might set a limit on total copies purchased in order to preserve some balance in materials acquisition and the consequent effect on the budget. That balance between the demand of the users and the welfare of the collection as a whole for all the users must be finely adjusted and constantly examined.

Some examples of how libraries handle demand for particular materials include: 1) establishing a policy of purchasing an additional copy for a certain number of accumulated reserves, e.g., one for each five; 2) using McNaughton, Baker & Taylor, or another rental plan to acquire additional copies for as long as they are needed; 3) purchasing additional copies quickly by making arrangements to buy them locally; 4) purchasing paperbacks in quantity, when available, to meet demand for "classic" titles or popular subjects; 5) requesting deposits of materials on popular subjects or for school assignments from regional system libraries; 6) requesting deposits from nearby libraries; 7) limiting the loan period for materials in demand; 8) telephoning users when material is available in order to keep the item moving; 9) having users fill out postcards for reserves, thereby saving staff time; 10) charging for postcard reserves to discourage bulk reserving by users.

Librarians are cautioned against a condescending attitude toward those who will read only the bestsellers no matter how many recommendations they receive about similar authors and similar titles. They must also guard against a discriminatory policy toward bestsellers no matter how poor the writing and the reviews. Librarians are not at the library to tell people what they should read, but to provide them with what they want to read.

BEYOND THE SHELF: INTERLIBRARY LOAN

"If we don't have it, we can get it for you." The small library, in particular, needs to encourage this attitude in its staff and promote interlibrary loan service to its users. How interlibrary loan is actually provided depends on such local factors as access to, and relations with, nearby libraries, membership in regional or statewide systems, and state programs for networking and resource sharing. Although the mechanics of interlibrary loan will vary from state to state, the service is as simple as offering interlibrary loan for any item the library does not have, or offering to call a nearby library for a shelf check and user pickup. Even the largest library does not pretend to stand alone, and small libraries have a special obligation to make access beyond their limited collections possible for users. Librarians should not be reluctant to reveal their resource limitations. Interlibrary loan and referral are basic and legitimate parts of a library's reader service. After all, users really don't care where the material comes from, just that they get it.

ON DISPLAY

Supermarkets know it; department stores spend lots of money on it; bookstores rely on it: marketing. Libraries can, and should, show their wares, bringing books and users together in creative ways that don't have to be expensive.

Visible space can be allocated in a high traffic area for the display of library materials. It need not be large. It can be a countertop, a section of shelves, or tabletop; wall space with display cabinets or brackets; floor space with a book truck or display rack; or even boxes stacked to create a display island. It can be outside the library's doors: in store windows, another department of a special library, the school office, a corridor.

There are tools which make display easier; browsing through a catalog of library furniture and equipment is a good way to become familiar with them. Titles can be displayed as bookstores do: cover out. Zig-zag shelves will turn a regular bookshelf into a display shelf and leave room for spineout shelving as well. Small easels will support books on tables, countertops, and desktops—wherever there's space. Metal bookends can be used as stands to display individual books.

The list of topics for display is endless. Knowing the collection, the community, the interests of users, following current events, locally and beyond, and the seasons, and using the tried and true—all help to make choices for display.

Many librarians use displays to feature "good stuff from the stacks," such as: Librarian's Choice; Oldies but Goodies; Lonely Books; If You Enjoy Victoria Holt, You'll Like These; Sure Bets for Mystery (SF, Romance) Lovers; Bestsellers of Yesteryear; Rediscoveries; Never Out of Style; People You Know; The Staff Recommends; Prizewinners of the Past; and not least, "Good Stuff from the Stacks."

Because library users are often looking for what's new, there should be a section set aside for new books. Other ways to feature new books are displays of: this year's prizewinners, e.g., ALA Notable Books, American Book Awards, National Book Critics Circle Awards; new nonfiction on a popular or seasonal subject; new fiction titles with other titles by the same author; and titles "Recommended by . . . " the *New York Times Book Review,* the local paper, or some other source. Some libraries display all new books for one week, with no checkout, giving everyone who comes in an opportunity to see what's new in the collection. The policy on reserving these titles should be decided in advance.

Other possible topics for display are suggested by community needs and library use. A library which sees a lot of parents and children passing through should try displays of books on child care and education, child development and psychology, sports for young people, clothes, furniture, and games for children. Other popular subjects are home improvement and decorating, gardening, travel, and cooking. The important point is to select displays with the users of the library in mind.

Time is needed not only to select and set up a display, but also to take care of it. Marketing principles apply here; the display should look good, earn its space, and meet the user's needs. The display does not require sophisticated visuals or elaborate backgrounds, although it does need to attract attention. After all, the books and other library materials are what users are looking at, not the actual shelf or cabinet or book truck. The display area can be designed to be used over and over again with little effort on the part of the librarian. Time spent working out flexibility of display space will be valued in the future when a change of selection and sign is all that's needed for a new display.

Time is needed to make selections, to call attention to them, to monitor them, and to weed and replace items in the display. Keep track of the display; fill in gaps, rearrange it, pull off titles that are just sitting and replace them with other choices. If the materials in the display are not being taken out, they should be returned to the shelves and a new display made. Users should not be insulted with an attitude of "they ought to be interested"; librarians must interest them!

Signs can be a difficult problem. Librarians are usually not artists or graphic designers, and access to professional services may be difficult, given a library's location and its limitation of funds. A "tacky" sign may be worse than no sign at all. This suggests one answer. Chances are users will be drawn to displays by their location, contents, and arrangement, and not by the sign at all. Something very dramatic, but simple, such as a giant, colorful arrow pointing to the display area, will serve better than hundreds of time-consuming homemade signs done for specific displays.

Some topics do require identification, such as Notable Book displays or former bestsellers. This problem can be solved by designing or having designed an all-purpose sign with attractive but neutral graphics, library identification, and space to write in information. Many vocational-technical schools have graphics programs and students who welcome some real-life experience. Several hundred can be printed cheaply. When compared to the cost of staff time, posterboard, and magic markers, they are probably a bargain. This kind of sign can be used in-house and outside the library; it can be part of the library's image in the community.

Neither booklists nor bulletin boards are as effective as actual book displays in getting books and users together. A book can be picked up, examined for length, print size, illustrations, subject; the blurb and jacket statements tell the reader "This is (or is not) my kind of book." Bulletin boards and booklists do not offer this hands-on experience. However, if they are placed outside the library, they can serve as advertisements intended to attract people to the library, just as newspaper ads invite people to department stores for clothing. It is actual clothing that they look at and choose from when they get there, however; they are not interested in being handed a list of possible choices. This is true of library users as well.

Bulletin boards in particular are labor intensive and require some expertise to keep them from looking homemade and tacky. It must be remembered that today's library user has been exposed to some of the most expensive and sophisticated marketing techniques in the world. To be effective, bulletin boards must be done well. For those who want to use this kind of display, there are ideas in the professional literature which can be copied or adapted.

Booklists also should be placed outside the library and, again, they should not look homemade and amateurish. There are many sources for printed lists and many ideas for professional quality design. Giving the list another use (a bookmark with library hours and services or a recipe card with a list of cookbooks on the back) will make it more "pickupable."

An annotated booklist is more than a list; it can serve the user as a selection guide. To create a good one, however, is time-consuming. Purchased booklists and those produced by library associations, regional systems, and publishers are often well-designed and attractive, although they present the dilemma of either advertising books the library doesn't own or having to buy books just because they're on the list. This is also true of the American Library Association's newsletter, *Openers,* but it is attractive, professional, up-to-date, of popular interest, and gives the public a good impression of libraries. Many libraries place most of their "advertising" materials—whether *Openers,* booklists, or other publicity—in locations where people wait: a doctor's office, laundromat, city or town hall, barber shop, beauty parlor. Very few are kept in the library itself.

Two kinds of book talks benefit users of libraries. One is the talk that takes place before a club or organization, school group, nursing home residents, or an audience in the library's own program room. Users learn of titles and subjects perhaps new to them, see and handle those— and other—books, and talk about their own favorites with each other and the speaker. Topics for book talks, as with book displays, can be as various as the collection permits, although the nature of the audience will determine the actual choice of subject.

To give successful book talks, there are three requirements. The librarian must be a skilled speaker, comfortable in front of an audience, and enthusiastic about the materials chosen. There are a number of ways to develop speaking skills and, once done, the other requirements will fall into place. If one of the requirements is missing, however, it is best to forget the book talk. It won't have the desired effect.

The other kind of "book talk" is the one that takes place at the card catalog, circulation desk, library lobby, new book shelves, browsing area, book displays, and the stacks. It is very much a part of the reader advisory service. Time spent talking with users about library services and users' needs is not wasted. During these casual conversations, the librarian has an opportunity to learn what users like, what they would recommend (or not recommend) to others, what they find missing. There is also the opportunity to say "I read this and enjoyed it," "This author writes like your favorite," or "I haven't read it yet, but I plan to since it had such good reviews." This kind of "book talk" shows that the librarian understands user needs, and is available, approachable, and at their service.

KNOWING THE READER

Implicit in the concept of reader service is that the librarian knows what readers want. A planning program which challenges the status quo, includes community analysis and needs assessment, identifies the roles a library can serve in a particular community, and bases the library's program of service on the results of the process is a major step in providing what readers want.

Some ongoing methods of staying aware of what users want are: talking to users at every opportunity; putting their suggestions and ideas into a consideration file for possible purchase; setting up a suggestion box for anonymous ideas; demonstrating that suggestions produce results, e.g., a title purchased or a change in shelving location; providing comment sheets for user evaluation of new titles; surveying user needs and satisfaction from time to time; and reviewing the book selection policy regularly in light of changing user needs.

A three- or four-question user survey can provide a quick picture of users, their needs, and their level of satisfaction. There are many examples of surveys available. Any survey should be designed to elicit the specific information that is desired and will be used.

Some typical questions might be:

1. I use the library for
   _____   popular fiction
   _____   popular nonfiction
   _____   children's books

_____   information for my daily life
_____   school assignments
_____   information on a particular subject
(specify) _____

2. I find what I am looking for
_____   all of the time
_____   most of the time
_____   occasionally
_____   seldom
_____   never

3. Today I wanted (specify) _____
I would rate my satisfaction of today's request as
_____   highly satisfied
_____   somewhat satisfied
_____   not at all satisfied

4. I would like to suggest
_____   title (specify) _____
_____   subject (specify) _____

TIME FOR READER SERVICE

Librarians should not spend time reinventing the wheel, but should use all the resources available to improve user services. They should talk to other librarians and copy their ideas; go to library conferences and workshops and discover new ideas; read the library literature and adapt the ideas; look around at supermarkets and bookstores and steal their ideas; and talk to library users and try their ideas.

Finally, librarians must spend time getting to know their users and their needs. Time spent on a book talk or booklist on the wrong subject or on selecting materials no one wants to borrow is wasted. Time spent learning who users are and what they want from their library and then providing the service needed is not. Reader service begins with the readers.

Service to Adults

Lois Siebersma

Adults need public library service for information and recreation. Often a book (or other library material) or a specific program serves both purposes. In the last ten years, a dramatic shift in emphasis has taken place. Libraries are now information centers for their communities, and are able to serve all citizens. This role of information center is appropriate to libraries because their scope is unlimited; they are free from partisan control; and their operators are specialists who serve the public impartially.

Public library service to adults takes on additional importance when considered in the light of continuing education. For most adults, formal schooling stops after 13 or 17 years. After that, the best source of informal self-education is the library, and the library's potential clientele includes all the adults in its service area.

While the possibilities for library services to adults are seemingly limitless, library budgets commonly have severe limitations. Each year at budget time the library director, with the board of trustees, carefully consider and reconsider whom to serve with what. Each year new ways to access information appear on the market; entertainment and information appear in new and exciting formats; publishers produce new magazines, new reference materials, more state-of-the-art advice on everything imaginable, more opportunities for cultural enrichment. Even the smallest library must plan for continuing updates and improvements.

ACCESSIBILITY

The first, most basic service that a library can perform for the adults in its community is to make the library's collection useful. No matter what kinds of materials are found in a library, they serve the populace poorly if they are not accessible. Accessibility includes careful cataloging according to an acceptable system, up-to-date maintenance of a print (or computer) catalog, adequate shelving, easy access to the

Lois Siebersma is Director of the Sioux Center Public Library, Sioux Center, Iowa.

building and all of its areas, space between shelving for browsing, and seating in all adult areas. It also involves the use of highly visible signs identifying areas and specific collections and even and adequate lighting. Other important concerns are correct filing and shelving of all materials, as few restrictions as possible on public use of materials and equipment, maintenance of the collection by weeding, updating, and repair, and, perhaps most important, library hours which are most useful to the citizens, taking into account their work schedules and lifestyles.

MATERIALS SELECTION

Just as a good collection of materials is virtually useless if not accessible, so an accessible collection will remain unused if it does not fit the needs of the citizens. The library staff in a small community has the advantage of personal acquaintance with many adult library patrons. The selection of useful materials for adults not only involves setting aside adequate time to read professional book reviews, e.g., in *Library Journal, ALA Booklist, Kirkus Reviews,* and the continuous monitoring of books appearing on bestseller lists and promoted in the media, but listening to what patrons are asking for, and reviewing all interlibrary loan requests for possible future acquisition. All circulation personnel have to maintain familiarity with books on a large variety of topics, and for diverse interests, and should engage in periodic checking of circulation records and materials on reserve to determine demand. Above all, self-discipline on the part of the director (and others responsible for selection) is necessary so that the collection reflects community, rather than individual, interests, and supports the library's long-range plan.

SPECIFIC SERVICES AND ACTIVITIES

Eleven specific activities and services which most small libraries can undertake on behalf of the adults in their communities are presented below.

Information. Few small libraries have research library capabilities, but all can establish a useful collection of materials to answer the kinds of questions that are asked most often. These include, but are not limited to, information concerning:

a. Government, especially how to contact senators and representatives.
b. Local, state, and federal government agencies.
c. Health, nutrition, and fitness.

d. Personal and business law.
e. Employment, job opportunities, how to write résumés and applications.
f. Welfare and Social Security.
g. Education, including local opportunities, national directories, and careers.
h. Business and consumer affairs.
i. Housing, including maintenance and repair.
j. Hobbies and sports.
k. Personal and family crises.

Interlibrary loan. All small libraries must take advantage of county, regional, and statewide networks established for borrowing among libraries. Adequate service to adults includes telling the patron, "If we don't have it, we'll borrow it for you," and the subsequent efficient handling of all requests.

AV equipment. In small communities, the public library is often the only source for borrowing projection equipment. Basic needs are for 16mm, slide, and overhead projectors. There may also be a demand for video players. A microreader printer is useful in towns where newspaper files are on microfilm, or where there is a demand for census records.

Other equipment. Essential to every public library, regardless of size, is a photocopier for public use, and the more versatile the copier, the better. Decisions on fees for use should be made by the library director, with the approval of the board. A typewriter for public use is also a valuable service for adults. A public-use computer in the library provides an opportunity for computer literacy and/or enables adults who are considering personal purchase to use a computer and a variety of software, without sales pressure. Circulating software (e.g., filing systems) and portable computers are excellent adult services if the budget permits.

Films, videodiscs and videocassettes. Films, especially 16mm, are still in demand as entertainment or information for large groups. Acquisition of 16mm films is prohibitively expensive for most small libraries, but they can be provided to patrons at low or no cost from state or regional collections, or through film cooperatives. This should be a routine library service. The films may be instructional (e.g., water safety or fire prevention) or entertaining (e.g., travel or old-time comedies). Frequent users of films include service and civic organizations, church groups, and nursing homes.

Availability and popularity of videodiscs is declining, while demand for videocassette tapes increases. Provision of these tapes for either inhouse individual viewing, or for circulation is an excellent service for adults, but in small libraries it will depend on budget, public demand, and library priorities.

Art and art exhibits. A circulating collection of art works is a legitimate cultural function of a public library, especially in cities and towns too small to support public or private galleries. Acquisitions can be the works of local artists, or reproductions of well-known masters. These are most useful to patrons when loan periods are at least three months.

Art exhibits for public viewing are an excellent service for public libraries with sufficient exhibit space. Often these may be obtained, for transportation fees only, from state arts councils, college and university art and photography classes, and local artists. An exhibit can be introduced at a special "opening" or can be viewed by the public during regular library hours.

Special collections and formats. Adult public demand for paperback books is increasing steadily. Cataloging need not be extensive, but title and author listing in the catalog is strongly recommended. Acquisition of other kinds of special collections will depend on community needs and interests. Large-print books, which are essential for libraries serving a population with a high percentage of elderly, are sometimes available in rotating collections from state or regional agencies. Collections for specific interests (e.g., genealogy, mountain climbing, horse racing, music) will depend on community demand and on the ready availability of similar material from other sources.

Programs. In every community, library personnel must be available for presentations to adult community groups. Some of the possibilities are: parent/teacher organizations, religious groups, women's clubs, veterans organizations, business and professional clubs, social and service clubs. Libraries may also offer in-library programs that meet the needs and interests of the community. Some examples are: book discussion groups, informational programs on hobbies (e.g., gardening), travel shows, poetry readings, and author/autograph parties. Care must be taken to work in cooperation with, rather than in competition with, other city agencies and organizations.

Service to the elderly. Especially important in library service to older adults is the delivery of books and other materials to home-bound persons. This must be done by a staff member or volunteer who is familiar with the library's collection and who is patient and understanding with the elderly. There should be a regular schedule, with sufficient time allowed for each visit. Collections of library materials can also be carried to senior citizen centers and the community rooms of housing for the elderly. Such library visits must be announced in advance, and provision made for accurate record keeping of borrowed materials. A visit by the library staff might include a film or other program. Information available to the elderly and their families should cover how to contact state agencies which provide specific services (e.g., talking books) for the blind and physically handicapped.

Meeting rooms. The American Library Association's *Bill of Rights* states: "As an institution of education for democratic living, the library should welcome the use of its meeting rooms for socially useful and cultural activities, and discussion of current public questions. Such meeting places should be available on equal terms to all groups in the community regardless of the beliefs and affiliations of their members." This position should be adopted by all public library boards of trustees. Generally, activities taking place in the library's meeting rooms are open to the public and are not private social events. Provision of a meeting room for the above purposes is an essential library service for adults in small communities.

Bulletin board. To be most useful, the library's public bulletin board should be located in the lobby, or if it is weather-protected, outside the building. One section can be reserved for announcing library events, but most space should be available for posting information about community happenings. Rules for inclusion may be established, but restrictions should be as few as possible.

PUBLICITY

An excellent collection of materials, and well-planned programs of service will be of little use if they are not continuously publicized and promoted. Publicity should be planned on a regular basis, and include maintenance of an annual, monthly, and weekly calendar. All available local media—television, radio, newspapers, and the bulletins and newsletters of community organizations—should be kept informed of library activities. Marketing techniques that are successful for business should be explored and used where appropriate. And finally, every opportunity, both formal and informal, should be made the most of to tell about the library's programs and services.

Successful library service to adults in all small communities depends on the policies established by the library board, the planning and administrative skills of the director, and the friendliness, helpfulness, and expertise of the circulation and reference staff. All of these working together can continually expand and alter library services, thus insuring the relevance and major importance of the public library to its community.

Service to Children and Young Adults

Brenda McElroy Pacey

Meeting the informational, recreational, and cultural needs of children and young adults, youth service professionals, and parents is a high priority for most public and school libraries as well as many hospital and institutional libraries. In smaller and rural communities, children and young adults are especially dependent upon libraries since they lack easy access to bookstores, theaters, museums, universities, entertainment and computer centers, and social service agencies found in larger communities. Therefore, it seems ironic and overwhelming that smaller libraries with less staff, space, and resources must attempt to serve a rather captive audience of youth who rely heavily upon libraries to meet their service needs.

The American Library Association (ALA) Task Force on Excellence in Education's document, *Realities: Educational Reform in a Learning Society,*[1] reinforces the assertion in the now-famous 1983 *Nation At Risk* report that lifelong learning is the key to effective educational reform. The four realities outlined by ALA stress the importance of preschool learning, libraries in schools, library availability to people throughout their lives, and public support for libraries to provide a strong foundation for community development in a democracy. Therefore, the role of children's and young adult library services is a crucial one, a first link in the chain of independent lifelong learning.

It is often assumed by the general population that libraries are "desirable" and "good," especially in providing services to youth. In some ways, then, the decisions facing the administrator of a small library concerning youth service and program planning is not whether to offer such a service, or whether there is a need or interest, but rather on setting realistic priorities in order to provide the best service by the most efficient means. Youth services are time-consuming and labor intensive—providing readers advisory to ever-growing and maturing youth;

Brenda McElroy Pacey is Library Consultant, Lincoln Trail Libraries System, Champaign, Illinois.

supervising patrons for general safety; program preparation and presentation; circulation and shelving of high turnover items in a variety of unique formats; teaching reference and search skills in both formal and informal settings; and much more. While general library policy, procedures, and staffing should apply to patrons of all ages, additional or unique services for children and young adults, as well as for adults who work with youth, should be considered.

PLANNING, POLICY, AND PROCEDURES

Children and young adults are library patrons, just as adults; therefore, it would seem to go without saying that library staffs should review general and specific planning, policy, and procedural matters to ensure that young patrons are offered quality service and access to library resources. The first issue to consider is just Who is Served under the umbrella of "children's and young adult (YA) services." Without going into semantic arguments over what ages constitute childhood or YA status, anyone up to at least 18 years should be considered. Prereaders, readers, nonreaders, non-English speaking youth, handicapped and special needs youth—all types of young people with all types of information needs fall into the service category. In addition, librarians serving youth serve the many adults who work with and are concerned about youth—parents and family, teachers, day care and nursery school staff, youth group leaders, clergy, health and social service professionals. This impacts on reference and adult collection development as well as children's and young adult collection development, readers advisory activities, and program planning.

Registration and circulation policies and procedures greatly affect how young people can best use libraries. May youth borrow materials from all sections of the library? Are they required to have parental permission to obtain library cards or to borrow certain materials? At what age may youth obtain individual library cards? How does this policy relate to provision of preschool services, day care, or other institutional services? If there are limits, numbers, or types of materials and equipment which can be borrowed by youth, why? Do youth carry the same weight when requesting reserve materials or interlibrary loan?

Libraries have the responsibility to protect the tenets of intellectual freedom for youth. Are ALA Freedom to Read and related youth service interpretative statements applied to youth services? For instance, the circulation and access policy questions raised above are perfect examples of day-to-day functions of libraries affecting youth access to information. In small communities without bookstore or commercial access, it is even more important that libraries provide a range of materials not easily available otherwise.

Staff and volunteers in small libraries often wear several hats, so sensitivity to, and competence in, youth services should be an integral part of all staff planning and training. Staff and volunteers should be encouraged to "read, read, read" and to "listen, watch, do" in order to become familiar with books, magazines, recordings, films, games, and youth issue interests. It's the old adage, "you've got to love 'em to serve 'em!" Area teachers or counselors should be asked to meet with staff to discuss child development stages. One youth age group should not be slighted at the expense of another. Small libraries do not have the luxury of being able to provide endless streams of preschool story hours and weekly teen film programs and year-round Junior Great Books discussion programs. However, that is not a viable reason for slighting any age or interest group by concentrating only on one clientele category. Often young adults are slighted; more captive audiences of lower-grade class groups or preschoolers seem more easily definable and manageable to the two-person library staff who are trying to provide all services. Plans should include a variety of age groups. Talented volunteers should be accepted with open arms and with specifically outlined expectations. Artists, storytellers, book talkers, and dramatics leaders can help the small library staff immeasurably.

Planning, evaluation, and advisory input are as essential to youth services as they are to adult services. Youth must be included in advisory groups, surveys, statistical reports, output measure sampling—in all aspects of library service. In fact, youth patrons are often willing and capable volunteers to assist with conducting such projects. The library's policy on youth advisory groups or volunteers—the purpose of, and responsibility for, such programs—should be clearly stated and youth must have the opportunity to feel they are truly contributing. A year-round planning calendar is helpful to keep track of school, scout, 4-H, recreation department, church, sports, and other events in order to avoid unnecessary conflict in small communities where many of the same people are involved in a great number of organizations. Young people need adequate lead time to plan for library events. The calendar also helps library staff to get an overall picture of just what is being offered for youth, thus affecting the type, number, and scope of library programs to be planned. The library's schedule should be shared with other groups, too, to avoid conflicts.

Formal and informal cooperation with other agencies should be pursued in order to more efficiently provide quality youth services. The most obvious network tie for youth services is between school and public libraries. Even if there is only one staff person in each facility in the community, it's a good idea to meet for coffee or lunch once a month to keep in touch, to share new materials, to deliver flyers for distribution in each other's library, or to exchange professional journals and catalogs. This can lead to staff exchanges, a joint school/public reading club, loan of materials and equipment, faculty teas and information sessions, and more. Other important contacts are mental health and counseling staff, scout leaders, 4-H and cooperative extension staff, nursery school and day care center personnel, church group leaders and clergy, PTA, and any other local youth connections. A card file of officers, addresses, and telephone numbers should be kept current and names added to the library's mailing and distribution lists. In turn, they can provide valuable information.

If the library is a member of a larger unit (countywide public library, school district, multitype cooperative system, bibliographic utility network), making human network contacts with other librarians becomes a little easier. It may require some schedule and time juggling in order to participate in activities in such an arrangement, but the effort will be rewarding in idea-swapping, rejuvenation, and reinforcement.

MATERIALS, PROGRAMS, AND SERVICES

Setting priorities for activities is essential. How do youth services correlate with adult services in the library? What major programs will be provided in the coming year in each age or interest category? How will this impact collection development? These are some of the questions to be kept in mind when determining what activities to plan for youth.

Materials of interest to children and young adults range from print to poster to popular music, and more. If at all possible, plans should include a variety of formats.

In the print category, books are a major resource for children and young adults. Hardbacks dominate nonfiction and reference for all ages, as well as picture books and juvenile fiction. Paperbacks have wide appeal for older elementary school readers and young adults. Fiction reprints and genre originals (especially science fiction, romance, mystery, and adventure) are very popular and should be an integral part of any collection. Board books, cloth books, and/or plastic books are intended for babies and young children—a growing segment of library patron populations. It is also important to become acquainted with the latest in periodical titles for youth; as with adult magazines, the young people's market is always changing and diversifying.

Sound recordings, both record and audiocassette, are very popular. Children's literature and music standbys will be used again and again by several generations of young patrons. Young adult popular rock titles, however, become outdated much faster. This should be kept in mind when developing and maintaining a collection if it is to be of any real value to patrons.

Books-on-tape and book/cassette sets are two formats which are becoming more easily obtainable. The younger library clientele adores picture book/cassette packets and the library may wish to circulate an inexpensive cassette player or have one with earphones in the library. Curriculum-related and life skills tapes are of interest to post-high school age adults as well as to young adults. Providing a variation in format such as this helps to reach a variety of patrons.

Films are most often purchased by larger libraries or cooperative groups for loan to smaller libraries for programs. Filmstrips are more affordable and holiday stories, author, and picture book adaptation titles are most appropriate for longevity in smaller libraries with limited budgets. And videotapes are hot items, popular with YA's (feature films especially) and with parents and younger children (entertainment).

Microcomputer software is appearing in more and more areas, with small public and school libraries often leading the way in providing public access microcomputers. Few libraries circulate software, but the interest and expertise of children, young adults, parents, and teachers is high for in-library use.

Toys, games, puzzles, flannelboard sets, posters, and other realia are some of the more unique library material formats associated with youth services. A toy lending service "is an effective way to serve young pre-readers and a way to stimulate intellectual growth early in the child's life," asserts Dr. Leslie Edmonds of the University of Illinois Graduate School of Library and Information Science.[2] Libraries can provide toys inhouse, in story hour programs, and/or for circulation. Lekotek library programs are gaining more notice throughout the country; Lekotek focuses on developmental toys of special value to handicapped children and their families. The local library should be an informed referral source, if not a provider, for such developmental opportunities.

The best way to keep up with reviews and availability of new materials for youth (especially in regard to nonprint resources) is through professional journals such as *School Library Journal, Voice of Youth Advocates (VOYA), Booklist, Top of the News, Emergency Librarian, Hornbook,* and *Library Journal.*

The standard "best of the year" award lists for children's and young adult print and nonprint materials are compiled by the Association of Library Service to Children (ALSC) and the Young Adult Services Division (YASD), divisions of the American Library Association. These lists include: Notable Children's Books, Notable Children's Recordings, Notable Children's Filmstrips, Notable Children's Films, Best Books for Young Adults, and Selected Films for Young Adults. Annotated lists of these recommended materials appear in the journals mentioned above, and are available in pamphlet format in quantity from ALA. Using these award lists (and other highlighted topical bibliographies which frequently appear in the recommended journals) as a starting point for collection development, readers advisory, and staff discussion and training is a practical and time-saving practice for small libraries with limited resources.

Providing readers advisory, displays, and bibliographies of materials for children and young adults is a helpful and often-requested service. Displays of new books, award lists, book review excerpts, dust jackets, and thematic or genre groupings is one way to alert patrons to materials. Even the smallest library staff can use simple colorful signs, such as "Have you read these"? on available counter or table space. Booktalks are an exciting form of readers advisory. Files of titles and booktalk outlines should be kept for use in the library, in classrooms, or community group settings. Booktalks are designed to whet the appetite of readers and, although it takes a little practice, each person develops his or her own style which helps literature to come alive for others. Bibliographies can be creatively designed to include brief annotations and catchy graphics. "Books like _____" lists appealing to topical interests, "Especially for Parents," "Hottest Hits" suggestions by teens for summer reading, and "New at the Library" formats can be distributed at the library, in classrooms, at day care centers, in PTA or Chamber of Commerce newsletters, and Welcome Wagon packets. ALA award lists and *Booklist* bibliographies can be purchased for distribution or in-library display and readers advisory as well.

Story hours, reading programs, and literature discussion groups provide children and young adults with the chance to experience the world vicariously, to learn to think and express themselves creatively, to appreciate literature, and to become acquainted with the library as a lifelong learning place. Each of these services can be adapted for large or small groups, can incorporate many media formats, and can involve staff, volunteers, parents, teachers, and others in the community served by the small library.

The story hour format is one of the best ways to introduce young children to reading and the library. Story hours are most effective if aimed at specific age groups, such as toddlers (18–36 months with parents participating), preschool (3–5 years), grades K to second or third, and older elementary. In small library settings, scheduling may result in a broader age range of participants than outlined here, but one characteristic of any story hour presenter is the ability to roll with the punches. Aiming programs at specific ages does help in planning for the most appropriate fingerplays, stories, puppets, films, songs, and activities for each developmental stage. Advertising desired age ranges in a positive way when registering individuals or groups can be effective.

A series should be tied together by following similar formats each week to help young patrons become familiar and comfortable with the library. Repeating the same introductory fingerplay or always distributing nametags is reassuring. Scheduling weekly series with "time off" provides variety and breathing room for library staff and children alike; e.g., six weeks of 30-minute morning and afternoon preschool sessions in October and November, four weeks of parent/toddler bedtime story hours in January, etc. Another approach is to present a special one-time program centering around a theme or event (Christmas, Halloween, teddy bears, fairy tales); these are especially effective if repeated in afternoon and evening sessions, or weekdays and Saturday.

Some hints for successful programs are to include a variety of activities (media, active and passive stories, long and short poems, etc.), keep the story hour moving along, and avoid programs which are too long for children's attention span; 20 to 30 minutes for preschoolers and 30 to 45 minutes for older children is more than enough for structured programs. Additional time before or after the story hour should be allowed for browsing. Enlisting one or more staff or volunteers to assist with book selection and circulation, crafts and games, and "traffic control" helps to make things go smoothly. The key to successful programs is parent or child care provider awareness of and involvement in the story hour goals and reading/playing followup. Distributing fingerplay handouts, highlighting new parenting or child development materials at the circulation desk, and encouraging adults to join in on songs are all good ways to involve and educate adults in the intellectual stimulation of youth in the community.

Reading programs, incorporating story hours, special activities, and reading incentive awards are often associated with elementary and junior high school-aged patrons (although preschoolers enjoy being a part of a read-to-me focus offshoot of such programs), and are most often sponsored as a summer public library program or as a joint school/public library year-round program. Reinforcing reading skills and the enjoyment of literature is a major goal of such programs. Small libraries can benefit from thematic program manuals compiled by state professional association children's services groups, or state and regional libraries (such as in Illinois, Ohio, Wisconsin). With themes such as "Be a Star! Read!" or "Readers on the Move" (Illinois themes), which can be expanded or adapted in a variety of settings, manuals provide time-saving high quality program ideas, graphic designs, activity sheets, resource lists, and more. Librarians should watch for notices in professional journals for availability of such resources at reasonable costs and add them to the library's programming shelf for use again and again.

A helpful source of reading promotional materials is the Children's Book Council (67 Irving Place, New York, NY 10003), a nonprofit group which produces posters, bookmarks, booklists, and other thematic items. In recent years, commercial sponsors such as Pizza Hut have begun to produce thematic promotional materials (and free coupons) for children's reading programs in schools and libraries. Such "ready-made" programs should be evaluated and adapted to meet local library goals and policies.

Literature discussion groups may be a part of summer or year-round theme program. Informal book-talk and discussion sessions can be a great way for youth and library staff to get to know one another. Lunchtime brown bag groups in school libraries or popcorn and pop evening sessions in public libraries may provide the right atmosphere for older children and young adults. The more structured Junior Great Books program is ideal for small library use, if a library staff member, teacher, or community volunteer completes leadership training; contact Great Books Foundation, 307 N. Michigan Ave., Chicago, IL 60601 (312-332-5870) for training and publication information. Successful sponsorship of a Junior program may open the door to adult and young adult participation in other discussion programs of the Foundation or other groups, such as the "Let's Talk About It" series of the National Endowment for the Humanities.

Joint parent/child reading and discussion programs (such as the Madison, Wisconsin, elementary school "Family Reading Nights"[3] and in the nationally recognized "Communicate Through Literature" teen/parent thematic discussion groups created by Pat Scales[4]) meet a community need and help to further community, school, and family support of the importance of reading and the freedom of expression of ideas. Informal family read-aloud nights can be encouraged by the library, reinforced by distribution of suggested age-appropriate booklists and helpful reading tip outlines.

Special events, programs, and services offer children, young adults, and adults who work with youth many opportunities to experience literature and media in creative ways and to meet informational, educational, and recreational needs in a variety of ways. As with reading and story hour programs, coordinating programs to meet local library needs and goals is essential. Possibilities are almost endless, but a few examples are summarized here.

1) Celebrate Children's Book Week (sponsored annually in November by the Children's Book Council), National Library Week (annually observed in April by ALA), and National School Library Media Month (annually observed in April by ALA's American Association of School Librarians) with special displays, film programs, open houses and refreshments, book discussions, local celebrity read-a-thons (invite the

mayor, local clergy, football coach, etc.), newspaper and radio coverage of events, bookmark design contests, etc.

2) Sponsor special one-time or annual events to focus library energy and staffing in an organized and concentrated fashion. Balloon launches, "battle of the books" quiz contests, book character entries in annual homecoming parades, career or health or craft fairs, "stump the librarian" reference week, paperback book fairs (a source of additional income for library Friends or school student librarian groups, as well as an opportunity for community members to purchase books if no book stores are readily available), and science fiction film festivals are all possibilities. Public and school librarians have also found annual participation in the Reading Is Fundamental (RIF) book distribution program for children to have an important impact on support for reading in their communities, with library and/or community organization financial support for paperback purchases for targeted groups of children to choose and keep. (Contact Reading Is Fundamental, Smithsonian Institution, Washington, DC 20560.)

3) Provide youth with access to media and technology. Film and film/book discussion programs, public access microcomputers, musical and performing arts presentations by or for area youth, videocassette circulation, and in-library programming offer a range of format options. Ask youth to review/preview software, using their interest and expertise in current culture and technology for the benefit of other patrons. Young adult participation in the videotaping of library programs, creation of computer-generated graphic banners for library events and displays, or presentation of a film series help young patrons gain experience as well as allowing library staff to carry out ideas that might not otherwise be possible to implement.

4) Offer ongoing reference and referral services. Ensure that reference collection purchases keep pace with needs and that new and special interest titles are added as well as general encyclopedias; offer tours and orientation/skills sessions periodically; provide interlibrary loan, database/searching, and other services to youth as a matter of course; keep social service agency information files and vertical file materials up to date and prominently displayed for easy youth browsing access. Develop "Assignment Alert" or "Quick Bib" bibliography format sheets to be distributed to faculty and libraries to increase two-way communication about reference and research needs and available resources.

5) Serve the needs of young handicapped and special needs patrons in a variety of ways. Librarians must make special efforts to identify these special populations through cooperation with local and state agencies, institutions, hospitals, schools, social service and rehabilitation groups, and then "reach out" with publicity to bring these potential patrons into the library or provide service to the home-bound. Blind and

physically handicapped citizens of any age are eligible for free Talking Book and Braille books from the National Library Service for the Blind and Physically Handicapped (Library of Congress, Washington DC 20542). Record and tape players, recordings, and Braille books are provided by mail directly to patrons. Each state is served by at least one National Library Service regional library which can follow up on referrals made by libraries of all sizes.

Adult new reader materials are also important resources for the learning disabled and developmentally disabled young adult. These can be featured in special orientation tours of the library or prominently displayed for easy browsing access, along with Large Print resources. Mainstreaming handicapped youth in library experiences and programs reminds us that the library should be an integral part of daily life for all citizens. Specific adaptations may sometimes need to be made (signing or captioned films, sensory activities, developmentally appropriate vs. age-appropriate stories or booktalks, special library skills sessions for special education class groups, etc.), but overall general sensitivity toward the fact that everyone learns from a variety of formats or at a unique pace will help to better meet the needs of more patrons.

Librarians also must be sensitive to the increasing numbers of "latchkey" children, teen parents, physically and sexually and emotionally abused youth, youthful drug and alcohol abusers, juvenile criminal offenders, and institutionalized youth. Prominently displaying information and hotline resources, sponsoring speaker programs and safety demonstrations, and creating a comfortable and nonthreatening atmosphere for youth in the library are all ways in which to better serve special needs. Collection development should reflect awareness of, and support for, the diverse needs of today's youth.

References

1. American Library Association Task Force on Excellence in Education, *Realities: Educational Reform in a Learning Society* (Chicago: American Library Assn., 1984).
2. Leslie Edmonds, "Child's Play as a Library Service: The Value of Toys to the Developing Child," *Top of the News* (Summer 1985): 347.
3. April Hoffman, "Families that Read Together Overcome Rift," *American Libraries* (October 1985): 647–49.
4. Pat Scales, *Communicate Through Literature: Introducing Parents to the Books Their Teens are Reading and Enjoying* (New York: Pacer/Putnam, 1984).

Reference Services

Robert E. Boyer

In the small library, all services seem to blend into one. Reference service is a natural part of basic patron assistance and hardly seems a separate function. Excellent reference service is dependent on two elements: a librarian who is skilled in understanding people and a base collection of appropriate materials. Two very basic principles are know the patrons, and know the collection. The service rendered will range from finding factual answers to short questions through finding materials for a deep study of a topic. Questions about the local community, school, or business are to be expected. Permanent printed materials as well as periodicals, ephemeral, or nonbook items could hold the answers. The librarian should be prepared to go beyond the local library to track down the answers. The skill of the librarian or any helpers in interviewing the patron will affect the success of reference service.

KNOWING THE PATRONS

In order to choose appropriate materials for acquisition, the librarian must know the audience and the community being served, be thoroughly versed in the materials already in the library, and keep abreast of new publications. The librarian must be aware of the reading level of the patrons and purchase reference materials written at that level. Even if reading levels are low, responsible librarians can deal with this creatively. Adult and juvenile nonfiction materials can be mixed together on the shelves. The children's books usually contain good factual material explained very clearly. Adults will see these materials and be more likely to consult them than if they were housed in a separate juvenile section. The economic base of the community determines many of the patrons' practical questions. A rural area will have reference questions on agricultural topics; urban centers will be reflected in questions asked about local industries.

The student body of the school or academic library will seek information related to the curriculum. A good understanding of the topics being

Robert E. Boyer is Assistant Director of the Arlington, Texas, Public Library, Arlington, Texas.

taught and of the expectations of the faculty must be gained, first by studying written materials explaining the program and then following up with personal visits and interviews with the faculty members who make assignments. In many cases, however, this fails to provide sufficient information as to what will happen in reality or to give enough lead time to do anything about it.

In all types of libraries, enlisting the help of "spies" may be necessary. Student pages, family members of staff, neighbors, members of civic, business, and religious organizations, and members of Friends groups may all be conscripted into an early warning corps to help the librarian brace for an attack of patrons all wanting answers to a common assignment, interest, or trend. Copies of the actual assignment sheet should be sought to avoid misunderstandings and wasted time.

A central file of frequently asked questions with dates and sources of solutions should be compiled. The dates will help in determining cyclical or perpetual questions. Just as important are the questions which could not be answered. If there are no sources, this becomes a guide for future purchase decisions. The file need not be elaborate; pages in a three-ring notebook or cards in a desk drawer will do the job. The important thing is to write down questions and sources and to have a regular time, such as quarterly, to examine these notes.

KNOWING THE COLLECTION

The best way to learn the collection is to study each item, including reading over the introduction to determine the stated scope and approach, and then examining the indexes and contents by applying several test cases. From time to time, it will be necessary to go back to the items in the collection in light of the list of unanswered or frequent questions. When the collection is small, it is important to squeeze every bit of usefulness out of every item. It follows that knowledge of the circulating items is equally important for sources of reference answers.

In a small community, it is both helpful and personally rewarding to become so well-versed in a favorite field that the librarian achieves a local reputation as an authority on that subject. If members of the community have confidence in the librarian's competence in one area, they will certainly turn to the library for assistance in that topic, and possibly other topics as well. As Margaret Waring, the director of the public library in Comanche, Texas, said, "In the small public library, you have to do it all. I've helped build the building, and I've helped write the books to go in it."[1] By publishing several books on the local cemeteries and genealogical records, she has established her interest and competence in local and Texas history.

With as little spare time as there is in the operation of a small library, it is still important to keep up with new publications and reference sources. When the budget allocation for reference materials is very small, the librarian should be on the lookout for items which fill several specific needs as evidenced by the file of unanswered or frequent questions. It is important to catch new items with a short run before they go out of print. This is an area in which a trusted volunteer may be able to help by examining the journals and bringing to the librarian's attention those items fitting a special need. The final decisions need to be made by the librarian, but assistance in screening the market can be extremely valuable. Since some questions may be referred to other libraries, it is important to know that certain reference tools exist, even if they are not appropriate for the local library.

Occasionally an opportunity will arise for a gift or donation to the library. Since donors may recommend a title or set which they associate with some other prestigious library—but which may never be needed locally—they should be directed toward items which the library truly needs and the patrons will use. Knowing the patrons, the collection, the gaps, and the available products will insure a wise selection and guarantee satisfaction on behalf of both donor and librarian.

THE COLLECTION AND READY REFERENCE

The noncirculating reference collection should contain items which are consulted so frequently that a copy absolutely must remain in the building at all times. In the small library, the number of items qualifying may be small. Sometimes items are placed in reference because their price makes them almost too expensive to use—a practice which can backfire if no one ever has the opportunity to look at the items. Other materials, such as indexes, are used only in conjunction with the rest of the library and could not be used alone. Some local, ephemeral, and archival materials should be placed in reference for security and preservation. There should be some policy, however, for allowing certain items to leave the building in special circumstances. Knowledge of the community is important in forming this policy. A large cash deposit might be required and the policy might exclude rare or archival items. Older copies of materials replaced or updated could be included in the circulating collection, but they should carry a notation that more recent information is available in "Reference."

The answer to a reference query may be a short fact or the research material for a thesis. Ready reference materials should include general almanacs, an unabridged dictionary, an atlas, and telephone directories for quick factual answers. Abridged dictionaries are sometimes frequently updated and many contain concise information in charts, such as historical periods, planets, weights and measures, or flags. Lists of elected and appointed officials are essential.

An encyclopedia set is a good tool to begin a deeper study. Articles explain general concepts and name the terms associated with a topic. Some encyclopedia articles include a bibliography of additional sources. One-volume encyclopedic works, such as the *Columbia Encyclopedia,* or encyclopedias of a specific topic, such as biographical dictionaries or sets on gardening or home repair, help to answer short, specific questions. There is always an interest in identifying things from garden pests to old coins, just as there is always interest in family health or in repair of appliances and automobiles. Patrons have been known to bring a snake into the library to be compared with pictures in the reference books. If the general reading level of the community is low, an encyclopedia geared for school children can meet the factual needs of both children and adults. If the library can afford one encyclopedia with an American slant and another with a British or European slant, then both hemispheres will be covered for historical and literary topics. Encyclopedias should be updated on a cyclical schedule until all titles in the collection have been updated. Some information in an encyclopedia never goes out of date, but other sources should be relied upon for the latest information in quickly changing fields. A "new" edition of an encyclopedia may have only a few articles added or completely rewritten. It takes many years for the bulk of a general encyclopedia to show much difference between editions.

Ready reference service also involves giving answers over the telephone. Very long answers, such as entire recipes, are seldom given since it takes time away from other patrons waiting for assistance. A general rule of thumb is to give walk-in patrons first priority and to ask telephone inquirers requiring lengthy answers to wait for a return call. Skill in locating specific factual answers quickly enhances the librarian's reputation for proficiency.

DEEPER REFERENCE LEVELS

Finding more materials for a patron is a deeper level of reference service than ready reference. Most often this involves the use of indexes and bibliographies. The most obvious index is the card catalog itself. The importance of good subject cataloging cannot be emphasized enough. The smaller the collection, the more added subject references and "see also" references are needed. Subject cataloging in a small library should be supplemented whenever additional references can lead patrons to part of a book or part of a set which answers their questions. If the collection is too small or there is not enough money or potential use for the printed indexes, such as the Wilson and Gale products, the local library may have to construct card indexes to plays and short stories in collections. This project, which volunteers can do, will have immediate and lasting results. A general comprehensive tool, such as the *Subject Guide to Books In Print,* may be used to identify authors or a series for which there may be a local holding. Good acquisitions choices which reflect the recurring questions coming from the community are necessary for good reference service.

Providing information on local topics, particularly for small public libraries, is a serious obligation. Access to local information may have to be constructed locally, too. Vertical file clippings, pamphlets, lists of community services and their corresponding leaders and contact persons must be collected and kept up-to-date if there is no other agency doing it. The work of historical preservation may fall on the librarian, and close cooperation with local historical societies is necessary to insure that items are preserved, to prevent duplication, and to divide the labor.

Old local telephone books, city directories, and high school year books are valuable sources of information which should be collected and preserved now if they are to be available for researchers in the future. If there is no space to store long runs, paper copies can be collected for a few years and then microfilmed. Sometimes the local government or police can do this, or they can refer to a regional governmental agency which has microfilming equipment. Often the state library agency will help with microfilming in exchange for a copy of the final product. Copyright restrictions should be checked for the most recent years. Recently, photocopy rights have been reserved for another party which may offer the item already copied onto film or fiche.

A viable library contains not only permanent bound books with lasting value, but also frequently updated and up-to-the-minute sources of information. Updated reference items such as state almanacs, highway maps, and periodic reports will ensure currency.

Reference involving periodicals includes reliance on the *Abridged Readers' Guide* for magazines. Few newspapers are indexed, and sometimes coverage of national events is accessed better through news magazines. Current events may be handled best through a service such as *Facts on File.* Local newspaper indexing is always a problem for small libraries which cannot afford a microfilm service such as *Newspaper Index* or which do not carry the titles referred to in the service. At the very least, the obituaries in the local paper should be indexed by volunteers.

Government publications are important to reference service. *U.S. Government Organization Manual, Statistical Abstracts, Occupational*

Outlook Handbook, Congressional Directory, and the *ZIP Code Directory* are particularly useful. Other census publications are helpful to businesspeople and planners if the library can afford them. Legal materials are expensive and difficult for laypeople to interpret, but sometimes are desirable. A small library may find itself designated a depository for a county law library or even a partial depository for U.S. documents. The best policy is to start small, keeping in mind the community and the reading level.

DISPLAYING THE COLLECTION

As for the physical location of reference books, if patrons need the information badly enough, it does not matter where the materials are placed. For the borderline user, however, convenience can make the difference. The most prominent display area is usually best assigned to highly circulating and requested items, particularly if the library lives or dies by its circulation statistics. For reference books to be used, proximity to writing surfaces, the photocopy machine, and the librarian is crucial. If there are only single copies of ready reference works which must be shared with telephone reference, placing them on a neutral side shelf is preferable to housing them directly on the reference desk. Although space is always at a premium, the arrangement of the items on the shelves will influence their use. The closer to the floor, the less likely they will be consulted by adults.

EXTENDED REFERENCE

No one library can answer all reference questions, and particularly not a small library. The librarian and all library workers should be aware of resources beyond the local library that can be tapped. Most public libraries can turn to the state library agency for reference assistance, and many libraries belong to systems and consortia whose purpose is to promote extended reference and interlibrary loan. State library agencies can help with suggested core lists of reference books, evaluation tools, and sharing of withdrawn but still useful titles.

Another recent development in extended reference service is computer databases and long distance telecommunication services. A product such as *Easynet* permits a small library to access a variety of index services and full-text reference sources while either passing the cost on to the patron or absorbing the operating expense, depending on which philosophy the library adopts and can afford. Sometimes computer services are the only way a small library can afford to provide current and thorough business reference. In a special library where time is money, computer reference service is cheaper, more accurate, and more efficient than trying to collect similar materials in house.

REFERENCE INTERVIEWING

No matter how complete the collection of materials, the skill of the librarian in fielding questions and drawing out the precise needs of the patron is the key to good reference service. Attitude has a great impact on first-time library users. The impressions received will determine whether or not they return and what they tell the rest of the community about the library. This is why it is important for all library workers to be counseled in techniques for successful reference interviewing. As Mike DuCharme of Bloomfield, Iowa, explained in *The Unabashed Librarian*,[2] it is possible to win patrons over as Friends of the library, even if none of their questions are answered, just by the way they are treated.

A question and a questioner should be taken seriously and in a pleasant and unhurried manner, no matter what the librarian is actually feeling. Repeating the question back can clarify misunderstandings. Getting the patron to narrow down the request by asking open-ended questions and questions leaving a choice can save the librarian hours. Determining the quantity of information needed and any time limits for its delivery is also helpful. The librarian cannot do the work for students, but they can be guided to the tools and sources they will need. If no answer can be found, the librarian should say so honestly but offer to continue seeking through networks and interlibrary loan.

Library staff should practice asking reference questions of one another to see how effective some of these techniques can be. This will assure smooth delivery of answers and material by a reference staff which knows its community, is prepared with an appropriate collection, and is skilled in matching the two.

OTHER REFERENCE AIDS FOR THE LIBRARIAN

Many excellent bibliographies have been published in book form and several journals contain seasonal issues or regular columns devoted to new reference publications. The American Library Association's *Reference Sources for Small and Medium-sized Libraries*[3] is an excellent tool which gives brief descriptions along with the citations. *Library Journal* includes reference titles in its reviews, and one issue in the spring includes a list of outstanding reference sources for the year compiled by *LJ's* book review staff. *Wilson Library Bulletin* contains a regular feature reviewing new reference items. It is also helpful to attend professional association meetings which host the Combined Book Exhibit where a variety of material can be examined firsthand.

Now 25 years old, but still clear, helpful, and concise is the booklet, *Reference Service in a Small Public Library* by Hannah Severns.[4] The content and suggestions apply to many types of small libraries. For extensive treatment of the subject, see also the fifth edition of Bill Katz's *Introduction to Reference Work*.[5]

References

1. Personal interview with Margaret Waring at the Comanche Public Library, Texas (pop. 7,850) on June 14, 1986.
2. Mike DuCharme, "The Reference Interview," *The Unabashed Librarian* (Consecutive issue no. 55, 1985): 13–14.
3. American Library Association. Ad Hoc Committee for the Fourth Edition of Reference Sources for Small and Medium-sized Libraries. *Reference Sources for Small and Medium-sized Libraries*. 4th ed. (Chicago: American Library Assn., 1984).
4. Hannah Severns. *Reference Services in a Small Public Library*. No. 9 in a series of pamphlets of the Library Administration Division's Small Libraries Project. (Chicago: American Library Assn., 1962).
5. Bill Katz, *Introduction to Reference Work*, 5th ed., 2 vols. (New York: McGraw Hill, 1987).

Library Instruction

Danielle Clarke

Librarians are really teachers, whether they feel comfortable with
that job title or not. They teach staff and volunteers how to run the
library; they teach board members, administrators, faculty members,
and other assorted commanders about the intimate details of the
library's operation; and they teach users about the library's contents. It
isn't easy for the manager of a small library to find time to design an
attractive brochure or conduct a tour in addition to keeping snow off the
sidewalk and the lightbulbs beaming, but difficult as it might be to
schedule, teaching how to use the library is one of the most important
parts of the manager's job. A case could be made that proper instruction
can justify the very existence of the library. Users who feel comfortable
and acclimated to their library might be inclined to support the library
financially. A library can be a very intimidating place, and the average
person has certain misconceptions and anxieties about using it. No one
enjoys looking ignorant; many people feel that asking questions makes
them appear so. Sometimes the very atmosphere of the library can
negate questions and discourage users. Negativism can be combatted by
good library instruction and library managers must take an active part
in such instruction. It is in everyone's best interests.

Library instruction can mean different things to different administrators. As a general term, however, it is quite simply that instruction in
the use of a library which can be applied to libraries of different sizes,
types, and specialties. In a small library, the manager will be responsible for both the planning and execution of most of the library instruction
ideas, projects, and designs. Each manager should know the importance
of such instruction: it is the key to full utilization of the library itself.
Knowing how to find information is every bit as important as the
information itself.

LIBRARY ORIENTATION

Every library should provide orienting details to the user. Anyone
who walks into a strange building needs information about where

Danielle Clarke is the Director of the North Salem Free Library, North Salem,
New York.

things are. The physical arrangement of library services and collections is a primary concern for the new user. Various departments and the staff who run them need to be highlighted. Specific services should be enumerated. Hours of operation should be clearly stated. Pertinent library policies should be publicized (overdue, reserves, renewals, etc.). The method used in cataloging the collection should be briefly outlined. All of this information can help stimulate the patron's return visit or future use. If the orienting process is presented in a pleasant, helpful way, the user will leave the library feeling well-informed and welcome to return.

Perhaps the best test for determining what orientation is needed for a specific library is to walk "in someone else's moccasins"—visit the library as if it were the first time. Glaring omissions will jump out, confusing details will be noticed, conflicting information will jar. Jot down notes while walking through the building. A good round discussion with staff (perhaps they should try the moccasins, too) will add further suggestions for areas in which the very first impression of the library can be improved.

A logical, first-step orientation to any new place is the guided tour. This can be a one-on-one tour by a staff member with each new user, given on an as-needed, spontaneous basis, or a pre-arranged group tour, given at pre-set times. In a small library where the manager will most likely be the tour guide, the group approach is probably the most efficient use of time. Some libraries schedule tours on a regular basis once a month; the actual times of the tours vary between week and weekend days and mornings, afternoons, and evenings. Whoever conducts the tour must be familiar with both the physical layout of the building and the collection. Groups are more effective if no more than 15 people are included. Since people are often reluctant to ask questions in large groups, the librarian must encourage an open atmosphere and welcome questions.

The audiotape, self-guided tour is another option. Users check out a cassette player with a long, comfortable shoulder strap (which frees both hands) and a set of earphones and are guided through the building at their own pace. The machine can be stopped at various points for the user to look up a certain title in the card catalog or watch a few moments of a videotape which might be playing at the time. And, portions of the tape can be replayed if the user doesn't understand the first time. Interesting bits of background about the library can be interjected in the dialogue: for example, a brief history of the library, its buildings, or the institution of which it is a part; funding sources; special collections; or other unique characteristics. The quality of the audiotape is very important: it should be friendly in tone and clear enough to be informative, but not so long that it explains too much. Producing audiotapes requires much planning, but they are inexpensive to produce and equipment costs are minimal. Even the smallest library could offer this form of self-guided orientation.

The overall effectiveness of both styles of tours can be enhanced by providing written handouts as well as "hands-on" experience at specific points to reinforce learning. A map or floorplan of the library is a basic necessity, no matter how small the library. One might be posted on the wall, but it is important to give the user a take-home copy. It is difficult for many library users to march up to the reference/circulation desk to ask where something is—especially if it is a topic which could be considered "embarrassing." The floor plan, with a brief listing of the basic divisions of the collection, will solve this problem by allowing the user to find what is needed independently. Another handout could list the complete name of the library, address, telephone number, hours of operation, the various departments or services, and the names of the staff for each. It might also include the most sought-after special features such as the photocopier, microfiche backfiles, computer-based searches, etc.

Another idea for a handout for independent use is an explanation of the card, microfiche, or computer catalog. Using as an example the entry of an author, directions would be given for searching the catalog in step-by-step fashion. Diagrams would show the actual appearance of the entries, with arrows leading to explanations of the parts of the entry. Underneath all directions, the fact should be stressed that "The librarian will be glad to help—ask questions."

Quick guides (such as the catalog idea) can offer individualized library instruction for the independent user. A serious researcher could gather as many of these handouts as possible to form a notebook of procedures for a specific library or for his specific needs. A person who only wants to know how to find a magazine article on one subject need only pick up the handout on searching for an article in a serial (or magazine—a much friendlier word). Other quick guides which could be developed are: how to use the computer (online catalog), how to use microform equipment, how to find a book or microform backfiles or audiocassettes or 35mm slides, etc.

Commercially-produced handouts are available and while they may save time, they do not reflect the specific qualities of an individual library. Producing handouts tailored to a particular library is easy. Volunteers or other staff can design graphics; a professional person on the staff can draft step-by-step directions; and photocopiers can be used for reproduction. Some hints for creating such handouts are: they should be brief, simple, clear, and appealing. They should also be compatible in style with other library-produced materials; be dated and authorship credited; and finally, they should be reviewed periodically for currency.

In the academic setting, specific subject search outlines called "pathfinders" are an excellent instructional aid. On a single sheet, one topic can be explored throughout the library's collection. For example, on the topic of Drinking Age, a brief discussion of the scope of the subject heads the page. Reference books containing information can be listed and locations highlighted within the particular cataloging system of the library. Subject headings (Sears or LC) should be cited (e.g., Drinking and Traffic Accidents—United States, Youth—United States—Alcohol Use, or Liquor Laws—United States). Often the trickiest part of research for the uninitiated library user is under what subject headings to look for what topics. Specific titles of books on the subject can be listed, giving the location symbols. Guides to finding appropriate indexes for journal articles should list the subject headings used in each index: Alcohol and Youth, Alcohol and Automobile Drivers, Mothers Against Drunk Drivers (MADD), etc. The user should be warned that subject headings change with each different index, and examples should be given which are pertinent to the specific index used in the guide. Information/vertical file subject headings should be included as well. By offering these quick tips on a single topic, the pathfinder can save the user hours of wasted energy and time which can be used more productively in reading the materials carefully rather than struggling to find them.

Commercial firms produce workbooks, handbooks, guides, and programmed instruction for library use. Since the quality of such materials varies, previewing is strongly recommended. Frequently, these materials contain sources which are unavailable in a small library; it would seem, therefore, that locally produced materials would be a better idea. Before any original projects are begun, it is highly recommended that the library manager contact LOEX for samples. This clearinghouse collects all sorts of library instructional materials and generously shares them. Contact Library Orientation Exchange, Center for Educational Resources, Eastern Michigan University, Ypsilanti, MI 48197, (313) 487-0168.

A frequent mistake librarians commit when orienting users is dispensing too much information. The rule of "Less is more" aptly applies to library instruction. Before a tour is conducted, members of the group should be questioned to determine their needs, and then the tour tailored to answer those questions. They should not be overwhelmed with information which they may not need at this point. An orientation is an acquainting, a brief introduction, a quick rundown of offerings— the most basic directions to the parts of the collection and necessary features about the building. By encouraging questions and by keeping it brief and to-the-point, the orientation tour guide will avoid driving away new users by intimidating them with too many unfamiliar terms or too much information. Friendliness, clarity, and brevity cannot be stressed enough to insure the success of the library orientation process.

LIBRARY INSTRUCTION

Although it may be considered a fine distinction, there is a difference between library orientation and library instruction. Public libraries often do not wish to promote too "school-like" an atmosphere. Emphasis on orientation methods which are less threatening to the user and can often be used independently are logical for the small public library. Of course, all libraries should orient their users with the suggestions already discussed, but school and academic libraries will utilize more advanced techniques.

Courses in library instruction may already exist in the curriculum or in other coursework. In either case, the following methods of teaching are usually included: lecture/demonstration methods which incorporate hands-on activities and exercises, workshops devoted to a specific topic, and term-paper clinics. Audiovisual presentations are very effective in this more intense form of library instruction. Slide-tape shows, films, videotapes, and audiotapes can serve as excellent teaching aids. Whenever possible, instruction in the use of the library should take place *in* the library. Expecting a student to retain information heard in a classroom and transfer it to the library at a later time is unrealistic. The attitudes of clarity, openness, friendliness, and helpfulness should prevail during lectures. Studies have proven that any learning is reinforced with hands-on experiences: the lecture can be stopped; a search assigned; and the students allowed to find out for themselves what points have just been made. Class size should be small; this allows for more attention to the student and encourages the students to ask questions.

Small, one-hour workshops on specific materials are another way of introducing good library use. Topics which present problems for students—audiovisual materials, microforms, abstracts, and indexes—should be selected and one concentrated on for an hour. Questions should be accepted throughout, and reinforced with specific hands-on activities. Worksheets for independent searching after the workshop can be distributed.

Term-paper clinics often include several sessions to instruct students in the various steps of preparing a research paper. These clinics are often successful because students have an immediate goal in mind (often a specific assignment) and so their attention is focused. The sessions are practical and reveal the helpfulness most librarians feel for students but often don't communicate. Brevity is important; the student should not be overwhelmed with unnecessary information.

Audiovisual materials can enhance any library instruction effort. Small libraries often do not have the resources or personnel to produce original, locally-specific materials; however, there are alternatives. Commercially produced materials are available, but should be previewed carefully. If these prove to be nonspecific or expensive, it might be possible to coordinate efforts with a local school or community college with an audiovisual department. Students could produce library instructional aids as part of their coursework in AV production classes. A side benefit for them would be greater understanding of library research techniques; a benefit to the small library would be a wider scope of individualized library instruction.

There are many types of materials to consider; each has its own advantages and disadvantages. Sound, 16mm films are very expensive to produce and require maximum planning and execution, so they are not suitable for the small library. However, the explosion within the videotape production world holds great opportunity for the limited budget. Less expensive than film to produce and fairly easy to shoot, videotape is adaptable for individual as well as small group screenings. Among the advantages of live-action aids are increased audience interest and the actual use of equipment within the library. It will be easier for a student to learn how to operate a microform reader after watching a user on tape and hearing the instructions. The student can immediately reinforce this learning by trying out the real thing. Since medium and larger libraries are now investing in their own videotape equipment, perhaps the small library could borrow equipment from a neighboring library or library system.

Slide/audiocassette shows are a popular form of orientation and instruction. They can be stopped for discussion with the audience, they are fairly inexpensive to produce, and are suitable for individual or group showing. The slides can feature "live-action" shots of people using the library as well as written materials (outlines, step-by-step directions, bibliographies) for discussion purposes. If staffing allows it, the slides can be used without the audiocassette soundtrack and narrated in person by the instructor. This more personal approach increases audience interest levels and encourages questions.

The audiocassette used alone still presents the best choice for the small library. It is very inexpensive to produce and can be tailor-made for specific library needs. When it is accompanied by handouts, exercises, posters, printed aids, flip charts, or worksheets, it can be a very effective tool. As with all the other audiovisual aids, quality of production is very critical. A poorly planned and produced item can have a negative effect on the student. If there is no one on the staff with a good speaking voice, someone outside the library should be found to read the script. It is imperative that the voice be clear and pleasant. Too many things should not be attempted on one tape; remember the "less is more" rule. Hands-on experiences immediately after the students have heard the tape will reinforce learning.

There are alternatives to classroom or group instruction. For the small library, it is especially important to consider the following concepts of library instruction: point-of-use, self-paced activities, learning packages, and programmed instruction. These methods require learners to assume more responsibility for their own instruction. Certainly the library staff can assist or answer questions, but basically learners concentrate on the areas in which they feel the need to learn the most.

Point-of-use library instruction focuses on one particular library tool, e.g., the card catalog, microfilm reader or other equipment, various guides to literature, indexes, abstracts, etc. They may be printed on AV materials, such as audiotape or slides. Those which involve the use of expensive audiovisual equipment are unrealistic for the small library. However, handsome illustrations and clear lettering on charts, posters, or handouts could provide as needed, on-the-spot information when placed strategically near the items they describe. Photography should not be overlooked for illustration purposes. Since it is possible that the library staff will be unaware of students' use of these materials, they must be self-explanatory, written in such a way that people of differing abilities will be able to understand them. Brevity is stressed and the description should cover only what is absolutely necessary for the student to know about the particular tool. A periodic review is necessary to ensure that the materials accurately reflect the item described.

Self-paced activities are materials which assign a learner certain tasks to lead him or her through steps of research in the library. The materials include questions to be answered by using the various library tools. In school or academic libraries, the completed assignments can be graded or required for classroom credit. In public libraries, the user is invited to submit the completed work for discussion with a staff member, or it can be left at the desk and the results mailed to the user later. School librarians could use this method to introduce students to the public library under the guise of a fact-finding field trip. Sometimes these materials are collected into workbooks which are the required text for an English class. Care must be taken to provide enough differently planned workbooks so that the students will not be able to use each others' answers. One real benefit of the workbook is that it may be kept by the student once it is completed and corrected, and then used for future referrals and brush-ups on specific tools. Since a quality product is important to effectiveness, LOEX should be contacted for exemplary models.

The *learning package* is yet another extension of the self-paced method which adds audiovisual aids. This term can simply mean a workbook accompanied by an audiocassette or a slide/audiotape presentation with exercises to complete afterwards. Since this is even more time-consuming and complicated to produce, the small library should consider purchase of ready-made programs or enlistment of the aid of other departments within the school or college.

Programmed instruction is another refinement of the learning package by which answers are provided in the materials and individuals learn by correcting their own mistakes. This seems inappropriate for the small library since personal contact and instruction by the staff would more likely reinforce learning. However, programmed instruction materials could be reviewed for ideas when a manager is developing the library's own product. What distinguishes programmed instruction from other methods is that if learners choose a wrong answer, they are immediately informed of this fact and instructed to reread the explanations which could help them choose the correct answer next time.

A further development of programmed instruction is computer-assisted instruction (CAI) which converts the learning process into machine-readable form and stores it in a computer. Learners simply sit at a terminal and proceed as they would in written programmed instruction. The immediate feedback and the limitless patience of the computer are two advantages; however, studies have indicated that CAI is not significantly better than other methods.

Games which teach library instruction should not be overlooked if the small library has younger users. There are commercially produced varieties which can be used to teach research strategies within the library itself or in the classroom. These games can be formally introduced to students or can be left available for them to use while visiting the library. There's nothing written which says library instruction can't be fun.

Because there are so many materials and techniques available for library instruction, there is much controversy over which method or style is best. By exploring the various methods mentioned and contacting LOEX for more information, library managers can find the most practical and effective method for their particular needs. The various methods are evaluated in ALA's *Bibliographic Instruction Handbook* (1979), prepared by the Policy and Planning Committee, Bibliographic Instruction Section of the Association of College and Research Libraries (ACRL). Another useful ALA/ACRL publication, *Library Instruction Clearinghouses 1986: A Directory* gives information on obtaining guidance and materials to develop library instruction programs.

There is agreement that using many forms of media is the most effective method of teaching and reinforcing library instruction as well as library use. It cannot be stressed enough that librarians must view their role as teachers whose duty goes beyond introducing the building and its various parts. (At the end of this chapter ALA's policy statement on library instruction has been reprinted.)

BIBLIOGRAPHIC INSTRUCTION

This term is used for the third, most scholarly approach to library instruction. BI is a formal course which many colleges and universities offer as part of their curriculum. It is unlikely that such a sophisticated level of coursework would be developed and taught by the manager of a small library, but it is worthy of brief mention here. The BI courses can be required for all students or optional for certain students who need remedial help or specific research techniques for their majors. Whatever their nature, all courses would be structured and organized in such a way to force students to complete assignments which would be graded (possibly for credit). As an expansion of library instruction, the course would include more specific needs for the serious researcher such as outlining techniques, the planning of the research paper, note-taking, style, footnotes, references, bibliographies, search strategies, and the actual writing of a research paper. A typical text for such a course might be Jean Kay Gates' *Guide to the Use of Libraries and Information Sources* (5th ed., McGraw-Hill, 1983). For a person planning such a course, Anne F. Roberts' *Library Instruction for Librarians* (Libraries Unlimited, 1982) is recommended for its thorough design of a bibliographic instruction course, complete with helpful suggested assignments and readings at the end of each chapter. No matter how complicated the coursework, the same principles of an open, friendly classroom atmosphere to encourage questions will engender the most positive attitudes toward librarians and libraries.

USER-FRIENDLY SIGNS

The small-library manager should not underestimate the importance of the design of the library building itself as a factor in educating the user. Since the most effective instruction takes place right in the building, features which are "user-friendly" should be planned in the architectural design as well as the interior decoration. It is a given that libraries are known to intimidate people; sometimes the building itself is forbidding and confusing. When planning a new building or renovating an old one, negative features should be eliminated. Ways to offer services and direct locations for maximum efficiency need to be devised. Physical impediments to full utilization must be redesigned.

Signs can be the most obvious problem and solution. Do people read signs? Are there enough signs for them to read? What is the first thing they see upon entering the library? Is the terminology used on the signs appropriate to first-time library users? Are the signs clear? Attractive? Legible? It behooves each library manager to try those moccasins again to answer these questions. A walk through the library can reveal both problems and successes in signs. If the manager tries not to be a librarian when reading the signs, do they still make sense? Do the words "Reference Desk" have a clear meaning to a nonlibrarian? Why not use the term "Information" instead? Everyone knows what that means and the user would be directed to a place where both directional and reference questions would be answered.

Signs can teach, orient, direct, and identify. Much thought must go into the planning of a sign system for a library. Signs should be brief and consistent in color scheme, lettering, language, and placement. Other considerations are the number of signs (too many or too few will confuse); visibility for special users (Can children or wheelchair-occupants see them?); obstructions (Are display cases or plants in the way?).

Limited finances and staff might tempt a small-library manager to prepare hand-lettered signs. This practice is heartily discouraged by the experts because these signs are often poorly planned, illegible, and inconsistent with each other. The price might be right, but homemade signs communicate a less than professional atmosphere. Neighboring art departments in schools or artists in the community could be contacted for locally produced signs. If it is necessary for budgetary reasons to have fewer signs, at least have them professionally prepared.

In considering what signs to prepare, the staff at the reference/circulation desk should be polled on the most frequently asked questions. By rank-ordering their responses, priorities will emerge. The actual wording of the signs should be discussed with the staff; their suggestions might be more practical since they speak with the public every day. The literature on the subject should be consulted; and the library's needs discussed with a sign construction company (preferably one which has made library signs before). Some other suggestions: consider the use of symbols, picto'graphs, and Braille signs; choose materials which are easy to maintain; and select designs which allow for change in the future. Press-type lettering on plastic surfaces can be removed and relettered if the library's needs change; this is more cost-effective than signs for one-time use only.

Since the most successful library instruction programs take place *in the library,* a manager who is constantly aware of the users' perspective is one who will create the ideal atmosphere of professionalism coupled with friendliness. In planning a library instruction plan, the manager of a small library must determine first what is wrong or confusing or threatening about the library and then systematically develop approaches to the physical as well as the intellectual needs of the users.

Policy Statement: Instruction in the Use of Libraries*

Utilization of information is basic to virtually every aspect of daily living in a democratic society, whether in the formal pursuit of educational goals or in independent judgment and decision making. In our post-industrial, increasingly complex society, the need for information daily becomes greater.

Libraries are a major source of information; however, their effective use requires an understanding of how information is organized and how individuals can retrieve that information. Many individuals have an inadequate understanding of how to determine the type of information needed, locate the appropriate information, and use it to their best advantage.

Instruction in the use of libraries should begin during childhood years and continue as a goal of the formal educational process in order to prepare individuals for the independent information retrieval essential to sustain life-long professional and personal growth.

It is essential that libraries of all types accept the responsibility of providing people with opportunities to understand the organization of information. The responsibility of educating users in successful information location demands the same administrative, funding, and staffing support as do more traditional library programs.

The American Library Association encourages all libraries to include instruction in the use of libraries as one of the primary goals of service.

*American Library Association, Council Document #45, 1980. Reprinted by permission of the American Library Association.

Community/User Studies

Blane K. Dessey

All public libraries, regardless of size, exist to serve their communities and their residents. In fact, libraries are evaluated increasingly upon their responsiveness to community need and citizen wants. Over the past several years, several techniques and books have attempted to instruct public libraries in how to become more proactive in their approach to community service. The concept of Community Analysis has been popular for several years. The American Library Association (ALA) has published both *A Planning Process for Public Libraries* (1980) and *Output Measures for Public Libraries* (1982), two texts that are designed to improve a public library's self assessment and community performance. They have, in fact, become the de facto standard for public library measurement.

A public library has the responsibility to assess both the community and the library itself. By doing this, the library decision-makers can be assured that the library services offered are the best. Community/user studies are actually two different activities and should be treated as such. Whether or not one or both activities are undertaken is decided by the library administration, library board, and, in some cases, the local funding officials.

COMMUNITY ANALYSIS

The premise of community analysis is very simple. In evaluating and planning library service, the community must be analyzed so that proper decisions may be made. After all, how can a community service organization make decisions about service if that agency hasn't learned about the community? Studying the community in all of its aspects gives the library decision-makers insight and information into how the community is composed—past, present, and for the future. Before conducting a community analysis, the library staff should understand the type and extent of the activities to be done and should think of those activities in terms of available library resources.

Blane K. Dessey is Deputy State Librarian for Library Services, The State Library of Ohio, Columbus, Ohio.

Community analysis is generally composed of several steps. The first may be a community walk-around. In this activity, library staff wander around the community making notes of distinguishing features which may include various neighborhoods, commercial center(s), school locations, major streets, major geographic features, and community service agencies and institutions. The point of the community walk-around is to provide a broad brush overview of the community and its composition. It is not meant to supply definitive information, but rather an impression of the community and its facets. Community maps are sometimes used to display the findings of the community walk-around.

Another activity is the examination of community statistics and census data. Examining these types of data should provide community demographics such as ages, races, educational levels, major occupations and industries, and other significant information. Another source of community statistics can be local, county, or regional planning commissions which may have conducted surveys of the community and forecasted trends for the future. These planning offices are a rich source of information and should be consulted before library staff undertake their own community information gathering. The purpose of the statistical data is to provide more detail about the community than the walk-around. The statistical data should provide insight into the composition of the community and its major segments and characteristics. Other areas for study are patron registration and sampling of the library's shelflist. The major thrust of all of this is to obtain a picture of the community in enough detail that decisions about library service can be made in an informed manner.

USER SURVEYS

While many libraries conduct only a community analysis, many public libraries also decide to collect data about the library's operations and its users. For small public libraries which have never collected data before, it is advisable to begin slowly and to collect only as much data as can be used effectively and efficiently.

User surveys can be very beneficial to library staffs because they indicate the quality of library service being provided to users. Assessing users' opinions about library service and measuring such activities as title and subject fill rate can be very enlightening to library staffs and boards of trustees. What is important for the library staff to remember is that this data gathering must be well planned and coordinated. It is also important to remember that these types of user surveys can require a large amount of staff time and energy.

Before undertaking any surveys of the community or of library users, it is important that the librarian has an accurate assessment of its available resources and that the staff and board of trustees are truly committed to the importance of gathering information and acting upon it in a responsible fashion.

Rationale for the Studies

"Every library should be structured in response to community residents and their needs." No one would argue with this hypothetical commitment to library service, but are there more concrete reasons for undertaking the study of a community and its library users? Two basic reasons are the budget and public relations.

The library's budget is the annual operational plan for that institution; it should be based on the library's objectives for a given year. In many cases, however, librarians base their budgets upon either a simple incremental approach or continue to budget for programs and services which may or may not have viability. The most legitimate method for preparing a budget (or a yearly plan for spending) is to know how the money may best be spent in the community. The way in which that knowledge is gained is through community and user studies.

Consider for a moment the budget category of library acquisitions. How does a librarian begin to think about what needs to be done during the course of the next year in buying library materials? The simplest approach is to add an inflationary factor of a certain percentage to last year's budget amount. But that does not address the question of purchasing appropriate materials for the community. By collecting and analyzing data about the community and library users, the librarian can make decisions about adult and juvenile materials, print and nonprint materials, and other issues such as educational level of materials, collection weeding, and overall focus of the library's collection—not only short-term, but long-range as well.

Community and user data are invaluable in developing a library budget, but there is another corollary reason for constructing a budget upon such data. Without exception, there is some type of governmental review of public library budget requests, either by elected officials or by appointed officials of a political subdivision. There is no substitute for community and user data when defending a budget request: state and national standards, professional opinion, and counsel from a state library agency cannot compare to information about the community and library users when the library budget is presented.

When questioned about why the budget includes certain items— more acquisition money or more staff, for example—the librarian must be prepared to answer in terms of the local community. It is the local community which the funding authorities represent and to which they are accountable. While it is important to be aware of national trends and state developments, it is, in the final analysis, the quality of local information that will determine the outcome of a budgetary process.

Community and user information also have high value in terms of library public relations. When a public library studies a community, it interests a community. By conducting a community study and user studies in a preplanned, formal manner, the public library stands to gain increased visibility and to benefit from better relations with that community. In small communities there can be tremendous public interest in the studies that the local public library is conducting. Newspapers and radio stations can be a valuable ally, not only in helping to collect data, but in promoting the story that the public library cares enough to find out about the community. By collecting, analyzing, and distributing data about the library's studies, the librarian creates a very impressive amount of public relations material which can be used to the library's benefit. Generally, people are flattered when others are curious about them. Communities are no different. When elected officials and funding authorities learn of the library's activities they will generally be favorably impressed by the conscientiousness of the library staff and trustees. This, in turn, makes the budgeting process that much easier.

FIRST STEPS IN THE STUDIES

The first step in conducting community and user studies is to plan for them. This in itself requires several steps. Because the impetus for this kind of activity generally comes from the library director, that person should learn as much as possible about data-gathering activities by reading professional literature, attending meetings and workshops on appropriate topics, and speaking to other librarians who have done similar activities. The state library is often a good source of information for this purpose. The librarian should not propose a formalized study process until he or she has become well versed in the topic. And once proposed, the librarian should be prepared to answer many questions posed by the staff and the trustees: Why do we have to do this? Who is going to do all of the work? What sort of things are we going to collect? What will we do with the results? Hasn't this been done already? Aren't we too small a library to deal with this? What if we discover that people don't like the library? Isn't this a big waste of time and money?

Commitment to the project by all involved is absolutely essential. Before doing anything else, it is imperative that everybody realizes the importance of the activity and will contribute time and energy to the project.

In planning the process, several fundamental questions must be answered. First, will the study involve conducting a community analysis only or will it also involve library user studies? Both are very important, but in terms of staff time and effort, it may only be possible to conduct one. The librarian must have a very firm idea of what type of data-gathering activity is to be done. Once that decision is made, other questions ensue. How extensive will the data gathering be? How much data are necessary?

Before deciding which data to collect, ask two questions: What is necessary to know? and What library management decision would be made with that information? Since collected data do not always translate into improved library service, it is important to know beforehand exactly what is to be learned about the community and/or library users. It is generally better to start off by collecting small amounts of data and then collect it as needed rather than beginning by undertaking a huge data-gathering activity. It is also important to have planned which people will perform which tasks. Generally the library staff is used, but library trustees, library friends, volunteers, and students could also become involved.

At the very beginning of the process, the support of the local media should be enlisted; in most cases this will be the local newspapers and radio stations. They may be able to supply information or assist in gathering data; or, at the very least, they can help spread the news about the library's data-gathering activities. This is where the public relations of community and user studies comes into play.

It is also a very good idea to inform the local funding authorities about the data-gathering activities. Not only will this keep them informed about the library, but it may also provide access to other sources of information, such as local planning boards and commissions.

HELP IN PLANNING/CONDUCTING THE STUDIES

There are many individuals and agencies which can lend assistance in planning and conducting the studies. The library director should contact peers who may have done similar projects, any regional or state library personnel who can offer advice and suggestions, local planning experts who may have already conducted community studies, and any library-related organizations that could lend time and support. Contacting these sources not only will greatly expedite the planning process but will help prevent mistakes during the course of the studies.

When the time comes to conduct the studies, the library director, staff, trustees, and other local individuals should be involved. It may also be possible to recruit volunteers for this type of activity. Clubs and social service organizations are often looking for worthwhile projects. The secret of successfully involving people is to assure them that what they are doing is valuable and that they are contributing to something important. Every volunteer and every activity should be considered a part of the library's public relations.

Length of the Studies

Everyone, especially the library director, needs to know how much time and effort will be required to do the job. This is difficult to know in a general way because it depends on the local situation. For example, it may be that there is a wealth of community data already available, so the task is to analyze and disseminate, not to gather. Or there may be no existing data, and so much will have to be gathered. The library staff may have been gathering data for a long period of time and, as a result, very little work needs to be done. On the other hand, studying the library users may be a totally new concept and a great deal of work may be necessary.

Another factor to consider is how much data the librarian, staff, and board can constructively use. Too much data gathering leads to "data overload." As mentioned earlier, it is often wiser to explore a small area of data, act upon that in some fashion, and then proceed to collect another small amount of data. For example, it may be much better to conduct an analysis of previous years' budgets as a single activity than to conduct it as part of a larger library and community statistical survey.

There are several rules of thumb regarding the length of the studies: Never collect more data than can be actively used; never propose a study that is more than can be reasonably accomplished given present library resources; never begin to conduct a study without knowing its end purpose; never begin a study without the approval and commitment of all involved; always make sure that there are solutions to potential problems worked out in advance; maintain administrative commitment in light of problems; and always maintain a sense of humor.

USING THE DATA

Generally, there is one person who is designated as the "data coordinator." This individual oversees all of the survey activities, seeing to it that schedules are met and that all necessary resources are coordinated. This person is also responsible for the compilation, analysis, and presentation of survey results.

Great care must be taken when analyzing and presenting the survey results. Each resulting piece of data should be linked in some way to a library service question. This is very important since it will give library decision-makers a context in which to review the data. (Too often data are collected but not connected in any way to library service problems; then the data are not used, or, in some cases, decried.) For example, a review of community demographics should be connected to discussions of collection development issues or library program planning.

It is also important to know the intended audience. How data are analyzed and presented depends on whether the audience is library staff, library board, funding officials, or the general public. Who the audience is may mean that more or less detail is presented or that financial impacts may or may not be included. Since different audiences require different slants on the survey information, it is necessary to know the audience's expectations of the data. By anticipating this, the value of the data, the analysis, and the presentations have increased value. Data presentations should be preplanned and the discussion should be conducted with an emphasis on the improvement of local library service.

FREQUENCY OF SURVEYS

Community/user surveys should be done as often as needed to verify the appropriateness of the library's services. Some surveys should be conducted annually; others may be done much less frequently. While the survey time frame is dependent upon local library needs, there are some general rules of thumb which may apply. Communities change at a fairly slow rate; unless something drastic happens, demographics change slowly. Therefore, community surveys or analysis only need to be done once every several years—generally five. User studies and other types of surveys are generally conducted more frequently. It is important not to use library resources carelessly. Collecting data requires time, staff, some money, and much commitment. Too much data gathering is counterproductive and strains those resources. Remember: surveys are meant primarily to assist in the process of improving library services; they should not detract from the provision of those services.

Friends of the Library

Mark Y. Herring

Librarians are a peculiar sort of professional when it comes to money. First, they want as much as they can get to run their programs, an attribute for which they cannot be faulted. Second, they do not want to charge anyone for any of the expensive services they offer—*perhaps* another admirable wish. Third, and last, they do not want to *earn* or *raise* any of this money themselves; they want it given to them. If there be any truth in political stereotypes, librarians are true Democrats. They are the prototypes of spend, spend, spend, give me more, more, more. If professional librarians spent their personal funds in a manner similar to the way in which they spent their corporate ones, they'd all be filing for Chapter 11.

Perhaps it's not quite that bad. Any review of the literature, however, will reveal a propensity against any charges for services whatsoever.[1] One might think, then, that the rush to initiate Friends groups in every library would be overwhelming, but such is not the case. Even with the advent of such positive signs as the publication of the *Friends of the Library Sourcebook* and *Friends of Libraries USA National Notebook*,[2] Friends groups are still catching on. Most groups are small (under 250 members) and the majority (as much as 80 percent of them) originate out of public libraries. (Are we to conclude that academic libraries do not need any help?) Other data serve to show that these groups are not members of a huge national network, most do not even belong to a state group for lack of one to join,[3] and most groups have been formed since 1970.[4] In a word, Friends groups are usually small operations with a few members, run by a few hard-working people. It is clear that to have a successful Friends group one needn't be at a large library, have a huge staff, or find a multi-millionaire to get one started.

Legislation passed in the last two decades has made it certain that eleemosynary contributions would be harder, not easier, to make. With private interest groups chasing down churches with church-state separation orders, and the IRS chasing down individuals with fewer and fewer write-offs, it should come as no surprise that contributions to libraries have all but diminished.

The decision to have a Friends group is an important one and should

Mark Y. Herring is Director, E. W. King Library, King College, Bristol, Tennessee.

not be taken lightly. Successful Friends groups are fun, they can create quite a splash for the library, and they do attract a lot of publicity and encourage public relations and good will. But more than that, successful Friends groups require a dedicated staff, an involved director, and a good deal of time, patience, and even prayer. When one looks at all that can go wrong with Friends groups, adds to that the number of reasons for letting it die, and collates the number of opportunities in one year for pronouncing it dead, anyone can see that successful Friends groups are aberrations, the existence of which can only be accounted for by the miraculous.

Setting aside the miraculous, what constitutes a Friends group, and how does a librarian get one going? If the librarian is lucky enough, someone will come and ask for help in organizing one. More often than not the librarian will come to the profound conclusion that, given the library's budget, the probability for significant increases in that budget, and aspirations for the collection, someone will have to do something to help the library out. Realizing further that private foundations contribute only ten percent of their grants to educational outreaches, and most of that not going to libraries, the librarian will be duly impressed to move forward with plans for a Friends group.[5,6]

ORGANIZING STRATEGY

The first thing to be done is to have a conference with the staff to discuss their interest in working long hours during an event, their desire to organize special library outreaches, and to read their barometers for such service. It is always a difficult task for the "boss" to ask "subalterns" if they want to undertake a new task. Most often they will answer yes, fearing for their jobs or thinking that the affirmative answer is the only one the director wants. If the director has done a good job of communicating with the staff, it will be possible to assess whether or not they want to get involved in the organization of a Friends of the Library group. If the answer is positive, then the director must take the lead in the preparations. The quickest way to kill a nascent program is to ask if everyone is ready to get involved, and then turn the whole matter over to someone else. Staff members learn best by example. Delegating responsibilities will come soon enough.

The director must be honest during this meeting. Friends programs, if they are to be successful, take an enormous amount of time and planning. If anyone goes into the planning stages with a qualified disinterest in the project, it will be stillborn. Everyone should know that such a project requires more hours, most of them without extra pay. Do they, in fact, want that?

The next step is to identify a small cadre of "outsiders" interested in the library. Second only to an enthusiastic library staff is an enthusiastic small group outside the library who want to see the library prosper.[7] This group can be best identified through the Development Office in the academic library or through circulation records and word of mouth in the public library. Once several names (no more than two dozen) have been identified, the librarian should plan a tea or some other event during which the plans for establishing the Friends group is explained, a call for volunteers is made, and another meeting is scheduled.

Before the next meeting the director and a few other members should get together to discuss writing the by-laws and constitution for the Friends group. In addition, the number of officers, how long their terms of service will be, and whether the officers will be elected or appointed should be decided. The election of officers at this point would be premature. It is best to let the elections or appointments wait until a more substantial membership is available.

At the second meeting, the by-laws can be approved, not as a binding statement, but de facto until a vote of a larger membership can be taken. The group must be able to function in some manner in the meantime. It violates no law, however, to approve these by-laws as binding, fully aware that a larger membership may overturn or rewrite them at a later date. At the close of this meeting, a third one should be announced. Those in attendance should be encouraged to bring a friend, and plans made to put a notice in the local newspaper about the new group. Often, groups will make newspaper announcements long before this. Experience has shown, however, that when the public is invited, even to preliminary organizational meetings, they have little patience for the slipshod way these meetings inevitably must be run. Get the motor on the big machine running first, then invite others for a ride.

Dues are permissible if they are set low enough (five or ten dollars) to appeal to everyone, but they can also have an adverse effect. Many will feel that they have "paid their dues" when special drives come up. It is best to wait for a project to solicit money. Memberships, on the other hand, should be secured from everyone at least once. The fee for membership should be set in categories and be clearly distinguished from dues. The similarity between dues and memberships is a close one, but dues imply benefits, and benefits are exactly what the *library* is looking for. Later, when the Friends of the Library group is purring, members can be given special benefits, such as discounts on library paraphernalia and special markdowns on library book sales.

A third meeting might include a tour of the library building, an examination of a special collection, and a brainstorming session on the kind of Big Event the library wants to take on annually. Every Friends group needs such an event. It is the rallying point for the membership's activities; it is that one thing for which they plan all year; it is the culmination of all that they have been working for. This big event can be anything from a reception highlighting a local author to a major production showcasing an internationally known playwright or novelist. Whatever the choice, the Friends group must have something to look forward to; without it, the group may lose interest.

PLANNING THE BIG EVENT

Only the limitations of the director's imagination will cordon off the boundaries for this extravaganza. Unless patrons of the arts can be reeducated about how to be patrons, the whole ball of wax will melt in the director's hot little hand. Librarians must remember that the world of fundraising is vicious, if not by choice, then by the number of mouths wishing to be fed. Impressing upon prospective patrons a desperate need requires more than lip service. It requires someone willing to sound a bit brash.

This does not mean that the director stoops to poor taste or turns the library into a barn for talking animals. Libraries, despite what some librarians would have us believe, are still respites of culture, way stations of intellectual delight along the broken road of unreason. Librarians do not need to hire jumping clowns or dancing bears, but they simply cannot always offer the *Four Quartets* or dramatic readings from *The Faerie Queene*. Even when these are offered, librarians must be wary of how to reach their audience. If librarians are trying to reach the intellectuals, they will, no doubt, be found. They are a difficult lot to please, however, and as a group are largely parsimonious.

Librarians have to reach as large a portion of the public as possible. They cannot afford not to do so.[8] To do this effectively, the director has to appeal to the masses in two ways: in a way that does not *seem* highbrow but is, and in a way that entertains. Debates on controversial subjects satisfy these criteria by fulfilling the appearance of intellectual stimulation and offering what is ostensibly entertaining. In discussing what to do for the big event, librarians need to pay attention to what is both culturally significant and entertaining. In choosing events, librarians want to be certain not to select something that will, in effect, make them barbers in a town of bald-headed people.

This third meeting should close with someone assigned to the job of putting on the big event. This means responsibility for all of the publicity, the organization of events, and the ticket sales. It is not recommended to divide the tasks by having someone in charge of getting the event rolling, another in charge of publicity, and still another in charge of ticket sales. This division of labor, albeit wise in some cases, is not a brilliant move here. Only the person who is continuously involved with the annual gala affair will be able to design effective publicity. Only the one working in the trenches daily will be able to assess the flow of ticket sales and apply adjustments as needed. When the labor is fractured, the right hand often forgets, or is never told, what the left hand is doing. It is perfectly logical that the person in charge of the gala event should have several people working with him or her to run errands and type correspondence. Beyond this, however, that person had better have a sharp eye for details.

In a small library, that person will invariably be the director. The director of a small library, whether an ex officio member of the Friends group or not, should be ready to take over all the responsibilities of the Arrangements Committee. Directors who begin Friends groups with the idea in mind that "someone will eventually take over this show" should strive to write biographies that have titles like *Iacocca* or *Caesar*.

During these first three meetings, the director should get a good idea of the number of members in this executive committee who will really work. If they are not forthcoming, the director should not hesitate to assume the role. A word of warning: do not assume the role until you are certain the role will not be assumed by others. It is a fundamental trait of group mentality to get together to be led. Once it is clear that no one can or will assume the reins, the director must take them. For those directors who must face a committee member who thinks he or she can do the job, but in fact cannot, a word of advice: start checking the job advertisements. Angels fear before fools, we are told, but even fools have their thresholds of stupidity.

Those in charge of the Friends group should plan for one or two small events during the year, highlighted by the annual event. These small events might be book or bake sales, an exhibit, or an open house. Almost anything will work, as long as it attracts community members and brings in enough funds to cover the expenses. In an academic library setting, the president of the college or university should be invited to all these events, along with other ranking officials and their spouses. One sure way to interest the president in the library's Friends meetings is an invitation to speak to the group about his or her hobby. Be sure, however, that you can get a small crowd together. In a public library setting, the director should call on important townspeople to talk about their hobbies. For example, what is it that the mayor likes to pontificate about, and with reasonable accuracy?

NEWSLETTERS

If small events cannot be arranged because of time, then the librarian (or a personally chosen delegate) should begin immediately putting out a newsletter. Newsletters work best if they are published four times a year, coinciding with the seasons which can be used as themes. The library's needs should always be prominently placed in the letter, along with a membership card printed somewhere on the sheet. The most easily mailed newsletter measures 8 1/2″ x 17″, folded. It need not exceed four pages. If one is hard pressed for words or news or both, then an 8 1/2″ x 11″, printed on both sides, will suffice.

The newsletter must be neat, should adapt to the library's purpose and, if an academic library, should show off the school's colors. Pictures of good quality for reproduction are highly recommended. The director of the library should have a regular feature or write the editorial in the newsletter. If the newsletter showcases an academic library, it should contain contributions from faculty members. For a public library newsletter, invitations should be sent to the mayor, members of the town council, and legislators. From congresspeople representing the district, ask for articles that touch on the importance of the library. If your representatives are too busy for such an assignment (i.e., they haven't assigned it to one of their staff), mention should be made in the newsletter that, "Senator X has been invited to write a piece on the importance of reading in this district. We look forward to reading his encouraging words." Make sure that Senator X gets a copy. After weeks have passed and no column appears, mention it again.

The editor of the local newspaper should also be asked to write for the newsletter. The invitation is not only in good taste, but also encourages involvement beyond lip service in the library's activities.

Of all the things that go into the newsletter, the entire front page of at least one issue should announce the Friends' big event. The person responsible for the event might offer a lighthearted tale of the planning and implementation of it. The style should be informal, the grammar impeccable.

THE WRITER-SPEAKER APPROACH

Of all the annual events that can be chosen—book sales, auctions, exhibits, concerts, raffles, bake sales, _____-a-thons, tours, etc.[9]—the speaker-writer series is especially recommended because it emphasizes what the library is about (reading) and showcases what the library thrives on (those who write). Painfully clear to every librarian who has chosen this route, however, is that not all writers are good speakers. One can learn only by trying, and by calling others who have heard writers speak. Names of some speakers whose platform abilities are exceeded only by their writing talents are William F. Buckley Jr., Madeleine L'Engle, Michael Novak, Kathryn Koob, Alex Haley, and John Ehrlichmann. Some librarians may be frightened off by these names, owing to their fear of being unable to raise the funds needed to cover expenses. The success of such ventures—both in attendance and earnings—will be in direct proportion to the amount of publicity accompanying the event.

Do such writer-speakers need to be famous? The answer is a resounding, "Yes!" The reason is simple: no matter whether the librarian invites I. M. Kitsch or William F. Buckley Jr., the work necessary to pull off a successful dinner will be the same. A successful fundraiser for the library is just as hard to bring off for an audience of ten as it is for one thousand. It may make a local historian feel very good to read a 50,000 word essay on the importance of soybeans during the Civil War to a half dozen community members who have already heard it more than once, but why bother? Why not set the ideologies of the community on edge with a highly charged delivery by William F. Buckley Jr., or elevate the discussion of nuclear war to something higher than drivel with a masterful exposé by Michael Novak?

PUBLICIZING THE BIG EVENT

Publicity for the event should know no bounds. Notices in the college newspaper, the local newspaper, and emblazoned all over the library are staple avenues of approach, but are only the beginning. Friends members in charge of this event must call on as many community groups as are in the civic club directory. These groups must be informed by phone; by mail; by the group's newsletter; and in person. Even in a small city, this task becomes a huge one. But the Friends member who manages the available time wisely, or the director who is willing to go out at night, will be able to make all of these rounds. Groups with a special interest in the speaker need to be drawn into the process. Those in charge of the event must be bold and not hesitate to speak to these groups about the library, the weather, or the price of eggs anywhere in the free world, being sure, however, to take the time to talk about the Friends group.

Churches and synagogues are another way of publicizing Friends events. Special mailings should be made to pastors and rabbis, later followed up by phone calls. Radio and television should also be contacted. Advertisements should be taken out in newspapers. Free tickets should be sent to the media, but only two—one for a reporter and one for a cameraperson. If the person in charge of the event is not also in charge of tickets, then the big event may be a big financial flop, owing to a plethora of newspeople who have tickets for themselves and their spouses.

Wheedling special interest stories out of the news media may be the hardest task of all. In many small towns, only farmers growing 100-pound squash, raising cows with five legs, or possessing such unusual characteristics themselves, make the front page. All else is reserved for those who, in strange costumes, do things to various shaped balls—hitting, kicking, or throwing them. Unless the speaker-writer agrees to do an interview in a helmet, the publicity from the newspaper may be difficult to secure. If, however, the librarian has laid the proper groundwork, all should go well. That "proper" work includes such things as taking the editor to lunch, offering to write various pieces for the paper, or heading up a book or movie review column for the paper if there isn't one already. Even all of this will not guarantee publicity success, but without it, the event may come and go without the newspaper's blessing.

Publicity should also be directed at schools and colleges, and other "ready-made" groups. Unless these groups have a natural interest in the speaker or event, they need not be contacted more than once or twice. Corporations in the city, however, should be called on in person. During the meeting, the Friends representative, or, better yet, the chief librarian, should make an offer on block tickets for the employees of that corporation.

Arrangements for a book sale during this event should be made. Almost all writers appreciate them, and most will even endure an autograph session. Good will can be established between the community and the library if the librarian offers the celebrity to the local bookstore for an hour or two. The Friends group should get front billing, some of the proceeds, or both.

ARRANGEMENTS/LOGISTICS

The evening's festivities should not last more than three hours, say from 6:30–9:30 in the evening. It should be held at a time when the community calendar is the least busy, and on a night not likely to interfere with church/synagogue meetings or civic group get-togethers. Clear the date of the event with the Chamber of Commerce for the best possible potential for a strong turn-out. The event should include a welcome by the college or university president or mayor, if a public library, an invocation by a recognized member of the clergy, and the address by the speaker-writer. The introduction of the speaker can be made by the chief librarian, the chair of the board, or the chair of the Friends group. The head table should not exceed more than eight individuals, including spouses. Closing remarks should be made by the head librarian or the chair of the Friends group. Above all, emphasis should be placed on money or in-kind contributions to the library. Be frank and honest. Announcements about the next library-related event can bring the festivities to an end. Auctions of the table decorations and any book sales can be held as participants are leaving.

Paraphernalia about the library should be in abundance: have mugs and T-shirts with the library's logo or name and pencils or calendars with the library's crest available for purchase. Sell the more expensive items; give away the less expensive ones, like pens and pencils. Not all of these things have to be sold every year or at every meeting. Prices for the items should not be set much above cost; the point of the marketing is not to raise all of the library's budget, but to do something to make certain the library's name and needs stay within easy reach of the public's memory.

Planning for the speaker-writer should be done with care. It is a tired cliché, but little things really do make the difference. What is the speaker's favorite snack? Does he or she enjoy any special treats, such as Godiva chocolates or cut flowers? These extras create an impression of caring, and more, that the person in charge has really done some homework. Never mind that the speaker is charging the Friends group several thousand dollars plus expenses; the speaker is also giving the group something that, if successful, will return that investment several times over.

When planning the schedule of events, try to give the speaker at least three hours alone. If all of the day's events must be crammed into one afternoon and evening, then such a luxury is not possible. In that case, the program activities chair must interlard physically taxing events with quiet interviews. Going that extra mile often makes the difference between a so-so evening and an unforgettable experience.

AFTER THE EVENT

The year never stops for those involved with the Friends group; once one event is over, another must begin. In between the meetings and the small get-togethers, there is always the ongoing work of the newsletter and the personal contact with civic groups. It sounds like a full-time job, but it isn't. Like most seasonal work, it comes and goes in spurts. Friends groups can take as much time as one wishes them to, but a certain amount of time is required to make the group successful.

Some groups may want to incorporate their Friends organization so that they can legally receive tax deductible donations from interested patrons (although this may change with the new tax laws). A constitution and by-laws (see box on pages 312–13) are needed first. The by-laws should include the purpose of the organization, annual meeting date, structure, and some means of dispensing the assets of the group, should

A Sample Constitution and By-Laws
for a Friends of the Library Group

ARTICLE ONE: NAME

The name of this organization shall be the Friends of the _____
Library.

ARTICLE TWO: PURPOSE

The purpose of the above named group shall be:

a. To encourage the interest in, and the expansion of, the resources,
equipment, and physical facilities of the _____ Library;

b. To allow for participation by interested patrons in Library-related
events such as exhibits, programs, and publications;

c. To solicit gifts and bequests of books, materials, manuscripts, and
financial contributions above and beyond the library's annual budget, enabling the _____ Library to remain in a continual state of growth and
progress.

ARTICLE THREE: CONTRIBUTIONS

Contributions of $25 or more will entitle members to library check-out
privileges.

Contributions are tax deductible and will be used in accordance with the
purpose of this organization as outlined in Article Two. The expenditure of
Friends of the Library donations will be determined by a joint consensus of
the Library Committee, the Friends of the Library Committee, and the
Director or Chief Librarian.

In-kind contributions, such as gift book collections, must meet with the
approval of the Director or Chief Librarian before being accredited to the
Friends of the Library account. Without the Director or Chief Librarian's
approval, in-kind donations will not be recognized by the Friends of the
Library organization.

All noncash contributions become the sole property of_____ Library
and will be disposed of as the Director or Chief Librarian and the President of
the Friends of the Library adjudicate. Noncash gifts with restrictions (e.g.,
gift book collections that continue under the ownership of the donor, or gift
book collections that must remain in the library *in perpetuum* may be
refused).

All restricted cash contributions shall be spent according to the donor's
wishes (e.g., a $100 gift for books on European History will be spent on books

relating to European History). All unrestricted or undesignated cash gifts will be spent in accordance with the Friends of the Library and the Director or Chief Librarian's determinations.

ARTICLE FOUR: OFFICERS

The Friends of the _____ Library shall have the following officers: A President, a Vice-President for Program and Events, a Secretary, and a Treasurer. The Director or Chief Librarian and his Associate shall serve as ex-officio members. Officers shall be elected for a one-year term of service, but may serve up to three consecutive terms. Nominees for the above-named officers shall be presented to the membership by a Nominating Committee, appointed by the reigning President. Nominees shall be announced three weeks prior to the annual election meeting. Nominees shall be voted on at the annual election meeting.

The President of the Friends of the _____ Library shall preside at all meetings. The President of the Friends of the _____ Library shall have the full authority to appoint committees as necessary.

The Vice-President shall serve the President; shall act in the President's absence; shall be in charge of all annual meetings, regular events, and other programs presented by the Friends of the _____ Library.

The Secretary shall record the minutes of all meetings.

The Treasurer shall maintain the financial records of the organization and see that receipts are posted according to accepted accounting practices. The Treasurer shall also see that all acknowledgements are mailed.

ARTICLE FIVE: MEETINGS

Meetings shall be held at least three times a year at a time and place determined by the Friends of the _____ Library Committee.

Executive meetings shall be held at least twice a year.

Exhibits will be scheduled by the Vice-President or as required by acquisitions.

Robert's Rules of Order shall govern the conduct of these meetings.

ARTICLE SIX: AMENDMENTS

These articles may be amended by a quorum vote of the membership at the annual meeting, provided there has been written notification of at least three weeks prior to said meeting. The President of the Friends of the _____ Library may request the amendment, deletion, or emendation of any of these articles, approval granted by a quorum vote of the membership.

it dissolve.[10] The group must also qualify for tax exemption. Forms are available through the IRS; look for Form 990, filed by all philanthropic foundations, which must be completed and returned to the IRS. Once these forms are submitted, the group is well on its way to incorporation. For Friends groups closely allied with a parent institution, itself tax exempt and receiving tax deductible contributions, incorporation may be unnecessary. A call to the IRS or to the institution's attorney will clear up any questions.

All too often, librarians and other enthusiastic patrons run headlong into such ventures as Friends groups, thinking what fun this "little pastime" is going to be. Some Friends groups may have started out that way, but if those groups are still meeting, they are most likely not being run on someone else's spare time. These groups take a great deal of time, patience, and, in the beginning, some money. Without all three, the venture is predestined to failure. But what makes for a good Friends group and sets apart one group from another? The one element that successful Friends groups have over less successful groups is a library director willing to see to it that the group's activities are carried out. In some cases, this means that the director has to do everything, from planning the event, to delegating responsibilities; in other cases, it will simply require overseeing the operation, attending all the meetings, and providing moral support when the group's enthusiasm flags. Without this key support from the one in charge, the group doesn't stand a chance. The reasons why this is so will be readily apparent to those librarians who have undertaken the organization of a Friends group. For those only beginning, remember that you are your own best friend. No one else knows the library's needs better, and no one wants to see those needs met more quickly. Finally, no one will work as hard to see that those needs are eventually met, those goals obtained.

References

1. Faye Blake and Edith Perlmutter, "The Rush to User Fees: Alternative Proposals," *Library Journal* 102 (October 1977): 2005–08; Carol Hole, "To: All Library Patrons. From: YPL (Your Public Library). Re: Fees for Library Service," *American Libraries* 14 (December 1983): 1716–17; Peter Leckie, "A Dangerous Quest for Certainty: Fees for Service and the Public Library," *Canadian Library Journal* 37 (October 1980): 317–18; Lawrence J. White, "The Public Library—Free or Fee," *The New Leader* 62 (December 1979): 3–5.
2. Sandy Dolnick, *Friends of the Library Sourcebook* (Chicago: American Library Assn., 1980) and *Friends of Libraries USA National Notebook*. Quarterly (Chicago: American Library Assn.).
3. Sandy Dolnick, "The Present State of Library Friends," in *Organizing the*

Library's Support: Donors, Volunteers, Friends (University of Illinois, 1980), pp. 33–40.

4. Ann Guy, Anne MacArthur and Karen Furlow, "Friends of the Library," *College and Research Libraries* 36 (July 1975), p. 272.

5. Bureau of the Census, *Statistical Abstracts of the United States, 1986,* 106th ed. (Washington, D.C.: GPO, 1985), p. 385; the figures reported here are for 1984.

6. Pamela Bonnell, *Fund Raising for the Small Library* (Chicago: American Library Assn., 1983).

7. Guy et al., p. 273.

8. Norman E. Tanis and Cindy Ventuleth, "The Decline in Donations?" *Library Journal* 111 (June 15, 1986): 41–44.

9. Bonnell.

10. Della Wakefield, *So You're Wondering About Incorporating Your Friends of the Library Group* (Olympia: Washington State Library, 1976). 22p. Eric document, 122 724.

Library Promotion

Tom Simpson

Effective promotion is not much different from any other form of communication, whether between husband and wife, boss and employee, or library and community. You have to know something about the people you are trying to reach, what message you are trying to get across, what is the most effective way of expressing that message, and how you hope your audience will respond. Then you have to be willing to listen to their response and be ready to adjust your next message accordingly. Promotional activities can be straightforward, honest, public-spirited, and responsive to the community; or they can be manipulative, deceptive, self-serving, and out of touch—all depending on your personal style and ethical standards. Ultimately, however, manipulation and its kin lead to unnecessary ill-will and, more importantly, undermine the library's potential for service to the community.

The basic criteria in judging the success of a promotional effort is how well it supports the overall goals of the library. Short-term promotions may increase circulation, but prove to be short-sighted if they result in more books simply being checked out and never read. On the other hand, a promotional campaign to attract high school kids may have no effect on circulation yet introduce many new users to the library's facilities and reference materials.

Promotion is an essential tool for competent library service. It can make the difference between a library being a warehouse where books are stored or a resource that people use to full advantage.

THE IMPORTANCE OF PROMOTION

Small libraries as a group have a much higher per capita circulation than larger ones. They are often highly respected institutions in their communities and are very successful in serving their patrons' reading needs. Why devote scarce time and money to promoting something that already works?

Tom Simpson is Director of the Le Mars Public Library in Le Mars, Iowa.

A lot has changed over the past few years. The public library has more competition in providing recreational and educational opportunities and sources of current information. To list just a few: cable television and feature movie channels, VCRs and local video stores, community recreation programs, book store chains, supermarket paperback racks, book clubs, and personal computers and commercial databases. Add to these the more traditional sources which also feel the competition and have become much more aggressive in their efforts to serve their customers: magazines—through subscriptions or newsstand sales, local and area newspapers and radio stations, local businesses and area representatives of larger corporations, local hospitals and other public service institutions, special interest groups and nonprofit organizations, and local and area schools and colleges. In addition, people still rely heavily on their personal libraries and advice from friends and associates. The library is often quite far down the list of sources people use most frequently for information, leisure activities, or learning projects.

Many small libraries are changing in response to this. They are providing more reference and information services, more audiovisual and computer equipment and software, and more specialized resources aimed at specific groups, such as job seekers and people with handicaps. The rising cost of keeping library resources current and the uncertainty of funds make it critical for libraries to promote what they are and what they do for their clientele. Municipal governments are becoming more tight-fisted and are allocating monies according to demonstrated priority rather than tradition or habit. More voters are realizing that they can fight higher taxes and new bond issues and win. The increasingly high price of professionally trained people in other city departments and the technology needed to fight fires and crime, maintain roads and bridges, and manage even small communities all has to be paid out of the same pot. A public library viewed as "a traditional institution serving the passive recreational interests of a small segment of the community" is given a pretty low priority in comparison.

By far the most compelling reason for promoting the library, however, is that it truly is crucial to the community—in more ways than we can reasonably expect people to realize unless we make a concerted and consistent effort to let them know. No other public or private institution has the public library's commitment to providing access to the full spectrum of views, opinions, cultural perspectives, artistic expression, historical interpretation, instructional resources, and factual information. The public library is (or should be) the community's principal resource for enabling its residents to be informed, open-minded, and capable of a creative and constructive response to the problems and opportunities they must face together.

THE PROMOTIONAL PLAN

There are many sources of outstanding promotional ideas available to librarians planning a campaign. However, taking someone else's good idea and using it in a completely different setting can prove to be a costly mistake. Even the most inspired local promotions can fail miserably (and expensively) if not coordinated properly. A promotional campaign must be an integral part of an overall promotional plan tailored to the library's available resources and the community's needs and interests.

The benefits of a well-designed promotional plan are several: 1) it allows you to build on established themes and take advantage of the groundwork already laid; 2) you can avoid unnecessary duplication by using the same effort to promote several related resources or programs; 3) you can set priorities for limited money and time by weighing different goals and objectives against each other and judging their relative value, potential success, and overall cost; 4) you can make a more convincing case for the budget items needed for a successful promotional campaign; 5) you can decide where and how to cut costs when necessary with less risk to the overall promotion of the library; 6) you can better identify and plan for future promotional expenses; and 7) you can more clearly identify gaps, where certain areas of the library's resources and services are not being adequately promoted.

The goals and objectives of the promotional plan must begin with the library's goals and objectives: promotion must never be an end in itself. By starting with the library's plan, you have greater assurance that you are considering all areas of the library's resources and services.

Each goal and accompanying objectives and activities of the plan must identify the people you want to reach, the message you want to get across, the promotional tools and outlets you will use, and how you will evaluate the results. Promotional goals should be general statements directly related to a library goal. Don't be afraid to make your goals a bit idealistic; you might underestimate your ability—and that of the staff—to rise to a challenge.

Each promotional goal should have as many objectives as you need to reach your goal and can reasonably hope to accomplish in a given time frame. Though the terms "goal" and "objective" are often used interchangeably, it is important to make a clear distinction. Unlike a goal, an objective should be quite specific and attainable, with results that can be objectively measured or observed. Each objective should have its own deadline and every effort should be made to keep to that schedule.

Each promotional objective should have as many activities or tasks assigned to it as are needed to successfully complete it within the deadline. If more than one person is available to help with promotion, each task should include the name of the individual responsible for its completion. These tasks should be as detailed as that individual needs to do them properly.

Figure 1 is an example of how promotional plans grow out of library goals.

FIGURE 1   Library Goals—Promotional Plan

LIBRARY GOAL: Provide resources, services, and programs to meet the informational needs of young people in junior and senior high school and encourage them to do more recreational reading and pursue independent learning projects using the public library.

Promotional Goal 1: Attract young people to the library, so they can discover its resources, and use them in constructive ways.

Promotional Objective 1a: Invite junior high and senior high student council members to the library for a special tour of the facility and a brainstorming session for ways the library can improve materials, programs, and services for young people (by September 15).

Promotional Objective 1b: Include an article about what's new in the library in each issue of the schools' newspapers (by September 15).

Promotional Objective 1c: Visit each junior and senior high school homeroom to talk about the library and answer students' questions (by October 15).

Promotional Goal 2: Create an atmosphere in the library that is inviting to young people and effectively draws their attention to the library resources available to help them pursue their interests and cope with problems and issues that concern them.

Promotional Objective 2a: Construct an attractive and functional "young adult bulletin board" to display useful and interesting information for this age group and call attention to relevant library resources, services, and programs (by September 1).

Promotional Objective 2b: Establish an on-going series of displays of library materials for young people (by September 15)

Promotional Objective 2c: Publish an annotated list of new books and other resources for young people to be posted on the bulletin board and updated every month (by October 1).

Task 1 (PO 2c): Make up extra shelf list card for each new junior and YA hardback or paperback book, record, and cassette; put it with the item when it's on the workroom shelf for staff inspection. Be sure each card has brief annotation. (Bonnie: on-going, begin September 15)

Task 2 (PO 2c): Remove the shelf list card and put it in the box labeled "New Jr and YA" when the item is put in the stacks or on the display shelf. (All staff: on-going, begin September 20)

Task 3 (PO 2c): Put cards by format, Dewey number, and author; type them up; make copies; post them on the bulletin board; and place extra copies on study tables. (Tom: last week of each month, begin last week in September)

FINDING YOUR PUBLICS

Regular library users: Despite efforts to serve everyone, most public libraries primarily serve people who read a lot. They are the true believers, the ones who are most likely to seek out the library under any circumstances. Yet, no library can afford to take them for granted. These regular patrons should be a prime target for promotional activities. They need to know about new materials, equipment, services, and programs. They also need to be encouraged to try different areas of the library rather than walk directly to the paperback racks, the genealogical area, or the photocopier. The paperback reader might like to carve wood as a hobby, but not know the library has several books and an instructional videocassette on the subject. The genealogist might be keenly interested in the disarmament issue, but not know the range of periodicals, books, and pamphlets the library has relating to it. The photocopier user might be looking for a new job, but not know about library resources to help him choose the best field, write a résumé, and conduct a successful job search. It might be that none of these people know about the library's telephone reference service or interlibrary loan program.

Special Populations: Every community has certain special populations that are nonetheless "standard." Senior citizens, people with various handicaps, people who are confined to their homes or an institution, people in the business community, preschool children, school-aged children, young adults, parents—the list can be as long as you want to make it. In addition to these, many communities have less common special populations: personnel stationed at a local military facility, local college or private school students and faculty, migrant workers, various ethnic groups, displaced farmers, people who are functionally illiterate, and many others. Some special populations may be characterized by beliefs rather than situation: religious faith, political persuasion, personal values, and lifestyles.

Nonusers: An overly conscientious librarian can easily be demoralized by failed efforts to turn everyone in the community into an active library user. No study of human motivation or market analysis has come up with an easy way of determining why promotional efforts are wasted on certain people. This is where small libraries have an advantage. It is much easier to identify and reach nonusers in a population of five hundred, or even ten thousand, than in a metropolis of half a million or more. You can more readily tell whether a promotional activity aimed at a group of nonusers is actually working, simply because you know whether or not they've been in the library. Efforts to promote the library to nonusers are particularly dependent on guidance from the library's goals and objectives. If one of your goals is to support economic development in the community, there's more justification for targeting local businesspeople. If your goals do not include providing academic support for a local college, you won't want to spend time trying to promote public library reference service on campus.

MARKET SEGMENTATION

Some television commercials are so ineffective with certain people that they never consider buying the product being advertised; yet, the same commercial can succeed in convincing just as many other people that the same product is the only one for them. That's usually no mistake; it's a conscious effort on the part of the advertiser to tailor a promotion to appeal to a specific segment of the viewing audience. In professional parlance, this is called market segmentation.

Even though public libraries are mandated to serve the entire community, they have to serve different segments in different ways. The same is true in promotion: a poster on a bulletin board in a laundromat may not be the best way to reach nursing home residents looking for inspirational reading, nor will an article on job hunting guides in the Chamber of Commerce newsletter have much of a chance of being read by unemployed people looking for work.

A community survey can be an extremely effective way of identifying the personal characteristics, interests, and preferences common to different groups in your service area, but it can also be very expensive and time-consuming. It can be dangerously misleading or just plain worthless if it isn't designed, conducted, and interpreted by someone with expertise in the area. A less expensive alternative (and one that should be used even with a community survey) is to garner the information already compiled by local businesses and institutions. Local radio and TV stations, cable TV franchises, newspapers, and shopper's publications have to know what segments of the population they reach most effectively with their respective media. Each one has a variety of tricks in their bags that they have found to be more effective for some groups than for others.

The local Chamber of Commerce often has up-to-date information on the community which is sent to businesses, industries, or professional people who are scouting good locations. Much of this same data can be found in census records that you may have in your library.

Perhaps the most reliable information can be obtained from local businesses that rely on effective promotions to survive. They are not as likely to overstate the effectiveness of specific promotions and promotional media as, for instance, the radio station that sold it to them. Below is a list of factors that can be used to identify special groups or segments of the community that require different promotional approaches:

Distribution of age groups

Population growth/decline in different age groups

Attendance at local schools, colleges, or technical schools

Educational attainment of out-of-school adults

Family income

Housing

Marital status and family make-up

Religious beliefs

Political persuasions/activity

Racial heritage

National/ethnic background

Occupation/employment status

Physical/mental disabilities

Reading, listening, and viewing habits

Information sources

CHOOSING A MESSAGE

What should you tell people about the library? The answer is not as obvious as it might seem. Even the smallest library can have a unique assortment of resources that goes far beyond the usual collection of books, while the largest can have surprising deficiencies in fundamental areas. You need to know what you have before you decide what to promote and what not to promote. This last point is crucial, but often overlooked: don't promote if you're not sure you can deliver. A common but costly error in many promotional efforts is the assumption that the library has something it doesn't. This can be a book that's not yet processed and ready for circulation; an area of the collection that is outdated or underdeveloped; a service the library staff is untrained to deliver; or a piece of equipment that is in need of repair. An inventory of the library's principal resources is an essential aspect of any promotional campaign. It will help you decide what to promote and identify priorities for remedial action.

FINDING PROMOTIONAL RESOURCES

Promotion doesn't have to break your budget. Using what you already have available in your library, resources in your community, and support from other library agencies, you can create very effective promotions. Figure 2 is a list of promotional resources to which you should add possible sources according to the code provided.

PROMOTIONAL OUTLETS

The best promotional message imaginable will fail if it's not where people will see or hear it and let it sink in. Small communities have

FIGURE 2   Promotional Resources

EQUIPMENT	SUPPLIES & SOFTWARE	HUMAN RESOURCES
_____ Telephone	_____ Graphics &	_____ Graphic art &
_____ Typewriter	word processing	calligraphy
_____ Photocopier	software	_____ Writing
_____ Computer	_____ Clip art	_____ Newsletter
_____ Printer	_____ Ready-made	layout
_____ Camera	slide, slide/tape	_____ Photography
_____ Darkroom	& video	& photo
_____ Light Table	presentations	development
_____ Graphic drawing	_____ Ready-made	_____ Videography
& layout tools	news releases &	& video editing
_____ Ditto or	radio spots	_____ Public
mimeograph	_____ Ready-made	speaking
machine	brochures &	_____ Dramatic arts
_____ Laminating	pamphlets	_____ Computer
machine	_____ Ready-made	graphics
_____ Slide Projector	posters & book	_____ Creative ideas
_____ Overhead	marks	_____ Folding,
Projector	_____ Films & blank	stapling,
_____ VCR	videocassettes	labeling,
_____ TV	_____ Poster board	stamping
_____ Video camera	_____ Press-on	
_____ Video editing	letters & stencils	
equipment	_____ Graph paper &	
_____ Automatic slide/	different colors	
tape machine	of bond paper	
_____ Headline maker	_____ Types of clear	
_____ Typesetter and	tape and glue	
press	_____ Colored markers	
_____ Other		

SOURCE CODE: 1–in the library; 2–in the parent agency or organization; 3–local school system; 4–local businesses; 5–library "Friend" or volunteer; 6–local club or organization; 7–board of trustees; 8–local or area newspapers; 9–local or area radio stations; 10–local or area TV stations; 8–area college; 9–regional or network library; 10–state library agency; 11–state library association; 12–American Library Association; 13–library supply dealer; 14–other.

many effective outlets for promotion, but they have to be used judiciously. Remember that different people use different media, shop in different stores, attend different functions, and open different mail. Even a front-page article in the local newspaper will be missed by a lot of people.

People tend to pay attention to the same thing in the same place for a relatively limited time. The same poster, the same bookmark, the same radio spot all lose their effect after a while. They blend into the background noise that we all have learned to tune out. It's important, therefore, to change the location of promotions periodically. If you are only able to create a few different bookmarks or buy a few posters, don't wear them out. Take some of the bookmarks out of circulation for a while and rotate them. Change the location of the posters so that different people can see them for the first time and others can see them in a different context. Either way, they will attract more attention.

Many of the most effective outlets are outside the library and require the cooperation of local businesses and organizations. You'll stand a better chance of getting that cooperation if you provide them with well-designed promotions and keep them up-to-date. Don't leave a dated poster announcing your annual book sale in a store window after the sale is history. The shop owner will probably take it down after a while, but you create more good will if you or one of your staff members or volunteers removes it the next day.

Local and regional media such as radio, TV, and newspapers are especially valuable outlets for library promotions. Within certain guidelines, they provide free promotional time and space for nonprofit organizations. Because they are so dependent on the success of their paid advertising, they know what works and what doesn't, and can provide valuable guidance and advice.

Don't shun larger media serving your entire area. If you have a worthwhile activity to promote, you may find them very willing to give you air time. The impact is that much greater because local residents will be surprised and even proud to see their library get regional coverage. Most cable TV franchises are required to have a community access channel as a part of their contract. This can be an actual studio equipped to air live and video-taped activities or a stationary poster-type display with changing messages. If you are fortunate enough to have the former, it can be a dynamic outlet for library promotion and is often viewed by a significant percentage of the community.

Some of the most common outlets for library promotions and some of the ways they might be used are presented below.

The library: Outside banners and oversize signs; announcements, posters and graphics on bulletin boards; wall posters; bibliographies, brochures, flyers and newsletters in literature racks; hand-outs and bookmarks at the circulation desk; large directional signs; displays of books and other materials; equipment displays and demonstrations; tours and programs of all kinds; activities outside on the sidewalk or lawn, or in the parking lot.

Local and area newspapers: Distinctive fillers using library logo or library week clip art, book reviews, weekly column, news releases, public service ads, letters to the editor, photos of library activities, publication of winning entries in writing or photo contests, announcements of library programs and meetings.

Local and area radio stations: Promotional tapes from the American Library Association (ALA), locally recorded promotions, news releases, guest visits on talk/interview programs, live coverage of major library events.

Local and area TV stations: ALA video promotion, announcements of special events, live coverage or videos of newsworthy events, guest visits on talk/interview programs, brief poster displays using library logo.

Local cable TV channels: If a studio: book talks, video or slide/tape tour of the library, demonstrations of library equipment, videos of story hours or special events at the library, interviews with visiting authors about their own books, or local dignitaries about their favorite books. If a poster-type display: announcements of current activities, titles of new books, promotional slogans.

Local churches: In bulletins or on bulletin boards: announcements of reading programs for kids; information about library services to people who are handicapped or homebound; annotations of new books on religion, spirituality, or social issues.

Local clubs and organizations: Articles, fillers, or flyers in their newsletters or general mailings; hand-outs of library brochures or bibliographies; announcements of programs, book talks, slide/tape or video presentations; and demonstrations of equipment at meetings.

Local movie theater: Screen ad with general promotional photo and message, brochures and hand-outs at ticket window, library poster.

Schools: Articles and fillers in school newspapers, classroom presentations, class visits, hand-outs through teachers, posters on bulletin boards.

Local businesses: Posters in display windows or on bulletin boards, hand-outs at cash registers, articles or fillers in employee newsletters, flyers in mailings.

Lunch counters: Flyers or library newsletters on counters and in booths.

Waiting rooms: Flyers or library newsletters on tables, counter, or literature rack.

Fairs, sidewalk sales, homeshows and festivals: Library booth, on-going video or slide/tape presentation; remote telephone hook-up with demonstration of telephone reference service; hand-outs of library brochures, bibliographies and newsletters; open-air story time; puppet shows; equipment demonstrations; drawings and contests.

Parades: Library float; kids, teens, or adults showing off library material or equipment; clowns with oversize books or other material or equipment.

U.S. Mail: Bulk mailing of newsletters; personal greeting to new residents with library brochure enclosed; thank-you notes to volunteers, Friends, and supportive businesses with mention of new materials of interest.

Telephone: Call about new books, tapes, or programs of special interest to individuals or groups; express thanks for volunteer or financial support; follow-up to see if patron found reference source, referral to another agency, or if special material ordered through interlibrary loan was what they were seeking.

JUDGING SUCCESS

Small library funds are too scarce to waste on ineffective promotions. Your promotional plan, therefore, has to include some way to evaluate the results. This doesn't need to be formal. In most cases, all that is involved is reviewing your objectives and noting whether they were met or not. In other cases, the results might come very slowly, but they still come and the promotion might be a great success.

An evaluation lets you decide whether to continue with a long-term promotion or repeat a short-term one, and what changes should be made. Looking back over records of a year or more ago gives some help in deciding whether to try a promotion again or some variation.

When more than one person is involved in working on a promotion, it is helpful to have everyone meet for a wrap-up evaluation/brainstorming session after it's all over. People can come up with unexpectedly creative ideas and insights when they share ideas—especially when the promotion is still fresh in their minds. Often you'll end up with more than just an evaluation of what you just did; you'll have the makings for several new promotions as well.

This is the time to consider writing up your experience to share with other librarians through a regional or statewide professional publication. If your promotion was particularly inventive and successful, you might even want to send it to a national publication. This is more than just showing off. If you have done the necessary planning and evaluation, your sharing can make it possible for other librarians to benefit from your efforts. This kind of sharing has been the key to many successful promotions across the country.

SETTING PRIORITIES AND KEEPING PERSPECTIVE

When you're running a one-person, part-time library with barely enough funds to buy bestsellers, all of this talk of planning and evaluating can seem like a bad joke. When you are in a tiny, isolated community, many of the promotional resources and outlets mentioned here are simply nonexistent. Some situations may seem so desperate that any promotion might seem to court embarrassment: "Didn't he say, 'Don't promote what you don't have!'?" If that's the case, effective promotion may be the only way you can raise the funds to improve the library's situation. If you feel you're not being paid enough for this kind of work, effective promotion might be the best way to raise the community's awareness of your role. It may seem poor stewardship to spend money and time on promotion when it is so desperately needed to select, buy, and catalog books, but the alternative might be watching a good (and expensive) book sit on the shelves because people don't know the library has it.

PUBLIC RELATIONS AND PUBLICITY

The terms "public relations," "publicity," and "promotion" are often used interchangeably, even by professionals in these fields. It can be helpful, however, to make some distinctions.

Public Relations (or PR) is a matter of attitude; specifically, "What is the library's image in the community?" It concerns how users and nonusers alike think and feel about the library. Thus it is very subjective and much more difficult to measure than promotion. The importance of public relations becomes apparent when you need cooperation or support from different individuals or groups in the community, whether as volunteers, financial contributors, political friends, program collaborators, or promotional outlets. Public relations is particularly important when you must enforce an unpopular policy such as overdue fines or deal with a hot issue such as censorship.

The principal rule of thumb in PR is to keep in touch with the community: listen and then let the public know you heard. The Board of Trustees are an essential part of this process. They are responsible for setting library policies for the general welfare of the community. They also are the likely ones to receive calls from upset patrons. Good communication between the trustees and the librarian can help avoid public relations crises and keep little ones from blowing up.

The following are some ways to maintain good public relations:

- Make sure your policies are up-to-date, clearly stated, and available to the public.
- Be consistent in the administration of policies, yet able to be flexible when it's necessary.
- Keep your trustees informed of public response to library policies.

- Announce all board meetings and encourage the public to attend.
- Keep a suggestion box and simple forms near the circulation desk or card catalog.
- Write notes or call individuals to thank them for any volunteer help, contribution, or other special support for the library.
- Support other community organizations.
- Participate in civic development projects.
- Avoid involving the library in partisan issues.
- Be honest and forthcoming about library mistakes.
- Be pleasant and professional when talking with patrons.
- Go an extra bit to serve a patron with an urgent request.
- Don't overstate library promotions or make promises you can't keep.
- Keep the library interior and exterior as clean and attractive as possible.
- Make a special effort to get to know community leaders and solicit their suggestions and feedback on library service.

Publicity is more concrete than PR, but still on the subjective side. It involves keeping the library's name, resources, and services before the public eye and ear. It's keeping the community aware of what the library has or does. Like PR, it is aimed at nonusers as much as users, and can make a significant difference when bond issues or other library concerns come before the public as a whole.

The following are some effective publicity ideas:

- Submit photos of any special library programs to the local newspaper. If you call in advance, the paper will often be willing to send a photographer to cover an event.
- Submit news releases on any honors bestowed on the library, the trustees, or the staff, or any conferences or training programs attended by staff or trustees.
- Give away (or sell at cost) library bumper stickers or book bags.

OTHER CONSIDERATIONS

"What do I do when promotion works so well we can't handle the demand?" In many instances this can be avoided by taking inventory of your resources and not overstating a promotion. Having done this, if you still find yourself overwhelmed with the response, it's usually because there was great need or interest in the community just waiting to be tapped. This might be ample justification for reassessing your budget priorities or seeking additional funds.

"What if I'm not at all creative?" Creativity can sometimes spell the doom of a promotional plan. If there is too much creativity and too little organization, then the plan will be nothing more than a list of good ideas that never happened. It is actually easier for an organized person to scavenge creative ideas from other sources than it is for a creative person to find organization. Organization skills will help to keep the plan on schedule and assure that none of the details are missed. Creativity is fun and very rewarding, but only if the creation actually happens. If you're not creative, focus on your organizational skills and begin scouting out creative people from among your staff, trustees, or community. The same is true for any other promotional skill you may be lacking, whether it's public speaking, writing, or even typing.

"Why not go all the way in my promotion and pay for an ad campaign?" If you've got bucks to burn, you are sure to get the attention of the advertising department of any newspaper, TV, or radio station. Be prepared, however, to spread it around evenly or give up your free public service spots. Public service directors are not going to be very warm toward you if you bought time or space from someone else and then expected it free from them. If you do have money—from a special bequest, for instance—earmarked for promotion, you might consider spending it either on promotional supplies for a newsletter or a series of brochures, or to hire a reputable consultant who will help on the creative stuff. If you do the latter, a few cautions are in order. Don't assume that consultants know what they're doing because they're so successful in some metropolitan area. If you're in a small rural community, it may require a completely different approach to reach an entirely different public.

5
Computers to Lasers

A Primer on Microcomputers and Automation

Bernard Vavrek

In this introduction to the use of microcomputer technology, the small public library will serve as the model for discussion, although the intent is to relate to small libraries of all types. Ironically, the author finds himself eating a prophetic interpretation offered a few years ago stating that small libraries would rarely be able to afford the use of computers. The international stock market in electronics and the present application of microcomputers in the library have proved him to be in serious error. The reader will kindly discount this inability at crystal ball gazing, however, in judging the usefulness of the following commentary.

About 20 percent of the public libraries in the United States located in populations of 25,000 or fewer people have microcomputers on-site, according to research conducted by the Center for the Study of Rural Librarianship. In 60 percent of these locations, Apple microcomputers can be found. IBM-compatible machines comprise the remaining presence of hardware. Although the availability of microcomputer technology for library use is still in its relative infancy, it is clear that this is an area of great interest among library staff members. This obvious conclusion has been confirmed through conversations in the field and in research. For example, in an audit of continuing education preferences, librarians in small communities—rural and otherwise—are primarily interested in workshops/conferences dealing with technology, which for the most part translates into something dealing with microcomputers.

Before proceeding to the topic of "all one ever wanted to know about microcomputers," it should be acknowledged that, in addition to these introductory insights about technology, there are already available many useful texts dealing with microcomputers and microcomputer

Bernard Vavrek is the Coordinator of The Center for Rural Librarianship, College of Library Science, Clarion University of Pennsylvania in Clarion, Pennsylvania.

applications in libraries.[1,2,3] This obviates the need and usefulness of reviewing here all of the practical minutiae dealing with hardware (computer equipment) and software (computer programming). What follows is intended to serve as a planning document—a discussion of considerations for library management, both immediate and long range. To this end, the reader will excuse the author's immodesty by initially citing a pertinent article whose title admonishes the wary to "Beware of Microcomputeritis."[4] If this malady has not been encountered as yet, be thankful. While the symptoms of microcomputeritis cannot be located in any available lexicon, it is, nevertheless, a violent affliction. Simply stated, it is a disease that robs an individual of her or his will to resist the takeover of one's life by microcomputers. Librarians are particularly susceptible.

DETERMINING NEEDS

Readers (and would-be library technocrats) should consider two questions: What are those goals and objectives that one wants to achieve in the library? and Does one need a microcomputer to help achieve those definable goals and objectives? Timing is everything and sometimes these questions are asked too late—only after the local "do-gooder" organization decides to make the librarian the recipient of its successful fundraising project by donating a microcomputer to the library, without any other supporting equipment. This is not to ridicule charitable efforts, but to suggest that frequently even the most ambitious planning (or intent) is negated by outside efforts. In circumstances that can be controlled, however, it is clear that public librarians spend more time in applying library services than planning for them. While this problem has had its effect in all of librarianship, it is a major deficiency among public librarians in small communities around the United States. In fairness, and as partial explanation, it should be noted that severe staff limitations—the national average being three full-time staff members per library—decidedly impedes even the best intentions of long-range planning. There are simply too many daily services to which staff time needs to be dedicated, precluding the opportunity to think about the future.

Answering the question, Does one need a microcomputer in the library? is obviously a relative matter. It is a type of question that library managers, including those in the one-person library, do not ask often enough. As a consequence, we have received more than one alert from a librarian who has been the recipient/purchaser of a microcomputer and then asks what can be done with it. Remember the rule of thumb, "software goeth before hardware": always identify a need first and then look for a program (software) that will most efficiently meet that need. Then, and only then, is the local computer outlet consulted for appropriate choices of equipment (hardware) on which that program will operate most conveniently. As always, compromise is an implicit consideration. For example, the ideal program and microcomputer may not be accessible in a rural community that lacks a shopping center filled with computer outlets.

RAISON D'ETRE

After positing the view that not enough up-front concern is related to the issue of need, it is then of some interest to consider what motivates a librarian to make a commitment toward the purchase of a microcomputer and library technology. Note that the following are not exclusive categories.

First, it is a trendy thing. We live in a society which is immersed in information. It is natural, then, that the library would want to take possession of the icon of the information age—the microcomputer. We must acknowledge, however, that sometimes competition among librarians is also a significant concern.

Second, by purchasing a microcomputer, the library will be seen as a modern entity—one which is freed from the cultural tradition of an institution based in the milieu of books. A corollary of this attitude is that the librarian is also transformed into a new symbol as, for example, updating the image of Betty Crocker or changing the logo of the U.S. Postal Service.

Third, consumer demand is another reason that librarians purchase microcomputers. While the emphasis in this chapter relates to staff use, one cannot discount requests that library patrons make to employ the new technology as an extension of existing services.

Fourth, microcomputers imply a level of efficiency and sophistication not inherent in traditional (manual) methods. The companion analog for this incentive to buy a microcomputer is closely related to the concept that technology ultimately saves staff time which can be reallocated to patron needs on an interpersonal level.

Fifth, writers in library science periodicals, keynote speakers at conferences, and workshop leaders all tell us that there is little future without the application of technology, particularly as it is facilitated by microcomputers.

To the above list, one could certainly add further factors. The essential question, however, becomes one of asking which is the *real* reason to adopt technology through the presence of a microprocessing device. Obviously, as with most issues, the answers are interrelated as opposed to being discrete. Making a decision may actually include a little of all of the instances cited above. There is one myth, however, that should be clarified—if only in a biased fashion. "In itself, microcomputer technology does not save staff time, it redistributes it." It is widely assumed that the lightning fast microprocessor saves personnel time which can be applied to the human side of library services. What is forgotten in this simple model is that time saved almost inevitably must be circuited to keep the mechanical beast "alive and well." The reference here is not so much to mechanical upkeep (although it is a prime concern) as to a commitment of time and energy relating to the culture of considerations that a microcomputer brings with it. It is definitely not neutral. It makes one want to read magazines such as *Personal Computing, Nibble, Byte,* etc. As a result of this excessive reading, one is tantalized and frustrated by all of the ads identifying new products. One may also be tempted to seek out a computer club where other groupies join their voices and begin to speak in tongues with expressions such as "upload" and "download."

HARDWARE DECISIONS

Once the matter of need is considered and the investment of time and energy is understood, one faces the pleasant but confusing consideration of hardware options. (We have already assumed that because software goeth before hardware that viable programming options have been identified.) Earlier it was noted that there are abundant examples of texts that describe the components of microcomputers including such things as memory size, parallel printers, disk drives, etc. Added to those texts are resources such as *Small Computers in Libraries* and *Library Software Review* that specifically address library needs.[5] For individuals who are unable to afford these two publications, valuable information can be found in the *Wilson Library Bulletin, Library Journal, Booklist, The Bottom Line,* etc. My particular all-around favorite is *Personal Computing,* a nonlibrary science publication.

There is little question that this is a favorable time for microcomputer purchasers. A cooling of the microcomputer industry, in relation to constantly increasing demand, and competition among manufacturers have provided favorable circumstances for consumers. IBM, Apple, Tandy, Compaq, Leading Edge, etc., are all vigorously vying for new customers. At this writing, prices for hardware are approximately one-half of what they were just a few years ago. The inevitable question arises: whether it is actually prudent to wait to join the technical age as prices continue to drop and microcomputer power increases. While this continues to be a valid question, one may be doing a personal disservice by not acting now—if the technology is needed.

In addition to the information that may be obtained from the published literature or from a membership in a computer club, significant experience can also be provided through participation in local workshops/conferences, visiting other libraries/places where microcomputers are being used, talking with colleagues, and visiting the local computer store. While some librarians look around for a computer consultant, it strikes me—at the initial stage of implementation—as being unnecessary, unless one is acquainted with someone who will volunteer her or his time. In any event, regardless of the many sources of insight that can be utilized, do not purchase a microcomputer unless you have tried it yourself. Consumer products have a "feel" about them which should not be underestimated in the haste of buying. This author can recall the personal episode of returning a purchase because the keyboard didn't feel comfortable to the touch. It had nothing to do with the quality of manufacturing; it just felt clumsy.

An important consideration in the purchase of electronic hardware is to buy locally, even if the price is higher than an inviting advertisement in a computer magazine. It is hoped that a local purchase implies that one may have had an opportunity to "try out the thing." A local purchase—even if a hundred miles away—should provide some insurance that service and assistance are available. As distance from a supplier increases—a problem in many small communities around the country—the philosophy of local purchase begins to lose its usefulness. In this case, an order by mail will be just as viable and may, in fact, be the only option. The concern for local purchase is to insure that some modicum of immediate service is available. Microcomputers do fail regardless of subtle propaganda to the contrary. It makes all the difference if the dealer sets up the equipment and tests it for you (and is close by for assistance thereafter) as opposed to your emptying the carton which has just been received and discovering that something has been jarred in transit. Microcomputers are very durable but equally sensitive as precision equipment.

After the initial installation, one is confronted with the question of what happens when the system fails. It cannot be stressed too strongly that one must be prepared for that eventuality—equipment failure— even to the point of having a second microcomputer, printer, etc., ready to be placed into the breach of everyday use. This is essential if one begins to rely exclusively on any system. Unless a library is prepared to implement an alternative approach, such as going back to a conventional circulation routine, duplicate hardware must be available to keep the library beat going. Another alternative, a further advantage of local purchase, may be for the nearby vendor to loan the library needed equipment until repairs have been made.

It is hoped that the reader is not totally frustrated by what appears to be the pessimism inherent in the preceding paragraphs. One can be a cheerleader of technology as long as it is understood that if things can go wrong, they will. This law of Mr. Murphy's is quite accurate. The issue is not only one of malfunctioning equipment, but also of finding pieces of equipment that are compatible with each other. In reality, the situation is much easier than described. In most instances there will be a single microcomputer system functioning in the library. Once that is established, the significant matter is upkeep. The single microcomputer installation, however, does not mitigate future temptations to enhance the system. One can become easily distracted with a wish list of needs relating to things that are bigger, faster, and more powerful. In any event, it still is fun.

SOFTWARE DECISIONS

The admonition regarding the seminal importance of first making a choice of a program before doing anything else bears repeating. This simple advice is a bit more troublesome to put into practice because of the considerable availability of application software. "Application" programs include the three most popular types of software: word processing, data management, and the spread-sheet. In each category, there are hundreds of choices. The novice microcomputer user will find the PFS series of software, *PFS: File, PFS: Report,* and *PFS: Write,* to be quality choices.[6] The standard sources of information mentioned earlier, such as computer clubs, magazines, etc., all provide strategies for learning about software.

Facts on File issues an interesting service that makes available public domain software. These programs are no longer protected by copyright and have been debugged, according to the company. While this publication is a bit too expensive for most small libraries, it is mentioned in order to introduce the fact that a lot of software is available as freeware—not from *Facts on File,* however. "Freeware" or "public domain" software is available from a number of different outlets, including computer clubs. Parenthetically, the Boston Computer Society, c/o Proteus Software, 363 The Great Road, Bedford, MA 01730, has a 100-page catalog of public domain software available for $10. The problem that sometimes occurs with public domain software is that it may not work properly. The major reason for this is that it has been passed from person to person with the possibility of errors being introduced along the way. The lack of documentation is also sometimes a problem with this category of software. Freeware should not be confused with illegally copied programs that are shared among friends and colleagues.

"Shareware," by comparison, is a much better investment. The concept behind shareware is most interesting. The user is encouraged to make copies available for distribution to friends and colleagues, and also to pay a modest sum (voluntarily) to the program owner for its use. The cost and future improvement of this type of software is then "shared" by the users. The following examples of shareware, to identify just a few, are recognized as quality items: *PC Talk III,* The Headland Press, Box 862, Tiburon, CA 94920, available at $35; *PC DBMS,* Paul Kobrin, Kware, Box 16206, Arlington, VA, available at $28; and *DOSaMATIC,* Marin Pacific Software Company, 1001 Bridgeway #514, Sausalito, CA 94965, available at $39.

Software does not have to cost a lot to provide a satisfactory return to the user, but it should be recognized that program sophistication and power usually are expensive. While there are companies that rent software, the basic problem remains that there is no inherent privilege among suppliers enabling buyers to try out software before the final purchase. Earlier, a case was made for purchasing hardware locally. Regarding software, the temptation is strong to recommend that the buyer look for the most competitive price, not excluding mail order. However, a major software "catalog" company recently filed for protection under the provision of the bankruptcy laws. Because of the general cooling of the microcomputer marketplace, local purchase is also suggested for software. However, it is actually more important, regardless of the locale of the purchase, to determine the degree of support (i.e., is there someone available to answer questions when you need help) that the dealer will provide. If the local dealer promises none, look elsewhere.

COMMUNICATIONS DECISIONS

The microcomputer industry has produced a plethora of books and related learning materials. One of the best choices, particularly on the topic of the role of microcomputers in communications, is the book by Alfred Glossbrenner, *The Complete Handbook of Personal Computer Communications* (New York: St. Martin's Press, 1985). Since this chapter has been organized as a primer, comprehensiveness has not been the overriding goal in attempting to identify all hardware/software options. After one has purchased a microcomputer and printer, enabling the system to reach out online is an important next consideration. Communicating with an online database such as Dialog, BRS, and Wilsonline requires three basic considerations: availability of a private telephone line—a problem in some small communities where the local telephone system has only party lines; a modem—a small device connected between the telephone and the microcomputer; and, communications software. (*PC TALK III,* mentioned earlier, is a good choice for those using IBM-compatible machines.)

The ability to communicate with other microcomputers or mainframe computers (the largest type in relation to memory size) is a topic being pursued with great interest inside and outside of librarianship. The desire to create and/or augment already existing networks with microcomputers is another reason to be familiar with the principles of electronic communications. Keep in mind, however, that the real question relates to what needs to be communicated. One may look skeptically upon electronic communications as just another gimmick or toy if nothing is to be gained or enhanced. The question is "Will librarians have anything more to communicate—electronically?" This is an unfair question, however, in that microcomputers enable files of data to be transmitted online, as well as providing a substitute for voice transmission. Any number of imaginative applications are possible. There is little doubt, however, that isolated libraries can benefit greatly from the facilities provided by online communications.

LIBRARY SOFTWARE

As stated at the outset, the armature around which everything should wind begins with goals, objectives, and needs. The next considerations are cost and the degree to which electronic techniques are more efficient than manual methods currently being applied in the library. Efficiency is really a relative matter. For example, a community library consisting of only one staff member may, in the long run, find that a circulation system implemented on a microcomputer has a salutary effect on library services, but the present system of check-out is satisfactory and there's no time that can be allocated to implementing anything new. One must be pragmatic, of course. In any event, decisions must be made locally.

Opportunities exist to enhance local library operations utilizing the major types of software mentioned earlier. Data-management programs can be used to compile bibliographies, prepare community resource directories, develop a list of registered borrowers, etc. Word processing software can be employed to send notices to delinquent borrowers as well as to compliment a donor for a recent contribution to the library's annual fundraising appeal. The electronic spreadsheet can be utilized for effective budget planning, fiscal control, and preparing "award winning" presentations for the local town meeting. Communications programs, on the other hand, can be targeted for consulting a union catalog at the headquarters library, sending and receiving interlibrary loan requests, as well as accessing remote data files.

In addition to the "generic" software available to today's librarian, one may also choose from more specific library-oriented programs. Among the types currently available are those intended to print library cards, *Avant Cards*[7] and *Librarian's Helper*[8]; prepare bibliographies, *Bibliography Writer* and *AV Catalog Writer*[9]; produce overdue notices, *Overdue Writer*[9]; compute statistics for output measures, *OUTPUTM*[10]; and keep a record of books in circulation, *Circulation Plus*[11] and *Winnebago Circ.*[12]

At the present, circulation software may be of the greatest interest because it emulates technology found in larger libraries. There are at least two satisfactory circulation programs currently available for microcomputers: *Circulation Plus* and *Winnebago Circ.* The bad news is that both pieces of software sell for approximately $1,000 each. Added to the expense of the program is the cost of hardware support.

Another trend currently emerging is a desire to have a fully integrated system available in the library instead of implementing functions, such as circulation, acquisitions, etc., on an incremental basis. While such software is available in libraries that can pay a minimum of $125,000, there is presently no affordable microcomputer-based system for integrated applications in the small library. This will change in the near future. Competition among library software vendors will bring this type of product into the marketplace at an affordable price.

PARTICIPANTS OR PLAYERS?

Within a decade, microcomputer technology has developed from its relative infancy to a multi-billion dollar industry. Librarianship has an opportunity to share in this creativity in exciting new ways. It is clear that we are all participants. The question then remains, to what extent should we be players?

References

1. Donald H. Sanders, *Computers Today* (New York: McGraw Hill, 1985).
2. Betty Costa and Marie Costa, *A Microcomputer Handbook for Small Libraries and Media Centers* (Littleton, Colo.: Libraries Unlimited, Inc., 1983).
3. Lawrence A. Woods and Nolan F. Pope, *The Librarian's Guide to Microcomputer Technology and Applications* (White Plains, N.Y.: Knowledge Industry Publications, Inc., 1983).

4. Bernard Vavrek, "Beware of Microcomputeritis," *Library Journal* 110 (November 1, 1985): 164–165.
5. Both of these publications are available from Meckler Publishing, 11 Ferry Lane West, Westport, CT 06880, at $30 each for personal subscriptions.
6. PFS software is available from Software Publishing Corporation, 1901 Landings Dr., Mountain View, CA 94043. One can also purchase this software locally and through catalog distributors.
7. *Avant Cards* is distributed by the Addison Public Library, 235 North Kennedy Dr., Addision IL 60101-2499.
8. *The Librarian's Helper* is distributed by Scarecrow Press, 52 Liberty St., Metuchen, NJ 08840.
9. *The Bibliography Writer, The AV Catalog Writer,* and *The Overdue Writer* are available from The New Follett Software Company, 4506 Northwest Highway, Crystal Lake, IL 60014. While not exclusively illustrating Follett software, Nancy Everhart's *MMI Preparatory School Computerized Model Library,* Freeland, PA 18224, available at $7.50, is a case study describing the automation of a small library.
10. *OUTPUTM* is a product of the College of Library Science, Clarion University of Pennsylvania, Clarion, PA 16214.
11. *Circulation Plus* is also distributed by The New Follett Software Company.
12. *Winnebago Circ,* as well as other circulation software, is available from Winnebago Software Company, 121 S. Marshall, Caledonia, MN 55921. On a relative basis, Winnebago seems to be the most dynamic library software producer at the moment.

Laser Technology

Ron Jordahl

We have an easy familiarity with traditional media, but the new optical formats bring with them a vocabulary studded with acronyms and initialisms which tends to bewilder the uninitiated. This medium is very much with us and will be increasing in importance. It is essential that librarians be conversant in this area because it holds great potential for library services. In June of 1986 it could be said:

> In the past year CD-ROM has gone from being an obscure acronym to one of the hottest topics in the information industry. . . . CD-ROM is now on the agenda as a topic at every major national information conference in 1986 and has spawned at least two specialized industry-level conferences a month through at least the first half of 1986.[1]

Librarians in smaller libraries sometimes write off new technologies as inappropriate, supposing them to be applicable only to very large libraries. This is a mistake, for even a small library may find technology can make available vast amounts of materials and information which was previously inaccessible to them; and it may save time and money. Furthermore, much of the new technology can be utilized without extensive training, and some vendors offer telephone assistance on help lines.

Pressure on libraries to utilize this medium will come from two directions. Improvements in the industry and availability of services and materials will make the advantages obvious. From the other side, public demand will force librarians to consider this medium. Laser disks are of immediate use to libraries in technical services, reference work, and lending collections, and new applications and products are reported regularly.

MATERIALS AND PROCESSES

It is not necessary to understand all the technical details of laser technology to make good use of it, nor is it difficult to gain sufficient

Ron Jordahl is at the Prairie Bible Institute, Three Hills, Canada.

knowledge to make intelligent decisions. Before discussing library applications, it will be helpful to review some terminology and technology.

Optical Disk.[2] The term "optical" in this context refers to the physics of light rather than to the human eye and vision. Optical media are formats in which data are recorded and retrieved by means of a light source. An optical disk is a plastic or metal platter on which information is impressed, usually by laser but sometimes photographically with incandescent light. The disk is "read" by means of a light source and the information manipulated as necessary for audio, visual, or electronic output.

Reflective. Disks may be recorded on both sides just as with phonograph records and floppy disks. There are two kinds of double-sided laser disks, reflective and transmissive. Reflective disks have a mirror-like surface and must be turned over to read the second side.

Transmissive. Transmissive disks are translucent and do not need to be turned over; the reading head refocuses on the second side through the disk. Transmissive disks are not in common use.

Laser Disk. A laser disk is an optical disk on which information is encoded by a laser beam which burns billions of microscopic pits into the disk. Copies may be mass-produced by pressing as with phonograph records. A low-power laser reads the information encoded by the pits from the center of the disk outward.

Videodisk. Optical disks and laser disks are named for the operating systems, but videodisks are named for their content—visual information. Videodisks may contain audio and digital data as well as visual information.

Capacitance Disk. Not all videodisks are optical disks; some are capacitance video disks, which may be grooved or grooveless and rely on a mechanical stylus for playback.

Analog. The encoding of information on a disk may be in one of two forms. An analog disk is one on which the length of the pits and the spaces between them vary according to the FM signal. This is the means used for encoding audiovisual materials to be played back on TV.

Digital. A digital recording consists of encoding by means of regularly spaced binary bits; spaces of uniform length either contain markings or they do not. This kind of coding is used by computers.

CD. Compact disks (CD) are so called because of their small size— 4.75 inches or sometimes 5.25 inches—in distinction from larger formats. Philips and MCA were pioneers in the field, both introducing prototype players in 1972. In 1976, these companies and others agreed that disks should be 30 cm. in diameter. Other standards were set as well. However, disks are available in various sizes including 14, 12, 8, 5.25, and 4.75 inches. The larger formats are used for videodiscs, eight inches is popular for rock videos, and the smaller sizes for digital records, compact disks. Though physical standards are being established, there is no agreement on how data are formatted on the disks. It is hoped that more standards will be established to prevent the kind of confusion and incompatibility of systems which developed in computer technology.

ROM. Read-only memory (ROM) indicates that the information on a disk is fixed, and cannot be added to or deleted.

Track. Information is placed on a disk in spiral form from the center outward. Each 360° portion is called a track.

CAV. There are two formats for filling the tracks. Constant angular velocity (CAV) means that the disk rotates at a constant speed. Thus the longer, outer tracks receive the same amount of recording (and reading) time as the inner, shorter tracks. Each track, regardless of length, has the same capacity.

CLV. The other format is constant linear velocity (CLV), which means that as the recording (or receiving) head moves outward to longer tracks, the rotation speed of the disk decreases. The speed of the disk head over the track is constant regardless of whether it is a long or short track. The result of CLV is that a longer track can contain more information than a shorter track. A CLV disk can accommodate twice the information of a CAV disk.

The advantage of more efficient use of disk space with CLV is offset by the difficulty of locating information on it. If a CAV disk track is divided into, say, eight sectors, a new sector begins with each 45° rotation of the disk, regardless of which track the head is focused on. With CLV, on the other hand, each sector is of equal linear length with more sector per track as the head moves outward. This makes it more difficult to locate any given sector.

OPTICAL MEDIA

Four kinds of optical media have become prominent, and another two types are being refined, all of them laser disks.

The first medium to reach the commercial market was the *videodisk,* which arrived with a certain amount of fanfare. *Popular Science* typically announced, "Here at Last—Video-Disk Players" (February 1977); and *Rolling Stone* introduced it with an article called, "Video Disc Is Here" (September 20, 1979). *Business Week* was more sensational a year later: "Videodisc Will Revolutionize Data Storage" (July 7, 1980); and *High Fidelity* concurred in a special report, "Video Discs: Where the Action Is" (April 1981).

Videodisks are analog recordings with the audio and video format of the FM television signal. This provides the flexibility to record the sight and sound of motion pictures. With that capability it can incorporate all types of information—motion, still pictures, audio, and digital—in a single program, a total of 54,000 frames per side with CAV and 108,000 with CLV.

Two uses for videodisks have become clearly identified. The first is for entertainment. A CAV videodisc can play a 30-minute movie per side, and a CLV disc can run 60 minutes. Videodisks are used for feature films, but in spite of the big kick-off, videodisks have failed to make inroads into the market dominated by videocassettes. The other use is interactive: the user may interact with the presentation rather than passively view it. Such applications include training programs, video games, and commercial presentations.

Compact audio disks (CD), digital audiorecordings, are now quite well known. They were an instant hit with the public because the sound reproduction is incredible, they are damage-resistant, and reasonably priced. The player converts the digital coding to an analog signal which is amplified in the conventional manner. The excellent sound is due to optical recording which eliminates the hisses and clicks of conventional mechanical recordings.

Thousands of recordings are available and the list is rapidly growing. The industry is unable to produce disks fast enough to meet market demands. A mail order dealer informed its customers in July 1986 that a major supplier such as Polygram is able to fill 70 percent of its orders, but other producers are shipping only five percent of their announced disks.

Another type of digital disk is distinguished by its applications. *Compact disk read-only memory (CD-ROM)*[3] designates laser disks containing machine-readable data. This format devotes a portion of its space for error correction, and more space to coding schemes than do audio disks. A CD-ROM player can be connected to a personal computer and its monitor. CD-ROM entered the scene early in 1985 and within two years has established itself as essential. It is an ideal medium for storing large amounts of information.

The required disk drive costs little more than a conventional floppy disk drive. A single compact disk can store about 550 megabytes of data, equivalent to about 1,600 floppy disks or 200,000 single-spaced pages. This opens a new era for personal computers via compact disks.

A fourth kind of optical media, the *optical digital disk,* is also distinguished by its application. The focus here is on massive, computer storage of data, the function up to now of magnetic disk and tape. This application is distinguished by the need to add information to the disk as necessary. This capability is provided by *write-once-read many (WORM)* disks and erasable disks; when a WORM disk is full, no more can be written on it. *Erasable disks* are being developed to compete with magnetic disks and tapes.

ADVANTAGES

Laser disks have a number of advantages that commend them to library applications. Without dealing with each type individually, we can cover a number of general favorable features. Efficient storage is a plus in an environment which is space-conscious. Laser disks are compact and superior to other media in relation to storage capacity. Versatility is an attractive factor. Laser disks can store multimedia materials. All types of black-and-white and full color images, sound, and machine-readable data can be included on a single disk. This medium is a wonder because not only is it super efficient in capacity and versatile with regard to media, but it also affords high resolution playback. The images are excellent and the sound, including stereo, is unsurpassed in quality.

Durability is an important quality where materials are open to public use and loaned out—laser disks pass the test. The disk consists of a base layer of plastic with an ultrathin aluminum coating which is pitted with encoded data. This delicate film is overlaid with a clear, protective plastic coating. A double-sided disk is two of these laminated back to back.

Those who claim that disks are indestructible know little about four-year-old children. Disks can warp in heat and be scuffed on the surface, but they certainly are resistant to wear. They are safe from magnetic fields, require no special climate beyond normal temperature ranges, and survive handling very well. Quality is not altered by constant use, and storage life is excellent.

Random access is relatively fast and precise. Freeze frame is simple and can be held indefinitely without damage to the quality. A factor that enhances the value of laser disks is that a user cannot accidentally erase them.

DISADVANTAGES

There are some disadvantages which will likely be overcome soon. It is expensive to create a master disk. Replication is not expensive, and mass production will make the price competitive with audio cassettes. Different formats such as analog, digital, CD-ROM, and videodisk are incompatible. This is partially overcome by the necessity of having players in different locations for different applications. For example, it is not generally convenient to use the same equipment for technical services and for public use anyway, so if they are for different formats, there is no loss. Combination players are, of course, being developed.

WEIGHING THE OPTIONS

Writing about software development for CD-ROM as compared with magnetic formats, Bill Zoellick, manager of software research at TMS Inc., observes:

> When the design work is done well, the payoff can be impressive: the CD-ROM enables you to move very large databases out of book form, out of centralized time-sharing systems, and off microforms. It provides convenient access to data inexpensively through mass distribution, and it offers exceptionally fast, convenient retrieval of these databases on very small computers.[4]

The applicability of the medium is limited by the recorded materials available and the cost of the hardware. Both of these problems are diminishing as competition becomes keener.

APPLICATIONS

This new technology was publicized in the early 1970s, but it took a decade for products to be developed and marketed. While compact audio disks are a booming business, some other applications are still in exploratory stages.

Librarians must assess the value and potential of this new medium and decide if and when to adopt various applications. Jumping in too soon can be an expensive experiment in underdeveloped and overpriced hardware and software; waiting too long can result in failure to take advantage of more economical systems and the expense of later building disk collections quickly. The market will become more competitive and prices can be expected to come down in some areas. One needs to keep up with library literature and commercial developments to ascertain when reasonable standards are reached and when prices are stabilized in any given area. The major library journals provide information on the status of developing technologies.

Of the four formats discussed—videodisks, compact audio disks, CD-ROM, and optical data disks—the first has not proven commercially popular, though it may yet capture a market for educational use. Audio disks and CD-ROM are proving themselves significant in both public and academic libraries of all levels. Optical data disks will doubtless also soon take their place in libraries, even in small libraries.

We turn our attention now to specific applications of the technology in small libraries. Applications as yet beyond the reach of small libraries, such as creating a publicity disk and archival preservation, will not be discussed except where application may soon be relevant, as in the case of WORM disks.

Lending Collections

Libraries having or considering LP record and music cassette collections should evaluate the applicability of CDs. Certainly the durability of CDs make them attractive to librarians frustrated with worn and damaged records and tapes. CDs are attractive to users because of their recording quality and the fact that players can be programmed to play selections in any order.

At this stage, the compact disk must not be considered a replacement for conventional recordings. Not all of the existing music will be transferred to this new medium, and it will be some time before the majority of new releases are available in this format. It is well to remember that transferring a poor recording to a compact disk will not make it a good one.

Instead of investing in more of the conventional hardware, LPs, and cassettes, it is worth considering the purchase of CDs and players. It is arguable that CDs at about $10–$15 are already more economical than LPs because of their longevity and the fact that they require less care. Without doubt, costs will be further reduced in the future. The CD has a 75-minute capacity compared with 45 minutes for an LP. As record companies begin to fill up the space, rather than simply supply the equivalent of an LP, the CD becomes a better buy.

Videodisks are another potential medium for lending collections. Included here are materials ranging from rock videos to aerobics, from auto mechanics to feature films. Prices for videodisk films are competitive with videocassettes, which is a fraction of the cost of 16mm. films.

Portable CD players are available for $300 or less. A CD player is about the same size as a cassette deck and can be plugged into the auxiliary or tape monitor input of a stereo system or any amplifier with an auxiliary input.

Since manufacturers have agreed upon standards for audio CDs, there is no problem of compatibility among different disk releases and players. All the major record companies are now releasing music simultaneously in CD and traditional formats. Recording on CDs is not restricted by class of music—pop, rock, classical, etc. are all available.

When shopping for a CD player, begin by reading a current general review. An example is *Changing Times'* "Compact Disc Players."[5] In addition to comparing various models available at the time, the article has continuing value for its warnings against off-brand, obsolete, and bare bones machines. Also included are features to consider such as programmability, remote control, audible scan, indexing, etc. Players range from battery operated models with headphones (5 x 5 x 1.25 inches) to sophisticated models with options such as ability to play six CDs at a time.

Before buying, read test reports in sources such as *High Fidelity*. This magazine also regularly reviews audio CDs as well. Robert Curtis offers some practical advice on building CD collections in an article called "Revolution Now? Classical Recordings and Compact Discs"[6] and Bruce Connolly goes further by recommending a list of 40 titles to start with in his article, "Popular Music on Compact Disc: A 'First-Purchase' Discography."[7]

Some observers caution that digital audio-tape (DAT) will compete favorably with CDs, providing comparable quality with the added advantage of being able to record.[8] The digital cassette with two-hour playing time is one-third smaller than conventional cassettes but carries the purity of digital sound. The technology has been around for years, but products have not been marketed until now to avoid confusing consumers with too much new technology.[9] Manufacturers are reportedly working on a CD player that can double as a recorder using erasable disks, and digital tape is still tape, so CDs are not likely to soon become obsolete.

If the market is any indication, compact disks are in. The Spring 1986 Schwann catalog listed 6,000 of them. First marketed in 1983, they claimed up to 15 percent of all sales of recordings within two years, and are expected to reach sales of $1 billion in 1986.[10] At least one library is finding CDs a good investment. The San Bernardino City Library reports that their 150 CDs have circulated more times than their 4,000 LPs.

Educational/Interactive

Materials for educational use have been available from the early days of the technology. In 1984, the National Gallery of Art released a videodisk for $95 which contained over 1,600 still pictures and a documentary on the development of the museum. The Center for Aerospace Education had by this time begun work on aerospace and astronomy series. Educational materials are available on all levels of instruction from home gardening to surgical techniques. Regional extension libraries are beginning to lend laser disks, sometimes with a nominal rental fee. Videodisks are ideal for instructional purposes because of their flexibility. In classroom use, the instructor can easily access information anywhere on the disk, and can hold an image indefinitely on the video screen. The student working alone can easily control the program for his own purposes.

This medium can involve the user at various levels, making it interactive. The user has more control than with conventional media, and can "talk back" to it. When linked with a personal computer, the possibilities are astounding. Learning rates were enhanced by 50 percent through interactive media, according to a research project with college biology students.[11]

An exciting development is the introduction of CD-I (compact disc-interactive). Robert Mason gives an example of the potential:

> Imagine a 30-minute narrated tour of London on the new CD-I. If we wish, we can simply listen and watch still pictures in a kind of slide show. But there is a difference: we can choose which street to follow at an intersection, or, upon reaching Westminster Abbey for example, we could choose to go inside for a more detailed tour. If we were interested in even more detail, we could request additional information and have it presented in text form on the screen. Or we could specify that we want the tour to continue, but we would like to see what this street was like in Shakespeare's time, and the visuals would switch to an Elizabethan street scene.[12]

In addition to consulting education journals, the librarian can locate educational videodisks through *The Educators' Handbook to Interactive Videodisc*.[13]

Reference

One of the most significant applications of the new technology is the potential of CD-ROM in reference work. A CD-ROM reader is used with a computer, generally an IBM-PC or a PC compatible, and a printer. Having made that investment of around $4,000 in hardware, the library can begin to enjoy substantial savings in indexes, reference materials, etc. Some of the CD-ROM materials are sold in packages with the hardware.

A 620-page book entitled *CD-ROM: The New Papyrus* (Microsoft Press, 1986) was prepared for the first Microsoft CD-ROM Conference. To demonstrate the potential of compact disks, a CD-ROM version of the book was produced. Mastering and pressing 50 disks cost only $4,000.[14] Since the book filled only 0.4 percent of the disk and only 50 copies were made, it is easy to appreciate the value this medium promises for normal publishing runs of databases and special collections.

It is not likely that many full-text conversions will soon be made to CD-ROM format. The first to appear, Grolier's *Academic American*

Encyclopedia, has received a lot of publicity. The entire nine million words of the 20-volume set are included on a single disk priced at $199, in comparison with $450 for book form. Type in the subject you desire and within five seconds the appropriate article appears on screen, having been located by automatic computer search of the 155,000-word index.

Indexes and abstracts are an ideal application of laser disk storage and retrieval. Dozens of such databases are now available or in test modes.[15] Most comprehensive systems and specialized databases are beyond the reach of small libraries. It may be expected, however, that before long CD-ROM periodical indexes and other databases will be competitive in price with printed subscription rates. University Microfilms International has been running a pilot project on optical disk storage of abstracts and articles. By early 1987 *Dissertation Abstracts* will be available on two CD-ROM disks. This will provide access to the entire database of citations as well as abstracts.

Some of these services have been available online, but there is the obvious advantage of owning the database with the freedom to search at no connect-time costs. Silver Platter Information Inc. is producing several CD-ROM databases including ERIC. The ERIC database will consist of permanent disks for pre-1986 materials and quarterly updates for current materials. Separate disks will contain the indexes, *Resources in Education* and *Current Index to Journals in Education.* Search software built into the ERIC database will permit search by subject descriptors, words in title or abstract, author, etc., with Boolean capability. It is expected that many small academic libraries will find this affordable. Other bibliographic utilities such as BRS are also developing CD-ROM products.

Cost effectiveness can be easily determined by comparing the cost of current indexes, reference sources, searching, etc. with the comparable resources on laser disks. Remember that this medium is limited by the number of reader stations available. Also, it is necessary to keep up with the field because what is not available or affordable this year may be next year. More information can be found in the *Optical/Electronic Publishing Directory,* which contains information on all aspects of CD-ROM, including databases.[16]

Technical Services

All areas of technical services may well be the first in the library to enjoy substantial economic benefits from the new technology. Cost savings in cataloging may be dramatic. It is easy to overestimate the savings in labor, however; sufficient time must be allowed for training and adaptation.

Acquisitions will be easier. Bowker has introduced their first CD-ROM product—*Books in Print.* A single compact disk contains *Books in Print, Subject Guide to BIP, BIP Supplement, Forthcoming Books,* and *Subject Guide to Forthcoming Books* with quarterly updates. The seemingly high price of $795 might not seem a bargain to smaller libraries, but before rejecting the idea, consider whether the retrieval system will save money in generating orders from *BIP* directly onto a printer.

BiblioFile, the system developed by The Library Corporation, also includes a book acquisitions system using their ANY-BOOK database. The system can be used to search the database of 1.5 million English language books by author, any word in the title, ISBN, or LCCN. It will print orders and maintain accounting records. Some book jobbers receive orders from libraries using such acquisition systems via telephone. The library's personal computer relays the order through a modem.

Introduced in January of 1985, BiblioFile will revolutionize catalog production for small libraries. It contains the entire MARC books database with author, title, LCCN, ISBN, and ISSN indexes on two CD-ROMs. The system is marketed as a package including the database, CD-ROM player, and cataloging software to interface with an IBM PC. The database is kept current through quarterly or monthly updates. The user must have an IBM-PC or PC compatible computer and printer. The user can retrieve MARC records, edit them if necessary, and generate original cataloging where necessary. Card sets and labels can be automatically printed with headings according to local specifications from the data, the records can be stored on diskette, or the records can be downloaded to another library system. If there is a bargain for small libraries in automation, it is BiblioFile. The advantage of this CD-ROM system over microcomputer cataloging programs is that instead of having to enter cataloging for each record, the cataloger can quickly find prepared cataloging for the majority of books.

Several automated library systems based on BiblioFile are being developed. These systems utilize BiblioFile ANY-BOOK for acquisitions, and MARC records for the catalog and circulations systems. It is worthwhile for small libraries to examine what these systems have to offer.

The time is propitious for the librarian managing a small library to consider alternative formats for library catalogs. The card catalog is very expensive. Card sets must be purchased and edited, if necessary, or they must be produced, which is a labor intensive method requiring typing and proofreading. Filing is time-consuming, and storage cabinets are expensive.

The library using the CD-ROM MARC database has a variety of

options in relation to public catalogs. The library can interface a printer with a microcomputer to print card sets and labels. Another option is to print labels only and store cataloging records on floppy disks. The floppies can then be used themselves as catalogs or they can be sent to a vendor for conversion to COM-fiche (computer output microfiche). Many libraries are using COM catalogs. The cost of conversion from magnetic tape or floppy disk to COM is not prohibitive, and additional copies of the COM master are a pittance. An online catalog must have an adequate number of user stations—microfiche readers for COM catalogs and microcomputers for floppy disk or hard disk catalogs.

CD-ROM is an attractive option. In 1986, several libraries began the move to CD-ROM catalogs. Among them is Los Angeles County which can place its entire catalog of five million books on one disk. This demonstrates the capacity of the medium, but is not an indication that the method is applicable only to large libraries. The cost of write-once compact disks is coming down and it is entirely within the reach of a small library to create its own online CD-ROM catalog. Using BiblioFile, the cataloger would locate cataloging records on the CD-ROM database, edit as necessary, and type in once the data for books not found in the database. These records are then transferred electronically to the library's WORM disk through a CD writer. That CD becomes the catalog for the library. Library users read the compact disk by means of a personal computer. Interfacing a printer makes it easy to create bibliographies from the catalog. Consult *Byte* (May 1986) for an introduction to write-once disks explaining how to get the most out of them in relation to updating, capacity, access time, etc.[17]

The initial cost of hardware—a CD-ROM player, multi-PC controller, and PCs for access—and software to utilize it will seem prohibitive. Once in place, however, such a system may cost only a fraction of the annual costs of supporting a card catalog. Several vendors are offering online laser disk-based catalogs, and some of them, such as Brodart and Gaylord, are appealing to "the smallest of libraries." Using such a service, the librarian may be spared much of the details and hardware involved in producing an online catalog locally. Laser disks also provide an ideal format for preserving masses of library materials. Richard Chapin, Director of Michigan State University Libraries, sees great promise in this field; "In the area of preservation of library materials, I see the video disc as the technology of the future. I think that microfilm will soon be a dead technology."[18] It is not yet feasible for a small library to utilize this means for custom work. However, it can be expected that more and more historical and special collections will become available on CD-ROM. It holds great promise for archival preservation. The technology is changing so rapidly that one must keep up with library literature to be informed of new developments and products. The annual feature, "Automated Library System Marketplace," by Robert Walton in *Library Journal* will likely give more space to CD-ROM-based systems in the future.

LASER LITERACY

Laser technology is so practical in its infancy that librarians dare not neglect looking to its maturity. Laser disk readers will find increasing use as computer peripherals in libraries, and we will see leaps and strides when WORM disks and erasable systems become generally available. We can also expect electronic publishing to make available a wide range of databases, reference works, and AV materials for local access.

Of special appeal to librarians lacking opportunity to study new technology is the fact that much of this material is user friendly. Carol Hanson Fenichel makes it sound easy:

> CD-ROM systems cost thousands rather than tens of thousands and are being sold as "turnkey" packages which include the disk with the database, the CD-ROM drive, the retrieval software, and the interface and cabling required to connect the drive to a personal computer. This significantly reduces the level of technical expertise needed to manage the systems, a cost saving at least as important as the actual cost of the systems themselves.[19]

Major problems in this developing new field revolve around pricing, copyright, and conditions of usage. Costs have been calculated in the past on the basis of number of pages or connect time to a computer database. Now that databases are being sold, the industry must develop some criteria for determining prices. The supplier has little control over the use of the product. Policies governing use, reproduction, sharing, etc. are generally not well defined.

Every librarian needs to be literate in this field. A place to start is with the ERIC document, *Videodisc and Optical Digital Disk Technologies and Their Applications in Libraries.*[20] Another excellent introduction is Nancy K. Herther's article, "CD-ROM Technology: A New Era for Information Storage and Retrieval?"[21] Other materials include *Optical Disk Technology and the Library,* published by the National Library of Canada;[22] and a pamphlet called "Disc Could Be Your Library,"[23] a mini guide to books, bibliographies, periodicals, conferences, and professional associations. There is a wealth of information of laser disk products in Bruce Connolly's four-part "Laserdisk Directory" in *Database* and *Online.*[24] Periodical literature, both professional and popular, is essential for keeping abreast of developments in this promising technology.

References

1. Nancy Herther, "The Silver Disk," *Database* 9 (June 1986): 87.
2. There is no agreement on how to spell disc/disk. "Disc" is favored by audiophiles, "disk" by information scientists.
3. This is written variously as CDROM, CD ROM, and CD-ROM.
4. Bill Zoellick, "CD-ROM Software Development," *Byte* 11 (May 1986): 188.
5. "Compact Disc Players," *Changing Times* 39 (December 1985): 59, 62–63.
6. Robert Curtis, "Revolution Now? Classical Recordings and Compact Discs," *Library Journal* 111 (May 1, 1986): 85–88.
7. Bruce Connolly, "Popular Music on Compact Disc: A 'First-Purchase' Discography," *Library Journal* 110 (November 15, 1985): 42–48.
8. Manuel Schiffres, "From TV to Tape Recorders, Digital Steals the Show," *U.S. News & World Report* 100 (March 17, 1986): 49.
9. Len Feldman, "Here Comes DAT," *Popular Science* 229 (August 1986): 82.
10. "A Compact Sonic Boom," *Newsweek* 106 (December 16, 1985): 48–49.
11. Peter Dworkin, "Videodisc Goes to School," *U.S. News & World Report* 100 (June 16, 1986): 62.
12. Robert Mason, "Woodstock in Seattle? CD-ROM & CD-I," *Library Journal* 111 (May 15, 1986): 51.
13. Ed Schwartz, *The Educators' Handbook to Interactive Videodisc* (Washington, D.C.: Association for Educational Communications & Technology, 1985).
14. Craig L. Stark, "CD-ROM Conference: Lured by 600 Megabytes on Disk," *PC Magazine* 5 (April 29, 1986): 42.
15. Carol Tenopir, "Databases on CD-ROM," *Library Journal* 111 (March 1, 1986): 68–69.
16. *Optical/Electronic Publishing Directory* (P.O. Box 1032, Carmel Valley, CA 93924: Information Arts, 1985).
17. Jeffrey R. Dulude, "The Application Interface of Optical Drives," *Byte* 11 (May 1986): 193–99.
18. Richard Chapin, "Future Automation Services in Academic Libraries," in *The Future of Library Automation: A Symposium* (West Newton, MA: CL Systems, Inc., 1984), p. 11.
19. Carol Hanson Fenichel, "For Optical Disks and Information Retrieval the Time Is Now," *Database* 9 (June 1986): 6–7.
20. Information Systems Consultants Inc., *Videodisc and Optical Digital Technologies and Their Applications in Libraries* (Washington, D.C.: Council on Library Resources, Inc., 1985). Available in paper copy or microfiche as ERIC document ED 257 433.
21. Nancy K. Herther, "CD ROM Technology: A New Era for Information Storage and Retrieval?" *Online* 9 (November 1985): 17–28.

22. *Optical Disk Technology and the Library,* Canadian Network Papers; no. 9 (Ottawa: National Library of Canada, 1985).
23. Clarke Davis, *Disc Could Be Your Library* (2 Court Street, Nashua, NH 03060: Nashua Public Library, 198?).
24. Bruce Connolly, "Laserdisk Directory," Part 1, *Database* 9 (June 1986); Part 2, *Online* 10 (July 1986); Part 3, *Database* 9 (August 1986); Part 4, *Online 10* (September 1986).

Searching for Small Libraries: A Selective Bibliography, 1977–87

Robin Kinder

Reviewing the literature on small libraries of all types is a fairly easy task since there is so little of it to review. The parameters of this bibliography could have been extended by removing the dates of inclusion; but the constraint of ten years kept this bibliography to a list of the most current and useful sources on small libraries.

The areas of administration, automation, public services, and technical services were searched to obtain those sources most appropriate for application to small libraries. Those materials specifically designed for small libraries are not all included in the bibliography. Instead, general sources were sometimes considered more valuable because of their methods of providing information. General, introductory monographs are included only when considered the most representative of a wide range of library literature on the subject.

Articles were discounted after a dismaying search through the literature. Few were found to provide the length that could be considered even a basic manual; and the general self-studies and how-to-do-it articles were either too specific or too shallow to be of use. The bibliographies published by the Center for Rural Librarianship at Clarion University of Pennsylvania, Clarion, Pennsylvania, provide a full range of articles.

"Readers" were generally excluded because of their unevenness in presentation: these sometimes exist as half-manual, half-theoretical forms of literature. This bibliography itself is a manual; it strives to be as clear and helpful as possible, providing just enough sources to assist the librarian working in the small library.

State manuals designed to aid small libraries have been included as

Robin Kinder is a reference librarian at Darien Library, Darien, Connecticut.

a separate section in this bibliography, the result of my request for manuals sent to 65 state and provincial public library agencies and 60 state school library agencies in the U.S. and Canada. Fifty-eight agencies responded with letters only; 27 submitted materials not included here; 15 provided manuals substantial enough for inclusion.

Librarians may find these manuals helpful, regardless of place of publication or intended audience. While many states' library laws and regulations are included in the manuals, they usually appear in appendixes and do not interfere with the content. All of the manuals are well-written, comprehensive, and clear—unless otherwise noted in the annotation. The area of technical services is one particularly well-served by these guides, in contrast to commercially printed sources. The only drawback may be where breadth of coverage prohibits any in-depth descriptions of processes and procedures. Considering the lack of basic, introductory manuals for small libraries that may have untrained personnel, these handbooks fill void.

No bibliography is ever complete. This one merely introduces the most basic sources for small libraries. It is hoped that the librarian will find it useful. As a last remark, this bibliographer would like to address librarians working in small and even not-so-small libraries around the country: a journal begun only a few years ago deserves special mention for its focus on small libraries. *Rural Libraries,* published by the Center for Rural Librarianship, presents concise, useful articles relating specifically to rural libraries. The publication is serious in intent and appearance and is a welcome relief from the glossy library magazines of today. With the assistance of Bernard Vavrek as coordinator, this journal may prove to be the most enlightening for all librarians working in small libraries.

BOOKS

Ahrensfeld, Janet L., Elin B. Christianson and David E. King. 2nd ed. *Special Libraries: A Guide for Management.* New York: Special Libraries, 1986. 85p. ISBN 0-87111-318-X

A basic introduction to the field, this volume describes the general purpose and functions of the special library. Emphasis is placed on procedures involving acquisitions, organization, and dissemination of materials. Staffing, space and equipment, and budget conclude the handbook. Administrative concepts and methods are excluded from discussion. Indexed.

Altman, Ellen, ed. *Local Public Library Administration.* 2nd ed. Chicago: American Library Assn., 1980. 245p. ISBN 0-8389-0307-X

A collection of essays exploring both theoretical and practical aspects of management at the local level. The former covers subjects such as contemporary society, political processes, community analysis, and decision-making. The latter describes personnel procedures, finance and budget, and management tools and techniques, to name only a few. A strong list of contributors. Indexed.

Bierman, Kenneth John. *Automation and the Small Library*. Small Libraries Publication No. 7. Chicago: Library Administration and Management Association (LAMA), American Library Assn., 1982. 10p. ISBN 0-8389-5604-1.

General approaches to automation, along with applications in areas such as interlibrary loan, acquisitions, cataloging, circulation, and information retrieval. One of the many booklets issued by LAMA as guides for small libraries.

Bloomberg, Marty and G. Edward Evans. *Introduction to Technical Services for Library Technicians*. 5th ed. Littleton, Colo.: 1985. 417p. ISBN 0-87287-486-9.

A manual for the paraprofessional or the lone librarian who must master all tasks within the library. This standard text covers all areas of technical services, including automation, acquisitions, bibliographic verification, order procedures, accounting, and record-keeping. The second half of the volume is devoted solely to cataloging and classification. A companion volume to the authors' *Introduction to Public Service for Library Technicians*. Indexed.

Boucher, Virginia. *Interlibrary Loan Practices Handbook*. Chicago: American Library Assn., 1984, 195p. 0-8389-3298-3.

Designed as a handbook for those unfamiliar with interlibrary loan, chapters examine management, procedures, and instructions, and the more abstract areas of reproduction and copyright. Ruth Freitag provides a comprehensive bibliography of verification sources. Indexed.

Breivik, Patricia Senn. *Planning the Library Instruction Program*. Chicago: American Library Assn., 1982. 146p. ISBN 0-8389-0358-4.

Directed to librarians who are responsible for planning and implementing a library instruction program, this volume is both a practical and theoretical guide. Steps in the process are reviewed as is the wider area of politics and education, and their role and effect on the library instruction program. Indexed.

Broadus, Robert. *Selecting Materials for Libraries*. 2nd ed. New York: H.W. Wilson, 1981. 469p. ISBN 0-8242-0659-2.

A comprehensive source for the small- to medium-sized library, with a progression of the general and theoretical to the more specific, practical application of selection. Principles and background to book selection are explored; types of print and nonprint materials and selection by subject field conclude the volume. Extensive notes for each chapter are listed in the back. Indexed.

Chan, Lois Mai. *Cataloging and Classification: An Introduction.* New York: McGraw-Hill, 1981. 397p. ISBN 0-07-010498-0.

A comprehensive text on the principles of cataloging and classification. Descriptive cataloging, subject cataloging, classification, and the production and organization of cataloging records comprise the major areas of discussion. A fine, clearly written work. Indexed.

Chernik, Barbara E. *Procedures for Library Media Technical Assistants.* Chicago: American Library Assn., 1983. 280p. ISBN 0-8389-0384-3.

A work designed as a textbook on library operations and in-service training. Circulation procedures, shelving and inventory, AV media and equipment, mending and binding, serials and filing in catalogs provide a basic introduction to library operations. Indexed.

Corbin, John. *Managing the Library Automation Project.* Phoenix: Oryx, 1985. 274p. ISBN 0-89774-151-X.

Planning, organization, and steps to implementing automation for those untrained in library systems development provide the major emphasis. Parts III and IV—System Procurement and System Installation and Operation—explain the practical progression from a theoretical base of planning and organization. Indexed.

Costa, Betty, and Marie Costa. *A Micro Handbook for Small Libraries and Media Centers, 2nd ed.* Littleton, Colo.: Libraries Unlimited, 1986. 325p. ISBN 0-87287-525-3.

A thorough review of micros in the small library with the novice particularly in mind. Introduces software and hardware in simple terms. Application of microcomputers include word processing, database management, and accounting programs for use in acquisitions, cataloging, circulation, administration, and serials control. Three case studies are included. An extensive list of resources, glossary, computer care, and alternative funding for purchasing computers makes this a basic computer resource for small libraries. Indexed.

Curley, Arthur and Dorothy Broderick. *Building Library Collections.*

6th ed. Metuchen, N.J.: Scarecrow Press, 1985. 339p. ISBN 0-8108-1776-4.

Revised edition of Bonk and Magrill's previous work, this text is a basic introduction to the fundamentals of collection development. Not geared toward small libraries specifically, it is nevertheless a comprehensive source for librarians wishing to learn collection development the easy way—with a readable text. Chapter 5 on "Variations by Type of Library"—describes the characteristics of university, college, community college, school library media centers, and special libraries. Indexed.

Curley, Arthur and Jana Varlejs. *Akers' Simple Library Cataloging.* 7th ed. Metuchen, N.J.: Scarecrow Press, 1984. 375p. ISBN 0-8108-1649-0.

A new edition of Susan Grey Akers' practical guide continues to focus on small libraries. Covers all aspects of cataloging, with final chapters emphasizing more specialized topics: nonbook materials, authority files, commercially printed cards, and arrangement of entries to the catalog. Includes reproduction of cards. Indexed.

Daniells, Lorna. *Business Information Sources.* Berkeley and Los Angeles: University of California Press, 1985. 673p. ISBN 0-8108-1649-0.

Revised edition of the classic Daniells text, this guide supplies selected, annotated listings of business sources published since 1976. Emphasis is on English-language materials. The scope is larger than that needed for a small library, but as a basic business reference tool, this source is the most outstanding. Chapter 21 on "A Basic Bookshelf" provides a listing of sources for collections in the small or corporate library. Indexed.

Dority, G. Kim. *A Guide to Reference Books for Small- and Medium-Sized Libraries: 1970–1982.* Littleton, Colo. Libraries Unlimited, 1984. 410p. ISBN 0-87287-403-6.

1,179 titles selected by subject specialists reviewing titles for *ARBA* and Sheehy's *Guide to Reference Books* (10th ed, American Library Assn.), arranged by subject-oriented chapters. Annotations are evaluative and citations to reviews are listed at the conclusion of each annotation. Indexed.

Fraley, Ruth and Carol Lee Anderson. *Library Space Planning: How to Allocate and Reorganize Collections, Resources, and Physical Facilities.* New York: Neal-Schuman, 1985. 158p. ISBN 0-918212-44-8.

A practical guide to space planning for all types of libraries with an emphasis on planning within existing facilities. A step-by-step progression from goals and objectives to moving and final procedures outlines in detailed form the requirements for successful planning. Attention is given to the often-overlooked problem of communication. Tables and charts illustrate the more difficult concepts. Indexed.

Gorman, Michael. *The Concise AACR2*. Chicago: American Library Assn., 1981. 164p. ISBN 0-8389-0325-8.

The guide to simplifying the intricacies of *AACR2* for use in small library cataloging. In an attempt to weed out the most extraneous material in *AACR2*, the author has devised a practical manual to meet everyday needs of catalogers. While this work has had its critics, it nonetheless provides catalogers with an accessible tool for the cataloging rules. Indexed.

Greenfield, Jane. *Books: Their Care and Repair*. New York: H.W. Wilson, 1983. 204p. ISBN 0-8242-0695-9.

The author illustrates the techniques of book repair in this practical manual. Expanded from a series of pamphlets, and written with the small institution in mind, the work covers basic repairs, the structure and care of books, and recommended equipment and supplies. Indexed.

Jennerich, Elaine Zaremba and Edward J. Jennerich. *The Reference Interview as a Creative Art*. Littleton, Colo.: Libraries Unlimited, 1987. 107p. ISBN 0-87287-445-1.

This work, aimed at novice and professional librarians alike, introduces the basic skills and fine-tuning devices which make the reference interview a true art. Chapter headings reflect the theatrical title; the text offers one of the few thorough examinations of the reference interview, notwithstanding articles and portions of other library texts. Chapters include skills, characteristics of librarians, types of interviewing, the setting, dealing with the handicapped and non-English speaking, follow-up, and performance evaluation. Indexed.

Katz, William. *Introduction to Reference Work*. Vols. I & II. 5th ed. New York: McGraw-Hill 1986. Vol. I: 397p. ISBN 0-07-033537-0. Vol. II: 237p. ISBN 0-07-033538-9.

Since 1969, the various editions of these texts have become a standard source for reference materials and services. Volume I, subtitled *Basic Information Sources,* focuses on specific reference sources and their uses to the librarian. The majority of this volume examines the bibliographies, indexing, and abstracting services, encyclopedias, ready reference, biographical works, dictionaries, geographical sources, and government documents.

Volume II, *Reference Services and Reference Processes,* consists of four major areas of reference work: information and the community, interviewing and searching, online services and library instruction, and evaluation of reference services. Chapters in both volumes provide suggested readings and extensive footnoting. Clarity of presentation and writing style, and the wealth of information, make these volumes indispensable.

McClung, Patricia A., ed. *Selection of Library Materials in the Humanities, Social Sciences and Sciences.* Chicago: American Library Assn., 1985. 405p. ISBN 0-8389-3305-X.

A comprehensive discussion of general sources and procedures and the techniques of materials selection in the basic disciplines. Twenty-nine essays provide information on specific sources as well as more general explanations of collection building. Each of the three disciplines is examined separately, followed by a special formats section which includes government publications, small presses, microforms, nonprint media, and machine-readable files. This reference work will be followed by a volume on interdisciplinary subjects and applied professional literature. Somewhat specialized for small public libraries, college libraries need this tool. Indexed.

Matthews, Joseph. *Choosing an Automated Library System.* Chicago: American Library Assn. 1980. 119p. ISBN 0-8389-0310-X.

A planning guide for small- and medium-sized libraries which discusses needs analysis, alternatives, selecting the system, contracts and installations, and implementation. Summaries conclude each chapter. Appendixes provide information about the functions automation may assume in acquisitions, cataloging, circulation, etc. Indexed.

Morehead, Joe. *Introduction to United States Public Documents.* 3rd ed. Littleton, Colo.: Libraries Unlimited, 1983. 309p. ISBN 0-8727-359-5.

The basic text on government publications, with general information concerning the role of the federal government in publishing, detailed references to government and commercial sources, including micro-publishing, and information on depository libraries. Online services and the various publications of each branch of the federal government are discussed. Indexed.

Rawles, Beverly A. *Human Resource Management in Small Libraries.* Hamden, Conn.: Library Professional Publications/Shoe String Press, 1982. 136p. ISBN 0-208-01966-9.

Staff management techniques for the inexperienced director of the small library focus on affirmative action, staff development and deployment, performance appraisal, communications, planning, budgeting, and programming. School library media centers are discussed in a separate chapter. Chapters are somewhat brief but useful. Indexed.

Renford, Beverly and Linnen Hendrickson. *Bibliographic Instruction: A Handbook*. New York: Neal-Schuman, 1980. 192p. ISBN 0-918212-24-3.

Primarily for the academic library, this practical manual addresses the activities which comprise the bibliographic instruction program. Orientation, printed guides, course instruction, and computer-assisted instruction are examined. Small libraries nonetheless should take note of the need for instruction in the use of library materials.

Rochelle, Carlton. *Wheeler and Goldhor's Practical Administration of Public Libraries*. rev. ed. New York: Harper & Row, 1981. 464p. ISBN 0-06-13601-4.

The standard work for library supervision and management, beginning with general administrative topics: planning, management, personnel, and finance. Part II focuses on services to the public with analyses of departmental services. Chapter 14 is devoted to small libraries. Concludes with support services, including technical services and the measurement and evaluation of library services. Indexed.

Sachse, Gladys. *U.S. Government Publications for Small and Medium-Sized Libraries: A Study Guide*. Public Library Reporter No. 20. Chicago: American Library Assn., 1981. 206p. ISBN 0-8389-3268-1.

A series of lessons designed for library assistants who are responsible for developing and integrating government documents into the local library collection. Designed as a training manual, each section includes performance objectives, discussions, and testing. Limited to federal publications. Selection aids, acquisitions procedures, processing, and publicizing government documents are a few of the topics covered. Indexed.

Sager, Donald. *Public Library Administrators' Planning Guide to Automation*. Dublin, Oh.: OCLC Online Computer Library Center, 1983. 133p. ISBN 0-933418-43-4.

Basic techniques for planning automation systems are addressed for the administrator of the small- and medium-sized library. Examines the procedures to study the benefits of automation, alternative goals and methods, financing, estimating cost, and assessing factors in addition to cost. Sager authored *Managing the Public Library* (1984). Indexed.

Schlessinger, Bernard. *The Basic Business Library: Core Resources*. Phoenix: Oryx Press, 1983. 232p. ISBN 0-89774-038-6.

A core list of printed business reference sources, a bibliography, and eight essays written with small libraries in mind. Some 156 titles are listed and every-other-year of purchase is suggested where applicable. Citations are annotated and evaluative. Each section contains its own index. The essays are informative and useful, particularly "Business Periodicals: A Core Collection for the Smaller Library" by Louise Sherby, which contains 49 annotated titles.

Serebnick, Judith, ed. *Collection Management in Public Libraries.* Proceedings of a Preconference to the 1984 ALA Annual Conference, June 21–22, 1984. Chicago: Resources and Technical Services Division, American Library Assn., 1986. 98p. ISBN 0-8389-3321-1.

A collection of addresses given at the ALA Annual Conference on such topics as guidelines, automation, resource sharing, management, and book selection. Each essay contains practical advice relating to libraries of all sizes. Although this is not a set of guidelines or a structured manual, the advice is wise and provocative.

Sinclair, Dorothy. *Administration of the Small Public Library.* 2nd ed. Chicago: American Library Assn., 1979. 156p. ISBN 0-8389-0291-X.

This is aimed at the new, inexperienced public library administrator. Attention is geared toward finance and planning and less to services, reflecting the rise in more complex management techniques. Individual chapters discuss the community, library objectives, governance, policies, finance, personnel administration, objectives to service and operations in support of service. A fundamental source for directors of small libraries. Indexed.

University Press Books for Public Libraries, 1986. 8th ed. New York: American University Press Services for the Public Library Association, American Library Assn., 1986. 96p. ISBN 0-8389-6388-9.

Titles are selected by librarians under the auspices of the Small- and Medium-Sized Libraries Section of ALA, with selection geared toward the general public. Over 500 monographs and 19 journals comprise the choice of hard and paper backed books. Annotations and reviews are included with standard bibliographic citations and purchasing information. Indexed.

Van House, Nancy A. *Output Measures for Public Libraries: A Manual of Standardized Procedures.* 2nd ed. Chicago: American Library Assn., 1987. 99p. ISBN 0-8389-3340-8.

A publication developed by the Public Library Development Program of PLA, designed to assist librarians in assessing library services. Methods included are data collection and analysis, interpretation and reporting of data. A self-help manual which can be used in conjunction with the program's companion volume *Planning and Role Setting for Public Libraries,* (Chicago: ALA), 1987. Indexed.

Wynar, Bohdan S. *Recommended Reference Books for Small and Medium-Sized Libraries and Media Centers, 1987*. Littleton, Colo.: Libraries Unlimited, 1987. 282p. ISBN 0-87287-597-0.

An annual publication now in its seventh year, this volume lists 577 titles with critical annotations selected from reviews in *ARBA 87*. The author calls this work an "abridged" version of *ARBA*. Excluded are reference titles in literature and fine arts dealing with individual artists, reference books in genealogy, and regional guides in botany and zoology. References to reviews are included with each title. Divided into four parts—General Reference, Social Sciences, Humanities, and Science and Technology—and arranged alphabetically, titles are subdivided by form. A general listing of sources heads each topical division. Librarians may also wish to consult an earlier reference source edited by Jovian Lang and Deborah C. Masters, *Reference Sources for Small- and Medium-Sized Libraries* (4th ed., ALA, 1984). Indexed.

Wynar, Christine Gehrt. *Guide to Reference Books for School Media Centers*. 3rd ed. Littleton, Colo.: Libraries Unlimited, 1986. 407p. ISBN 0-87287-545-8.

Designed for librarians and teachers of grades K–12, this comprehensive source contains evaluative annotations, notations to other reviews, and full bibliographic information. Arranged by topic, it contains 2,011 titles, as a result of new subjects such as the disabled, which this year carries its own subject heading. One of the few reference sources that deals specifically with reference materials and aids for the school library center.

Young, Virginia. *The Library Trustee: A Practical Guidebook*. 3rd ed. New York: R.R. Bowker, 1978. 192p. ISBN 0-8352-1068-5.

Examines the various responsibilities of trustees, their role in library policy making, planning, and finances. All areas receive attention including buildings, politics, public relations, automation, and Friends of the Library. Excellent appendixes ranging from trustee orientation to budget checklist to suggested readings for trustees. Indexed.

STATE MANUALS

Alaska

Kolb, Audrey P. *A Manual for Small Alaskan Libraries*. Fairbanks: Division of State Libraries and Museums, Alaska State Library, Department of Education. 1986. 150 + p.

The author, Librarian/Coordinator of the Northern Region of the Alaska State Library, generously provided the initial four chapters of a manual in progress (interim title above), which include establishing the library, the library building, the library collection, and the nuts and bolts of operating a library. From mission statements and goals and objectives through the neglected world of small library buildings to collection development and materials selection, this manual explains the rudiments of librarianship without the jargon confusing to the novice. Short bibliographies are included at the end of each chapter.

Alberta

Guidebook to Cataloging and Classification for Small Public Libraries. Edmonton, Canada: Alberta Culture, Library Services Branch, 1984. 24p. ISBN 0-919411-20-7.

Designed for use with DDC and Sears List of Subject Headings, this booklet provides a concise account of the process of making a library's materials accessible to the public. Cataloging includes descriptive cataloging, main and added entries, and classification; Dewey numbers are described by Tables, Outlines and Relative Index. Provides questions and answers to familiar problems in classification. Illustrations of cards are included. The intended audience is the para-professional as the contents are too shallow for trained librarians.

Colorado

Miller, Edward P. et al. *Education for Directors of Small Public Libraries. A Training Manual.* Denver: Colorado State Library, Colorado Department of Education and the University of Denver Graduate School of Librarianship and Information Management, 1985. Var. pg.

Issuing from an institute/seminar held in May 1985, this manual is a substantial review of library administration and management. Each of the five sections include a glossary of applicable terms and bibliographies for further reading. Sections are divided into broad subjects: Library and Community, Management Concepts, Public Relations, Putting Information in the Library, and Library and Government. Figures, forms, samples, and examples offer practical guidance. Described as a self-teaching tool for those without formal education, it would be instructive for the new library director of a small library as well.

Hawaii

Recommended Basic Reference Collections for Community and Commu-

nity-School Libraries. Honolulu: Hawaii State Library System, Hawaii Department of Education, 1985. 26p.

An update of recommended reference books. Arranged by Dewey number with author and/or title, edition, publisher, year, and price. Most helpful are the alphabetic notations given to each title to distinguish among libraries serving different populations. These notations signal highly recommended books for designated collections; they are not mandatory, however.

Illinois

Illinois: Recommended Standards for Educational Library Media Programs. Springfield, Ill.: Illinois State Board of Education, 1983. 32p.

A statement of standards with qualitative recommended standards, general overview of standards concerning staff, programs, collection and selection of materials, reference materials, nonprint media, and films and video recordings. Of special importance is the section on consideration for low-enrollment school districts which explores alternatives in personnel, materials, and equipment for districts still in developmental stages in library media building. Categories of quantitative standards include professional and support staff, selection of materials, instruction, books, periodicals, and district library media expenditures. An assessments guide provides forms for completing phases, short- and long-range plans, by category and grade.

Iowa

Iowa Certification Manual for Public Libraries. Des Moines: Continuing Education/Certification Advisory Committee of the State Library of Iowa, State Library of Iowa, 1985. 22p.

Divided into five parts describing the following areas: competency statements, levels of certification, time frames for certification, recertification, and continuing education for public librarians. Competency statements considered basic to fulfilling the mission of the library include general and administrative services, and public and technical services. Glossary. Appendixes provide charts for certification time frame, explanation and samples of forms, and descriptions of how to apply for certification.

Public Library Measures of Quality. Des Moines: State Standards Committee, State Library Commission of Iowa Standards Committee, State Library of Iowa, 1985. 45p.

Based on Illinois' *Avenues to Excellence,* broad, definitive standards for public libraries identify 13 areas and tasks, levels of service and output measures required. Stresses the development of a mission statement. Sections include structure and governance, finances, and administration. Output measures for this publication were based on the PLA's *Output Measures for Public Libraries*.

Kansas

Gardiner, Allen. *The Handy Book for Kansas Public Libraries and Trustees*. Topeka: State Library of Kansas, 1983. 78p.

Developed by a consultant for the State Library of Kansas, this reference tool outlines the issues and legislation affecting public libraries within the state. Cited alphabetically, with cross-references, terms are annotated with the opinions of the attorney general, statutes, rules and regulations, and outside sources for further reading. Questions and answers collected from queries most often asked by librarians and trustees are also included. Quick index. 1985 supplement.

Kentucky

Klee, Ed and Jean Wiggens, ed. *Policies and Procedures for the Public Library: A Sample Collection, 1985*. Frankfort, Ky.: Division of Field Services, Department of Libraries and Archives, 1985. Var. pg.

Section I on Personnel Policies contains 31 chapters with detailed discussions on objectives, financial support, organizational structure, work week and salaries, leaves, insurance, health, disability, and termination of services, etc. Extensive appendixes provide forms for evaluation and performance appraisals, exit interviews, information on sex and pregnancy discrimination, EEOC, etc. Section II on Procedures outlines processes for public relations, circulation, display space exhibits, materials selection, weeding, inventory, gifts and appraisals, etc. An excellent source of information for any library to compare with its own policy or as an aid in developing a new policy.

Massachusetts

Bolt, Nancy and Corinne Johnson. *Options for Small Public Libraries in Massachusetts: Recommendations and a Planning Guide. A Full Report.* Quincy, Mass.: Options for Small Libraries Committee. Massachusetts Department of Education.

Developed by a committee whose members serve communities with populations of less than 1,500 people, this document provides choices and modified planning processes for small libraries. The latter includes simplified data collection, sources of information, critical success factors (e.g., adequate hours, staffing, materials, etc.), critical success factors by role—in essence, by different types of centers, and automation. This report is useful for local planning and assisting small libraries in role decisions.

New York

Library Trustee Institute. Albany, N.Y.: New York State Association of Library Boards and the University of the State of New York, New York State Library, State Education Department. Var. dates.

A looseleaf binder providing sections on Trustee Readings, Microcomputer Update, Director-Board Relations, Basic Duties and Responsibilities, and Planning Process Policy. Each contains miscellaneous articles, pamphlets, reviews, and booklets appropriate for the library trustee. Integrated Library Systems, Youth Service Standards, Library Cost, Planning and Budgeting, Literacy, Lobbying-Public Relations, Conservation-Preservation, Running an Effective Board Meeting, Intellectual Freedom, and Construction are also divided into separate sections which are updated.

Oklahoma

Procedures Manual for School Library Media Centers. Oklahoma City: Oklahoma State Department of Education, 1982. 239p.

An excellent review of procedures for selection and acquisition of materials, processing, equipment selection, circulation, and general services. Discusses maintenance of library materials, including inventory, repair, and weeding. Glossary. Bibliography.

Pennsylvania

A Handbook for Public Library Trustees. 2d ed. Harrisburg, Penn.: State Library of Pennsylvania, Pennsylvania Department of Education, 1983. 79p.

Originally published in 1979, this handbook provides information, ideas and procedures useful to the experienced and novice trustee. The objectives of the guide are to heighten trustee awareness, suggest useful practices, and to serve as a source of legal and general information.

This guide is an extremely useful and clear approach to the business of the trustee, with discussions on personnel matters, planning and evaluation, finance, legislative processes, and the board's duties. References to further reading are provided throughout the text. Index.

Vermont

A Library Media Guide for Vermont Schools. Montpelier, Vt.: Vermont Department of Education, 1981. 122p.

Primarily a technical services manual outlining sample worksheets for all aspects of library operations. Topics include curriculum, care of materials, parts of a book, card catalog, reference materials and AV equipment. Designed for administrators, school board members, and media directors, this typeset manual is contained in looseleaf binders for updating. Bibliography.

Wyoming

Wyoming Interlibrary Loan Manual. Cheyenne, Wy.: Wyoming State Library, 1984. 98p.

This guide provides information on protocols for borrowing among Wyoming libraries, reference and interlibrary loan procedures, copyright essentials for ILL, ILL procedures for genealogy requests, and policy sheets containing ILL information. The policy sheets are clear, full-page reproductions of ILL policies for individual Wyoming libraries.

Wyoming Public Library Trustees Handbook. Cheyenne, Wy.: Wyoming State Library, 1985. 70p.

Describes the responsibilities of trustees and library directors, including personnel, budgeting, and public relations; types of libraries, professional organizations, financing, budgeting, legislative processes, and a do-it-yourself survey for the small library. Glossary. Basic resources list divided into essential and helpful literature. Wyoming has created the most readable and handsome library manuals of those included in this bibliography.

Bibliography

The following list of books and articles are suggested readings provided by the contributors to *The How-to-Do-It Manual for Small Libraries*. It is keyed to the four sections of the book having to do with the daily operations of a small library: administration, collection development and technical services, public services, and computers to lasers.

ADMINISTRATION

Association of College and Research Libraries. *Standards for College Libraries*. Chicago: American Library Assn., 1986.

Association of College and Research Libraries and the Association of Research Libraries. *Standards for University Libraries*. Chicago: American Library Assn., 1979.

Association of College and Research Libraries and Association for Educational Communications and Technology. *Guidelines for Two-year College Learning Resources Programs*. Chicago: American Library Assn., 1981.

Association of Specialized and Cooperative Library Agencies. *Multitype Library Cooperation State Laws and Regulations, An Annotated Checklist*. Chicago: American Library Assn., 1983.

Bolt, Nancy and Corinne Johnson. *Options for Small Public Libraries in Massachusetts, Recommendations and a Planning Guide*. Chicago: American Library Assn., 1985.

Cherrington, J. Owen. *Accounting Basics*. Boston: Kent Publishing, 1981.

Cohen, Elaine and Aaron Cohen. *Automation, Space Management, and Productivity: A Guide for Librarians*. New York: R.R. Bowker, 1981.

Dahlgren, Anders. *Planning the Small Public Library Building*. Small Libraries Publication, No. 11. Chicago: American Library Assn., 1985.

Dessy, Blane K. "Small Public Libraries and Long-range Planning: a Rationale," *Illinois Libraries* (May 1984): 210–12.

Draper, James and James Brooks. *Interior Design for Libraries*. Chicago: American Library Assn., 1979.

Emerson, Carol, ed., *Iowa Trustees' Library Guide,* 2nd ed., State Library of Iowa, 1985.

Hoffman, Herbert H. *Simple Library Bookkeeping*. Newport Beach, Calif.: Headway Publishing, 1977.

Knieval, Helen A., ed. *Cooperative Services: A Guide to Policies and*

Procedures in Library Systems. New York: Neal-Schuman Publishers, 1982.

Lynch, Beverly. *Management Strategies for Libraries.* New York: Neal-Schuman Publishers, 1985.

Lynch, Mary Jo, ed. and Helen M. Eckard, Project Officer. *Library Data Collection Handbook.* Chicago: American Library Assn., 1981.

Lynn, Edward S. and Robert J. Freeman, *Fund Accounting: Theory and Practice.* 2nd ed. Englewood Cliffs, N.J.: Prentice-Hall, 1983.

Leighton, Philip and David Weber. *Planning Academic and Research Library Buildings.* Chicago: American Library Assn., 1986.

Mallery, Mary S. and Ralph E. DeVore. *A Sign System for Libraries.* Chicago: American Library Assn., 1982.

Palmour, Vernon E., Marcia C. Bellassai, and Nancy V. Dewath. *A Planning Process for Public Libraries.* Chicago: American Library Assn., 1980.

Pierce, William S. *Furnishing the Library.* New York: Marcel Dekker, Inc., 1980.

Robbins-Carter, Jane and Douglas L. Zweizig. "Are We There Yet?: Evaluating Library Collections, Reference Services, Programs and Personnel." *American Libraries* 16 (October 1985): 624–27.

St. Clair, Guy. *Managing the One-Person Library.* Stoneham, Mass.: Butterworth, 1986.

"What's a Good Boss?" *Library Administrator's Digest* XXI (February 1986): 14.

Zweizig, Douglas and Eleanor Jo Rodger. *Output Measures for Public Libraries.* Chicago: American Library Assn., 1982.

COLLECTION DEVELOPMENT AND TECHNICAL SERVICES

American Library Association. Committee on Cataloging: Description and Access. *Guidelines for Using AACR2 Chapter 9 for Cataloging Microcomputer Software.* Chicago: American Library Assn., 1984.

American Library Association. Filing Committee. *ALA Filing Rules.* Chicago: American Library Assn., 1980.

American Library Association. Office of Intellectual Freedom. *Intellectual Freedom Manual.* Chicago: American Library Assn., 1983.

Anderson, David C., "Deciding the Future of the Catalog in Small Libraries." *Library Journal* 105 (October 1, 1980): 2034–38.

Anglo-American Cataloguing Rules. 2d ed., Ed. by Michael Gorman and Paul W. Winkler. Chicago: American Library Assn., 1978.

Anglo-American Cataloguing Rules, Second Edition, Revisions 1985. [by] Joint Steering Committee for Revision of AACR. Chicago: American Library Assn., 1986.

"The Basics: Paperback Reference Books" in *Rural Libraries,* Vol. 5, No. 1, 1985.

Bauer, Marion D. "The Censor Within." *Top of the News* 4 (Fall 1984): 67–71.

Bosmajian, Haig, ed. *Censorship, Libraries, and the Law.* New York: Neal-Schuman Publishers, 1984.

Bosmajian, Haig, ed. *The Freedom to Read Books, Films, and Plays.* The First Amendment in the Classroom Series, No. 1. New York: Neal-Schuman Publishers, 1986.

Bosmajian, Haig, ed. *Freedom of Religion.* The First Amendment in the Classroom Series, No. 2. New York: Neal-Schuman Publishers, 1987.

Carter, Mary Duncan and Wallace John Bonk. *Building Library Collections.* Metuchen, N.J.: Scarecrow Press, 1969.

Caster, Lillie D. *The Classifier's Guide to LC Class H: Subdivision Techniques for the Social Sciences.* New York: Neal-Schuman Publishers, 1986.

Chan, Lois M. *Immroth's Guide to the Library of Congress Classification.* 3rd ed. Littleton, Colo.: Libraries Unlimited, 1980.

———. *Library of Congress Subject Headings: Principles and Application.* 2nd ed. Littleton, Colo.: Libraries Unlimited, 1985.

The Children's Catalog. 1981 and annual supp. New York: H.W. Wilson, 1981.

Cianciolo, Patricia Jean. *Picture Books for Children.* 2nd ed. Chicago: American Library Assn., 1981.

Comaromi, John P. et al. *Manual on the Use of the Dewey Decimal Classification.* Albany, N.Y.: Forest Press, 1982.

Consumer Information Catalog. Consumer Information Center-Y, Box 100, Pueblo, CO 81002.

Crawford, Walt. *MARC for Library Use: Understanding USMARC Formats.* White Plains, N.Y.: Knowledge Industry Publications, Inc., 1984.

Dodd, Sue A. and Ann M. Sandberg-Fox. *Cataloging Microcomputer Files: A Manual of Interpretation for AACR2.* Chicago: American Library Assn., 1985.

Downs, Robert B. and R.E. McCoy, eds. *The First Freedom Today: Critical Issues Relating to Censorship and to Intellectual Freedom.* Chicago: American Library Assn., 1984.

Doyle, Robert P. "Censorship and the Challenge to Intellectual Freedom," *Principal* 6 (January 1982): 8–11.

Dreyer, Sharon. *The Book Finder: When Kids Need Books; Annotations of Books Published 1979 through 1982.* Circle Pines, Minn: American Guidance Service, 1985.

Ellman, Barbara, ed. *Popular Reading for Children II: A Collection of Booklist Columns.* Chicago: American Library Assn., 1986.

Fleischer, Eugene and Helen Goodman. *Cataloging Audiovisual Materials: A Manual Based on the Anglo-American Cataloguing Rules II.* New York: Neal-Schuman Publishers, 1980.

Friedberg, Joan Brest, June B. Mullins, and Adelaide W. Sukiennik. *Accept Me As I Am: Best Books of Juvenile Nonfiction on Impairments and Disabilities.* New York: Bowker, 1985.

Frost, Carolyn O. *Cataloging Nonbook Materials: Problems in Theory and Practice.* Littleton, Colo.: Libraries Unlimited, 1983.

Futas, Elizabeth. *Library Acquisition Policies and Procedures.* 2nd ed. Phoenix: Oryx Press, 1984.

Ganly, John V. and Diane M. Sciattara. *Serials for Libraries: An Annotated Guide to Continuations, Annuals, Yearbooks, Almanacs, Transactions, Proceedings, Directories, Services, Second Edition.* New York: Neal-Schuman, 1985.

Gillespie, John T., and Christine B. Gilbert, eds. *Best Books for Children Preschool through the Middle Grades, 2nd ed.* New York: Bowker, 1981.

Halliwell, Leslie. *Halliwell's Film Guide.* 4th ed. New York: Scribner, 1985.

Hoffman, Frank William. *Development of Library Collections of Sound Recordings.* New York: Dekker, 1979.

Hoffman, Herbert H. *Small Library Cataloging.* Metuchen, N.J.: Scarecrow Press, 1987.

Johnson, Thomas L. "Cataloging Service Contracts: the Riverside Experience." *Technicalities* (June 1986): 13–15.

Jones, Delores Blythe. *Children's Media Market Place, Third Edition.* New York: Neal-Schuman Publishers, 1987.

The Junior High School Catalog. 1985 and annual supps. New York: H.W. Wilson, 1985.

Katz, William A. *Collection Development: The Selection of Materials for Libraries.* New York: Holt, 1980.

Mahoney, Ellen and Leah Wilcox. *Ready, Set, Read: Best Books to Prepare Preschoolers.* Metuchen, N.J.: Scarecrow, 1985.

Manheimer, Martha, ed. *OCLC: An Introduction to Searching and Input, Second Edition.* New York: Neal-Schuman Publishers, 1986.

Miller, Shirley. *The Vertical File and Its Satellites.* Littleton, Colo.: Libraries Unlimited, 1979.

National Council of Teachers of English. *Books for You; A Booklist for Senior High Students.* Urbana, Ill.: NCTE, 1982.

———. *High Interest—Easy Reading, 4th ed.* Urbana, Ill.: NCTE, 1983.

Olson, Lowell E. "Blind Spots in Collection Development." *Top of the News* 41 (Summer 1985): 371–76.

O'Neill, Edward T. and R. Aluri, "Library of Congress Subject Heading Patterns in OCLC Monographic Records." *Library Resources & Technical Services* 25 (January–March 1981): 63–80.

Osborn, Jeanne. *Dewey Decimal Classification, 19th edition: A Study Manual.* Littleton, Colo.: Libraries Unlimited, 1982.

Perritt, Patsy H. and Jean T. Kreamer. *Selected Videos and Films for Young Adults: 1975–1985.* Chicago: American Library Assn., 1986.

Phalen, Heather. "Supplementary Resources for Enhancing Reference Service." *OLA Bulletin* (July 1985): 17–19.

Richardson, Selma. *Magazines for Children: A Guide for Parents, Teachers, and Librarians.* Chicago: American Library Assn., 1983.

———. *Magazines for Young Adults: Selections for School and Public Libraries.* Chicago: American Library Assn., 1984.

Rogers, Jo Ann V. *Nonprint Cataloging for Multimedia Collections: A Guide Based on AACR2.* Littleton, Colo.: Libraries Unlimited, 1982.

Roman, Susan. *Sequences: An Annotated Guide to Children's Fiction in Series.* Chicago: American Library Assn., 1985.

Segal, Joseph P. *Evaluating and Weeding Collections in Small and Medium-sized Public Libraries: The Crew Method.* Chicago: American Library Assn., 1980.

Selected U.S. Government Publications. Washington, D.C.: Superintendent of Documents, U.S. Government Printing Office.

The Senior High School Catalog. 1982 and annual supps. New York: H.W. Wilson, 1982.

Shaloiko, John. "Independent School Network Joins OCLC." *OCLC Newsletter* (June 1986): 10.

Shapiro, Lillian L., ed. *Fiction for Youth: A Guide to Recommended Books.* 2nd ed. New York: Neal-Schuman Publishers, 1986.

Smallwood, Carol. *Free Resource Builder for Librarians and Teachers.* Jefferson, N.C.: McFarland & Co., 1986.

Smith, Adeline Mercer. *Free Magazines for Libraries.* Jefferson, N.C.: McFarland & Company, 1985.

Thomas, Joy. "Rejuvenating the Pamphlet File in an Academic Library." *Library Journal.* (October 15, 1985): 43–45.

Vertical File Index. New York: H.W. Wilson Co.

West, Celeste. "The Secret Garden of Censorship: Ourselves." *Library Journal* 108 (September 1, 1983): 1651–53.

White, Nancy I. "Cataloging the Serial Collection," in *Introduction to Serials Management.* ed. by Marcia Tuttle. Greenwich, Conn.: JAI Press, Inc., 1982.

Wynar, Bohdan S. *Introduction to Cataloging and Classification.* 7th ed. by Arlene G. Taylor. Littleton, Colo.: Libraries Unlimited, Inc., 1985.

PUBLIC SERVICES

American Library Association. "Policy Statement: Instruction in the Use of Libraries." Council Document 45, 1980.

American Library Association. Young Adult Services Division. Intellectual Freedom Committee. *You Are Not Alone—Intellectual Freedom Issues and Library Services to Youth.* Chicago: American Library Assn., 1986.

Association of College and Research Libraries. *Bibliographic Instruction Handbook.* Chicago: American Library Assn., 1979.

Association of College and Research Libraries. *Library Instruction Clearinghouse 1986: A Directory.* Chicago: American Library Assn., 1986.

Auster, Ethel. *Managing Online Reference Services.* New York: Neal-Schuman Publishers, 1986.

Baechtold, Marguerite and Eleanor Ruth McKinney. *Library Service for Families.* Hamden, Conn.: Library Professional Publications, 1983.

Barber, Peggy, ed. *68 Great Ideas: The Library Awareness Handbook.* Chicago: American Library Assn., 1982.

Bauer, Caroline. *Celebrations: Read-aloud Holiday and Themebook Programs.* New York: H.W. Wilson, 1985.

Bodart, Joni. *Booktalk Two: Booktalking for All Ages and Audiences.* New York: H.W. Wilson, 1985.

Broderick, Dorothy. *Library Work with Children.* New York: Wilson, 1977.

Bronson, Que. *Books on Display.* Washington, D.C.: Metropolitan Washington Library Council, 1982.

Carlson, Ann D. *Early Childhood Literature Sharing Programs in Libraries.* Hamden, Conn.: Shoe String Press, 1986.

DuCharme, Mike. "The Reference Interview," *The Unabashed Librarian* (consecutive issue no. 55, 1985): 13–14.

Edsall, Marian S. *Library Promotion Handbook.* Phoenix: Oryx Press, 1980.

Franklin, Linda Campbell. *Publicity and Display Ideas for Libraries.* Jefferson, N.C.: McFarland, 1985.

Gates, Jean Kay. *Guide to the Use of Libraries and Information Sources.* 5th ed. New York: McGraw-Hill, 1983.

Katz, William. *Your Library: A Reference Guide.* 2nd ed. New York: Holt, Rinehart & Winston, 1984.

Kohn, Rita and Krysta Tepper. *You Can Do It: A PR Skills Manual for Librarians.* Metuchen, N.J.: Scarecrow Press, 1981.

Lubans, John, Jr. *Educating the Public Library User.* Chicago: American Library Assn., 1983.

Rice, James, Jr. *Teaching Library Use: A Guide for Library Instruction.* Westport, Conn.: Greenwood Press, 1981.

Roberts, Anne F. *Library Instruction for Librarians.* Littleton, Colo.: Libraries Unlimited, 1982.

Rummel, Kathleen Kelly and Esther Perica, eds. *Persuasive Public Relations.* Chicago: American Library Assn., 1983.

Sherman, Steve. *ABC's of Library Promotion.* 2nd ed. Metuchen, N.J.: Scarecrow, 1980.

Soltys, A. "Planning and Implementing a Community Survey." *Canadian Library Journal* 42: (October 1985) 245–49.

Tanis, Norman E. and Cindy Ventuleth. "The Decline in Donations?" *Library Journal* 111 (June 15, 1986): 41–44.

Turock, Betty J. *Serving the Older Adult: A Guide to Library Programs and Information Sources.* New York: Bowker, 1983.

Velleman, Ruth A. *Serving Physically Handicapped People.* New York: Bowker, 1979.

Wade, Gordon S. "Managing Reference Services in the Smaller Public Library," *The Reference Librarian* 3 (Spring 1982): 107–12.

Weingand, Darlene E., ed. *Marketing for Libraries and Information Agencies.* Ablex, 1984.

See under Collection Development and Technical Services for collection building tools.

COMPUTERS TO LASERS

Automation in a Small Public Library. 1986 PLA Conference cassette L18637AB. Chicago: American Library Assn., 1986.

Berk, Robert. *Management of the One Person Library.* Phoenix: Oryx Press, 1986.

Clark, Philip M. *Microcomputer Spreadsheet Models for Libraries.* Chicago: American Library Assn., 1985.

Cohen, Elaine and Aaron Cohen. *Automation, Space Management and Productivity.* New York: Bowker, 1982.

Dewey, Patrick. *101 Microcomputer Software Packages to Use in Your Library.* Chicago: American Library Assn., 1987.

Lovecy, Ian. *Automating Library Procedures: A Survivor's Handbook.* Chicago: American Library Assn., 1984.

Mason, Robert M. and Stephen C. Ennis. *The Library Micro Consumer: MRC's Guide to Library Software.* Dist. by Neal-Schuman, 1986.

Matthews, Joseph R. *Directory of Automated Library Systems.* New York: Neal-Schuman Publishers, 1985.

Reynolds, Dennis. *Library Automation: Issues and Applications.* New York: Bowker, 1985.

Rice, James. *Introduction to Library Automation.* Littleton, Colo.: Libraries Unlimited, 1984.

Saffady, William. *Introduction to Automation for Librarians.* Chicago: American Library Assn., 1983.

Walton, Robert A. and Nancy Taylor. *Directory of Microcomputer Software for Libraries.* Phoenix: Oryx Press, 1986.

Index